1

TEACHER'S GUIDE

D1073102

Paul Dummett

John Hughes

Helen Stephenson

Life Level 1 Teacher's Guide

Paul Dummett

John Hughes

Helen Stephenson

Publisher: Sherrise Roehr

Executive Editor: Sarah T. Kenney

Senior Development Editor: Margarita Mate

Director of Global Marketing: Ian Martin

Senior Product Marketing Manager:
  Caitlin Thomas

Director of Content and Media Production:
  Michael Burggren

Production Manager: Daisy Sosa

Senior Print Buyer: Mary Beth Hennebury

Cover Designer: Scott Baker

Cover Image: Sarah Palmer/Getty Images

Compositor: MPS Limited

Cover image

Sea nettle jellyfish swim off the coast
of San Francisco.
Photo by Sarah Palmer.

Teacher's Guide
ISBN-13: 978-1-305-25658-3

National Geographic Learning/Cengage Learning
20 Channel Center Street
Boston, MA 02210
USA

Cengage Learning is a leading provider of customized learning solutions with office locations around the globe, including Singapore, the United Kingdom, Australia, Mexico, Brazil and Japan. Locate our local office at **international.cengage.com/region**

Cengage Learning products are represented in Canada by Nelson Education Ltd.

Visit National Geographic Learning online at **NGL.Cengage.com**
Visit our corporate website at **www.cengage.com**

Printed in the United States of America
1 2 3 4 5 6 7 8 19 18 17 16 15 14

Contents

Introduction

National Geographic

National Geographic was founded in 1888 and defines its mission as "to inspire people to care about the planet." The National Geographic Society is one of the world's largest non-profit scientific and educational organizations. It reaches more than 325 million people in more than 30 languages through its magazines and other media. Proceeds from these activities have funded more than 9,000 scientific, conservation, and educational projects around the world. *LIFE* is published in partnership with National Geographic, using National Geographic's content and values to inspire people to learn English.

National Geographic topics

The topics are paramount and are the starting point for the lessons. These topics have been selected for their intrinsic interest and ability to fascinate students and teachers. Language objectives have been matched to the content and organized into a tried and tested syllabus. The richness of the content means that students are so engaged in learning and expressing their own opinions that language learning has to take place in order for students to satisfy their curiosity. This element of transfer from the topics to students' own realities and experiences converts the input into a vehicle for language practice and production.

People and places

LIFE takes students around the globe, investigating the origins of ancient civilizations, showing the drama of natural forces at work, and exploring some of the world's most beautiful places. These uplifting tales of adventure and discovery are told through eyewitness accounts and first-class reporting, with superb photos, maps, and videos.

Science and technology

Students learn about significant scientific discoveries and breakthroughs, both historic and current. These stories are related by journalists or told by the scientists and explorers themselves through interviews or first person accounts. Students see the impact of the discoveries on our lifestyles and cultures. Because the material comes from a huge archive that has been developed and designed to appeal to the millions of individuals who make up National Geographic's audience, it reflects the broadest possible range of topics.

History

History can be a dry topic, especially if it's overloaded with facts and dates. However, the National Geographic treatment of historical events brings them to life and there is often a human dimension and universal themes that keep the events relevant to students and to our time. History, or the re-telling of historical events, can also be influenced by a culture or nation's perception of the events. National Geographic's non-judgmental and culture-neutral accounts allow students to look behind the superficial events and gain a deeper understanding of our ancestors.

Animals

The animal kingdom is always an appealing and interesting topic. *LIFE* provides astonishing photos that give a unique insight into the hidden lives of known and lesser-known animals, offering rare glimpses of mammals, birds, bugs, and reptiles in their daily struggle for survival. It also informs and surprises with accounts of animals now extinct, species still evolving, and endangered species which are literally fighting for their existence.

Environment

It isn't always possible to find clarity in texts on the environment and climate change, or trust that they are true and not driven by a political agenda. National Geographic's objective journalism, supported by easy-to-understand visuals, presents the issues in an accessible way. The articles are written by experts in their fields. It's often true that those who have the deepest understanding of issues are also able to express the ideas in the simplest way. High-quality thinking and expertise are not synonymous with complicated concepts expressed through complicated language; in fact, usually the reverse is true.

National Geographic photography

We live in a world where images are used more than ever to reinforce, and at times replace, the spoken and written word. To present discourse without them is both unrealistic and unhelpful. Our memories work in pictures; our experiences and the things we learn about the world are stored using them. Raising awareness of this can help students to remember language more easily. All too often photos in books are cosmetic and without impact. National Geographic has great photography and powerful images at its core, so it seems natural that photographs in *LIFE* should serve as the starting point for each unit. The photographs in each spread are also integral to the written and recorded content and every opportunity has been taken to use photographs to stimulate learning.

In *LIFE*, there are photographs that:

- tell a story by themselves
- support understanding of a text
- provoke debate
- stimulate critical thinking by asking you to examine detail, think about what is not shown, or question the photographer's motives
- raise questions about the ethics
- support the language learning process by representing lexical sets or language functions

As a first exercise when handing out the new book to your students, ask them to flip through the book, select their favorite photograph, and then explain to the class what it is they like about it. Some suggestions for working with the photographs:

- pictures of people or animals capture a moment, so ask students to speculate on the events that led up to this moment and those that followed it
- pictures of places aim to capture their essence, so feed students the vocabulary they need to describe the details that together convey this (the light, the colors the landscape, the buildings)

National Geographic video

Each level of *LIFE* features National Geographic videos on a whole range of subjects. Each video is connected with the topic of a corresponding unit and can be used in conjunction with the video lesson pages in the unit. Video sections are divided into three parts:

Before you watch

This section leads students into the topic of the video and engages them in a pre-watching task.

While you watch

These exercises check comprehension of the video, both in terms of what a student sees and hears.

After you watch

This section allows students to respond to the video as a whole and take part in a productive speaking task using language and contexts from the video.

The videos are designed to form part of your lessons. However, if you don't have time in class to watch them all, you can ask students to watch the videos and complete many of the exercises on the page in the Student Book. This can form a useful part of their self-study. Students can also watch the videos again after seeing them in class. This is useful for review and students can focus on parts of the audio that particularly interest them.

For more variation with the videos, here are some more ideas you can use and develop:

- Play the video without sound. Students predict what the narrator or people are saying. Then play with sound and compare.
- Play the sound only with no video. Students predict where the video takes place and what is happening. Then play with the screen on and compare.
- Show the first part of the video, pause it, and then ask students what they think happens next.
- Give students a copy of the script for the video and ask them to imagine they are the director. What will they need to film and show on the screen? Afterwards, they can present their screenplay and finally watch the original.
- Write a short text on the same topic as the one in the video, leaving some information out. Students read the text and then watch the video. They make notes on any new information and rewrite the text so it includes the new details.
- With monolingual groups, choose part of the video with someone talking. Ask students to listen and write down what they say. Then, in groups, ask them to create subtitles in their own language for that part of the video. Each group present their subtitles and the class compares how similar they are.

National Geographic and critical thinking

There is a graded critical thinking syllabus in *LIFE* that starts in Level 2 and runs through all the later levels. The critical thinking activities appear in Lesson C of each unit. The syllabus covers areas such as reading between the lines, differentiating between opinion and fact, evaluating the reliability of source material, assessing the relevance of information, identifying the techniques used by an author to persuade the reader, weighing up evidence, etc. These activities require students to engage with the reading texts at a deeper level and to show real understanding, not just reading comprehension. This training in evaluating texts, assessing the validity and strength of arguments, and developing an awareness of authorial techniques is clearly a valuable skill for those students learning English for academic purposes (EAP), where reflective learning is essential. However, it is also very much part of the National Geographic spirit, which encourages people to question assumptions and develop their own well-informed and reasoned opinions. In this sense, it adds another dimension to the experience of learning English through National Geographic material.

LIFE methodology

Treatment of grammar

Target grammar is presented through reading and/or listening input in the first two spreads of each unit. This input is authentic, adapted for level as necessary, using the target language in natural and appropriate linguistic contexts. This not only aids comprehension, but presents good models for the learner's own language production through a variety of "voices" and genres.

The primary focus is on the topic content before the learner's attention is drawn to the target grammar structures. Learners are first directed to *notice* this language by various means, such as using highlighting within the text, extracting sample sentences, or having learners locate examples themselves.

A variety of task formats are used to lead learners to *analyze* the form, meaning, and use of the grammar structures, as appropriate. Such an approach can be highly motivational by actively engaging learners in the lesson and allowing them to share and discuss their interpretation of the new language. After this stage, clear paradigms or examples of form and use are given on the page in a simple summary box. This supports the learners and is a check point for the teacher and learners alike as it summarizes the information learners will have arrived at through completing the discovery tasks. A cross-reference is provided to more detailed information and additional exercises at the back of the book. These are suitable for use both in class and for self-study, according to the needs of the learners.

The grammar practice tasks within the unit are linked to the presentation text and topic and are thus content-rich in the same way. They move from more supported exercises through to more challenging tasks. Depending on the level, they have a differing emphasis on form and use. The practice tasks give learners an opportunity to *personalize* the structures and practice them in the context of their own experiences and situations. This anchors the new language in existing frameworks and leads to a clearer understanding of the usage of this new or revised language. Equally, the practice exercises incorporate a real reason to use the target structure, whether by devices such as quizzes, games, etc., or by genuine exchange of information between students.

A final task on each spread allows the learners to create their own output and is structured so that learners have the opportunity to use the target grammar as well as other target language, for example vocabulary, in a meaningful context. This final task has a variety of formats such as discussions, personal narratives, and task-based activities (ranking, etc.), and the emphasis from the learner's perspective is on content and fluency, rather than grammatical accuracy.

Aside from the two main grammar input spreads, the target grammar is also recycled in the subsequent spreads of each unit and beyond.

Treatment of vocabulary

LIFE teaches vocabulary in a range of different ways. This eclectic approach takes account of recent research, but doesn't abandon tried and tested methods. There is more practice of all of this vocabulary input (apart from words occurring in glossaries) in the Workbook.

1 Lexical sets

Some of the benefits generally associated with teaching words in lexical sets are:

- learning words in a set requires less effort
- retrieving related words from memory is easier
- seeing how knowledge can be organized can be helpful to learners
- it mirrors how such information is stored in the brain
- the meaning of words can be made clearer by comparing and contrasting them to similar words in the set

Each unit usually has two or more lexical sets. The lexical sets also cover commonly confused words. There is evidence to suggest that once students have learned one or more of the words that belong to a group of commonly confused words (e.g., *job* and *work*), it is useful to compare and contrast these words directly to clarify the differences (or similarities) in meaning. *LIFE* focuses on these groups of words as and when they come up.

2 Word focus

The *Word focus* sections take high-frequency words and give examples of the different meanings they can have according to the contexts in which they appear and the different words they collocate with. At higher levels, there is increased exposure to idioms and colloquial usage. This content is reinforced in the Workbook where appropriate.

3 Wordbuilding

The independent wordbuilding syllabus offers students another opportunity to expand their vocabulary. The *Wordbuilding* boxes in the units focus on areas such as prefixes, suffixes, collocations, parts of speech (e.g., noun→adjective), compound nouns, and phrasal verbs, and highlight examples from the reading or listening texts. The box gives a brief explanation and some examples, which is often reinforced in the Workbook.

4 Glossaries

Where certain words are important to the meaning of a text, but are above the level of the student, they are glossed. Students aren't expected to learn these words, but the short and simple definitions prevent them from being a barrier to understanding.

Learning skills

There is a comprehensive learning skills syllabus in the Workbook. This covers traditional learning skills, such as recording new vocabulary, using a dictionary, remembering new vocabulary, planning study time, assessing your own progress, etc.

Assessment

Students and teachers can assess progress in the following ways:

- Each unit in the Student's Book finishes with a one-page review where students do the exercises and complete a number of can-do statements linked to the objectives of the unit.

- There are photocopiable tests in the Teacher's Guide.
- There is a *Check!* section at the end of each unit in the Workbook for students to check what they have learned (general knowledge as well as language).

Overview of a Student Book unit

On the following pages, you will find a walkthrough of a unit of *LIFE*, from Level 2. The Student Book units follow this organization:

Opener: a one-page introduction to the unit that gets students interested in the topic

a and b: double-page lessons that teach grammar and vocabulary through reading and listening texts

c: a double-page lesson that focuses on reading comprehension

d: a one-page lesson that teaches a speaking skill and functional/situational language

e: a one-page lesson that teaches a writing skill and the features of a text type

f: a double-page lesson of video comprehension exercises

Review: a one-page lesson of practice activities and can-do check statements

Explore a Unit

Compelling **National Geographic images** open every unit and introduce the theme, while naturally promoting critical thinking.

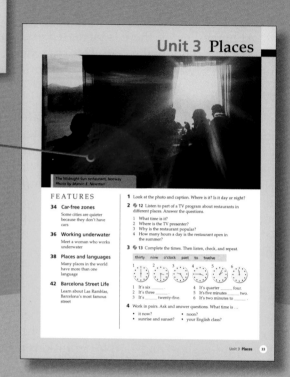

Lessons a and b

Lessons a and b deductively teach and practice the grammar and vocabulary needed to acquire the real-life functions of the unit.

Real-world images alongside **readings** develop visual literacy skills.

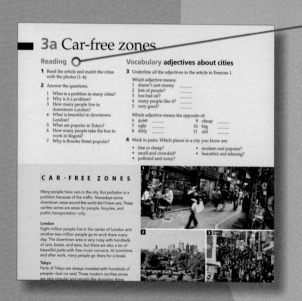

Grammar is presented deductively through a reading or a listening activity and then applied to relevant practice.

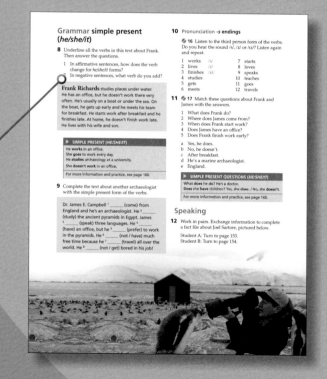

Lesson c

Lesson c teaches reading, vocabulary, and critical thinking skills while providing a full reading.

3c Places and languages

Reading and vocabulary

1 How many languages do you speak? Which language(s) do you speak in different places (e.g., at home, at school, at work)?

2 Read the article. What is it about? Choose the correct answer (a–c).

  a The languages people speak in different places
  b Places with new languages
  c Why English is important in different places

3 Read the article again. What do these numbers refer to?

  1 over 190   *countries in the world*
  2 about 7,000   _____
  3 over 1 billion   _____ and

  4 380 million   _____
  5 400 million   _____
  6 80%   _____
  7 65   _____
  8 109   _____
  9 1   _____

4 Find these words in the article and match them with the definitions (1–4).

  | ancient   first   official   second |

  1 the language you learn after your first language
  2 the main language that people in a place speak
  3 the language of the government
  4 a very old language

▶ **WORDBUILDING collocations**
We use certain words together. These are called *collocations*. Many nouns have adjective and noun collocations: *first language, official language.*

5 Discuss these questions as a class.

  1 What is your first language? Is English your second language?
  2 Does your country have an official language?
  3 What languages do people normally learn at school? Why do they learn these languages?

Critical thinking making connections

6 Read the article again. Add these sentences (a–d) to the end of each paragraph.

  Paragraph 1: ___
  Paragraph 2: ___
  Paragraph 3: ___
  Paragraph 4: ___

  a English is the world's biggest second language.
  b That's one point five languages for every island.
  c When he dies, his language dies.
  d Many people there speak Spanish as their first language.

Vocabulary cardinal and ordinal numbers

7 Look at these two sentences from the article. Which says how many and which says the order?

  1 In first place is China.
  2 There are over one billion speakers of Mandarin Chinese.

8 Work in pairs. Complete the sequence of numbers. Then tell your partner the numbers. Check your answers with your instructor.

  1   1 3 ____ 7 ____ ____ ____
  2   ____ 21 ____ 41 51 ____ 71
  3   21ˢᵗ 31ˢᵗ 41ˢᵗ 51ˢᵗ ____ ____ ____
  4   ____ 3ʳᵈ ____ 5ᵗʰ 6ᵗʰ 7ᵗʰ

9 **Pronunciation saying numbers**

  🔊 18 Listen and check your answers in Exercise 8. Then listen again and repeat.

Speaking

10 Write down three favorite numbers. Tell your partner why they're your favorites.

  My birthday is on June third.

38

Explicit **"Critical Thinking"** activities build the scaffolding that takes learners from understanding, to evaluating, and finally to creating their own texts in English. (Level 2 and on)

"Wordbuilding" boxes offer opportunities to expand vocabulary through an exploration of relevant prefixes, suffixes, collocations, parts of speech, compound nouns, and phrasal verbs.

Information-rich readings about real people and places, including National Geographic explorers, will engage and motivate learners.

PLACES AND LANGUAGES

First place and first languages

There are over one hundred and ninety countries in the world and about seven thousand languages. In first place is China. Over one billion people speak Mandarin Chinese as a first language. In second place is India with speakers of Hindi. And in third place is Spanish. Spain isn't a big country, but there are over four hundred million Spanish speakers around the world, especially in Latin America.

English as a global language

As a first language, English is in fourth place. About three hundred and eighty million people are native English speakers. But English is in first place as a second language. Over a billion people speak English for doing business, reading the news, or studying science and medicine. In some countries, English is not the native language but it is the official language for the government and in schools.

The other 6,996 languages

Chinese, Hindi, Spanish, and English are the "big" languages. About eighty percent of the world's population speak them. But what about the other 6,996 languages? Many countries have lots of different languages. For example, the sixty-five islands of Vanuatu in the South Pacific Ocean have one hundred and nine different languages!

The last speakers

Finally, there are some languages with only one speaker. They are old people and they speak the language of their parents and grandparents. For example, Charlie Muldunga lives in Australia. He speaks English but his native language is Amurdag. It's an ancient Aboriginal language and he is its last speaker.

ancient (adj) /ˈeɪnʃənt/ very old
last (adj) /lɑːst/ final
over (adv) /ˈoʊvər/ more than
about (adv) /əˈbaʊt/ approximately

新幹線
Shinkanse

Lessons d and e

Lesson d applies the language skills learned in Lessons a through c in relevant, real-world tasks.

3d The city of Atlanta

Vocabulary places in a city

1 Look at the map of Atlanta. Where do you do these things?

1 get tourist information
2 learn about history
3 relax outside
4 see a play or a musical
5 park your car
6 read a book
7 meet clients and colleagues
8 look at marine life

Real life giving and getting directions

2 ♪ 19 Listen to a conversation at the visitors' center. What places on the map do they talk about?

3 ♪ 19 Look at the expressions for giving directions. Listen again and complete the conversation at the visitors' center.

T = Tourist, G = Guide
T: Hi, we'd like to go to the aquarium. Is it ¹ _____ ?
G: It's ² _____ fifteen minutes _____ , but you go past some interesting places on the way. Here's a map. Go ³ _____ Decatur Street and continue on Marietta Street. ⁴ _____ Spring Street and ⁵ _____ Centennial Olympic Park Drive. The park is on your left. It's very nice. Go ⁶ _____ the top of the park and on the right there's the World of Coca-Cola.
T: Oh, that sounds interesting.
G: Yes, it is. Go past it and the aquarium is opposite.
T: Great. Thanks a lot.

▶ DIRECTIONS

Asking for directions
Where is...?
How do I get to...?
Is it near here?

Giving directions
It's near here. / It's about ten minutes away.

Go past the... ➡
Cross... ↗
Go straight on... ⬆
Turn left on... /Go left at... ⬅
Turn right on... /Go right at... ➡

4 Work in pairs. Ask for and give directions to different places on the map of Atlanta.

40

Lesson e presents various text types through a writing model and then teaches and practices a relevant writing skill.

Text types include emails, blogs, reports, and forms, while skills include organization, using descriptive words, and being polite.

3e Describing a place

Writing a travel website

1 Bella Potachouck writes for a travel website. Read about her favorite city. Mark the items she describes (1–6).

1 the name of her city
2 good places to visit
3 her favorite time of day, month, or season
4 places to meet friends
5 her favorite cafés and restaurants
6 good ways to travel around the city

WHY I LOVE MOSCOW

My favorite place in Russia is Red Square in Moscow because there are interesting museums and art galleries. But I also like other parts of Moscow. Krasnaya Presnya Park is great. On Saturdays in the summer, I meet friends there in the afternoon. We relax and play sports. Summer is between May and September, but I love winter. December is my favorite month because the snow is beautiful and we go ice-skating.

2 Writing skill capital letters

a Read the website in Exercise 1 again. Which one of these things 1–7 does not have a capital letter?

1 the word at the beginning of a sentence
2 the pronoun *I*
3 names of people, cities, or places
4 countries, nationalities, or languages
5 days and months
6 seasons and parts of the day
7 streets, roads, parks, and squares

b Rewrite this description with capital letters.

i'm from australia and i love sydney! there are over four million people here, but it's never crowded. that's because there's the harbor with the famous sydney opera house and there are beautiful beaches. my favorite season is summer because of the surfing. lots of people go to bondi beach, but on saturdays i go with my friends to narabeen beach. it's quiet and relaxed. afterwards we go downtown. there are over 3,000 restaurants with every type of food, from japanese to lebanese.

3 Write a description of your favorite town or city for a website.

4 Display the descriptions around the classroom. Read each other's descriptions and check the capital letters.

Lesson f

Each unit culminates with a National Geographic video that engages students while providing an opportunity to synthesize related topics between the unit and the clip.

3f Barcelona Street Life
Video

Las Ramblas in Barcelona, Spain

42

Each clip is supported by Before, While, and After viewing activities.

Before you watch

1 Look at the photo and read the caption. With a partner, describe what you see using the appropriate words from the list.

noisy	modern
polluted	small
beautiful	quiet
crowded	big
ugly	relaxing

2 In the video, people talk about the Ramblas, an important street in Barcelona, Spain. Look at the list of words in Exercise 1. Which words do you think describe the Ramblas?

3 Look at the word box below. Listen and repeat the words after your instructor.

While you watch

4 As you watch the video, check the people and things that you see.

☐ hospital
☐ musicians
☐ people dancing
☐ singers
☐ people sleeping
☐ buses
☐ flowers
☐ people in costumes
☐ museum
☐ trees
☐ performers
☐ outdoor café
☐ books
☐ paintings

5 Watch the video again. Complete the quotes with the missing words.

friend	living
lively	inspiring
music	entertained
street	way

a "There is always something going on. You can always find a _____ on the street. It's where _____ is."

b "You can go out in the street at night. It's always _____"

c "I felt somehow better than in Amsterdam, more alive... vital. That makes it very enjoyable... _____, too."

d "In the Ramblas you can find theater, _____ from Argentina, from Spain, from Africa..."

e "The Ramblas is the street in Barcelona, in Europe, and I think, in the world, that you're going to be _____."

f "Even the _____ is decorated."

g "It's a _____ of life."

6 Match the quotes from Exercise 5 with the person. Two of the people have two quotes.

1

2

3

4

5

After you watch

7 Work with a partner. Compare the Ramblas to a street in your city or town.

The Ramblas is crowded...

8 Your friend is traveling to Spain. Write an email to your friend. Explain why he/she should visit the Ramblas when he/she is there. Be sure to mention:

- where it is
- things to buy
- things to see or do during the day
- when to visit
- where to eat
- things to see or do at night

When you are in Spain, you can visit Barcelona. There is a very interesting street there ...

decorate (v) /ˈdekəˌreɪt/ to make an object attractive by putting something on it
enjoyable (adj) /enˈdʒɔɪəbəl/ something that is fun, nice, or pleasant
entertain (v) /ˌentərˈteɪn/ to amuse someone by singing, dancing, etc.
inspiring (adj) /ɪnˈspaɪərɪŋ/ causing people to want to do or make something
lively (adj) /ˈlaɪvli/ with a lot of movement and activity
performer (n) /pərˈfɔːrmər/ a person who acts, sings, dances, etc., for a crowd
vital (adj) /ˈvaɪtəl/ with a lot of energy
way of life (n) /ˈweɪ əv ˈlaɪf/ the habits and customs of a person or group of people

Review page

The review page after every unit informally assesses each skill taught in the unit.

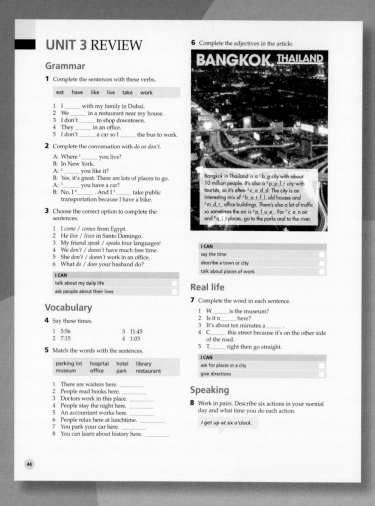

UNIT 3 REVIEW

Grammar

1 Complete the sentences with these verbs.

| eat | have | like | live | take | work |

1 I _____ with my family in Dubai.
2 We _____ in a restaurant near my house.
3 I don't _____ to shop downtown.
4 They _____ in an office.
5 I don't _____ a car so I _____ the bus to work.

2 Complete the conversation with *do* or *don't*.

A: Where ¹_____ you live?
B: In New York.
A: ²_____ you like it?
B: Yes, it's great. There are lots of places to go.
A: ³_____ you have a car?
B: No, I ⁴_____ . And I ⁵_____ take public transportation because I have a bike.

3 Choose the correct option to complete the sentences.

1 I *come / comes* from Egypt.
2 He *live / lives* in Santo Domingo.
3 My friend *speak / speaks* four languages!
4 We *don't / doesn't* have much free time.
5 She *don't / doesn't* work in an office.
6 What *do / does* your husband do?

I CAN
talk about my daily life ☐
ask people about their lives ☐

Vocabulary

4 Say these times.

1 5:56   3 11:45
2 7:15   4 1:03

5 Match the words with the sentences.

| parking lot | hospital | hotel | library |
| museum | office | park | restaurant |

1 There are waiters here. _____
2 People read books here. _____
3 Doctors work in this place. _____
4 People stay the night here. _____
5 An accountant works here. _____
6 People relax here at lunchtime. _____
7 You park your car here. _____
8 You can learn about history here. _____

6 Complete the adjectives in the article.

BANGKOK, THAILAND

Bangkok in Thailand is a ¹b_g city with about 10 million people. It's also a ²p_p_l_r city with tourists, so it's often ³c_o_d_d. The city is an interesting mix of ⁴b_a_t_f_l, old houses and ⁵m_d_r_ office buildings. There's also a lot of traffic so sometimes the air is ⁶p_l_u_e_. For ⁷c_e_n air and ⁸q_i_t places, go to the parks and to the river.

I CAN
say the time ☐
describe a town or city ☐
talk about places of work ☐

Real life

7 Complete the word in each sentence.

1 W_____ is the museum?
2 Is it n_____ here?
3 It's about ten minutes a_____ .
4 C_____ this street because it's on the other side of the road.
5 T_____ right then go straight.

I CAN
ask for places in a city ☐
give directions ☐

Speaking

8 Work in pairs. Describe six actions in your normal day and what time you do each action.

I get up at six o'clock.

44

For additional, independent practice tied to the lessons taught in the Student Books, learners can access:

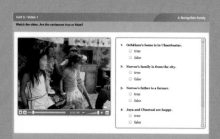

The Online Workbooks that feature each National Geographic video clip, additional activities, and tracked student progress.

The Student CD-ROMs offer the same video clips and activities as the Online Workbooks in an alternate format.

The Print Workbooks reinforce the vocabulary, grammar, and language functions taught in the Student Book.

NATIONAL GEOGRAPHIC LEARNING · CENGAGE Learning

Life 1

Paul Dummett
John Hughes
Helen Stephenson

NATIONAL GEOGRAPHIC LEARNING · CENGAGE Learning

Life 2

Paul Dummett
John Hughes
Helen Stephenson

NATIONAL GEOGRAPHIC LEARNING · CENGAGE Learning

Life 3

Paul Dummett
John Hughes
Helen Stephenson

NATIONAL GEOGRAPHIC LEARNING · CENGAGE Learning

Life 4

Paul Dummett
John Hughes
Helen Stephenson

NATIONAL GEOGRAPHIC LEARNING · CENGAGE Learning

Life 5

Paul Dummett
John Hughes
Helen Stephenson

NATIONAL GEOGRAPHIC LEARNING · CENGAGE Learning

Life 6

Paul Dummett
John Hughes
Helen Stephenson

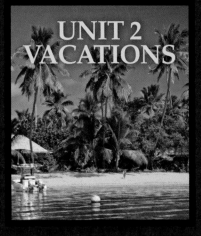

**UNIT 1
HELLO**

**UNIT 2
VACATIONS**

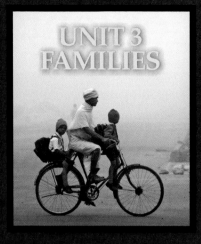

**UNIT 3
FAMILIES**

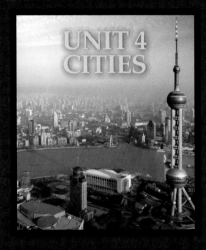

**UNIT 4
CITIES**

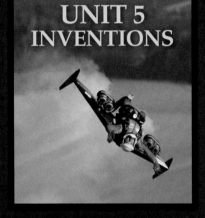

**UNIT 5
INVENTIONS**

**UNIT 6
PASSIONS**

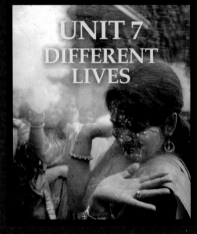

**UNIT 7
DIFFERENT
LIVES**

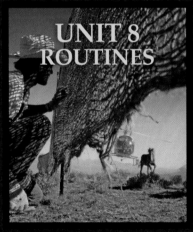

**UNIT 8
ROUTINES**

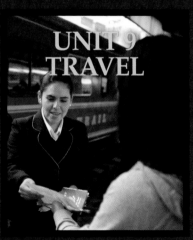

**UNIT 9
TRAVEL**

**UNIT 10
HISTORY**

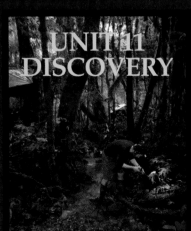

**UNIT 11
DISCOVERY**

**UNIT 12
THE WEEKEND**

Contents

PRONUNCIATION	LISTENING	READING	SPEAKING	WRITING
word stress questions	introductions	a description of two people in the Himalayas an article about phone calls from New York	personal information a quiz phone numbers	text type: an identity badge writing skill: capital letters (1)

we're, they're
isn't, aren't
be questions and
  short answers
plural nouns
syllables
	a description of a place
	a conversation on vacation
		a blog about a vacation
		a quiz about vacation
		  places
			vacation photos
			on vacation
			general knowledge
				text type: a form
				writing skill: capital
				letters (2)

possessive 's
linking with at
exclamations
	information about a family
	  from India
	a description of the Cousteau
	  family
		a description of a
		  wedding in Thailand
		an article about
		  population pyramids
		  in different countries
			your family tree
			a wedding
			your family pyramid
				text type: a greeting
				  card
				writing skill:
				  contractions

th /ð/
linking with can
	a description of Shanghai
	at a tourist information center
		information about a
		  town center
		a description of two
		  famous towers
		an article about times
		  around the world
			locations
			famous places
			times and timetables
				text type: a postcard
				writing skill: and

can/can't
numbers
	information about Yves Rossy
	an interview with a robot
	  expert
		an article about a robot
		a blog about
		  technology
		an article about
		  cooking with the sun
			your abilities
			your favorite object
			buying online
				text type: an email
				writing skill: but

do you … ?
likes, doesn't like
intonation
	information about soccer and
	  the World Cup
	an interview with a man
	  about his likes and dislikes
		an article about giant
		  vegetables
		a profile of a TV
		  presenter
		an article about racing
		  with animals
			a food survey
			things in common
			a sports event
				text type: a review
				writing skill: pronouns

PRONUNCIATION	LISTENING	READING	SPEAKING	WRITING
don't intonation in questions sentence stress	information about the Holi festival an interview with a teacher an interview with a student	an article about traditional life an article about the seasons of the year	you and your partner a survey activities in different seasons	text type: a profile writing skill: paragraphs
-s and *-es* verbs /s/ and /z/	an interview with a man about his job a conversation about a National Geographic explorer	an article about a typical day an article about a job in tiger conservation	routines your friends and family a quiz	text type: an email writing skill: spelling: double letters
there is/are *I'd like*	four people talking about travel a conversation in which two people plan a trip	an article about things in your suitcase an article about a Trans-Siberia trip	things in your suitcase hotel rooms travel tips	text type: travel advice writing skill: *because*
was/were weak forms strong forms sentence stress	information about an important moment in TV history a radio show about heroes	a quiz about "firsts" in exploration an article about the first people on the American continents	dates and events people in the past famous Americans	text type: a blog writing skill: *when*
-ed verbs *did you … ?* *didn't*	information about discoveries in Papua New Guinea a story about the investigation of a discovery an interview about discovering your local area	an article about an unusual discovery an interview with an adventurer an article about an accident in Madagascar	your family's past what did you do last year? telling a story	text type: an email writing skill: expressions in emails
going and *doing* *would you … ?*	information about the weekend in different countries a description of a family in Indonesia a conversation between two friends about this weekend	an article about helping people on the weekend	your photos next weekend a special weekend	text type: an invitation writing skill: spelling: verb endings

Life around the world

Unit 4 Where's that?

A video quiz about four cities.

Unit 6 At the market

Meet people at a market in an English city.

Unit 7 The people of the reindeer

Life with the Sami people in Scandinavia.

Unit 12 Saturday mornin in São Tom

Meet some local artists in this small African country.

Unit 3 A Mongolian fam

Meet a family in Mongolia.

Unit 1 My top te photo

A photographer talks about his favorite photos.

Unit 10 The space race

What was the "space race"? Find out in this video.

Unit 9 Along the Inca Road

Discover South America with writer Karin Muller.

Unit 5 The Owl and the Pussycat

A video about an unusual pair of friends.

Unit 11 Perfumes from Madagascar

Why do scientists love Madagascar?

Norway
UK
Mongolia
San Francisco
USA
Nepal
São Tome and Príncipe
Kenya
Peru
Madagascar
Antarctica

Unit 2 Antarctica

Vacations in Antarctica.

Unit 8 The elephants of Samburu

Meet a man who photographs elephants.

Pacific Ocean, Australia
Photo by David Doubilet

FEATURES

10 National Geographic people
People and jobs

12 People and places
Photos by Alex Treadway

14 International phone calls
Phone calls from New York

18 My top ten photos
A video about National Geographic photos

1 🔊 **1** Look at the photo. Listen and mark (✓).

a   Hi! My name's Mike.
b   Hello! I'm Mike.
c   Hi! I'm Mike. ✓

2 🔊 **1** Listen again and repeat.

3 Write your name.
Hi! I'm _____ .

4 Work in pairs.

Hello! I'm Meera.

Hi! My name's Jared.

Hello

Warm-up

Greetings

Use gestures to introduce *Hi, Hello,* and *Goodbye* to students. Walk toward three or four students, shake hands, and say: *Hello.* Then, as you walk away, wave and say: *Goodbye!* Then introduce *Hi* by waving and saying *Hi!* as you walk toward them. Once students have the idea, continue the gestures and have them call out the phrases. Finally, ask students to walk around the class, saying *Hi!* and *Goodbye!* to each other.

Getting to know you

Ask students to make name cards, using index cards or sturdy paper. Students fold the cards and place them on their desks. Write your name on the board. Say: *Hi, (Ana)!,* and students can respond.

Use the cards in "getting to know you" games. Collect the cards and hand them out at random. A student has to say *Hi, (Ana),* and (Ana) must reply *Hello!* or *Hi!* in order to reclaim the card.

PHOTO INFO

The diver is observing a large fish called a potato cod, on the Great Barrier Reef off the coast of Australia.

2 After completing the activity, go around the class, calling on students to say: *Hi! I'm (Ana).*

3 Encourage students to write the complete sentence on a separate piece of paper. Let them compare their answers in pairs.

4 First model the activity with a student by introducing yourself and eliciting a response. Then divide the class into pairs. Go around the class to monitor conversations and check pronunciation.

Extra activity

Extend Exercise 4 by asking students to stand up, walk around the room, and have conversations with five or six classmates.

Vocabulary notes

Hello and *hi* have the same meaning, but *hi* is informal.

I'm and *My name's* also mean the same thing. *I'm* is more common.

Teaching notes

Beginners know little or no English. They have also had very few, if any, English language lessons. Here are a few suggestions teaching beginners:

- Use gestures and visuals, such as flashcards, pictures, presentation slides, or an interactive whiteboard.
- Model activities. Simplify your language and limit your talking time.
- Vary lessons by combining listening, reading, basic writing, and speaking.
- Activities should be short and include pair and group work.

National Geographic people

Warm-up

Using words

Write the job-related words from Exercise 2 on the board. Read them aloud and have students repeat. Then act out each job for students to guess: pretend to take photos (photographer), pretend to do an experiment (scientist), etc.

For more practice, have pairs of students act out and say the jobs.

PHOTO INFO

Mattias Klum is a Swedish filmmaker and photographer. He was the first Swede ever to have his work on the cover of National Geographic Magazine.

Robert Ballard is an American ocean explorer. He has discovered the wrecks of the *Titanic* (1985), the German WWII battleship *Bismarck* (1989), and the aircraft carrier USS *Yorktown* (1998).

Mireya Mayor is an American anthropologist. She is a wildlife correspondent for the National Geographic Channel.

Carolyn Anderson was a writer and editor at National Geographic for many years.

Alex Treadway is a photographer. He is based in London but travels all over the world taking photographs, particularly in the Himalayas.

Pronunciation notes

Notice the stressed syllable in these words (underlined):

*ex<u>plo</u>rer   <u>film</u>maker
pho<u>tog</u>rapher   <u>sci</u>entist   <u>wri</u>ter*

Point out that *w* in *writer* and *c* in *scientist* are silent. Note also that *ph* has a sound equivalent to *f* in English.

1a National Geographic people

Vocabulary jobs

1 🔊 2 Look at the photos. Listen to the people.

Hi. I'm Mattias. I'm a filmmaker.

2 🔊 3 Listen and repeat the jobs.

e<u>x</u>plorer	<u>film</u>maker
<u>photog</u>rapher	<u>sci</u>entist <u>wri</u>ter

3 Look at the photos. Write the jobs.

1 Hi. I'm Carolyn. I'm a <u>writer</u> .
2 Hello. I'm Alex. I'm a <u>photographer</u>
3 Hi. I'm Mireya. I'm a <u>scientist</u>
4 Hi. I'm Mattias. I'm a <u>filmmaker</u>
5 Hello. I'm Robert. I'm an <u>explorer</u> .

4 Complete the sentence with your job.

I'm _____ .

5 Talk to four people in your class.

Hi. I'm Katya. I'm a student.

NATIONAL GEOGRAPHIC PEOPLE

Mattias Klum in Malaysia

Mattias Klum
filmmaker

Carolyn Anderson
writer

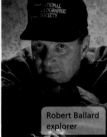

Robert Ballard
explorer

Mireya Mayor
scientist

Alex Tr
photog

10

Teaching notes

Here are three ways of checking comprehension:

1 Visuals: bring in pictures to show these jobs, hold them up or project them, and ask students to say the job.

2 Gestures: use the ideas in the warm-up to check understanding.

3 Examples: Say or write famous people who have the jobs included on page 10. Be sure to name people the students are likely to know.

Vocabulary

Vocabulary notes

Point out that we always use the indefinite article (*a / an*) with jobs.

We use *a* before nouns that start with a consonant sound. We use *an* before nouns that start with a vowel sound.

For more detailed practice, see the grammar section that follows.

Grammar *a/an*

6 Look at the grammar box and the example. Then look at the jobs in Exercise 2. <u>Underline</u> the first letter.

Example: <u>e</u>xplorer

A	AN
a + noun with b, c, d, f, …	an + noun with a, e, i, o, u
a filmmaker	an explorer
For more information and practice, see page 161.	

7 Complete the sentences with *a* or *an*.

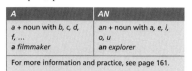

1 I'm ___*a*___ photographer.
2 I'm ___*a*___ doctor.
3 I'm ___*a*___ teacher.
4 I'm ___*an*___ artist.
5 I'm ___*an*___ engineer.
6 I'm ___*a*___ driver.

Listening

8 🔊 **4** Listen and put the conversation in order.

a Yes.   5
b Oh, you're a photographer!   4
c Hello.   *1*
d I'm Alex Treadway.   3
e Hi.   2

9 🔊 **5** Listen and complete the conversation.

you're   I'm   Hi   Hello

YOU: ¹ __Hi__ .
MATTIAS: ² __Hello__ . ³ __I'm__ Mattias Klum.
YOU: Oh, ⁴ __you're__ a filmmaker!
MATTIAS: Yes, for National Geographic.

Grammar *I + am, you + are*

▶ *I + AM, YOU + ARE*

I'm	Katya.
You're	a student.
(I'm = I am, You're = You are)	
For more information and practice, see page 161.	

10 Work in pairs. Look at the photos on page 10. Practice the conversations in Exercises 8 and 9.

11 Work in groups. Play a game. Take turns.
Student A: Act a job.
Students B, C, D: Say the job.
Take turns.

Vocabulary **the alphabet**

12 🔊 **6** Listen and repeat the alphabet.

Aa	Bb	Cc	Dd	Ee	Ff	Gg
Hh	Ii	Jj	Kk	Ll	Mm	
Nn	Oo	Pp	Qq	Rr	Ss	Tt
Uu	Vv	Ww	Xx	Yy	Zz	

13 🔊 **7** Listen and choose the correct name.
1 Paula /(Paola)   3 Shaun /(Sean)
2 (Bryan)/ Brian   4 Anna /(Ana)

14 Work in pairs. Spell your name.

15 Work in pairs. Spell words.
Student A: Turn to page 153.
Student B: Turn to page 157.

Speaking

16 Work in groups. Play a memory game. Introduce yourself. Then give information about other people.

> *I'm Katya.*
> *I'm a student.*

> *You're Katya. You're a student.*
> *I'm Paola. I'm a doctor.*

> *You're Katya. You're a student.*
> *You're Paola. You're a doctor.*
> *I'm Jason. I'm a scientist.*

---

11 Model the activity by acting out some of the jobs from Exercises 1 and 7 for students to guess.

Vocabulary

12 Point out that the vowels are in a different color.

Speaking

16 Model the activity by saying *I'm (Mike). I'm a teacher.* The next student must say *You're (Mike). You're a teacher. I'm (Elena). I'm a nurse.* And so on.

> **HOMEWORK** Ask students to write a few sentences to introduce themselves. Tell them to include their name and their job.

4 Start by writing *a student* and *a teacher* on the board. Point to yourself and say: *a teacher.* Point to a student and say: *a student.* Then elicit your students' jobs and write them on the board. Point out whether they need *a* or *an*, and point out word stress. Then ask students to complete the sentence with the name of their job.

> **Extra activity**
> Ask students to think of and write down the name of a famous explorer, scientist, writer, filmmaker, or photographer. Then ask students to walk around the class and introduce themselves as that person, e.g., *Hi. I'm Shakespeare. I'm a writer.*

> **Pronunciation notes**
> We use *a* before nouns that start with a consonant sound. We use *an* before nouns that start with a vowel sound.
>
> Be aware that it is the vowel **sound** that is important. For example, we say *an umbrella* but *a uniform.*
>
> Note that *a* and *an* are usually unstressed, so students should say /ə/ and /ən/.
>
> Note the word stress:
>
> doctor   teacher   artist
> engineer   driver

Grammar

> **Grammar notes**
> In spoken English, *I am* and *You are* are almost always shortened, so it is best to teach them in the short form with the apostrophe. The long form is used for emphasis or contradiction: *No! I am Katya!*
>
> Note the pronunciation: *I'm* /aɪm/ and *you're* /jɔ/.

People and places

Warm-up

Introducing the theme: countries and nationalities

Write on the board: *jobs, countries, nationalities*. Check students' understanding by eliciting the job, country, and nationality of your students. Then write on the board the names of famous filmmakers, artists, and writers. In pairs, have students match the famous people to countries and nationalities.

Reading

1 Ask students to look at the photos, read the article, and then complete the table. Check by writing the table on the board and having students complete it.

Background notes

Nepal is a country in the Himalayas, bordered by China in the north and India in the south. Mount Everest, the highest mountain in the world, is in Nepal.

Ladakh is a mountainous and sparsely populated region of Jammu and Kashmir in the far north of India, near the border with Tibet.

Vocabulary

2 Have students work in pairs to complete the table.

Teaching notes

Bring in a large world map or, if possible, project a map. That way you can check that students know each country's location.

Vocabulary notes

In English, most countries take no article and have a capital letter.

However, some countries use *the* because they are described as a set of states, islands, or kingdoms: the United States (the US), the United Kingdom (the UK), the United Arab Emirates (the UAE), the Philippines.

Reading

1 Read the article. Complete the table.

	Photo 1	Photo 2
Name	Manu	*Dechen*
Country	*Nepal*	*India*
Nationality	*Nepalese*	Indian

1 PEOPLE AND PLACES BY ALEX TREADWAY

Alex Treadway is a British photographer with National Geographic.

This is Manu. He's from Jagat. Jagat is in Nepal. Manu is Nepalese.
Photo by Alex Treadway

2

This is Dechen. She's from Ladakh. Ladakh is in India. Dechen is Indian.
Photo by Alex Treadway

 12

Vocabulary **countries and nationalities**

2 Complete the table.

British   China   Spanish   the United States

Country	Nationality
Brazil	Brazilian
Canada	Canadian
China	Chinese
Egypt	Egyptian
France	French
Germany	German
Great Britain	*British*
Italy	Italian
Japan	Japanese
Mexico	Mexican
Oman	Omani
Spain	*Spanish*
the United States	American

3 Pronunciation **word stress**

🔊 **8** Listen and repeat the countries from Exercise 2. Notice the stress.

Grammar *he/she/it + is*

▶ HE / SHE / IT + IS		
He		from India.
She	is	Indian.
It		in India.
(He's, She's = He is, She is)		
For more information and practice, see page 161.		

4 Complete the table for you. Then work in pairs. Complete the table for your partner.

	You	Your partner
Name		
Country		
Nationality		

5 Work in groups of four. Tell the other pair about your partner.

This is Kira. She's from France. She's French.

Background notes

Note that Americans generally call their country *the US* or *the United States*, or just *the States*.

Great Britain (or Britain) is made up of three countries: England, Scotland, and Wales. The more official name is *the United Kingdom* (*the UK*), which includes Great Britain and Northern Ireland.

Pronunciation

3 Play the recording. Students listen and repeat.

Grammar

Grammar notes

In spoken English, *he is, she is,* and *it is* are almost always shortened, so it is best to teach them in the short form with the apostrophe. We only give *is* its full value when we are emphasizing or contradicting.

6 Look at the photos (a–d). Then read the sentences. Write true (T) or false (F).
  1 Miu is from Japan. T   3 Jai is Indian. T
  2 John is French. F   4 Marita is from China. F

7 Write sentences (true or false) like Exercise 6. Read your sentences to your partner.

> Miu is a writer.

> False. She's a filmmaker.

a **WORLDWIDEFILMS**
T O K Y O   O F F I C E
MIU SAEKI
Filmmaker

b UNITED KINGDOM OF GREAT BRITAIN AND NORTHERN IRELAND
PASSPORT
Type Code Passport Number
P   GBR   956870043
Surname (1)
ALLBRIGHT
Given name(s) (2)
JOHN WILLIAM
Nationality (3)
BRITISH
Date of birth (4)

c People at IRT
Mumbai:
Jai Dimri
Writer

d **IT Engineers**
ITALY
MARITA NERO
12/06/13
MARITA NERO

Speaking and writing

8 Work in pairs. Do the quiz.

> Toshiba is French.

> False. It's Japanese.

QUICK QUIZ: TRUE OR **FALSE**

around the world

01 Toshiba is French.

02 Curry is from India.

03 Judo is American.

04 Flamenco is from Spain.

9 Work in pairs. Write an "Around the world" quiz. Write four sentences. Test the class.

4 Read through the grammar box with the class. Refer students to page 161 for more information and practice. Model filling in the chart by copying it on the board and filling in your information. Have students complete the *You* column; then divide the class into pairs and have them share information. Model by saying: *Hi. I'm (Mike). I'm from (the US). I'm (American).*

5 Have the pairs from Exercise 4 join another pair. Model the activity by introducing two or three students to the class. Show *This is...* by gesturing as you introduce each student.

Extra activity 1

If students find it difficult to speak fluidly in Exercise 5, give this drill:

This is Kira. [Students repeat.]

Haruko. [Students say: *This is Haruko.*]

Ana. [Students say: *This is Ana.*]

She's from France. [Students repeat.]

Japan. [Students say: *She's from Japan.*]

Brazil. [Students say: *She's from Brazil.*]

Extra activity 2

Bring into class some magazine pictures or posters of well-known people from different countries. Display the pictures and ask students to "introduce" the people to students in their group.

---

6 Before marking the sentences, ask students to look at the IDs, and elicit information. When checking, ask students to correct the false sentences *John is British; Marita is from Italy.*

7 Model the activity by writing an incorrect sentence on the board and asking students to correct it. Then give students five minutes to write their own sentences. Then put students in pairs to read and correct each other's sentences.

Speaking and writing

8 Tell students to take turns reading and answering the quiz items.

ANSWERS

1. F **2.** T **3.** F **4.** T
(Toshiba and judo are both Japanese.)

---

9 As a class, brainstorm categories, such as people, food, music, and sports. Then, as pairs write their sentences, monitor to help with language.

When checking, ask pairs to read aloud their sentences. The class decides if they are true or false and corrects the false sentences.

HOMEWORK Ask students to find a picture of a well-known person from their country. Tell them to write a description, giving their name, country, nationality, and job. In the next lesson, ask students to present their picture and description to the class.

International phone calls

Warm-up

Continents

Tell students to think about places, or geography, as you ask them a few questions about countries. Ask: *What do Brazil, Argentina, Venezuela, Peru, and Chile all have in common?* (They are all countries in South America.) Ask similar questions about Asia and Africa.

Vocabulary

1 Point to the continents on the map—a bird's eye view from the North Pole—and elicit their names from students. Then have them complete the items.

2 Have students point to the countries on the map.

ANSWERS

1 Asia
2 Europe
3 Europe
4 North America
5 South America

Grammar and pronunciation notes

Continents take capital letters but not definite articles.

Note the stress and pronununciation in American English: Africa, Asia, Australia, Europe, North America, South America.

3 Model the activity by writing three sentences on the board—two correct and one incorrect (e.g., *Germany is in Asia*)—for students to correct.

Extra activity

Divide the class into groups of four or five. Say a continent (e.g., *Asia*) and ask the groups to write down as many (Asian) countries as they can in one minute. When checking, write the countries on the board.

Vocabulary
continents

1 Look at the map on page 15. Complete the names of the continents.

1 Af**rica**
2 As**ia**
3 Au**stralia**
4 Euro**pe**
5 North **America**
6 S**outh** **America**

2 Look at the map again. Complete the sentences.

1 India is in _____ .
2 Italy is in _____ .
3 Germany is in _____ .
4 Canada is in _____ .
5 Brazil is in _____ .

3 Work in pairs. Write five sentences (true or false). Test your partner.

Brazil is in Africa.

Reading

4 Read the article on page 15. Underline the names of four countries.

5 Read the article again. Complete the sentences with the correct name.

1 _____ is a student.
2 _____ is Mexican.
3 _____ is an artist.
4 _____ is from Brazil.
5 _____ is from Canada.
6 _____ is a doctor.

1 Anne-Marie
2 Juan
3 Naomi
4 Nelson
5 Anne-Marie
6 Juan

6 Word focus *from*

Underline *from* in the sentences. Then match the sentences (1–3) with the pictures (a–c).

1 I'm <u>from</u> Spain. *b*
2 Pizza is <u>from</u> Italy. *c*
3 This phone call is <u>from</u> John. *a*

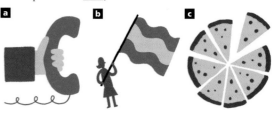

Vocabulary numbers 1–10

7 🔊 **9** Write the numbers (1–10). Then listen and repeat the numbers.

0	zero	*4*	four	*8*	eight
1	one	*5*	five	*9*	nine
2	two	*6*	six	*10*	ten
3	three	*7*	seven		

8 Work in pairs. Look at the map and say a number. Your partner says the country. Switch roles.

Grammar *my, your*

9 🔊 **10** Listen to the conversation. Choose the correct cell phone number (a–c).

a 619 507 7132.   ⓑ 619 408 7132.   c 619 401 6235.

10 🔊 **10** Listen again. Write the work phone number. *661-467-9285*

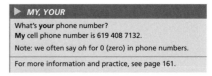

▶ **MY, YOUR**

What's **your** phone number?
My cell phone number is 619 408 7132.
Note: we often say *oh* for 0 (zero) in phone numbers.

For more information and practice, see page 161.

Speaking

11 Work in pairs. Ask and answer questions.

cell phone number   work number   home number

Background notes

The borders between continents are not always obvious. Some countries, for example, Russia and Turkey, span continental boundaries.

Officially, the Australian continent is formed by the countries of Australia and New Guinea. The larger continent of Australasia or Oceania also includes New Zealand, Polynesia, and Micronesia.

Reading

5 Have students compare their answers with a partner before discussing as a class.

Word focus

6 Ask students to look at the pictures. Ask: *What can you see?* Then ask students to complete the activity.

Extra activity

Write *I'm from…* on the board and ask students to write three sentences about themselves. Model the activity by saying: *I'm from (Boston). I'm from (the US). I'm from (North America).*

GEOGRAPHY

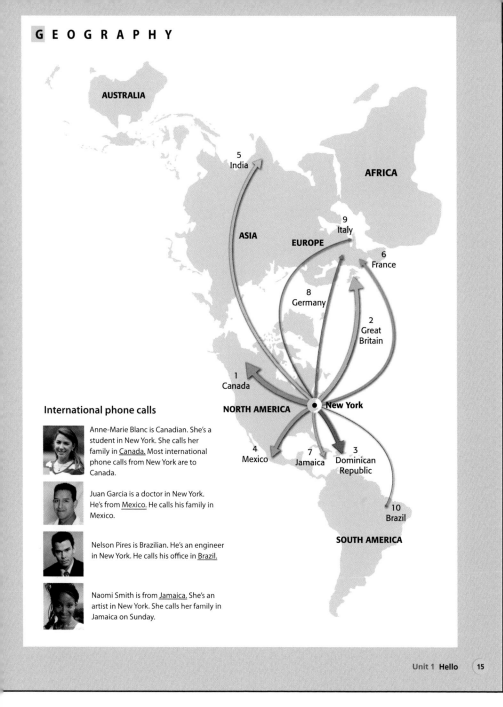

AUSTRALIA

5
India

AFRICA

9
Italy

ASIA

EUROPE

6
France

8
Germany

2
Great
Britain

1
Canada

NORTH AMERICA

New York

4
Mexico

7
Jamaica

3
Dominican
Republic

10
Brazil

SOUTH AMERICA

International phone calls

Anne-Marie Blanc is Canadian. She's a student in New York. She calls her family in Canada. Most international phone calls from New York are to Canada.

Juan Garcia is a doctor in New York. He's from Mexico. He calls his family in Mexico.

Nelson Pires is Brazilian. He's an engineer in New York. He calls his office in Brazil.

Naomi Smith is from Jamaica. She's an artist in New York. She calls her family in Jamaica on Sunday.

Grammar

9 Ask students to look at the three phone numbers and practice saying them. Then play the recording. Check by calling on a student to read the correct number aloud.

10 Read through the grammar box with the class. Refer students to page 161 for more information and practice.

Grammar notes

My and *your* are possessive adjectives, which describe nouns. They are always placed before the noun that they describe.

Speaking

11 Model the activity by asking *What's your…?* questions to several students. Make sure that you elicit *My* in their responses. Then divide the class into pairs and have them take turns asking and answering the questions. Encourage them to jot down the numbers; partners can verify that they are written correctly.

Vocabulary

Pronunciation notes

Point out the unusual spelling and pronunciation of *one two*, and *eight*.

8 Have students look at the map. Model the activity by saying a number between 1 and 10; students respond with the corresponding country.

Extra activity 1

Play these number games to practice numbers.

1 Write these math problems on the board and ask students to write the answers.

one + nine =

three + four =

eight − two =

2 Ask students to write the missing number in each list.

Two four … eight ten

One three five … nine

Two + four three + three

five + one six + …

Extra activity 2

Play "Buzz" as a whole-class activity. Students go around the room counting up to ten, but they cannot say *three* or *five* or multiples of three or five. Instead, they must say *buzz*. So, the first student says *one*, the second student says *two*, but the third student must say *buzz*. The fourth student says *four*, but the fifth and sixth students must both say *buzz*. The seventh student says *seven*. The next student says *eight*. Then the ninth and tenth students must both say *buzz*. The eleventh student says *one* and the count starts again.

If a student makes a mistake, he or she is out. Continue the game until students get so good that they stop making mistakes.

Nice to meet you

Warm-up

Introducing the theme: meeting people

Bring in large pictures of famous people (film stars, sports stars, etc.) and display them.

Walk up to one of the pictures and say *Hello*. Then have a brief imaginary conversation, pausing slightly to pretend that you're listening to a question or an answer (with Leonardo DiCaprio): *Hi, Leo... Oh, I'm fine, fine... I'm (Mike)... Oh, I'm a teacher. ...*

Repeat with another picture; then ask students to go to a picture and have an imaginary one-sided conversation. Point out that this is an open-ended activity, so they can be creative in their conversations.

Vocabulary

1 Drill the expressions for pronunciation practice.

Background notes

Good morning is a common expression. *Good afternoon* and *Good evening* are used in more formal situations; with family and friends, people tend to use *Hi* or *Hello*.

See you or *see you later* is a common alternative to *goodbye*.

Note the stress: *good morning, good afternoon, good evening, goodbye*.

People say *hi* or *hello* when they answer the phone.

Pronunciation

Pronunciation notes

When asking *Wh-* questions, students should generally use an intonation that starts high, rises, and then falls at the end.

4b Monitor carefully and make sure that students are attempting a good intonation pattern when asking the questions.

Vocabulary greetings

1 Write *Bye* and *Hello* in the correct places.

Good ✓ morning.

Good afternoon.

Good evening.

Hi. ✓
¹Hello .

Good night.

Goodbye. ✓
² Bye . ✓

Real life personal information (1)

2 🔊 11 Listen to the conversation. Mark (✓) the greetings in Exercise 1.

3 🔊 11 Listen again. Complete the visitor book.

Date	Name	Company	Signature
5/17/2015	Elias Brich	EB Consulting	E Brich
5/18/2015	Suzi Lee	New Start	Suzi Lee
5/18/2015	James Watt	New Start	James Watt
5/18/2015	Liam Schultz	Today	Liam Schultz

4 Pronunciation questions

a 🔊 12 Listen and repeat three questions from the conversation.

b Work in pairs. Look at the audioscript on page 169. Practice the conversation.

5 Look at the expressions for asking for PERSONAL INFORMATION. Complete the questions with these words.

first   name   phone

▶ PERSONAL INFORMATION

What's your name ?
What's your first name?
What's your last name?
What's your phone number?
What's your job?
I'm Liam. / My name's Liam.

Real life meeting people

6 🔊 13 Listen to the conversation. Put the conversation in order.

a Hi, Katya. How are you?   1
b Nice to meet you too.   5
c Fine, thanks. And you?   2
d I'm OK. This is Silvia. She's   3
   from Madrid.
e Nice to meet you, Silvia.   4

7 Work in groups of three. Practice the conversation from Exercise 6. Use your own names.

▶ MEETING PEOPLE

Hello. / Hi.
How are you?
Fine, thanks. / I'm OK.
This is X.
Nice to meet you.
Nice to meet you too.

8 You are at a meeting. Invent an identity: name, job, company, phone number. Talk to people. Write the names and phone numbers of people with the same job.

Good afternoon. I'm Vicente.

Nice to meet you.

Extra activity

If students still don't know each other well, mix the pairs so that students are with partners that they don't normally work with. Then ask students to practice exchanging information, using the questions in the Personal Information box.

Vocabulary notes

How are you? and *Nice to meet you!* are fixed expressions that students need to understand from context and learn by heart. They need no analysis. Make sure that students are attempting a friendly intonation pattern.

Teaching notes

Before starting the activity, write key language on the board at random (*How are you? What's your phone number? Nice to meet you!* etc.). Then, if students get stuck during the role-play, they can refer to the language on the board.

During the role-play, make note of common errors so that you can provide feedback.

HOMEWORK Tell students to write an imaginary interview with a famous star.

1e My ID

Writing an ID badge

1 Look at the ID (identity) badge and find:

1 the name of the company TD Films
2 the name of the visitor Carolyn Smith

2 Writing skill capital letters (1)

a <u>Underline</u> the capital letters on the ID badge.

b Write these words in the table.

Brazil	Nelson Pires
Brazilian	Rio de Janeiro
Portuguese	South America

a city	Washington _Rio de Janeiro_
a continent	North America _South America_
a country	the United States of America _Brazil_
a language	English _Portuguese_
a name	Carolyn Anderson _Nelson Pires_
a nationality	American _Brazilian / Portuguese_

c Rewrite the sentences with the correct capital letters.

1 riyadh is in saudi arabia. _Riyadh is in Saudi Arabia._
2 I'm chinese. _I'm Chinese._
3 He's from tokyo. _He's from Tokyo._
4 She's from canada. _She's from Canada._
5 I speak french. _I speak French._

3 Complete the IDs with the information. Use capital letters.

1 houston   sean booth

2 american   cathy newman

3 honolulu bangkok sydney   jan sastre

4 Write an ID badge for yourself.

5 Check your badge. Check the capital letters.

HOMEWORK
Write the following name and address on the board:

carlos lopez

26 clifford street

miami, florida

_us_

For homework, ask students to rewrite the name and address, using capital letters. Then have them write their own name and address.

My ID

Writing

1 Let students compare their answers in pairs before discussing as a class.

Vocabulary notes

An *ID card* is carried in your wallet or purse. An *ID badge* is fastened to your clothing.

Writing skill

2b Ask students to look at the table; point out that capital letters are used for words in all these categories. In a monolingual class, it is a good idea to point out situations where the use of capitals differs from the students' native language.

4 and 5 Students must decide what sort of ID badge they want to make (e.g., for their company or their school) and what information to include.

Monitor and help with ideas and vocabulary. Ask students to show their completed badges to a partner to check the use of capital letters.

My top ten photos

Videoscript

Tom Brooks: Hi. My name's Tom Brooks. I'm a photographer. This is my top ten, my favorite National Geographic photos of people and places.

Number 1 is a photo by Alex Treadway. The woman is from Nepal in the Himalayas. She's Nepalese.

Photo number 2 is in Asia, too. The man is from Mongolia. He's a hunter. This photo is by Charles Meacham.

This is photo number 3. It's by James Stanfield. It's in Mongolia, too. It's evening. The woman is happy.

Number 4 is a photo by Michael Melford. This is Ina Bouker. Ina is American. She's from Alaska in the United States. She's a fisherwoman.

Now number 5. This photo is by Jim Blair. He's an American photographer. This photo is in Dhaka in Bangladesh. It's a photo of water buffalo in a river … and a man.

Photo number 6 is fantastic. It's by Brian Skerry. The photo is in the ocean of New Zealand. It's a photo of a man and a whale.

Photo 7 is by Jimmy Chin. This is Kate Rutherford. She's from the United States. She's a climber.

And now three photos from Africa.

Photo number 8 is by David Cartier. He's Australian. He's a student. This is a photo of a student, too. She's a student from South Africa.

This photo is of people from Namibia in Africa. It's by Chris Johns. He's a National Geographic photographer. This is photo number 9.

Hello. My name's Isha.

18

And this is photo number 10. It's my favorite. It's by Chris Johns, too. It's a lion. It's in South Africa. It's the evening. The lion is beautiful. This photo is fantastic.

Before you watch

1 Work in pairs. Look at this photo. Complete the information about Tom Brooks.

Hi. My name ¹ **is** Tom Brooks. I'm ² **a** photographer. This ³ **is** my top ten—my favorite National Geographic photos of people and places.

While you watch

2 Watch the video. Mark (✓) the correct column for each photo.

	a man	a woman	people	an animal / animals
Photo 1		✓		
Photo 2	✓			
Photo 3		✓		
Photo 4		✓		✓
Photo 5	✓			✓
Photo 6	✓			✓
Photo 7		✓		
Photo 8		✓	✓	
Photo 9			✓	
Photo 10				✓

3 Work in pairs. Compare your answers from Exercise 2.

> Photo 2 is a man.   Yes, I agree.

4 Watch the video again. Choose the correct country.

Photo 1 (Nepal) / India
Photo 2 China / (Mongolia)
Photo 3 (Mongolia) / Nepal
Photo 4 (the United States) / Canada
Photo 5 Brazil / (Bangladesh)
Photo 6 Canada / (New Zealand)
Photo 7 Australia / (the United States)
Photo 8 (South Africa) / Namibia
Photo 9 (Namibia) / Kenya
Photo 10 Kenya / (South Africa)

5 Work in pairs. Read the sentences. Write true (T) or false (F). Then watch the video again and check.

Photo 1   The photographer is Alex Treadway. T
Photo 2   This man is a hunter. T
Photo 3   This woman is happy. T
Photo 4   This fisherwoman is from Alaska. T
Photo 5   This is a photo of water buffalo. T
Photo 6   This whale is in the ocean. T
Photo 7   This climber is Jimmy Chin. F
Photo 8   The photographer is South African. F
Photo 9   This photo is in Africa. T
Photo 10 Tom says, "This photo is my favorite." T

6 Watch the video again. Choose your favorite photo. Tell your partner.

After you watch

7 Complete the information about three of the photos.

Photo 5 is by Jim Blair. He's ¹ **an** American photographer. The photo is in Dhaka in Bangladesh. It's ² **a** photo of water buffalo in ³ **a** river and ⁴ **a** man.

Photo 7 ⁵ **is** by Jimmy Chin. This ⁶ **is** Kate Rutherford. She's ⁷ **from** the United States. She's ⁸ **a** climber.

Photo 8 is by David Cartier. ⁹ **He's** Australian. He's ¹⁰ **a** student. This ¹¹ **is** a photo of a student too. She's a student ¹² **from** South Africa.

8 Write about your favorite photo.

an **animal** (n) /ˈænɪməl/

a **climber** (n) /ˈklaɪmər/

fantastic (adj) /fænˈtæstɪk/

a **fisherwoman** (n) /ˈfɪʃərˌwʊmən/

happy (adj) /ˈhæpi/

a **lion** (n) /ˈlaɪən/

a **man** (n) /mæn/

an **ocean** (n) /ˈoʊʃən/

a **river** (n) /ˈrɪvər/

a **water buffalo** (n) /ˈwɔtər, bʌfəloʊ/

a **whale** (n) /weɪl/

a **woman** (n) /ˈwʊmən/

Before you watch

1 Ask students to look at the photo. Ask: *What can you see? What's his name?* Ask students to read through the paragraph silently. Then divide the class into pairs and have them fill in the missing words.

While you watch

2 Before playing the video, give students a moment to look at the table. Ask: *How many photos are there? Are the photos of people or animals?* Then play the video and have students mark the appropriate column for each photo.

4 Play the video again and ask students to choose the correct country.

5 Allow pairs a few minutes to read the sentences and decide if they are true or false. Then play the video again for them to verify their answers. When checking, ask students to correct the false sentences. *The climber is Kate Rutherford; The photographer is Australian.*

6 Divide the class into pairs. Ask students to watch the video again, choose their favorite photo, and tell their partner. When checking, ask questions to elicit the information: *What's your favorite photo? Where is it? What's his / her name?* etc. You could mention that photograph 6 (man and whale by Brian Skerry) was the winner in "The Underwater World" category of the BBC Wildlife Photographer of the Year competition.

After you watch

7 Tell students to read through each paragraph before completing it. Then have them read each paragraph again and check their work. Check by calling on different students to read aloud each sentence.

8 Model by bringing in a favorite photo. Pass it around the class and tell the students about it. Then ask students to write about their favorite photo. You may want to assign this task as homework. Ask students to bring their favorite photos to the to the next class and present their photo and description to the class.

UNIT 1 REVIEW

Grammar

1 Students complete the sentences with the words. Ask them to check that they used capital letters appropriately.

2 Students circle the correct option. Let them compare their answers in pairs before discussing as a class.

Vocabulary

3 Students complete the sentences with a job, country, or nationality.

ANSWERS
1 teacher, Italian
2 engineer, France
3 Great Britain, artist
4 photographer, Chinese
5 doctor, Mexican
6 the United States, driver

4 Students work in pairs and take turns to write and dictate numbers.

5 Students work in pairs to complete the names of the continents. They then take turns to spell the names to their partner.

Real life

6 Students complete the conversation with the options given. Let them compare their answers in pairs before discussing as a class.

ANSWERS
1 What's your name, please?
2 Can you spell your last name?
3 Nice to meet you too.
4 How are you?

Speaking

7 Students prepare and practice the conversation in Exercise 6.

UNIT 1 REVIEW

Grammar

1 Complete the sentences with these words.

I'm   you're   he's   he's   she's   she's   it's   it's

1 Hi. My name's Rosa. <u>I'm</u> from Brazil.
2 This is Carolyn. <u>She's</u> an engineer.
3 I'm from Ottawa. <u>It's</u> in Canada.
4 "My name's Claude Lefevre."
   "Oh! <u>You're</u> a writer!"
5 Mattias is a doctor. <u>He's</u> from Germany.
6 Marina is from Italy. <u>She's</u> Italian.
7 This is Nelson. <u>He's</u> a student.
8 John is from Sydney. <u>It's</u> in Australia.

2 Circle the correct option.

1 (a)/ an country
2 a /(an) explorer
3 (a)/ an family
4 a /(an) identity badge
5 a /(an) office
6 (a)/ an passport

I CAN	
introduce people (*be*)	
use *a* and *an* correctly	
use *my* and *your* correctly	

Vocabulary

3 Look at the pictures. Complete the sentences.

1 I'm a <u>teacher</u> . I'm from Italy. I'm _____ .
2 Lisa's an _____ . She's French. She's from _____ .
3 Joe's British. He's from _____ . He's an _____
4 I'm a _____ . I'm from China. I'm _____ .
5 Enrique is a _____ . He's from Mexico. He's _____
6 Sam's American. He's from _____ . He's a _____ .

4 Work in pairs. Take turns.

Student A: Write five numbers. Then say the numbers to your partner.

Student B: Write the numbers. Then check your answers.

5 Work in pairs. Complete the names of the continents. Spell the names to your partner.

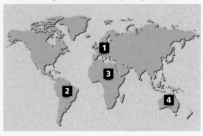

1 E u r o p e
2 S o u t h A m e r i c a
3 A f r i c a
4 A u s t r a l i a

I CAN	
talk about jobs, countries, and nationalities	
count to ten	
say the alphabet, and spell names and words	

Real life

6 Complete the conversations with the right option.

Can you spell your last name?
How are you?
Nice to meet you too.
What's your name, please?

A: Hello. I'm from *World Film* magazine.
B: Ah yes! Good morning. [1] _____
A: My name's Amy Lewis.
B: [2] _____
A: Yes. Lewis. L–E–W–I–S.
B: Thanks. Nice to meet you, Amy.
A: [3] _____
B: This is Chanda. She's a photographer.
A: Hi, Chanda. [4] _____
C: Fine, thanks.

I CAN	
ask for and give personal information	
meet and greet people	

Speaking

7 Work in groups of three. Practice the conversation in Exercise 6.

Extra activity

Students often have trouble spelling out loud and need to review often and early. To review, play a spelling circle game. Students sit in a circle of five or six. Say a job-related word (e.g., *artist*). Going clockwise around the circle, each student says a letter until the word is spelled. If a student gets a letter wrong, he or she is "out." Keep going until you run out of words or until all the students are out. This game is also a great way to review new vocabulary.

A beautiful beach on Robinson Crusoe Island in the Pacific Ocean
Photo by Richard Nowitz

FEATURES

22 My vacation
Vacation photos

24 Where are you?
A conversation with friends

26 A vacation quiz
A quiz about vacation places

30 Antarctica
A video about Antarctica

1 Look at the photo. Choose the correct option (a–c).

a This is in Canada. It's a beach. It's evening.
b This is in France. It's a city. It's night.
ⓒ This is in Fiji. It's an island. It's morning.

2 🎧 **14** Look at these two pictures. Listen and repeat the words.

3 Complete the sentences with words from Exercise 2.

1 Rio de Janeiro is a <u>city</u> in Brazil.
2 Titicaca is a <u>lake</u> in Bolivia and Peru.
3 Tahiti is an <u>island</u> in the Pacific Ocean.
4 Everest is a _____ in Nepal. mountain

4 Write four sentences about places and read them to your partner.

> Loch Ness is a lake in Scotland.

Vacations

2 Hold up your book and point to the geographical features. Ask: *What is it?* You could also include the word *boat* from the main photo.

Extra activity

An alternative way of introducing these words is to make flashcards with simple pictures of a beach, a city, an island, etc.

Hold up each flashcard and say: *What is it?* Elicit each word, model it for pronunciation, and ask students to repeat. After going through all the cards, hold them up and call on individuals to say what each one shows.

Pronunciation notes

Point out that an *island* uses *an* because the noun starts with a vowel sound. The *s* is silent. The stress in *island* and *mountain* is on the first syllable.

Background notes

Lake Titicaca, which lies in the Andes region on the borders of Peru and Bolivia, is the largest lake in South America (by volume).

Tahiti is the largest island in French Polynesia. It was formed by a volcano, which is why it has black sand beaches.

Mount Everest is the world's highest mountain. It is almost 8,800 meters high and is located in Nepal.

Loch Ness is a large, deep lake (or *loch* in Scottish dialect) in the highlands of Scotland. It's famous for the legend of a monster that is supposed to live deep in the lake.

4 Tell students to write about places they know well.

Extra activities

1 Ask students to write two true and two false sentences (e.g., *Titicaca is a mountain in Australia*). They read them aloud and their partner corrects the false ones.

2 Write ten geographical features from around the world that your students are likely to know, on the board (e.g., *Everest, Baikal, Andaman, Majorca, New York, Eiger, Paris, Ipanema*) and tell students to categorize them. Then tell students to add two more names to each category.

3 Write 10–20 different geographical features on the board. Divide the class into two teams. The teams take turns creating sentences that use a word from the board and a country name. (e.g., *Everest is a mountain in Nepal*). Teams get a point for each accurate sentence using a geographical feature and the name of a country.

2a

My vacation

MY VACATION BLOG *by Laura* 03 JAN

This is in Tunisia. It's beautiful! It's evening. I'm with Brad, Andy, and Jessica. We're on a beach. We're happy. Andy and Jessica are Canadian. They're doctors. They're on vacation too.

Materials

Ask students to bring in photos or have photos on their cell phone for Exercise 10.

Warm-up

Using words

With books closed, ask students to recall and describe the photo of a beautiful vacation spot on the first page of the unit. Once students have described the beach photo, ask them to name some other popular types of vacation destinations.

Reading

2 Ask students to look at the photo and read through the text. Check that students understand *blog* (a web log), *vacation*, and *happy*. Then have students scan the text to find the information.

Grammar

3 When checking, emphasize that *I* refers to Laura, *we* refers to Laura and her new friends, and *they* refers to Andy and Jessica.

Refer students to the information and practice on page 161.

Grammar notes

In spoken English, *We are* and *They are* are almost always shortened, so it is best to teach them in the short form with the apostrophe. We only give *are* its full value when we are emphasising or contradicting: *No! We are French!*

Pronunciation

5b Model sentences for the class: *We're in Moscow. We're from Russia. We're in class. We're happy.* Emphasize that all the sentences should be true.

Reading

1 Work in pairs. Look at the photos. Choose the place (a–c).

a North America b Europe c Africa

2 Read about the photo above. Find:

1 the name of the country Tunisia
2 the names of the people
  Brad, Andy, Jessica (and Laura)

Grammar *we/they + are*

3 Look at the grammar box. Then look at the blog. Underline the contractions *we're* and *they're*.

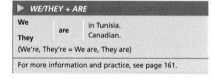

▶ **WE/THEY + ARE**

| We | | in Tunisia. |
| They | are | Canadian. |

(We're, They're = We are, They are)

For more information and practice, see page 161.

22

4 Complete the sentences.

1 This is Jane. This is Paul. They 're Australian.
2 I'm Meera. This is Suri. We 're from India.
3 In this photo, I'm with my friend Jack. We 're in Egypt.
4 Laura is with Brad, Andy, and Jessica. They're on vacation.
5 Jeanne and Claude are from France. They're French.

5 Pronunciation *we're, they're*

a 🔊 **15** Listen and repeat six sentences.

b Work in pairs. Write three true sentences with *We're*. Read your sentences to a new pair.

> *We're in Moscow.*

Extra activity

Bring in magazine photos showing two or more people in different places, ideally recognizable locations. Hand out the photos to pairs or groups and ask them to describe the people using *They're*.

6 Have pairs of students compare their corrected sentences.

ANSWERS

1 False. It is Tunisia.
2 True.
3 False. Andy and Jessica are from Canada.
4 False. Laura is in the photo.
5 False. They're (They are) happy.

6 Read these sentences about the photo on page 22. Write true (T) or false (F). Correct the false sentences.

1 It isn't Tunisia. F
2 They are on a beach. T
3 Andy and Jessica aren't from Canada. F
4 Laura isn't in the photo. F
5 They aren't happy. F

Grammar *be* negative forms

7 Look at the grammar box and the sentences in Exercise 6. Note the negative forms of *is* and *are*.

▶ BE NEGATIVE FORMS		
I	am not (I'm not)	
You	are not (aren't)	happy.
He/She/It	is not (isn't)	on a beach.
We/You/They	are not (aren't)	

For more information and practice, see page 162.

8 Complete the blog. Use these words.

not   aren't   isn't   isn't

In this photo, we ¹ _aren't_ in Tunisia. We're in Morocco. It ² _isn't_ a beach. It's the Sahara Desert. Andy and Jessica are on a camel trek. Brad ³ _isn't_ on the camel trek. He's in a tent. I'm ⁴ _not_ in this photo.

9 Pronunciation *isn't, aren't*

a 🔊 16 Listen and repeat the sentences.

b Write true sentences. Read them to your partner.

> We aren't on a beach.

	a student.
	a doctor.
I'm (not)	in a city.
	in a classroom.
You're	in Asia.
You aren't	happy.
	on a lake.
We're	on a beach.
We aren't	on vacation.
	from Morocco.

Speaking

10 Work in groups. Show a photo on your cell phone to the group. Tell the group about your photo.

> This is a photo of my friends, Carlos and Enrique. We're in Egypt.

Unit 2 Vacations **23**

Grammar

7 Read through the grammar box with the class. Ask students to find the negative forms in Exercise 6. Refer students to page 162 for more information and practice.

> **ANSWERS**
> The negative forms are *isn't* and *aren't*.

8 Ask students to look at the photo on page 23. Ask: *Where are they?* Elicit ideas. Ask students if they can point out the camels and the tents. If necessary, draw them on the board to check understanding. Then ask students to read the blog and fill in the blanks.

Pronunciation

9b Emphasize that students should write sentences that are true for them and their partner.

Write some sentences with *isn't* on the board to give students extra practice with this form, for example: *Today isn't Monday, He isn't George.* Point out to students the short vowel and /z/ sound. Correct pronunciation of this form immediately and regularly, making sure students repeat the correct pronunciation after you, as it is a pronunciation problem students regularly carry into higher levels.

Speaking

10 Model the activity first by bringing in some photos of your family and friends on vacation. Pass the photos around the class and describe them.

> **Extra activity 1**
> Draw a simple line drawing on the board, showing two stick figures sitting on a beach or walking in the mountains. As you draw, pretend you are showing two friends on vacation, and describe the picture, e.g., *This is Andy and Sue. They aren't in the US. They're on vacation in Peru. They're happy. The mountains are beautiful,* etc. Then ask students to make a similar drawing and describe their friends' vacation to a partner.

> **Extra activity 2**
> Review vocabulary from the previous section. Write on the board: lakes, seas, mountains, cities, islands. Divide the class into pairs. Each pair must choose a category (lakes, for example) and think of as many examples as they can in one minute.

> **HOMEWORK** Ask students to find a vacation photo that shows at least two friends or family members. Ask them to write a description of the photo.

Where are you?

2b Where are you?

Warm-up

Introducing the theme: numbers

Review numbers from 1 to 10 by playing "Buzz" (see the extra activity in 1c).

Introducing the theme: places

Review places from 2a by playing a *Pictionary*-like game. Start drawing a lake on the board and when a student guesses correctly, draw an island. Keep going until students have guessed all the place words.

Vocabulary

Pronunciation notes

Point out the unusual spelling and pronunciation of *twelve* and *eighteen*.

Note that the strong stress is on the last syllable (teen): *thirteen*, *fourteen*, etc.

2 Students write the numbers in order. Check and have them repeat the numbers.

Pronunciation notes

Note that the strong stress is on the first syllable: *sixty*, *seventy*, etc.

In English, you can say *one hundred* or *a hundred*.

Extra activity

Students at this level often mispronounce and mishear *sixty* and *sixteen*, *thirty* and *thirteen*, etc.

To check this, write this list on the board and remind students of the stress.

thirteen   thirty   fifteen   fifty

sixteen   sixty   nineteen   ninety

Then read aloud one word from each pair and ask students to indicate which one you are saying.

Alternatively, have pairs test each other.

Vocabulary numbers 11–100

1 Write the numbers. Repeat them after your instructor.

11	eleven
12	twelve
13	thirteen
14	fourteen
15	fifteen
16	sixteen
17	seventeen
18	eighteen
19	nineteen

2 Write the numbers in order. Check your answers with your instructor.

| eighty | fifty | forty | ninety |
| seventy | sixty | thirty | twenty |

one hundred — 100
ninety — 90
eighty — 80
seventy — 70
sixty — 60
fifty — 50
forty — 40
thirty — 30
twenty — 20
ten — 10
zero — 0

3 🔊 17 Look at the temperatures. Then listen. Are the numbers the same or different?

It's twelve degrees.
the same

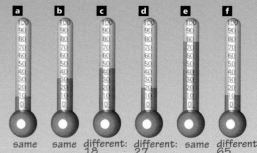

| a | b | c | d | e | f |
| same | same | different: 18 | different: 27 | same | different: 65 |

4 🔊 17 Listen again. Write the correct numbers.

5 Work in pairs. Say the correct temperatures to your partner.

6 Complete the sentences with *hot* or *cold*.

1 It's eleven degrees in London today. It's _cold_ .
2 It's eighty degrees in Sydney today. It's _hot_ .

7 Work in pairs. Make sentences with *hot* and *cold*.

Iceland is cold.

Cairo is hot.

24

---

3 Point to the thermometers and check that students understand the words *temperature* and *degrees*. Say: *What's the temperature?* and elicit the numbers in the pictures from the students. Then play the audio.

6 Write *hot* and *cold* on the board. Act out *hot* (wipe sweat from your brow) and *cold* (shake with teeth chattering) and point to the words. Say the words and ask students to repeat. Then have students complete the sentences.

Extra activity

Play bingo. Draw a simple bingo grid of 25 boxes (5×5) on the board and ask students to copy it. Tell students to write a different number (between zero and 100) in each square.

Then read aloud numbers from 0–100 at random. Students cross out numbers they hear that are on their card. When someone has crossed out a row of numbers (horizontally, vertically, or diagonally), they shout out *Bingo!* They're the winner.

Reading and listening

8 Lorna is Australian. She's on vacation in Europe. Read the conversation. Answer the questions.

1 Where's Lorna? *She's in the Alps.*
2 Where's Greg? *He's in Sydney.*
3 Where are Kara and Ona? *They're in Morocco.*

9 🔊 **18** Listen and choose the correct option.

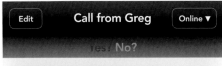

> Greg: Hi! <u>Where are you now?</u> <u>Are you in</u> ¹⟨France⟩/ *Italy*?
>
> Lorna: Yes, I am. I'm in the Alps. It's beautiful!
>
> Greg: <u>Are you OK?</u>
>
> Lorna: No, I'm not. It's ²⟨two⟩/ *seventy-two* degrees!
>
> Greg: Wow! <u>Is it</u> ³⟨cold⟩/ *hot* in your hotel?
>
> Lorna: No, it isn't. The hotel is nice.
>
> Greg: It's ⁴⟨eighty-six⟩/ *sixteen* degrees in Sydney today.
>
> Lorna: Oh! That's ⁵⟨hot⟩/ *cold*!
>
> Greg: <u>Are Kara and Ona in France?</u>
>
> Lorna: No, they aren't. They're on a ⁶⟨beach⟩/ *lake* in Morocco!

Grammar *be* questions and short answers

10 Look at the grammar box. Then <u>underline</u> the questions in Exercise 9.

▶ **BE QUESTIONS and SHORT ANSWERS**

Am I		Yes, I am. No, I'm not.
Are you/we/they	in France? cold?	Yes, you/we/they **are**. No, you/we/they **aren't**.
Is she/he/it		Yes, she/he/it **is**. No, she/he/it **isn't**.

For more information and practice, see page 162.

11 Put the words in order to make questions. Then match the questions (1–6) with the answers (a–f).

1 you / OK / are / ?
2 is / in France / Kara / ?
3 in Sydney / you and Paul / are / ?
4 in London / is / Greg / ?
5 Kara and Ona / in Morocco / are / ?
6 nice / your hotel / is / ?

a Yes, they are. 5
b No, he isn't. 4
c Yes, I am. 1
d Yes, it is. 6
e No, she isn't. 2
f Yes, we are. 3

12 Pronunciation *be* questions and short answers

a 🔊 **19** Listen and repeat these questions and answers.

b Work in pairs. Practice the questions and answers.

Speaking

13 Work in pairs. You are on vacation. Have a telephone conversation with your friend.

Student A: Turn to page 153.

Student B: Turn to page 157.

Reading and listening

8 Set the scene by asking: *Where is Lorna from? Where is she now?* Then ask students to read the conversation and answer the questions.

Grammar

10 Read through the grammar box with the class. Refer students to page 162 for more information and practice.

> **Grammar notes**
>
> Questions are formed with the verb *be* by inverting the subject and verb:
>
> | *Are* | *you* | *French?* |
> |---|---|---|
> | *Is* | *he* | *OK?* |
>
> In short answers, the speaker shortens the answer because it is unnecessary to repeat the information in the question:
>
> | *Are you French?* | *Yes, I am (French).* |
> |---|---|
> | *Is it cold?* | *No, it isn't (cold).* |

> **11 ANSWERS**
>
> 1 Are you OK?
> 2 Is Kara in France?
> 3 Are you and Paul in Sydney?
> 4 Is Greg in London?
> 5 Are Kara and Ona in Morocco?
> 6 Is your hotel nice?

Pronunciation

12a Point out the rising intonation on the *yes/no* questions and the falling intonation on the short answers.

> **Extra activity**
>
> Ask pairs to rewrite the questions in Exercise 11, using the names of people in the class. Students then practice asking and answering these personalized questions.

Speaking

13 Give students time to read the information at the back of their book. Student A prepares to describe a vacation. Student B prepares questions to ask. Circulate and help students. Have them practice the conversation and then switch roles.

Check by asking what is different about the two destinations.

> **HOMEWORK** Ask students to imagine that their best friend is on vacation. Tell them to write five texts or tweets that they will send to their friend (e.g., *Are you in Florida? Is it hot?*) and tell them to write their friend's short answers.

Warm-up

Test before you teach: colors

Find out whether your students already know colors by drawing (and labeling) the designs of four flags on the board, e.g., Japan, the US, India, and the country of most of the students. Have pairs of students say what colors are in the flag, e.g., *the Japanese flag is red and white*. If students don't know these colors, try this activity again later in the lesson.

Vocabulary

1 Have students check their answers in pairs.

If your students are already familiar with basic colors, challenge them by presenting some additional vocabulary, such as *light* and *dark* to describe shade, or *beige*, *silver*, and *gold*.

ANSWERS
1 red
2 blue
3 yellow
4 green
5 black
6 orange
7 brown
8 pink
9 white
10 gray

2 To follow up, say a color and have students point to an example of it in the classroom.

Reading

3 Ask students to read the quiz and match the photos to only four of the the sentences.

ANSWERS			
a 3	**b** 2	**c** 4	**d** 1

4 Remind students to use the words from the list to complete the sentences. Go over the pronunciation with them to help them.

La Defense, Paris, France

Vocabulary **colors**

1 Match the colors with the numbers.

1   **2**   3   **4**   **5**

black	blue	brown	green	gray
orange	pink	red	white	yellow

6   **7**   8   10

2 Find the colors in the photo.

Reading

3 Read the quiz on page 27. Match the photos with four sentences.

4 Complete the sentences in the quiz in pairs.

Grammar **plural nouns**

5 Look at the grammar box. Find these plural nouns in the quiz. Then find two more plural nouns in the quiz.

▶ **NOUNS**	
Singular	**Plural**
a lake	lakes
a car	cars
a country	cities
a beach	beaches
For more information and practice, see page 162.	

6 **Pronunciation plural nouns**

a 20 Listen and repeat these nouns.

/s/	/z/	/ɪz/
lakes	cars	beaches
airports	countries	buses

b 21 Write the plural of these nouns. Then listen and repeat.

a city	a doctor	a friend
a hotel	a mountain	an office
a phone	a student	a tent

7 **Word focus *in***

Write the expressions in the correct place.

in Australia	in French	in a hotel
in Japanese	in Moscow	in a tent

1 in English   in Japenese   in French
2 in Europe   in Australia   in Moscow
3 in a classroom in a tent   in a hotel

Speaking

8 Work in pairs. Test your partner. Take turns.

cities	countries	continents	lakes

Name three cities.

London, Lima, Bangkok.

26

Extra activity

Ask pairs of students to write two new quiz sentences using a color. Ask some pairs to read aloud their sentences without saying the color. The rest of the class says the color.

Grammar

5 Read through the grammar box with the class. Refer students to page 162 for more information and practice.

Grammar notes

Plurals are usually formed by adding *-s*.

Add *-es* when a noun ends with *-ch*, *-sh*, *-s*, or *-x* (*beaches*, *dishes*, *buses*, *taxes*, etc.).

When a noun ends with *-y*, change *-y* to *-i* and add *-es*.

A Vacation Quiz

airports	black	China
Cuba	lakes	London

1. In __Cuba__, cars are old.
2. In __London__, buses are red.
3. In Hawaii, beaches are __black__.
4. In Iceland, the __lakes__ are hot.
5. Hong Kong, Shanghai, and Beijing are cities in __China__.
6. John Lennon, Charles de Gaulle, and John F. Kennedy are __airports__.

A 1951 Chevy on Playa Ancon, Cuba

Vocabulary notes

In English, we use *in* to say where someone or something is located. So, we can say *in* with cities, countries, and continents, and with rooms, buildings, and means of transport.

Notice that we say *in a car* or *taxi* but *on a bus* or *train*. We can say *in* or *on a boat* or *plane*.

Speaking

8 Model the activity by saying: *Name three cities*, and elicit three answers from students.

Pronunciation

6a Make sure that students are attempting the correct pronunciation of the plural noun endings.

Pronunciation notes

After unvoiced sounds, *-s* is pronounced /s/.

After voiced sounds (vowel sounds and some consonant sounds), *-s* is pronounced /z/.

The *-es* endings is pronounced /ɪz/.

6b Ask students to write the plural forms. Do the first one as an example on the board, and let students compare their answers in pairs before playing the recording.

Extra activity

Review vocabulary by asking students to look back at Unit 1 and find five nouns. Then tell them to write the plural form.

ANSWERS

doctors
friends
cities
mountains
offices
phones
students
tents

Word focus

7 Open the activity by writing *in* on the board, and asking: *Where are you?* Elicit possible answers: *I'm in (Russia). I'm in a classroom. I'm in (Moscow)...*

Ask students to write the expressions in the table. Do the first one as an example on the board.

Here are your keys

Warm-up

Using words: letters and numbers

Review letters and numbers. Write these pairs on the board:

A	B
ITV	ATV
17	70
UAE	USA
0118723459	0118623459
CNN	CSN
BMW	BMX
50	15

Read aloud one set of letters or numbers in each pair. Students listen and indicate the one you said. Then have pairs of students test each other.

Vocabulary

1 Model and drill the words 1–5 to practice pronunciation.

2 Model saying an email address by writing yours on the board and having students repeat each part after you. Make sure that students take turns reading the addresses at random.

Pronunciation notes

Notice the pronunciation of these email symbols:

@ = at   . = dot

3 Model by asking questions with *What's your…?* to several students: *What's your email address? What's your address?*

Real life

6 Monitor carefully and make sure they are attempting a good intonation pattern when asking the questions.

Vocabulary **car rental**

1 Match 1–5 with a–e.

1 a license plate number *e*
2 an email address *d*
3 an address *b*
4 a zip code *c*
5 keys *a*

b 3 Park Street
Milton
c 02186

d To: jamesp@national.org

e MÉXICO SZ-27-627 QUINTANA ROO

28

2 Work in pairs. Take turns.

Student A: Read an email address.

Student B: Identify the email address.

1 smith23@hotmail.com
2 ryan.law@google.com
3 barry@yahoo.com
4 smnrss@msn.com

3 Work in pairs. Ask your partner his or her address, zip code, email address, and license plate number.

Real life **personal information (2)**

4 🔊 **22** Listen to the conversation. Answer the questions.

1 Is the man from Tokyo? Yes
2 Is he on vacation or on business? On business

5 🔊 **22** Listen again. Choose the correct option.

1 Name: Mr. Sato / Mrs. Ono
2 Zip code: 08597 / 170-3293
3 Email address: epsato@hotmail.com / ep@hotmail.com
4 License plate number: BD5 ACR / BD6 ATR

6 Work in pairs. Practice the conversation on page 169.

> ▶ **PERSONAL INFORMATION**
> This is my ID.
> Where are you from?
> Is this your (email) address?
> What's the zip code?
> What's your telephone number in the US?
> Sign here, please.
> Here's your key.
> The license plate number is BD6 ATR.
> Note: in email addresses we say *at* for @ and *dot* for "."

7 Pronunciation **syllables**

🔊 **23** Listen and repeat these words. Count the syllables.

vacation   va – ca – tion = 3

address 2 car 1 email 2 key 1 number 2 telephone 3

8 Work in pairs. Practice the conversation again with new information.

> Good evening.

> Hello, I'm Mrs. Ono.

Extra activity

Write these prompts on the board:

Name? From? Address? Email address? Phone number?

Vacation or business? Zip code?

Ask two students to act out the car rental conversation for the class. Prompt the student that is asking the questions by pointing at the word prompts.

Call on another pair. Keep the conversations brisk but correct errors.

Pronunciation

Extra activity

Test stronger students by writing some more difficult words on the board, and asking them to work out how many syllables there are: *registration, pronunciation, engineer, scientist.*

8 Ask pairs to look at the conversation on page 169 and think about which details they can change. Then ask them to practice the conversation.

> **HOMEWORK** Tell students to write an interview with a well-known politician using questions from the unit.

2e Contact details

Writing a form

1 Match 1 and 2 with the options (a and b).

a   a hotel online reservation form   2
b   an Internet profile   1

Enya Farrell

Call name:	enya123
Cell phone:	212-555-6957
Home phone:	212-555-5512
Email address:	enya@gmail.com
Country:	US
Contacts:	19

2

Title	Ms. ☑
First name	Enya
Last name	Farrell
Address	16 Park Avenue
City	New York
State	New York
Zip code	10021
Country	US ☑
Email address	enya@gmail.com

2   What's your title? Is it Mr., Mrs., or Ms.?

---

3 Writing skill capital letters (2)

a Look at the information in form 2. Underline the capital letters.

b Rewrite this information with the correct capital letters. *See form below.*

1   11 hill view   4   esposito
2   california   5   mr.
3   san francisco   6   ryan

4 Complete the college registration form with the information from Exercise 3b.

REGISTRATION FORM

Title   Mr.

First name   Ryan

Last name   Esposito

Address   11 HIll View

City San Francisco   State   California

Zip code   94122

Contact number   415 - 489 - 1453

Email address   ryan@aol.com

5 Complete the online reservation form with your own information. Check the capital letters.

Title	Choose… ☑
First name	
Last name	
Address	
City	
State	
Zip code	
Contact number	
Email address	

Contact details

2e

Contact details

Warm-up

Using words: numbers, letters, and email addresses

Use dictation to practice numbers, letters, and email addresses. Ask students to write the numbers 1 to 5 on a blank sheet of paper. Then read aloud each address twice, clearly but naturally. Let students check what they wrote with a partner before writing the email addresses on the board.

1   jimmy23@mail.pe
2   DBC397@newmail.co.au
3   SP34@BT.com
4   007@MI5.co.uk
5   JFK100@CIA.com

Writing

1 When checking, ask follow-up questions, e.g., *What is Enya's home phone number? What is Enya's zip code?*

Background notes

In US addresses, house numbers are written before the street name, and street names and cities always have a capital letter. State names are often written as two-letter abbreviations using capital letters, e.g., *New York → NY*.

A zip code is used to identify a mail delivery area in a US town or city. Zip codes start with a zero in the Northeast US, and gradually get higher (up to 9) as you move west. Zip codes are usually written as five digits (10021), but a nine-digit form can be given to indicate a more specific delivery area (10021-1264).

In the phone numbers on Enya's forms, the first three digits are called the *area code*. This is a number assigned to a geographical area of the US, Canada, or the Caribbean.

2

Background notes

On forms, men always use *Mr.,* but doctors may use *Dr. Mr.* is an abbreviation of *Mister* and is pronounced in the same way.

On forms, women generally use the title *Ms.,* or *Dr.* for doctors. *Ms.* does not indicate a woman's marital status. Some married women prefer *Mrs.* and some unmarried women use *Miss.*

Writing skill

3b When checking, have students say why each word is capitalized (street name, etc.).

Extra activity

Students interview a classmate and write down their personal information. Then they complete an online booking form with their partner's information. Finally, pairs check each other's information and make corrections.

HOMEWORK Ask students to find an English-language form online for something that they are interested in. Tell them to download the form and complete it.

Antarctica

Videoscript

Narrator: Antarctica is a continent. It isn't hot. It's cold.

The <u>temperatures</u> in Antarctica are below freezing. <u>Temperatures of 30 degrees below zero are typical</u>.

Antarctica is a good place for scientists and explorers, <u>but the people on this boat are on vacation</u>!

<u>Boats</u> to Antarctica come from South America, Australia, New Zealand, and South Africa.

Is it a good place for a vacation?

The <u>beaches</u> aren't beautiful yellow beaches.

And the <u>sea</u> is gray and cold.

But, the <u>animals</u> are amazing. These <u>whales and penguins</u> are from Antarctica.

In Antarctica, the mountains are white.

In the sea, the ice is white and blue.

The temperature of the sea is <u>from four degrees below zero to ten degrees</u>.

For the animals in Antarctica, cold temperatures are good.

Life is difficult for scientists and explorers.

But Antarctica is a beautiful continent.

People and penguins in Antarctica

30

Before you watch

1 Look at the photo and the caption on page 30. What are the animals? *penguins*

2 Look at the map. Write the number (1–4) next to the place.

Africa 2   Australia 4   New Zealand 3   South America 1

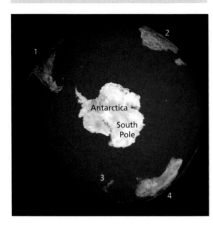

Antarctica
South Pole

While you watch

3 Watch the video without sound. Write at least five words.

4 Work in pairs. Read your words to your partner. Watch the video again. Check your partner's words.

5 Watch and listen to the video. Listen to information about these things. Put the words in the order you hear them.

a animals 5   d temperatures 1
b beaches 3   e the ocean 4
c boats 2

6 Read the sentences. Watch the video again. Write true (T) or false (F).

1 The typical temperatures in Antarctica are 90 degrees below zero. F
2 The people on the boat are scientists. F
3 The animals in the ocean are whales and penguins. T
4 The temperature of the ocean in Antarctica is from two degrees below zero to ten degrees. T

7 Read the sentences. Underline the correct option. Watch the video again. Check your answers.
1 Antarctica *is / isn't* a continent.
2 Antarctica *is / isn't* a good place for scientists and explorers.
3 The beaches *are / aren't* yellow.
4 Cold temperatures *are / aren't* good for the animals.

After you watch

8 Work in pairs. Test your memory. Ask and answer the questions.

1 Where are the boats from?
2 What color are penguins?
3 What color are whales?
4 What color is ice?

9 Work in pairs. Write questions about Antarctica with these words.

1 mountains / beautiful
2 beaches / nice
3 animals / amazing
4 Antarctica / a good place for a vacation

10 Work as a class. Ask three people your questions. Write their names and answers.

Are the mountains beautiful?

Yes, they are.   No, they aren't.

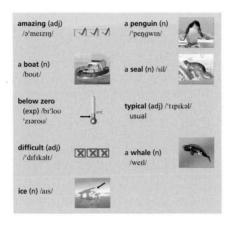

amazing (adj) /əˈmeɪzɪŋ/

a boat (n) /boʊt/

below zero (exp) /bɪˈloʊ ˈzɪroʊ/

difficult (adj) /ˈdɪfɪkəlt/

ice (n) /aɪs/

a penguin (n) /ˈpeŋgwɪn/

a seal (n) /siːl/

typical (adj) /ˈtɪpɪkəl/ usual

a whale (n) /weɪl/

Before you watch

1 Ask students to look at the photo on page 30. Ask: *What are the animals?*

2 Students look at the map and write the numbers (1–4) next to the places.

While you watch

3 Ask students to watch the video without sound and write at least five words (any words they can think of).

4 Give students some time to compare their words with a partner. Get feedback from the whole class and write the words on the board. Accept any correct answers.

5 Students watch and listen to the video. Ask students to put the words in the order they hear them. Check the answers as a class.

6 Read through the sentences as a class. Then play the video again. Students decide if the sentences are true or false.

7 Give students some time to read the sentences and underline the correct option. Then play the video again. Students watch, listen, and check.

After you watch

8 Divide the class into pairs. Ask: *What do you remember?* Students ask each other the questions.

ANSWERS
1 Australia, South Africa, South America, New Zealand
2 black and white (and some orange)
3 gray
4 white and blue

9 Model the activity by writing the prompt *Antartica / cold* on the board. Guide students in forming the question: *Is Antarctica cold?* Go through items 1–4 as a class and have students say whether they will use *Are* or *Is* in each question. Then ask pairs to write questions.

ANSWERS
1 Are the mountains beautiful?
2 Are the beaches nice?
3 Are the animals amazing?
4 Is Antarctica a good place for a vacation?

10 Ask students to walk around the room and ask three classmates their questions. When checking, write the most popular answers on the board.

UNIT 2 REVIEW

Grammar

1 Ask students to complete the texts with the words, and match the photo with Greg or Kara.

> **ANSWERS**
>
> 1 'm
> 2 We're
> 3 not
> 4 isn't
> 5 They're
> 6 aren't
> 7 We
> 8 are
> 9 isn't

The photo matches Kara's description; it shows a famous landmark in Rio de Janeiro, and the beaches Kara describes are easily visible.

2 Students write questions.

> **ANSWERS**
>
> 1 Is your teacher American?
> 2 Are we in an office?
> 3 Are you from Europe?
> 4 Are your friends teachers?
> 5 Is this classroom cold?
> 6 Are you okay?

3 Students ask and answer the questions in Exercise 2.

4 Students write the plurals.

Vocabulary

5 Students write the numbers.

6 Students choose the correct color.

Real life

7 Students complete 1–4, then match 1–4 with a–d.

> **ANSWERS**
>
> 1 are; c
> 2 Is; d
> 3 zip code; a
> 4 your; b

Speaking

8 Student A must think of questions to ask. Student B must think of how to give the information. Then have them switch roles.

UNIT 2 REVIEW

Grammar

1 Complete the texts with the words. Then match the photo with Greg or Kara.

> 'm   isn't   not   we're

GREG
I'm in the mountains. I ¹_____ with my friends. We're in Canada. ²_____ on vacation. I'm ³_____ happy—the hotel ⁴_____ nice.

> are   aren't   isn't   they're   we

KARA
I'm in Brazil with my friends Jorge and Ana. ⁵_____ Brazilian. I'm on vacation. Jorge and Ana ⁶_____ on vacation. ⁷_____ 're in Rio de Janeiro. The beaches ⁸_____ beautiful. The ocean ⁹_____ cold—it's warm!

2 Write questions.

1 your teacher / American?
2 we / in an office?
3 you / from Europe?
4 your friends / teachers?
5 this classroom / cold?
6 you / OK?

3 Work in pairs. Ask and answer the questions in Exercise 2.

4 Write the plurals.

1	airport	airports	5	country	countries
2	beach	beaches	6	friend	friends
3	bus	buses	7	office	offices
4	city	cities	8	photo	photos

> **I CAN**
> talk about more than one person (*we, you, they*) ☐
> ask and answer questions (*be*) ☐
> use regular plural nouns ☐

Vocabulary

5 Write the numbers.

a eleven + twelve = twenty-three
b twenty-three + sixty = eighty-three
c forty-five + fifteen = sixty
d thirty-eight + fifty-one = eighty-nine

6 Choose the correct color.

1 My car is *red* / yellow.
2 My phone is *gray* / black.
3 The buses are *yellow* / green.
4 The lake is brown / *blue.*
5 The boats are *orange* / red.

> **I CAN**
> count from eleven to one hundred ☐
> say the colors of objects ☐

Real life

7 Complete 1–4 with four of these words. Then match 1–4 with a–d.

> a   are   is   my   your   zip code

1 Where _____ you from?
2 _____ this your address in the US?
3 What's the _____?
4 Here are _____ keys.

a 10007.
b Thank you.
c I'm from Poland.
d Yes, it is.

> **I CAN**
> ask for and give personal information ☐
> rent a car ☐

Speaking

8 Work in pairs.

Student A: You are a car rental agent.

Student B: You are a customer.

Ask and answer questions to complete the car rental form. Take turns.

SuperCar

title	
first name	
last name	
address	
city	
state	
zip code	
contact number	
email address	

Extra activity

Have students write a description of a vacation destination that they know, without saying the name of the destination. They should describe the weather, geography, and any well-known attractions. Pre-teach *there is/there are* if necessary. Then have them read their descriptions aloud to the class to see if they can guess the location.

Unit 3 Families

A father in India takes his two sons to school.

FEATURES

1 🔊 24 Look at the photo and read the information about the family. Complete the information for Ravi and Mohan. Then listen and check.

Danvir and Mohan are brothers. Ravi and Danvir are father and son. Ravi and Mohan are <u>father</u> and <u>son</u>.

2 Write the words in the correct place.

daughter   parents   sister

♂	♀	
brother	<u>sister</u>	
son	<u>daughter</u>	
father &	mother	= <u>parents</u>

3 Complete the sentences with a family word.

1 I'm a _____ .   2 I'm not a _____ .

4 Work in pairs. Read your sentences to your partner.

I'm a father. I'm not a brother.   *I'm a sister. I'm not a mother.*

Families

Warm-up

Introducing the theme: families

Bring in photos of people in your family. Pass the photos around the class and encourage students to ask questions, e.g., *Who is he? What's his name? What's his job? Where is he from? How old is he?*, etc. Answer the questions.

1 Hold up your copy of the Student Book. Point to the adult in the photo and say: *This is Ravi.* Point to the children and say: *This is Mohan and this is Danvir.* Then have students complete the activity.

2 Before beginning the activity, make sure that students understand the symbols for male and female.

Pronunciation notes

Note the strong stress and pronunciation: *brother, sister, daughter, father, mother, parents.*

Note that *parents* can be a false cognate in some romance languages, where similar words can have a more general meaning of "relatives."

3 Model the activity by writing two true sentences about yourself on the board and reading them aloud.

Extra activity 2

Pick a famous family from your country and write the names of the people on the board. Pre-teach some vocabulary by saying and writing the names of the relationships between the people. For example, if you use the British Royal family, point to Prince William and then Charles, and say *father and son;* then William and Harry, and say *brothers;* then William and Elizabeth and say *grandson, grandmother.*

Extra activity 1

Bring in photos of pairs of famous family, or write their names on the board. In pairs, have students say how they are related. For example:

Julio and Enrique Iglesias (father and son)

Bill and Chelsea Clinton (father and daughter)

Jake and Maggie Gyllenhaal (brother and sister)

Unusual families

Materials
Ask students to bring in photos of their family to use in Exercise 10.

Warm-up
Using words: families
Briefly review family-related words. Draw a male symbol and a female symbol on the board and ask students to write three words under each one

Vocabulary

1 ANSWERS
grandchild, granddaughter, grandfather, grandmother, grandparent, grandson

Pronunciation note
Grand is stressed: <u>grand</u>son, <u>grand</u>father, etc.

Extra activity
Check the meaning of *grand* by writing your name on the board and pointing to yourself. Then write your parents' names above yours and ask: *Who is he? Who is she?* to elicit *mother* and *father*. Then write the names of one of your parents' parents to elicit *grandmother* and *grandfather*.

2 Ask students to look at the family tree. Ask a few focus questions, e.g., *What is the family's last name?* (Cousteau); *What is Jacques' job?* (marine explorer); *What is Philippe's job?* (writer). Then have students complete the activity.

ANSWERS
Jacques & Simone
Philippe Jr. & Fabien
Alexandra & Celine
Philippe & Jean-Michel
Alexandra, Philippe Jr., Fabien, & Celine

3a Unusual families

Vocabulary **family**

1 Look at the words. Add *grand-* to six of the words to make words for more family members.

brother	child	cousin
daughter	father	mother
parent	sister	son

2 Look at the Cousteau family tree. Find the names of:

1 the grandparents
2 two grandsons
3 two granddaughters
4 two brothers
5 four cousins

The Cousteau family

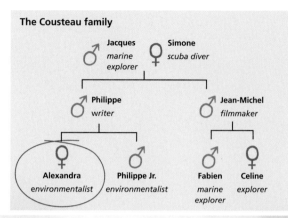

Reading and listening

3 🔊 **25** The woman in the photo is Alexandra Cousteau. Look at the family tree. Mark (✓) the correct options (a–d) about Alexandra. Then listen and check.

Who's Alexandra?
a She's Jacques Cousteau's daughter.
b She's Philippe's daughter. ✓
c She's Philippe Jr.'s sister. ✓
d She's Simone's mother.

34

4 🔊 **25** Listen again. Match A and B to make sentences.

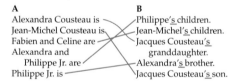

A
Alexandra Cousteau is
Jean-Michel Cousteau is
Fabien and Celine are
Alexandra and
    Philippe Jr. are
Philippe Jr. is

B
Philippe's children.
Jean-Michel's children.
Jacques Cousteau's granddaughter.
Alexandra's brother.
Jacques Cousteau's son.

Background notes
Jacques Cousteau (1910–1997) was a famous French marine explorer who wrote books and made films and TV series about marine life. He helped develop the aqua-lung and was a pioneer of marine conservation. Cousteau's sons and grandchildren have all become involved with exploration and environmentalism.

Note that *Jr.* is short for *junior*, and is used when a son has the same name as his father. It is commonly used in the US but not in other English-speaking countries.

Reading and listening

3 Ask students to look at the photo. Ask: *What's her name?* Then point to names in the family tree and ask: *Who's this?* Ask students to indentify their relationship to Alexandra (*father, grandmother, grandfather*, etc.).

Grammar

5 Read through the grammar box with the class. Ask students to work in pairs to find and underline examples of *'s* in Exercise 4. When checking, point out and model the pronunciation of *'s*. Refer them to the information and practice on page 162.

Grammar possessive 's

5 Look at the grammar box. Then look at the sentences in Exercise 4. Find 's five times.

> **POSSESSIVE 'S**
>
> Alexandre Cousteau is Jacques Cousteau's granddaughter.
>
> For more information and practice, see page 162.

6 Explain the use of 's in these sentences.

1 Who's Celine?
2 She's Fabien's sister.

7 Work in pairs. Test your memory.

> Who's Jacques?

> He's Alexandra's grandfather.

8 Look at the photo. Then look at the example. Write sentences about this family.

Example: Bolormaa – Bat
Bolormaa is Bat's mother.

1 Bat – Sukh
2 Bat – Bolormaa
3 Bold – Bat
4 Bolormaa – Sukh

9 Pronunciation possessive 's

🔊 26 Listen and repeat the sentences.

Speaking and writing

10 Work in pairs. Draw your family tree. Tell your partner about people in your family.

> Who's David?

> He's my sister's son.

11 Write about your family tree.

Three generations of a family in Mongolia

Sukh

Bolormaa

Bat

Bold

Unit 3 Families   35

6 Discuss the sentences as a class. When checking show the use by writing *Who is* and *She is* on the board.

> **ANSWERS**
>
> In *Who's* (Who is) and *She's* (She is), 's is an abbreviated form of is.
> In *Fabien's*, the 's is possessive.

7 First model the activity with books open. Ask a few questions: *Who's Celine? Who's Simone?* Then do the same with books closed. Begin the activity. Monitor students to check their use and pronunciation of 's.

> **8 ANSWERS**
>
> 1 Bat is Sukh's grandson.
> 2 Bat is Bolormaa's son.
> 3 Bold is Bat's brother.
> 4 Bolormaa is Sukh's daughter.

Speaking and writing

10 Model this activity by drawing your family tree on the board, or have students use the Cousteau family tree as a model. If possible, have them include photos and label each person's job.

11 Ask students to write a few sentences to describe their family trees. Monitor and help with spelling and vocabulary.

Extra activity

Ask students to draw their family trees on one piece of paper and write their descriptions on another. Then ask students to display their trees and descriptions on different walls or desks of the classroom.

Have students walk around and match each description with its family tree.

HOMEWORK Ask students to do online research about a famous family from their own country. Have them draw the family tree and write a short description of the people.

3b Celebrations

Vocabulary **months and ages**

1 Look at the calendar. Write the months in the correct place.

August   December   February   June   November

FAMILY EVENTS

January	
February	Jim's birthday (49)
March	Rory's birthday (34)
April	Sue and Colin's wedding anniversary
May	Jack and Rosie's wedding anniversary
June	Matt's birthday (19)
July	
August	Eve's birthday (21!)
September	
October	
November	Kate and Paul's wedding anniversary
December	our wedding anniversary

2 Work in pairs. Look at the calendar. Ask and answer questions.

When's Sue and Colin's wedding anniversary?

In April.

3 Write a list of five family members. Then work in pairs. Exchange lists. Take turns to ask and answer questions about people's ages.

mother
grandmother
sister – Pilar
sister – Erika
brother

How old is your sister Erika?

She's twenty-three.

Reading

4 Look at the photo of a wedding. Find:

the bride   the groom   a boy   a girl

5 Read about the wedding. Complete the sentences with five of these words.

bride   cousin   groom
husband   wedding   wife

1 This is Jao and Sunisa's <u>wedding</u>.
2 The <u>bride</u>'s name is Sunisa.
3 The <u>groom</u>'s name is Jao.
4 Deng is Jao's <u>cousin</u>.
5 Deng's <u>wife</u> is at the wedding.

Celebrations around the world

This is a wedding in Thailand in October 2010. The bride is 23 years old. Her name's Sunisa. The groom is 30 years old. His name's Jao. Their family and friends are at the wedding. Jao's cousin Deng is there with his wife and their children. "Today we are all happy," says Deng.

Warm-up

Using words: families

Draw a family tree on the board with only two names supplied, and blank boxes for the other people. List the remaining names next to the tree. Tell students to copy the family tree and then listen as you read aloud sentences describing the relationships, e.g., *Dan is Matt's grandfather.* Students complete the family tree based on what they hear.

Vocabulary

2 Begin by checking comprehension of *wedding anniversary* and *birthday* with gestures and examples. For example, if you are married, write the year you got married on the board, hum the wedding march, and point to your wedding ring. Then write the date and this year and act out giving flowers.

Pronunciation notes

Note the strong stress and pronunciation:

A<u>pril</u>, <u>July</u>, <u>Au</u>gust, Sep<u>tem</u>ber, Oc<u>to</u>ber, No<u>vem</u>ber, De<u>cem</u>ber, <u>Jan</u>uary, <u>Feb</u>ruary

Extra activity

Practice the use and pronunciation of months:

- Provide sequences of months. Students must give the next month in the sequence, e.g., *February, March, April...* (May); *December, March, June...* (September).

- Give different temperatures. Students name a month with that typical temperature.

- Bring in pictures of well-known events or festivals. Hold up the pictures and ask students to name the months.

- With a small class, get students to line up according to their birthday months. They must ask each other *When's your birthday?* and arrange themselves in a line from January to December.

Reading

4 Ask students to look at the words. Read them aloud and have students repeat. Then point to different people in the photo and get students to guess which word describes them.

5 After completing the activity, check the meaning of *wife, husband,* and *cousin* by eliciting Deng's family tree from students and drawing it on the board. Alternatively, refer back to the Cousteau family tree and point out that Alexandra and Celine are cousins.

Pronunciation notes

Note the stress and pronunciation:
woman, cousin, husband.

Cousin is used with both males and females.

Note that *man* and *woman* have irregular plurals: *men, women* /ˈwɪmɪn/.

Grammar *his, her, our, their*

6 Look at the sentences in the grammar box. When do we use *his* and *her*? When do we use *our* and *their*?

> ▶ **HIS, HER, OUR, THEIR**
>
> He is the groom. **His** name's Jao.
> She is the bride. **Her** name's Sunisa.
> They are from Thailand. This is a photo of **their** wedding.
> We are married. **Our** wedding anniversary is in June.
>
> For more information and practice, see page 162.

7 Complete the sentences with *his, her, our,* and *their*.

1 Deng's daughter is three. Her ___ name's Areva.
2 Sunisa's father is fifty. His ___ name's Thaksin.
3 This is a photo of my father. His ___ name's Andrew.
4 Kate and Paul are parents. Their ___ baby's name is Louisa.
5 My sister and I are twins. Our ___ birthday is the same day.

8 Look at the answers. Complete the questions about the people in the photo with these words.

her	his	their	they

1 "Where are they ___ ?"
   "In Thailand."
2 "What's his ___ name?"
   "Jao."
3 "What are their ___ names?"
   "Sunisa and Areva."
4 "What's her ___ husband's name?"
   "Jao."

Speaking

9 Work in pairs. Ask and answer questions about two weddings.

Student A: Turn to page 153.

Student B: Turn to page 157.

Grammar

6 Read through the grammar box with the class. Elicit rules of use from the students. Refer students to page 162 for more information and practice.

> **Grammar notes**
>
> *His* and *her* are second person singular possessive adjectives. *His* refers to a male possessor. *Her* refers to a female possessor. Emphasize this point to Romance language speakers: the gender of third-person singular possession adjectives agrees with the possessor, not the object.
>
> Note that *its* is used to show possession with animals, objects, countries, etc.
>
> *Their* is the third person plural possessive adjective. *Our* is the first person plural possessive adjective. Unlike some languages, *Their* and *our* are used regardless of the gender of the possessor.
>
> In English, possessive adjectives do not change form when the noun is singular or plural, e.g., *their cousin* and *their cousins*.

> **Extra activity 1**
>
> Play a memory game to practice possessive adjectives. Have the class stand in a circle. The first student says his or her name and the name of a family member. For example, *I'm Sarah and my mother's name is Anne*. Then the next student must repeat the information and add their own: *Her name is Sarah and her mother's name is Anne. My name is Brian and my sister's name is Linda.* Then the next student must repeat all of the previous information and add their own. For example: *Her name is Sarah and her mother's name is Anne. His name is Brian and his sister's name is Linda. My name is Michael and my brother's name is David.* Keep notes to prompt students when they forget and encourage them to go quickly to make it more fun. It might seem like the first student got lucky, but you can have him or her repeat the whole class's information at the end.

Unit 3 Families 37

> **Extra activity 2**
>
> In pairs, students write other answers based on the information in the text, e.g., *She's 23. Sunisa. Sunisa's father.* Pairs exchange their answers with other pairs, who write the corresponding questions.

> **HOMEWORK** Ask students to find a photo of a wedding they attended. Tell them to write five sentences about the people in the photo.

Young and old

Warm-up

Using words: describing people

Bring in magazine photos of many different people. Display an interesting photo and introduce the person to the class, e.g., *This is my cousin. His name's Raul. He's American. He's from Los Angeles and he's an artist. He's twenty-five. He's happy. His wife's name is Jill and she's an engineer.*

Divide the class into small groups. Give each group a set of magazine photos and ask students to choose a photo to describe to their group.

Vocabulary

1 Ask some questions about the pictures, e.g., *Where is he? How old are they?* Then ask students to match the adjectives.

> **ANSWERS**
>
> **1** young
> **2** rich
> **3** old
> **4** big
> **5** small
> **6** poor

> **2 ANSWERS**
>
> young / old, rich / poor, big / small

3 Model by writing sentences about yourself on the board, e.g., *My family is big*.

Extra activity

Ask students to write three sentences (two true, one false) about themselves and/or their family. Have them read aloud the sentences to a partner, who must guess which sentence is false. Were there any clues that gave away the false item?

3c Young and old

Vocabulary adjectives

1 Match these adjectives with the pictures (1–6). Then check your answers with your instructor.

> big   old   poor   rich   small   young

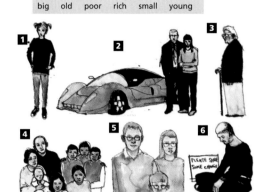

2 Find three pairs of opposite adjectives in Exercise 1.

3 Write three sentences with words from Exercise 1. Then read your sentences to your partner.

> *My grandfather isn't young.*

Reading

4 Read the article on page 39. Choose the correct option (a or b) for what the diagrams show.

ⓐ The ages of people in two different countries.
b The family size in two different countries.

5 Read the article again. Answer the questions.

1 Where are families big?   Uganda
2 Where are people old?   Japan

6 Work in groups. Answer the questions.

1 Are families in your country big or small?
2 Are people old or young?

> *I'm from Italy. In my country, families are small.*

Grammar irregular plural nouns

7 Look at the grammar box. <u>Underline</u> examples of two of these nouns in the article on page 39.

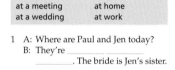

> ▶ **IRREGULAR PLURAL NOUNS**
>
> a child → two **children**
> a man → three **men**
> a woman → four **women**
> a person → five **people**
>
> For more information and practice, see page 163.

8 Choose the correct option.

1 Daughters and mothers are men / women.
2 Grandsons are men / women.
3 Boys and girls are children / men.

9 Word focus *at*

Look at the expressions with *at*. Complete the exchanges with two of the expressions. Check your answers with your instructor.

at a meeting	at home
at a wedding	at work

1 A: Where are Paul and Jen today?
   B: They're _____
   _____. The bride is Jen's sister.

2 A: Where are you?
   B: We're _____ ! My parents are here.

10 Pronunciation **linking with** *at*

🔊 **27** Listen and repeat these sentences.

1 They're at␣a wedding.
2 He's at␣a meeting.

Speaking

11 Work in pairs. Draw a population pyramid for your family. Tell your partner about it.

> *The people in my family are all young.*

Grammar and pronunciation notes

Note that adjectives do not change according to the gender or number of a noun, e.g., *a young man* and *a young woman; a rich brother* and *rich brothers*. Watch out for errors of this type.

Reading

6 Model the activity by talking about your country. Then divide the class into small groups to ask and answer the questions.

FAMILIES AROUND THE WORLD ARE DIFFERENT

This is Mulogo and his friends. They are from Uganda. Their families are big—with seven or eight children. Mulogo's brothers and sisters are under sixteen years old. In Uganda, people are young. Half the people are under fifteen. Uganda is a poor country.

UGANDA

| 85 and older |
| 80–84 |
| 75–79 |
| 70–74 |
| 65–69 |
| 60–64 |
| 55–59 |
| 50–54 |
| 45–49 |
| 40–44 |
| 35–39 |
| 30–34 |
| 25–29 |
| 20–24 |
| 15–19 |
| 10–14 |
| 5–9 |
| 0–4 |

JAPAN

| 85 and older |
| 80–84 |
| 75–79 |
| 70–74 |
| 65–69 |
| 60–64 |
| 55–59 |
| 50–54 |
| 45–49 |
| 40–44 |
| 35–39 |
| 30–34 |
| 25–29 |
| 20–24 |
| 15–19 |
| 10–14 |
| 5–9 |
| 0–4 |

This is Amaya. She's Japanese. Her family is small—one daughter, one son, and one grandson. Japan is a rich country. In Japan, people are old. Twenty percent of the people are over sixty-five. In rich countries, people are old.

Grammar

7 Read through the grammar box with the class. Model the pronunciation of the irregular plurals. Refer students to the information and practice on page 163.

Vocabulary notes

Note the stress and the change in the pronunciation of the vowel sound between these singular and plural forms: *child, children; woman, women; person, people.*

Word focus

9 Read the expressions aloud and ask students to repeat. Then ask students to complete the exchanges.

ANSWERS

1 at   a   wedding
2 at   home

Extra activity

Write on the board: *Where are your parents? Where are your brothers or sisters? Where are your friends?* Ask students to provide answers using *at* (or *in*).

Pronunciation

10 Point out the linking symbol between *at* and *a*.

Pronunciation notes

Note the use of the *schwa* sound and the way that the consonant /t/ in *at* links with the vowel sound /ə/ in *a*.

They're   at a   wedding.
          /ə tə/

Speaking

11 Model by drawing your own population pyramid on the board and describing it briefly.

Extra activity

In pairs, assign a country to students. Ask them to research the age distribution of the population and make their own age pyramid. Have them bring it up and present it to the class, or just hang them up and give students time to look and compare.

HOMEWORK Ask students to write sentences about people in their population pyramid.

3d

Congratulations!

Warm-up

Introducing the theme: special occasions

Write three dates on the board that are special for you, e.g., your birthday or wedding anniversary, your brother's birthday.

Write *special occasions* on the board and check that students understand its meaning by giving examples (birthdays, weddings, etc.). In pairs, have students guess why the dates are special for you.

Vocabulary

1 Read through the list as a class. Check comprehension by acting out the words. Then play the recording and have students name the occasion.

Extra activity

Give students some extra expressions and ask them to match them to events. Suggestions: Good luck / First day at a new job; Break a leg! / Appearing in a play; Bravo! / Giving a performance; Well done! / Passing an important test; Welcome! / The first day of class; Bon voyage! / Leaving for a trip.

Pronunciation notes

Note the strong stress in the long words: *birthday, party, wedding, anniversary, engagement*.

Real life

3 ANSWERS

1 an engagement
2 a wedding anniversary
3 a birthday

3d Congratulations!

Vocabulary **special occasions**

1  28 Look at these words. Then look at the photo and listen to a conversation. What's the special occasion?

> a new baby
> a birthday
> a party
> a wedding
> a wedding anniversary
> an engagement

2 🔊 28 Put the conversation in order. Then listen again and check.

a Ah, she's lovely. What's her name? 3
b Congratulations! 1
c Hello, Juba. 5
d It's Juba. 4
e Thank you. We're very happy. 2

Real life **special occasions**

3 🔊 29 Listen to three more conversations. Number (1–3) the occasions in Exercise 1.

4 🔊 29 Look at the expressions for SPECIAL OCCASIONS. Listen again. Write the number of the conversation.

▶ SPECIAL OCCASIONS	
Congratulations!	1
Happy birthday!	3
Happy anniversary!	2
I'm very happy for you.	1
How old are you?	3
When's the wedding?	1

5 Pronunciation **exclamations**

a 🔊 30 Listen and repeat three expressions for SPECIAL OCCASIONS.

b Work in pairs. Practice the conversations on page 170.

40

Real life **giving and accepting presents**

6 Work in pairs. Answer the questions.

1 Is it traditional to give presents in your country?
2 What are some special occasions for giving presents?
3 What's a good present for these special occasions?

> a new baby
> new parents
> your best friend's birthday
> your cousin's wedding
> your parents' wedding anniversary

7 Look at the occasions in Exercise 1. Which expression would you use for each one?

▶ GIVING AND ACCEPTING PRESENTS
This is for you / the baby.
That's nice / very kind.
You're welcome. / My pleasure.
Thanks. / Thank you very much.

8 Work in pairs. Choose a special occasion. Create a conversation. Take turns.

> Hi. This is for ...

Pronunciation

Pronunciation notes

Note the strong stress: *congratulations, anniversary*.

These expressions are used very positively to express pleasure, so they require an exaggerated intonation pattern. Students should start their intonation high. It rises then falls.

Real life

6 Check comprehension of *presents* by drawing a wrapped gift on the board. Model this activity by having the class ask you the questions and giving answers for your country. As students discuss the questions, monitor and help with any vocabulary students need to describe gifts from their country.

8 Have a few pairs role-play their conversations for the class.

3e Best wishes

Writing a greeting card

1 Writing skill **contractions**

a <u>Underline</u> the contractions in these sentences. What's the missing letter?

1 <u>I'm</u> Mexican. a
2 <u>She's</u> French. i
3 It <u>isn't</u> my birthday. o
4 <u>What's</u> your name? i
5 <u>They're</u> engaged. a
6 <u>Who's</u> this? i
7 You <u>aren't</u> married. o
8 <u>Where's</u> your husband? i

b Find and <u>underline</u> eight contractions in these messages.

> **1**
> <u>It's</u> Javi's birthday tomorrow. <u>He's</u> with his grandparents in Chicago. <u>What's</u> their address?

> **2**
> Diana and Albert are engaged. <u>They're</u> really happy! The engagement <u>party's</u> at Albert's house.

> **3**
> Ingrid and Karl's <u>wedding's</u> in June. <u>Sonia's</u> the bridesmaid. <u>I'm</u> the best man!

c Rewrite these messages. Use contractions.

> **1**
> It is Karin's birthday tomorrow. She is twenty-one. Where is her present?

> **2**
> I am engaged to Miguel. Our wedding is in May.

> **3**
> Hi. What is Katya's husband's name? Is it Bruno or Silvio? Thanks.

2 Read the greeting. Answer the questions.

1 What's the occasion? birthday
2 Who's the card from? Katya and Bruno
3 Who's the card to? Javi

3 Write a card for Diana and Albert, and for Karin. Use these words. You can use some words more than once.

best wishes	birthday	congratulations	
engagement	from	love	
happy	on	to	your

4 In pairs, read your cards. Check the capital letters.

5 Work in pairs. Compare your cards with your partner's cards.

1c Rewrite the first sentence on the board as a class.

> **ANSWERS**
>
> 1 It's Karin's birthday tomorrow. She's twenty-one. Where's her present?
> 2 I'm engaged to Miguel. Our wedding's in May.
> 3 Hi. What's Katya's husband's name? Is it Bruno or Silvio? Thanks.

3 Read through the words with the class and elicit possible combinations (e.g., *Congratulations on your engagement, Love from*).

> **SAMPLE ANSWERS**
>
> To Diana and Albert
> Congratulations on your engagement!
> Love from…
> To Karin
> Happy birthday!
> Best wishes from…

> **HOMEWORK** Ask students to write a card to a friend or family member who has a birthday or other special occasion coming up soon.

Best wishes

Warm-up

Test before you teach: contractions

Write a set of sentences on the board, e.g.

My teacher is American.

She is from New York.

She is married.

She is twenty-five years old.

We are friends.

Ask students to suggest where and how the sentences can be contracted. Then ask them to change the sentences so that they are true. They could change the information or use negatives. They will need to ask you questions to check the information.

Writing

1b When checking, point out that *Javi's*, *Albert's*, and *Karl's* are not contractions—they are examples of possessive *'s*.

> **Background notes**
>
> In the US, couples sometimes have an engagement party with family and friends to announce that they are getting engaged to be married.
>
> At a wedding, the groom has a best man. The best man is usually a close friend, brother, or cousin. It's his job at the wedding to stand next to the groom and carry the ring, and to make a speech at the reception that follows the wedding.
>
> The bride's equivalent is a maid of honor. She stands next to the bride during the wedding and holds the bride's flowers during parts of the wedding ceremony.

A Mongolian family

Videoscript

Narrator: This is Ochkhuu's home. It's a ger in Ulaan Baatar.

Ochkhuu's daughter, Anuka, is six years old.

Ochkhuu's wife's name is Norvoo.

Norvoo's family isn't from the city.

These are her parents.

Their ger is in the country.

This is Jaya—Norvoo's father. He's a farmer.

Jaya and his wife, Chantsal, are sixty-five years old.

They are happy in the country.

Jaya's life and Ochkhuu's life are very different.

Ochkhuu is a taxi driver now.

Mongolian children in Ulaanbaatar

Before you watch

1 Read about Mongolia. Complete the article with three of these words.

> country   family   hot   people

Mongolia

Mongolia is a ¹ _country_ in Asia. It's big. It's cold in January and it's ² _hot_ in July. Sixty percent of the ³ _people_ are under thirty. Forty percent of the people are in Ulaanbaatar, the capital.

2 Look at the word box in the next column.

3 Look at the photo on page 42. Find:

> a ger   children   houses

While you watch

4 Watch the video. Mark (✓) the things you see.

> ✓ a ger   a city ✓
> ✓ children   a wedding
> ✓ animals   mountains ✓

5 The young man's name is Ochkhuu Genen. Watch the video again. Match the names with the people.

1 Anuka ———— his wife's mother
2 Norvoo ———— his daughter
3 Jaya ———— his wife's father
4 Chantsal ———— his wife

6 Watch the video again. Choose the correct option.

1 Where is Ochkhuu's ger?
   ⓐ in Ulaanbaatar   c in the mountains
   b in the country

2 How old is Ochkhuu's daughter?
   a two years old   c ten years old
   ⓑ six years old

3 How old are Norvoo's parents?
   a fifty-five years old ⓒ sixty-five years old
   b sixty years old

4 What is Norvoo's father's job?
   a a taxi driver   c a teacher
   ⓑ a farmer

5 What is Ochkhuu's job?
   ⓐ a taxi driver   c a teacher
   b a farmer

After you watch

7 Work in pairs. Answer the questions.

1 Is Ochkhuu's family big or small? small
2 Are Norvoo's parents young or old? old

8 Work in pairs.

Student A: Look at photo A. You are in Mongolia. These people are your neighbors. What are their names and ages? What are the relationships?

Tell your partner about the people in the photo.

A

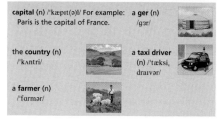
B

Student B: Look at photo B. You are in the United States. These people are your neighbors. What are their names and ages? What are the relationships?

Tell your partner about the people in the photo.

capital (n) /ˈkæpɪt(ə)l/ For example: Paris is the capital of France.

the country (n) /ˈkʌntri/

a farmer (n) /ˈfɑrmər/

a ger (n) /gɜr/

a taxi driver (n) /ˈtæksi, draɪvər/

8 Divide the class into pairs. Give students time to look at the photos and think of the names and ages of, and relationships between, the people. Then students tell their partner about the people in the photo. Check by having students share their descriptions with the class. You may want to have the class vote for the best description.

Before you watch

1 Ask students to look at the photo on page 42. Ask: *What can you see? Where are the people?* Then ask students to complete the article with the missing words. When checking, ask questions to elicit the information, e.g., *Where's Mongolia?* Then have a volunteer read the fourth sentence aloud. Ask students how Mongolia is similar to Uganda, which students read about in 3c on page 39. (Answer: Both Mongolia and Uganda have young populations.)

2 Read the words aloud and have students repeat.

3 Explain the meaning of *ger* (a type of house). Ask students to look at the photo and find the things.

While you watch

4 Give students time to read through the list. Check their understanding of the words. Play the video. Students watch and listen and mark the things they see.

5 Students watch the video again and match the names with the descriptions. When checking, ask questions to elicit the information, e.g., *Who is his daughter?*

ANSWERS

1 Anuka is his daughter.
2 Norvoo is his wife.
3 Jaya is his wife's father.
4 Chantsal is his wife's mother.

6 Give students some time to read the questions. Play the video again. Students choose the correct option to complete the sentences.

After you watch

7 Divide the class into pairs. Students answer the questions.

UNIT 3 REVIEW

Grammar

1 Students complete the sentences.

> **ANSWERS**
> **2** Sandra's car
> **3** Toni's keys
> **4** Diana's phone
> **5** Michael's passport
> **6** Enya's email address

2 Students complete the sentences with the words.

Vocabulary

3 Students match the words for women with the words for men.

4 Students work in pairs to say the months in sequence.

5 Students choose the correct option.

Real life

6 Students put the words in order to make questions and sentences. Then they match 1–4 with a–d.

> **ANSWERS**
> **1** When is the wedding?
> **2** How old are you?
> **3** This is for you.
> **4** Thank you very much.
> **c** It is in July.
> **b** I am eighteen.
> **d** That is very kind.
> **a** You are welcome.

7 Students work in pairs to practice the exchanges in Exercise 6. Remind them to use contractions.

Speaking

8 Students write the names of people from three generations in their family. Then they ask and answer questions with a partner.

Grammar

1 Complete the sentences.

1 Look at the photo. This is ___Jin's family___ .
   (Jin / family)

2 This is _____ .
   (Sandra / car)

3 They're _____ .
   (Toni / keys)

4 Is this _____ ?
   (Diana / phone)

5 This is _____ .
   (Michael / passport)

6 Is this _____ ?
   (Enya / email address)

enya@bt.com

2 Complete the sentences with these words.

> he's   his   our   their   they're

1 This card is for Ellie and Greg. What's ___their___ address?
2 Suzi and Ryan are engaged. ___They're___ very happy!
3 It's David's birthday. The party's at ___his___ house.
4 Dirk and I are married. It's ___our___ anniversary in March.
5 It's my grandfather's birthday today. ___He's___ eighty-nine.

> **I CAN**
> talk about families and possessions (possessive 's and possessive adjectives)   ☐
> use irregular plural nouns   ☐

Vocabulary

3 Match the words for women and men.

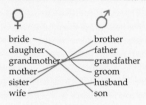

> ♀   ♂
> bride   brother
> daughter   father
> grandmother   grandfather
> mother   groom
> sister   husband
> wife   son

4 Work in pairs. Take turns.

Student A: Say a month.

Student B: Say the next month.

5 Choose the correct option.

1 Our class is *big* / *small*—3 students!
2 "Are your grandparents *old* / *young*?"
   "Yes, they are. They're 89 and 92."
3 We aren't rich. We're *big* / *poor*.
4 This wedding is *rich* / *small*—the bride and groom and their families.

> **I CAN**
> talk about my family   ☐
> talk about months and ages   ☐
> describe people   ☐

Real life

6 Put the words in order. Then match 1–4 with a–d.

1 the / is / wedding / when / ?
2 are / how old / you / ?
3 for / this / is / you / .
4 you / much / thank / very / .

a are / welcome / you / .
b am / eighteen / I / .
c in / is / July / it / .
d very / kind / is / that / .

7 Work in pairs. Practice the exchanges in Exercise 6. Use contractions.

> **I CAN**
> talk about special occasions   ☐
> give and accept presents   ☐

Speaking

8 Write the names of people from three generations in your family. Then work in pairs. Ask and answer questions using *who* and *how old*.

Unit 4 Cities

The Pearl TV tower and the Huang Pu River in Shanghai, China
Photo by Justin Guariglia

FEATURES

46 In the city
Places in a town

48 Tourist information
Two famous towers

50 Time zones
Times around the world

54 Where's that?
A video about four cities
around the world

1 Look at the photo. Find these things:

> buildings   a river   a tower

2 Read the photo caption. Find the name of the city and the country. Shanghai, China

3 🔊 **31** Listen. Are these items true (T) or false (F)?

1 Shanghai is the capital of China. F
2 Shanghai isn't rich. F
3 The buildings in Shanghai are old. F
4 The Pearl TV tower is famous. T

4 Work in pairs. Tell your partner about famous things in your city or town.

> *I'm from Tokyo. Mt. Fuji is famous.*

Cities

Warm-up

Introducing the theme: cities

Bring in a large picture (or pictures) of a well-known city that shows buildings, towers, bridges, etc. Display the picture and ask pairs of students to describe it to each other in as much detail as they can. When checking, write interesting words or phrases on the board.

1 Ask students to look at the photo. Point to the tower, buildings, and river and ask: *What is it? What are they?*

3 Give students a moment to read through the sentences. Then play the audio. Students listen and write *T* (true) or *F* (false) next to the sentences.

4 Model by talking about your town or city. Then divide the class into pairs. Give students a minute or two to think of things to say, then ask them to speak to their partner. If your students all come from the same city, ask them to work in pairs to prepare sentences to describe the city, then ask a few pairs to say their sentences for the class.

Extra activity 1

Play Twenty Questions as a class. Students take turns. One student comes up and thinks of a city but doesn't say the name of it. The rest of the class asks yes/no questions until they guess the name of the city. Remind them the topics that they know that they can ask about: size, location, weather, and some landmarks. For example.

—Is it in Europe?   —No.

—Is it in Latin America?   —Yes.

—Is it in Mexico?   —No.

—Is is very big?   —Yes.

—Is it on an island?   —Yes.

—Is it very old?   —Yes.

—Is it Santo Domingo?   —Yes!

Extra activity 2

In a class with a variety of nationalities, you could ask students to write three sentences about their city, without revealing its name. Collect the descriptions and read them aloud. The class must listen and identify the city and, if possible, the student who wrote the sentences.

In the city

Test before you teach: places in a city

Draw a simple word web on the board. Write *city* in the middle circle. Ask: *What's in a city?* Elicit a few words from students (*cars, people, buildings,* etc.) and have students write them in the web.

Have students brainstorm more words in pairs or groups. Have them share their words with the class. Write the most useful terms on the board.

Vocabulary

1 Ask students to look at the photos and the words. Ask them to work in pairs to match words and pictures. Students write the number of the correct photo next to each word.

Pronunciation notes

Remind students that we use *an* in front of vowel sounds, e.g., *an information center.*

Note the strong stress: *station, market, museum, information*

Note the pronunciation: *café* (an imported French word that retains its accent)

2 If students are in a large city, ask about the local area. Ask for the names of movie theaters, cafés, museums, etc.

3 ANSWERS

1 café
2 market
3 museum
4 park

Extra activity

Ask students to think of places in their hometown or where they live now. Review places and adjectives by asking questions such as: *Is the museum old? Is it good? Is the park big? Is it beautiful?*

4a In the city

Vocabulary places in a town

1 Match the words and the pictures. Check your answers with your instructor.

a bank 8
a café 3
a movie theater 10
a museum 9
an information center 5
a bus station 6
a parking lot 2
a market 4
a park 1
a train station 7

2 Are the places in Exercise 1 in your town? What are their names?

Reading

3 Read the information about downtown Northville. Complete the sentences with the places in the comments.

1 The _____ is great.
2 The _____ is new.
3 The _____ is old.
4 The _____ is on Milk Street.

ⓐ bank
ⓑ Transportation Museum
ⓒ bus station
ⓓ café
ⓔ parking lot
ⓕ City Information Center
ⓖ Roxy movie theater
ⓗ Central Market
ⓘ train station
ⓙ Green Park

 The museum isn't very good. It's old. It's <u>near</u> the train station. *Berta*

This café is great! It's <u>next to</u> a movie theater. *Artem*

Grammar

4 Look at the grammar box with the students. Ask students to work in pairs to find and underline the prepositions. Refer students to the information and practice on page 163.

ANSWERS

1 It's <u>near</u> the train station.
2 It's <u>next to</u> a movie theater.
3 It's <u>across from</u> a bank.
4 It's <u>on</u> Milk Street.

Grammar prepositions of place

4 Look at the grammar box. Then look at the comments about Northville. <u>Underline</u> the prepositions.

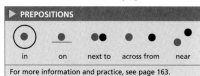

▶ PREPOSITIONS

| in | on | next to | across from | near |

For more information and practice, see page 163.

5 Look at the map. Are the sentences true (T) or false (F)?

1 The café is next to the movie theater.   T
2 The museum is in the park.   F
3 The park is near the information center.   T
4 The market is across from the movie theater.   F
5 The train station is on Exeter Street.   T
6 The transportation museum is across from the parking lot.   T

6 Look at the map. Choose the correct option.

1 The bank is *next to* / *across from* the market.
2 The movie theater is *on* / *near* South Street.
3 The information center is *next to* / *across from* the bus station.

4 The bus station is *in* / *next to* the park.
5 The train station is *across from* / *near* the museum.

7 🔊 **32** Listen to four conversations about these places. Write the number of the conversation (1–4) next to the places.

a bank   4
b parking lot   3
c information center   2
d train station   1

Speaking

8 Work in pairs. Ask and answer questions about places on the map.

Excuse me?

Yes?

Where's the market?

9 Work in pairs. Ask and answer questions about four places in your town.

Where's the Coffee Pot café?

I'm not sure!

DOWNTOWN NORTHVILLE

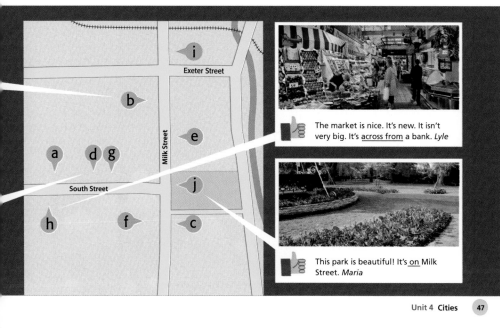

The market is nice. It's new. It isn't very big. It's <u>across from</u> a bank. *Lyle*

This park is beautiful! It's <u>on</u> Milk Street. *Maria*

Unit 4 Cities   47

Unit 4 **Cities**   47

Tourist information

Warm-up

Using words: places and prepositions of place

Write on the board the names of four places in the town or city where you and your students are studying. Point to a place, and say: *Excuse me. Where is the (museum)?* Students have to think of ways to answer, e.g., *It's on Walnut Street. It's next to the parking lot. It's across from the school.*

Listening

1 Have students read through the sentences. Then play the audio and have students write the correct number next to each sentence.

Background notes

Tokyo Tower is a communications and observation tower located in Minato, Tokyo. It is the second-tallest structure in Japan, and has a similar shape to the Eiffel Tower in Paris.

Grammar

Grammar notes

We use *this* to refer to a singular person or thing which is close to the speaker. We use *that* to refer to a singular person or thing which is more distant from the speaker.

Extra activity

Provide more practice of *this* and *that*. Walk up to a student and say *This is (Karin)*. Then point to a student across the class and say *That is (Tim)*. Then, in pairs, have students introduce people close to them and far away from them.

4b Tourist information

Listening

1 🔊 **33** Listen to the conversation and put it in order.

a Good morning. 2
b Is **this** a map of the city? 3
c Hi. *1*
d No, it isn't. **That's** a map of the city. 4
e OK. And where's Tokyo Tower? 5
f Yes, it is. 8
g Oh yes. Is it open on Sunday? 7
h It's near the Prince Park … here it is. 6

Grammar *this, that*

▶ **THIS, THAT**

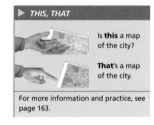

Is **this** a map of the city?

That's a map of the city.

For more information and practice, see page 163.

2 Complete the conversations with *this* and *that*.

Excuse me. Is **that** a map of Tokyo?

Yes, it is.

1

Is **this** a train schedule?

No, it's a bus schedule.

2

Is **that** guidebook in English?

Where?

The book next to you.

No, it isn't. It's in Spanish.

3

48

3 Pronunciation *th* /ð/

a 🔊 **34** Listen and repeat the conversations from Exercise 2.

b Practice the *th* sound in these words.

| this | that | there | they |

Vocabulary **days of the week**

4 Put the days of the week in order. Check your answers with your instructor.

| Friday | Monday | Saturday | Sunday | Thursday |
| Tuesday | Wednesday | | | |

5 🔊 **35** Read the questions about places in Tokyo. Then listen to the conversation and answer *yes* or *no*.

1 Are museums open on Monday? ⟨yes⟩ no
2 Are stores open every day? ⟨yes⟩ no
3 Are banks open on Sunday? yes ⟨no⟩

6 Work in pairs. When are places open—and not open—in your country?

Banks aren't open on Saturday or Sunday.

Pronunciation

Pronunciation notes

The *th* or /ð/ sound is tricky to say. It is a voiced consonant and produced by pressing the tongue against the top front teeth and withdrawing it. Students often approximate to /d/ or /z/ sounds.

If students struggle with this sound, tell them to place their index finger in front of their lips with their tongue pressing against the front teeth and just touching the finger. As they make the sound, they pull their tongue back.

3b Model the pronunciation of /ð/ in the words. Then ask students to practice saying them.

Vocabulary

4 ANSWERS

Monday, Tuesday, Wednesday, Thursday, Friday, Saturday, Sunday

Pronunciation notes

The stress on days of the week is always on the first syllable.

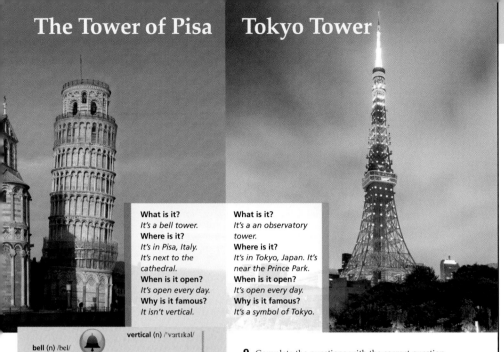

The Tower of Pisa   Tokyo Tower

What is it?
It's a bell tower.
Where is it?
It's in Pisa, Italy.
It's next to the cathedral.
When is it open?
It's open every day.
Why is it famous?
It isn't vertical.

What is it?
It's a an observatory tower.
Where is it?
It's in Tokyo, Japan. It's near the Prince Park.
When is it open?
It's open every day.
Why is it famous?
It's a symbol of Tokyo.

bell (n) /bel/

vertical (n) /'vɜrtɪkəl/

observatory

Reading

7 Read about two famous towers. Choose the correct option.

1 (Tokyo Tower) / The Tower of Pisa / both is an observatory.
2 Tokyo Tower / The Tower of Pisa /(both)is open to tourists.
3 (Tokyo Tower) / The Tower of Pisa / both is near a park.

Grammar question words

8 Look at the grammar box and the words in **bold** in the questions. Then look at the article about towers. Find the words in **bold** in the article.

> ▶ **QUESTION WORDS**
>
> | **What is it?** | **When is it open?** |
> |---|---|
> | **Where is it?** | **Why is it famous?** |
>
> For more information and practice, see page 163.

9 Complete the questions with the correct question word.

1 Q: __Where__ are you?
   A: I'm in the park.
2 Q: __When__ is the museum open?
   A: Every day.
3 Q: __What__ is the name of this street?
   A: Main Street.
4 Q: __Why__ is this place famous?
   A: It's very old.
5 Q: __Where__ is this?
   A: It's in Italy.
6 Q: __When__ is your birthday?
   A: In June.

10 Work in pairs. Ask and answer questions about two more towers.

Student A: Turn to page 154.

Student B: Turn to page 158.

Speaking

11 Work in pairs. Ask and answer questions about famous places you know.

Background notes

The days of the week are named after the sun (*Sunday*), the moon (*Monday*), and old Norse or Germanic gods (for example, Thor, the god of Thunder, and Woden, the lord of the gods, lend their names to *Thursday* and *Wednesday*).

Reading

7 Ask students to look at the photos. Ask: *What are they?* (elicit *towers*) *What are their names? Where are they?*

Ask students to read the information and choose the correct options. Let students compare their ideas in pairs.

Check the meaning of *vertical* (point to the tower of Pisa and show that it isn't vertical) and *cathedral* (point to the building next to the tower).

Grammar

> **Grammar note**
>
> After question words, the verb *be* comes **before** the pronoun, e.g., *What **is** it?*

10 Divide the class into pairs. Students read the information about two different towers on pages 154 and 158 of the Student Book. Then they take turns asking and answering the questions from the grammar box on page 49 to share the information.

Speaking

11 Ask students to think of a famous building in their city and write notes about it, using the information in Exercise 7 as a model. Then divide the class into pairs and complete the activity.

Extra activity

Tell half the class that they are working in a tourist information center. The other students "visit" the center and ask what places they can see in the city. Allow time for the information center employees to prepare their role, and for the tourists to prepare questions.

HOMEWORK Ask students to research a famous tower on the Internet (e.g., the Eiffel Tower in Paris, the Burj Khalifa in Dubai, or the Empire State Building in New York). Ask them to write a short article about the tower, using the article in this unit as a model.

Time zones

Warm-up

Test before you teach: times

Bring in a clock with moveable hands. Show different times (e.g., *twelve o'clock, six thirty, two forty-five,* etc.). Ask students, *What time is it?* Don't correct at this stage; use it as an opportunity to find out what students know.

Vocabulary

1 Ask students to look at the photo at the bottom of the page in the Student Book. Ask: *Where is it? What time is it?* Then ask students to match times and clocks.

Pronunciation note

Review the stress in numbers (e.g., *thirty* but *fifteen*).

PHOTO INFO

Grand Central Station is a commuter terminal in midtown Manhattan in New York. It first opened in 1870 but was rebuilt in 1913. More than 20 million tourists visit the station each year.

2 Ask students to listen and write down the times as numbers. Let students compare their answers in pairs before discussing as a class.

Extra activity

Create a listening activity. Write pairs of similar times on the board and read aloud only one in each pair. Students listen and identify the correct time. For example:

    a 5:30   b 5:40
    a 9:15   b 9:50
    a 1:45   b 1:55

Then have students write their own lists and repeat the activity in pairs.

4 Model by asking several students the questions.

Vocabulary the time

1 Match the times with the clocks.

- **a** 11:00
- **b** 9:30
- **c** 4:15
- **d** 7:45
- **e** 8:20
- **f** 3:55

- eight twenty
- eleven o'clock
- four fifteen
- seven forty-five
- three fifty-five
- nine thirty

2 🎧 **36** Listen and write the times.

1	5:00	4	9:45
2	1:30	5	2:20
3	7:15	6	6:00

3 Match the word with the time.

1 noon————————12:00 pm (☼)
2 midnight————————12:00 am (☾)

4 Work in pairs. Ask and answer questions.

What time is	your the	English class? office open? bus in the morning? train to work?

Grand Central Station, New York

Information

50

Reading

5 Read the article and look at the map on page 51. Where is the International Date Line?

6 Read the article again. Look at the time in London. Then write the names of the two cities.

London: 12:00 pm

1 _____ : 8:00 pm   2 _____ : 4:00 am

7 Work in pairs. It's noon in London. What time is it in these places?

Cairo   Sydney   Rio de Janeiro   Japan
Argentina   South Africa

In Cairo, it's two o'clock in the afternoon.

8 Word focus *of*

a Underline *of* in the sentences. Then match the sentences (1–4) with the pictures (a–d).

1 What's the name of this street? *c*
2 Rome is the capital of Italy. *d*
3 It's a symbol of Tokyo. *b*
4 This is a map of the city. *a*

b Complete the sentences. Then tell your partner.

1 The name of my street is _____ .
2 The capital of my country is _____ .
3 _____ is a symbol of my _____ .

Speaking

9 Work in pairs. Talk about your city at different times of the day. Take turns.

Student A: Say a time.

Student B: Make sentences.

Five o'clock in the afternoon.

Stores are open. Children aren't at school.

5 ANSWER

from north to south in the Pacific Ocean

6 ANSWERS

1 Hong Kong
2 Los Angeles

Reading

7 ANSWERS

Cairo: 2 pm Japan: 9 pm
Sydney: 10 pm Argentina: 8 am
Rio de Janeiro: 9 am South Africa: 1-3 pm

Background notes

The International Date Line (IDL) runs along an imaginary line from the North to the South Pole at 180° longitude. It deviates at certain points to go around various Pacific Island groups. It is on the opposite side of the Earth to the Prime Meridian, which passes through the Royal Observatory in Greenwich in southeast London. This is at 0° longitude.

TIME ZONES

In London, it's twelve o'clock noon. Stores and offices are open. People are at work. Children are at school. In Hong Kong, it's eight o'clock in the evening. Schools are closed and children are at home. People are in cafés and restaurants. In Los Angeles, it's four o'clock in the morning. People aren't at work. They're at home.

The time is different in the 24 time zones around the world. The International Date Line is from north to south "in" the Pacific Ocean. The Date Line is the end of one day and the beginning of the next day. It's 80 kilometers from Russia to Alaska, but Sunday in Russia is Saturday in Alaska.

Word focus

8a Ask students to look at the pictures. Ask: *What can you see?* Then ask students to underline *of* in the sentences. Check the answers; then ask students to match the sentences with the pictures.

8b Students complete the sentences so that they are true for them.

Speaking

9 Model the activity by saying a time and having the class provide sentences. Then divide the class into pairs. Ask students to make as many sentences as they can about each time of day.

Two teas, please

Vocabulary

2 Before starting the activity, see if students can identify the items. Have students close their books. Hold up a book so that students can see the images, but not the words. Point to each picture and ask: *What is it?* Elicit guesses, then say the word and have students repeat it. Then have students open their books and complete the activity.

ANSWERS

1 water
2 fruit juice
3 pastry
4 coffee
5 salad
6 tea
7 sandwich

Real life

3 Ask students to look at the photos in Exercise 2 and check that they remember the snacks. Then play the audio.

ANSWERS

1 coffee
2 water
3 tea, fruit juice, and pastries

4 Ask students to complete the conversations with the missing lines. Then play the audio again. Students listen and check.

4d Two teas, please

Vocabulary **snacks**

1 Look at the photo. Choose the correct caption (a–c).

a   Fruit juice, India   ⓑ Mint tea, Morocco
c   Black coffee, Turkey

2 Write the words with the pictures (1–7).

| pastry | coffee | fruit juice | water |
| salad | sandwich | tea | |

52

Real life **buying snacks**

3 🔊 37 Listen to three conversations. Number the snacks (1–3) in Exercise 2.

4 🔊 37 Complete the conversations with expressions for BUYING SNACKS. Then listen again and check.

1   A: Hi. Can I help you?
    B: ¹ *Two coffees, please.*
    A: ² *Large or small?*
    B: Small.
    A: Anything else?
    B ³ *No, thanks.*

2   A: Hi. Can I help you?
    B: ⁴ *Can I have a bottle of water, please?*
    A: Anything else?
    B: Yes. A salad.
    A: OK. ⁵ *Four dollars, please.*

3   A: ⁶ *Can I help you?*
    B: A tea and a fruit juice, please.
    A: ⁷ *Anything else?*
    B: Yes. Two pastries, please.
    A: OK. Here you are. Seven dollars, please.
    B ⁸ *Here you are.*

5 Pronunciation **linking with** *can*

🔊 38 Listen and repeat these sentences.

1   Can_I help you?
2   Can_I have a water, please?

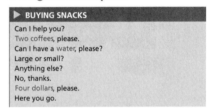

▶ **BUYING SNACKS**

Can I help you?
Two coffees, **please.**
Can I have a water, **please?**
Large or small?
Anything else?
No, thanks.
Four dollars, **please.**
Here you go.

6 Work in pairs. Take turns buying a snack from your partner.

Hi. Can I help you?

Two teas, please.

Pronunciation

6 Remind students to use the phrases in the Buying Snacks box.

4e See you soon

Writing a postcard

1 Read the postcard. Answer the questions.

1 Who is the postcard to? Sandra
2 Who is it from? Jen and Chris
3 Where are they? Thailand (Bangkok)

2 Read the postcard again. Underline:

1 two adjectives to describe the hotel
2 one adjective to describe the markets
3 two adjectives to describe the people
4 one adjective to describe the food

3 Writing skill *and*

a Read the postcard again. Circle *and* in three sentences.

b Look at the example. Then rewrite the sentences with *and*.

Example: The hotel is small. The hotel is new.
*The hotel is small **and** new.*

1 The museums are big. The museums are old.
2 The town is old. The town is beautiful.
3 It's famous in America. It's famous in Europe.
4 It's a drink with sugar. It's a drink with mint.

> Hi Sandra
> We're in Thailand. We're in Bangkok. It's great! Our hotel is big (and) new. It's near the market on this postcard. The markets are famous here. Thai people are nice (and) friendly. Oh, (and) the food is great too. See you soon.
> Jen and Chris

4 Choose a place you know. Write a postcard to your partner. Write about these three things. Use *and*.

- the town/city
- places in the town/city
- the food
- the hotel
- the people

5 Work in pairs. Exchange postcards. Where is your partner?

See you soon

Warm-up

Introducing the theme: postcards

Bring in some postcards, ideally ones that you have received from different places in the world. Pass them around the class and ask: *Who are they from? Who are they to? Where are they from? What's in the picture?*

Writing

> **PHOTO INFO**
>
> People from Thailand are called *Thai*. The picture shows a floating market in Thailand (which is a popular holiday destination in Southeast Asia).

2 When going over answers, check the meaning of the adjectives.

Writing skill

3b Read aloud the first two sentences in the example. Point out that joining two adjectives, nouns, or phrases avoids repeating words. Model by doing item 1 as a class.

> **Grammar note**
>
> Note that adjectives do not change according to whether they are describing singular or plural nouns.

> **ANSWERS**
>
> 1 The museums are big and old.
> 2 The town is old and beautiful.
> 3 It's famous in America and Europe.
> 4 It's a drink with sugar and mint.

4 Ask students to choose a place that they know well enough to write about. Tell them to use the postcard on this page as a model. To add authenticity, give students blank cards to write on; they can also draw a picture of the place on the other side. Alternatively, tell students to leave the name of the city blank. This way, when they exchange postcards with a partner, the challenge is to read and guess the city.

5 When checking, ask follow-up questions about the information on the postcards, e.g., *Is Ivan's hotel big? Is the food good?*

> **HOMEWORK** Ask students to write a postcard from a place that they have visited recently.

Where's that?

Videoscript

Narrator: Four cities around the world. What are their names?

City 1

F: OK, so this is in Asia.

M: Ah, it's at night. Look at the lights.

F: Yeah, they're shops. It's a shopping street.

M: And the cars and the people …

F: Yes, it's big. Well, it's the capital.

F: And this is in the day.

M: That's beautiful. Where's that?

F: It's in the city. It's a park with a lake.

M: Who's that? Is that you next to the lake?

F: No, it isn't.

City 2

M: And now this is in Europe.

F: Of course, this museum is really famous: the Prado.

M: Oh, yes! Is it an art museum?

F: Yeah, that's right. It's popular with tourists and local people, too.

M: Is that in the capital?

F: Yes, it is.

M: And where's that?

F: That's the train station.

M: Where are the trains?

F: Ah, this is the old station.

M: What's that? A park?

F: Well … a garden … and a nice café next to the garden.

M: Oh, yes. It's beautiful … for a train station!

City 3

F: Now we're in the United States.

M: That's a great photo.

F: I know. The bridge is famous.

M: It's the symbol of the city …

F: Yeah … this is about seven o'clock in the morning.

M: Look at the buildings in the city. And the mountains, too. Where's this? Is it in a parking lot?

Coffee and a sandwich, please.

54

F: No, it's a snack bar. It's near the beach. Look at the sign—eat, drink, surf.

M: Oh, yeah! Well, the surfing and the beaches are famous.

City 4

M: Ooh, that's cold!

F: Yes. Well, it's Europe!

M: What's this building? Is it a museum?

F: No, it isn't. It's old and famous but it isn't a museum.

M: Is that next to the river?

F: Yes, in the capital.

M: And look at the two people. Why are they there?

F: I don't know.

M: Aha! That's opposite the Houses of Parliament!

F: Yeah.

M: Look at the river and the bridges. Great! Who are the people?

F: Erm, they're tourists, I think.

Narrator: Four cities around the world. What are their names?

Before you watch

1 Look at the photo and the caption on page 54. Find the name for this place in the word box in the next column. *a snack bar*

2 Work in pairs. Are these places in your town? Where?

> a bridge   a shopping area
> a garden   a snack bar

3 Work in pairs. Mark (✓) what's in your city or town.

> a bank
> a bus station
> a café
> a parking lot
> a movie theater
> a market
> a museum
> a park
> an information center
> a train station

4 This video is a quiz about cities. What do you think the title will be?

> ☐ Where's that?
> ☐ Four cities around the world.
> ☐ What are their names?

While you watch

5 Watch the video. Are the things in your list from Exercise 3 in the video?

6 Watch the video again. Where are the cities? Write the number of the city (1–4) with the continent. Two cities are in one continent.

3	1	2,4
North America?	Asia	Europe

7 Work in pairs. What are the names of the four cities? Choose the correct option (a–c). Do you agree?

1 a Beijing   b Hong Kong   ⓒ Tokyo
2 ⓐ Madrid   b Paris   c Rome
3 a New York   ⓑ San Francisco
   c Washington
4 a Lisbon   ⓑ London   c St. Petersburg

8 Watch the video again and check.

After you watch

9 Look at the questions and answers from the video. Complete the questions.

A: That's beautiful. ¹ _Where_ 's that?
B: It's in the city. It's a park with a lake.

A: ² _Who_ 's that? Is that you next to the lake?
B: No, it isn't.

A: ³ _What_ 's that? A park?
B: It's a garden—and a nice café next to the garden.

A: Look at the two people. ⁴ _Why_ are they there?
B: I don't know.

A: ⁵ _Who_ are the people?
B: They're tourists, I think.

10 Match two places with each city from the video. Then write sentences about one of the cities.

> Atocha Station Madrid
> Fisherman's Wharf San Francisco
> Greenwich Naval College London
> Shinjuku district Tokyo
> the Golden Gate Bridge San Francisco
> the Imperial Palace Tokyo
> the London Eye and the Houses of Parliament London
> the Prado museum Madrid

11 Write a postcard from one of the cities in the video.

12 Send your postcard to a classmate.

a bridge (n) /brɪdʒ/   a sign (n) /saɪn/

a garden (n) /ˈgɑːd(ə)n/   a snack bar (n) /ˈsnæk ˌbɑːr/

lights (n) /laɪts/   surf (v) /sɜːrf/

---

11 Demonstrate the activity by writing an example on the board. Elicit suggestions from the class. Give students some time to write a postcard to one of their classmates.

12 Ask students to exchange the postcards.

Before you watch

1 Ask students to look at the photo. Ask: *What can you see?* Ask students to find the word for this place.

2 Write the categories of places on the board. When checking, fill in the names under each category.

3 Read through the list as a class. Then divide the class into pairs and have them check the places that are in their city or town.

4 Survey the class to find out the most popular answer.

While you watch

5 Play the video. Students mark the things from the video in their lists.

> **ANSWERS**
>
> a park, a museum, a train station, a café

6 Play the video again. Get students to match the cities with the continents.

7 Put students in pairs. Give them some time to read through the options and choose the correct ones.

8 Play the video again for students to check.

After you watch

9 Ask students to look at the questions and answers from the video and complete the questions.

10 Students match two places with each city from the video then write sentences about one of the cities.

> **SAMPLE ANSWERS**
>
> Atocha Station and the Prado museum are in Madrid.
>
> Fisherman's Wharf and the Golden Gate Bridge are in San Francisco.
> The Imperial Palace and Shinjuku district are in Tokyo.
>
> The London Eye, Greenwich Naval College, and the Houses of Parliament are in London.

UNIT 4 REVIEW

Grammar

1 Students read about the café. Then they complete the questions.

2 Students work in pairs to ask and answer the questions from Exercise 1.

3 Students look at the pictures and choose the correct option.

Vocabulary

4 Students fill in the missing letters to form words for places in a town.

5 Students work in pairs to talk about where the places in Exercise 4 are in their town.

6 Students take turns to say the days of the week in order.

7 Divide the class into pairs. Student A says a time and student B points to the corresponding clock.

8 Students complete the menu with the snacks.

Real life

9 Students complete the conversation in a café.

Speaking

10 Students practice the conversation in Exercise 9 in pairs.

> **Extra activity**
> Have students do a project on sister cities.

UNIT 4 REVIEW

Grammar

1 Read about the café. Then complete the questions.

New!

The Art Café

We are in the Modern Art Museum.
We are next to the Museum Store.

We are open Monday – Saturday,
10:00 – 6:00. On Sunday we are open
10:00 – 2:30.
Hot and cold snacks.

1 __What__ is the café's name?
2 __Where__ is the café?
3 __When__ is the café open?
4 __How__ old is the café?

2 Work in pairs. Ask and answer the questions from Exercise 1. Take turns.

3 Look at the pictures. Choose the correct option.

1 _Is (this) / that the bus to downtown?_

2 _Is this / (that) fruit juice?_

3 _Is this / (that) the train station?_

I don't know!

I CAN	
describe the location of places (prepositions of place)	☐
use *this* and *that* correctly	☐
ask and answer questions (question words)	☐

Vocabulary

4 Complete the words for places in a town.

1 tr**ai**n st**a**t**io**n   3 m**u**s**eu**m
2 p**a**rking l**o**t   4 m**o**vie th**ea**te**r**

5 Work in pairs. Where are the places in Exercise 4 in your town?

6 Work in pairs. Say the days in order. Take turns. Start with Monday.

7 Work in pairs. Take turns.

Student A: Choose a clock and say the time.

Student B: Point to the clock.

8 Complete the menu with these snacks.

| salad | fruit juice | coffee | sandwiches |

The Art Café

Hot drinks		Cold drinks	
¹ **coffee**	$2.50	mineral water	$2.50
tea	$2.00	² **fruit juice**	$3.00
		Snacks	
		³ **sandwiches**	$7.50
		⁴ **salad**	$7.50
		pastries	$3.00

I CAN	
talk about places in a town	☐
say the days of the week	☐
say the time	☐
talk about snacks	☐

Real life

9 Complete the conversation in a café with a–d.

a OK. Four dollars, please.
b Large or small?
c Thanks.
d Hello. Can I help you?

A: ¹ __d__
B: Can I have two teas, please?
A: ² __b__
B: Small, please.
A: ³ __a__
B: Here you are.
A: ⁴ __c__

I CAN	
buy snacks	☐

Speaking

10 Work in pairs. Practice the conversation in Exercise 9. Change the snacks.

Unit 5 Inventions

The "Jetman" in the air
Photo by Laurent Gillieron

FEATURES

1 Work in pairs. Look at the photo. What is it?

a   a toy
ⓑ   a person
c   a robot

2 🎵 **39** Listen to the information about the photo. Check your answer from Exercise 1.

3 🎵 **39** Listen again. Choose the correct option.

1   Yves Rossy is from *France /* Ⓢwitzerland
2   In the photo, he's above the Swiss Ⓐlps/ *capital*.
3   He's in the air for Ⓕive/ *nine* minutes.

4 Work in groups. Yves Rossy is an inventor. Name some inventors and their inventions.

> *Steve Jobs – iPod*

Unit 5 **Inventions**   57

Inventions

Warm-up

Introducing the theme: inventions

Write: *20th- and 21st-century inventions* on the board. Then ask: *What 20th- and 21st-century inventions are there in the classroom and in the school?* Elicit a list and write them on the board, e.g., *computers, laptops, cell phones, MP3 players, CD players,* etc. Ask students to rank the inventions from least important to most important.

1 Check the meaning of *toy* and *robot* with examples or gestures. Ask students to look at the photo and say what it is.

4 Divide the class into groups of four or five to think up a list of inventors and inventions. When checking, write students' ideas on the board.

Extra activity 1

Write these lists on the board:

car, plane, radio, bicycle, train

American, British, German, Italian, French

Ask students to match inventions and nationalities in pairs. When checking, see if students can name any of the inventors.

Answers:

car:	German (Daimler and Benz)
airplane:	American (Wright brothers)
radio:	Italian (Marconi)
bicycle:	French (Michaux and Lallement)
train:	British (Trescothick and Stephenson)

Extra activity 2

In pairs, ask students to name important inventions from their own country or countries. They should discuss the invention's name, approximate date, and the inventor, if known. Then bring the class together for a discussion.

Robots and people

Warm-up

Pre-teaching key words

Draw a simple diagram of a robot on the board and introduce it to the class, e.g., *This is Robbie. He's my robot.* Ask: *What can he do?* Elicit ideas from students.

Reading

2 Students read the article and find the information.

> **ANSWERS**
> 1 Nabeshima Akiko
> 2 It can see, speak, move, and carry things.
> 3 It can't run.

Grammar

3 Ask students to choose the correct option to complete the sentence. Look at the grammar box with the students and refer them to the information and practice on page 164.

> **Grammar notes**
>
> We use *can* to express a general ability, and *can't* to express a lack of ability.
>
> *Can* and *can't* are modal verbs and are followed by the infinitive without *to*.

4 Read through the example with the class then ask students to write sentences. Let them compare their answers in pairs. They will check the answers in Exercise 5.

> **ANSWERS**
> 1 Robots can speak.
> 2 Robots can carry things.
> 3 People can't fly.
> 4 I can speak English.
> 5 My grandfather can't run.

ROBOTS AND PEOPLE

This is 69-year-old Nabeshima Akiko. She's in a supermarket in Japan. She's with a robot. The robot is from Keihanna Science City near Kyoto. This robot can see and it can speak. It can move, but it can't run. It can carry things—for example, Nabeshima's basket.

Robots are amazing. They can help people in their lives.

Photo by Randy Olson

Reading

1 Look at the photo. Find:

| two women | a robot | a child | a basket |

2 Read the article. Underline:
1 the woman's name
2 four things this robot can do
3 one thing this robot can't do

Grammar *can/can't*

3 Choose the correct option to make a true sentence.

Robots *can* / *can't* help people.

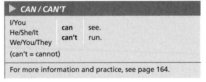

> ▶ **CAN / CAN'T**
>
> | I/You
He/She/It
We/You/They | can
can't | see.
run. |
>
> (can't = cannot)
>
> For more information and practice, see page 164.

4 Write sentences with *can* and *can't*.

Example:
robots / move ✓ *Robots can move.*
1 robots / speak ✓
2 robots / carry things ✓
3 people / fly ✗
4 I / speak English ✓
5 my grandfather / run ✗

5 Pronunciation *can/can't*

🔊 40 Listen and check your sentences from Exercise 4. Then listen again and repeat.

Pronunciation

5 Ask students to notice the different vowel sound in *can* and *can't*. Native speakers sometimes don't fully pronounce the final *t* in *can't*, and sometime even they need clarification. However, *can't* is usually a content word, with a longer, stressed vowel, while *can* is usually a function word with a shorter, unstressed vowel. For that reason, students can often determine which is being said even if the *t* in *can't* is minimized.

Vocabulary

6 Tell students to mark the sentences that are true for them. Then tell them to make the other sentences negative by changing *can* to *can't*.

7 When checking, ask students to tell the class about their partner, e.g., *Jaime can play soccer. He can't cook. He can drive a car.*

Vocabulary abilities

6 Mark (✓) the sentences that are true about you. Make the other sentences negative.

1 I can cook.

2 I can speak English.

3 I can play soccer.

4 I can drive a car.

5 I can ride a bike.

6 I can swim.

7 I can sing.

8 I can play the piano.

7 Work in pairs and take turns.

Student A: Read your sentences to your partner.

Student B: Write the number of the sentence. Then write ✓ (*can*) or ✗ (*can't*).

Listening

8 🔊 **41** Listen to an interview with Christine Black, a robot expert. Are the sentences true (T) or false (F)?

1 The robot's name is Tomo. T
2 Tomo is an American robot. F
3 Tomo is from a new generation of robots. T
4 "Tomo" is Japanese for "intelligent." T

9 🔊 **41** Listen again and answer the questions with ✓ (*can*) or ✗ (*can't*).

1 Can Tomo speak Japanese? ✓
2 Can she sing? ✓
3 Can she play the piano? ✓
4 Can she swim? ✗

Grammar *can* questions and short answers

10 Look at the grammar box. Write full answers to the questions in Exercise 9.

▶ CAN QUESTIONS and SHORT ANSWERS		
Can	I/you he/she/it we/you/they	speak Japanese? swim?
Yes, No,	I/you he/she/it we/you/they	can. can't.
For more information and practice, see page 164.		

Speaking

11 Work in pairs. Ask and answer questions about the abilities in Exercise 6.

Can you cook?

No, I can't.

Listening

8 Ask students to look at the photo. Ask: *What is it? What can it do?* Play the audio. Students listen and write *T* (true) or *F* (false).

Grammar

10 Look at the grammar box with the students. Then ask them to write answers to the questions in Exercise 9 using short answers. Check the answers and refer students to the information and practice on page 164.

ANSWERS
1 Yes, she can.
2 Yes, she can.
3 Yes, she can.
4 No, she can't.

Speaking

11 Model the activity by asking *Can you...?* questions around the class. Then divide the class into pairs to do the activity.

5b

Technology and me

Warm-up

Introducing the theme: technology

Show students any technological items you have with you, and describe one of them, e.g., *This is my cell phone. It's small and blue. It's new. It's Japanese.*

In groups, ask students to show and describe any technological items they have in their possession.

Vocabulary

Extra activity

Have students use their dictionaries to label the other objects in the photo on this page. Do they bring these things when they travel? What else do they bring?

Grammar

2 Read through the grammar box with the class. Ask students to choose the correct option. Let them compare their answers in pairs. Refer students to page 164 for more information and practice.

Grammar note

We use *have* and *has* to express possession.

We use *has* with the third person singular (*he, she, it*).

3 Check by asking different students to tell the class about their partner's possessions.

Reading

4 Organize the class into pairs to complete the sentences. Then ask students to read the text quickly and find the objects in the blog.

Vocabulary technology

1 Look at the objects. Number the words (1–5). Check your answers with your instructor.

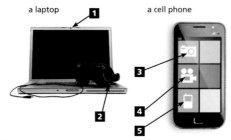

a camera 3   a video camera 4
headphones 2   a webcam 1
an MP3 player 5

a laptop   a cell phone

Grammar *have/has*

2 Look at the grammar box. Then look at the sentences. Choose the correct option.

1 This laptop *have* / *has* a webcam.
2 Cell phones *have* / *has* MP3 players.

▶ HAVE/HAS		
I/You/We/You/They	**have**	a camera.
He/She/It	**has**	headphones.
For more information and practice, see page 164.		

3 Work in pairs. Tell your partner about your laptop, cell phone, or computer.

I have a cell phone. It has a camera.

intelligent travel blog

We ask six travelers about their favorite piece of technology. Here are their comments.

This is my "mobile office." These things are in my backpack.
Posted by **Ian Walker**

I can take hundreds of photos with my new camera. It has a big memory.
Posted by **Sacha Brown**

I have an old webcam, but it's OK. I can see and talk to my family at home.
Posted by **Luis dos Santos**

I can work on the train with my laptop. It has a good battery.
Posted by **Adela Law**

My phone has a fantastic video camera. I can take great videos.
Posted by **Hon Yin**

My MP3 player is small and light. It's in my bag all the time.
Posted by **Adam LeBlanc**

a backpack (n) /'bæk,pæk/

60

ANSWERS

1 MP3 players
2 camera
3 video camera
Objects in the blog include: camera, webcam, laptop, phone, video camera, and MP3 player.

5 ANSWERS

new:	camera
big:	camera memory
fantastic:	video camera
great:	videos
small:	MP3 player
light:	MP3 player

Reading

4 Work in pairs. Complete the sentences with objects from Exercise 1. Then read the *Intelligent Travel* blog. Which objects are in the blog?

1 You can listen to music with _____ .
2 You can take photos with a _____ .
3 You can take videos with a _____ .

5 Read the blog again. Find these adjectives. What do they describe?

| new | big | fantastic | great | small | light |

Grammar adjective + noun

6 Look at the words in **bold** in the grammar box. Circle the adjectives and underline the nouns.

> **ADJECTIVE + NOUN**
>
> | My camera is fantastic. | I have an old webcam. |
>
> For more information and practice, see page 164.

7 Look at the example. Then write sentences.

Example:
This is my camera. It's new.
This is my new camera.

1 It's an MP3 player. It's new.
2 My phone has a battery. It's small.
3 They are headphones. They are light.
4 I have a video camera. It's digital.

Writing and speaking

8 What's your favorite piece of technology? Write a comment for the blog.

9 Work in groups. Talk about your favorite pieces of technology.

> What's your favorite piece of technology?
>
> My cell phone.
>
> Why?
>
> It's new and it has a great camera.

Grammar

6 Read through the grammar box with the class. Ask students to circle the adjectives and underline the nouns. Let them compare their answers in pairs. Refer students to page 164 for more information and practice.

7 Ask students to look at the example. Ask: *Which word is the adjective? Which word is the noun?* Students write sentences. Let them compare their answers in pairs.

> **ANSWERS**
>
> 1 It's a new MP3 player.
> 2 My phone has a small battery.
> 3 They are light headphones.
> 4 I have a digital video camera.

Writing and speaking

8 Check by asking students to read aloud their comments. Comments could also be displayed on the classroom walls.

9 Have students expand the discussion by ranking their favorite pieces of technology in order of importance. Why did they rank the items the way they did? Have the class share their rankings to explore any similarities and differences in students opinions.

Solar ovens

Warm-up

Using words

Write this sentence on the board: *I have a computer and a cell phone.* Divide the class into two teams. Team A must add two adjectives in front of each noun to produce an accurate sentence, e.g., *I have a new, Japanese computer and a big, blue cell phone.* Then it's Team B's turn. They must produce a sentence with different adjectives. Then it's back to Team A. Continue until one team repeats an adjective or can't think of any more adjectives to use.

Reading

1 Tell students to look at the photos 1–3 and then tell a partner the following information: Say which items they have seen before, which they have used before, and which are in their homes.

ANSWERS

1 *a gas oven*
2 *a microwave oven*
3 *an electric oven*

Teaching notes

This article provides a good opportunity to teach students how to use visuals as learning tools. Tell students that often visuals such as photos, pictures, and charts include important information. On this page, the visuals illustrate the article. They make the text easier to understand.

5c Solar ovens

Reading

1 Work in pairs. Match the words with the photos (1–3). Are these ovens popular in your country?

an electric oven   a gas oven
a microwave oven

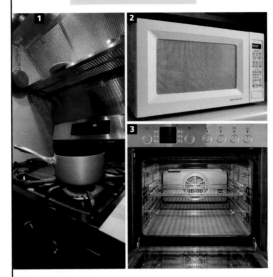

2 Read the article. Write this information for the two ovens.

	Bøhmer	HotPot
Number of parts	5	3
Price	$7	$100
Maximum temperature	90C/194F	150C/300F

3 Read the article again. Are the sentences true (T) or false (F)?

1 Solar ovens can heat water. T
2 You can buy the Bøhmer oven in stores. F
3 The Bøhmer oven has five parts. T
4 The HotPot oven has a glass bowl. T
5 You can buy the HotPot oven online. T

Grammar *very, really*

4 Look at the sentences in the grammar box. Which sentences are from the article?

▶ **VERY, REALLY**

This oven is **very** basic.   This oven is **really** basic.
It's **very** cheap.   It's **really** cheap!
Note: really great ✓ really fantastic ✓
BUT very great ✗ very fantastic ✗

For more information and practice, see page 164.

---

5 Put the words in order to make sentences.

1 basic / this / is / design / very
2 basic / this / a / oven / is / really
3 is / a / designer / very / he / good
4 phone / this / really / a / has / good / video camera

6 Word focus *this*

a Match the sentences (1–4) with the pictures (a–d).

1 This is my new camera. *c*
2 What's this in English? *a*
3 This is my sister Anita. *d*
4 Is the Plaza Hotel on this street? *b*

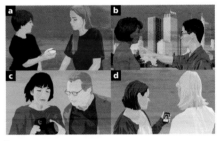

b Work in pairs. Change the underlined words in the sentences in Exercise 6a.

This is my new phone.   It's very nice.

Speaking

7 Work in pairs. Ask and answer questions about two microwave ovens.

Student A: Turn to page 154.

Student B: Turn to page 158.

---

2 Read the article with the class. Show students how the visual of the parts of the Bohmer oven to helps them understand the article. Point out the items (lid, pot, etc.) as you read the list in the second paragraph. Point out the labels and the icons that connect the labels with the images. Also explain the purpose of the glosses at the bottom of the page.

3 Have students correct the false item(s) in pairs.

Grammar

4 Read through the grammar box with the class. Ask students to say which sentences are from the article. Let them compare their answers in pairs. Refer students to page 164 for more information and practice.

ANSWERS

This oven is very basic.
It's really cheap!

TECHNOLOGY

Solar ovens

People in some parts of the world can't cook with gas or electric ovens, but they can cook with the sun! Solar ovens are really fantastic. They can cook food and heat water. Here are two solar ovens.

The Bøhmer oven

This oven is very basic. The designer is Jon Bøhmer. He's Norwegian, but he lives in Kenya. You can't buy this oven, but you can make it. It has five parts: a lid, a pot, two boxes, and newspaper. The total price of the parts is about $7. It's really cheap! The maximum temperature is about 90°C (194°F). This oven is very good for people in poor parts of the world.

The HotPot oven

The HotPot oven is a basic design too. It has three parts: a pot, a bowl, and aluminum panels. The pot is in the glass bowl. The maximum temperature is about 150°C (300°F). It's really hot! You can buy this oven online and in stores. The price is about $100.

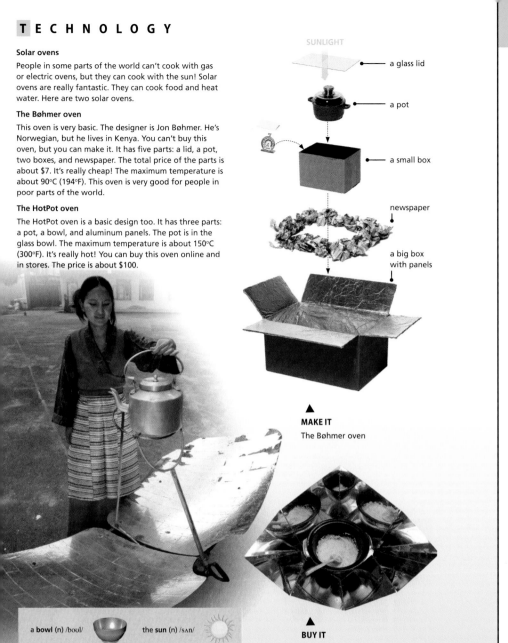

SUNLIGHT

a glass lid

a pot

a small box

newspaper

a big box with panels

▲ **MAKE IT**
The Bøhmer oven

a **bowl** (n) /boʊl/   the **sun** (n) /sʌn/

▲ **BUY IT**
The HotPot oven

5 Invite volunteers to write the completed items on the board. Have their classmates decide if the sentences are correct or need changes. Try not to lead students during this error-correction exercise; it's good practice for them to get used to approving/correcting their work without needing intervention.

> **ANSWERS**
>
> 1 This *design* is very basic.
> 2 This is a really basic oven.
> 3 He is a very good designer.
> 4 This phone has a really good video camera.

Word focus

6b Be sure that students understand that they should replace the underlined words with their own ideas.

> **Grammar notes**
>
> *This* can be a determiner (in this street) or a pronoun (This is my camera / my sister). We use *this* to refer to a person, thing, or place that is near the speaker. It is often used to introduce people for the first time, always in this singular, even if more than one person is being introduced. For example: *This is Gabriela. This is Gabriela and her husband Edward. This is Gabriela and Edward.*

Speaking

7 After checking answers as a class, personalize the activity by asking: *Do you have a microwave at home? What does it have? What can it do?*

> **ANSWERS**
>
> Student A (ProfessionalChef)
>
> 1 It has a big memory.
> 2 It has ten power options.
> 3 It can cook and heat food.
> 4 It can make cakes.
> 5 You can buy it online.
>
> Student B (EasyCook)
>
> 1 It can cook and heat food.
> 2 It has three power options.
> 3 It can't make cakes.
> 4 It has a digital clock.
> 5 You can buy it online.

> **HOMEWORK** Ask students to write a profile of one of their own domestic appliances. Then, in class, have them read the description to a partner, without naming the appliance. Their partner will guess what it is.

Vocabulary money and prices

1 Match the symbols with the money (currency).

1 $ ——— euros
2 £ ——— pounds
3 € ——— dollars

2 Work in pairs. What's the currency of these countries?

Australia	Brazil	China	the United States
Ireland	Canada	the United Kingdom	
Egypt	Germany	Saudi Arabia	

3 🔊 42 Listen and repeat the prices.

a $2.90 **b** £13.50 **c** €15.00
d €3.75 **e** $17.80 **f** $18.00

4 Pronunciation **numbers**

a 🔊 43 Listen and mark the correct price.

1 $13.00 $30.00   4 $16.00 $60.00
2 $14.00 $40.00   5 $17.00 $70.00
3 $15.00 $50.00   6 $18.00 $80.00

b Work in pairs. Take turns to dictate three prices to your partner.

Real life shopping

5 🔊 44 Listen to three conversations in stores. Write the number of the conversation (1–3) next to the product. There is one extra product.

an alarm clock 1   flash drives 3

speakers   a video camera 2

6 🔊 44 Listen again. Mark the correct price.

1 $15 $50 $80
2 $46.50 $65.60 $95.50
3 $5.99 $9.99 $99

7 Look at the expressions for SHOPPING. Write customer (C) or salesperson (S).

▶ SHOPPING

Excuse me. **C**
Can I help you? **S**
I'd like this video camera, please. **C**
How much is this alarm clock? **C**
How much are these flash drives? **C**
It's / They're 15 dollars. **S**
That's $95.50, please. **S**
Can I pay with pesos / cash / a card? **C**
Here you go. **C**

8 Work in pairs. Take turns to buy a product from your partner.

Salesperson: Decide the price of the products.

Customer: Decide how much you can pay.

a digital camera   headphones

an MP3 player   a webcam

64

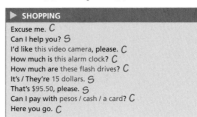

How much is it?

Warm-up

Introducing the theme: money

Bring in some money, either from the country where your students are studying, or your home country (if different). Pass coins and bills around the class and ask students to look at them carefully. Tell them to be prepared to answer questions about the money.

Collect the money. Hold up a bill or coin and ask: *How much is it? What color is it? Is it big or small? What's the picture on it? Who is the person on it?*

Vocabulary

2 ANSWERS

Australia: Australian dollar
Ireland: Euro
Egypt: Egyptian pound
Brazil: Brazilian real
Canada: Canadian dollar
China: Yuan Renminbi
Germany: Euro
United States: US dollar
United Kingdom: UK pound
Saudi Arabia: Riyal

Extra activity

Read aloud other prices using euros, pounds, and dollars. Ask students to write them down.

Alternatively, write some prices in number form on the board and ask students to read them aloud.

Pronunciation

4a Play the audio a second time if students have a difficult time selecting their answers.

Pronunciation notes

Note that *thirteen*, *fourteen*, *fifteen*, etc. have a strong stress on the second syllable.

Thirty, *forty*, *fifty*, etc. have a strong stress on the first syllable. The vowel in the second syllable has a shorter sound.

4b Tell students that they should dictate prices in the teens and tens (*13, 14, 30, 40*, etc.). You may want to have them dictate prices in dollars, pounds, and euros, so that their partners will practice writing all three symbols.

Real life

5 Ask students to look at the pictures and check that they know what the products are and can say the words.

8 Give students time to prepare in pairs before attempting the conversation. Monitor carefully and make sure they are attempting a good intonation pattern when asking the questions.

HOMEWORK Tell students to write a conversation between a customer and a salesperson in an electronics store.

5e Can you help me?

Writing an email

1 Read the emails and answer the questions.

1 Who is Eliza?
2 Who is Mike?
3 What is Eliza's question?
4 What is Mike's answer?

2 Read Mike's reply again. Complete the table.

	Positive +	Negative −
Tablets	small, _light_ _good_ screens special pen	expensive small screens
Laptops	_big_ screens keyboard	

Computer Life *Weekly*

can help with your IT questions.

Email mike@computerlifeweekly.com.

Hi Mike

I'm in my first semester at college and I'd like a new computer. My PC is old and slow. I can buy a laptop or a tablet. I can't decide. Can you help me?

Eliza

Hi Eliza

Tablets are small and light, but they are expensive. Tablets have good screens, but they are small. Laptops have big screens. Can you type? Laptops have a keyboard. Tablets have a special pen and you can write on the screen. This is great, but it's slow. Good luck in your studies!

Mike, Computer Life Weekly

screen

keyboard

3 Writing skill *but*

a Look at the example. Then underline two sentences with *but* in Mike's reply.

Example: Tablets are small and light. They are expensive.
*Tablets are small and light, **but** they are expensive.*

b Read the pairs of sentences. Which pair can you not rewrite with *but*?

1 This tablet is great. It's expensive.
2 Tablet screens aren't big. They are good quality.
③ This computer is old. It's slow.
4 With this phone, you can watch videos. You can't edit videos.

c Rewrite the pairs of sentences with *but*.

4 Write a reply to this email. Before you write, make notes on the two things. Use a table.

> Hi Jo,
> I'm in my first term at college. The bus to college is slow. I'd like a bike or a motorcycle. I can't decide. Can you help me?
> Billie

5 Work in pairs. Exchange replies. Is your partner's reply useful?

Can you help me?

Warm-up

Using words: computers

Ask students to look at the photograph of a computer on page 65 and introduce vocabulary. Check the key words: *computer, PC, laptop, tablet, screen*, and *keyboard*.

If there are computers in your classroom, point to parts of the computer and ask students to identify them. You could also review words like *webcam, headphones*, etc.

Writing

1 ANSWERS

1 *Eliza is a college student.*
2 *Mike works at* Computer Life Weekly.
3 *Eliza asks what sort of computer she can buy.*
4 *Mike answers with information about tablets and laptops.*

2 Ask students to read Mike's reply again and complete the table. Let them compare their answers in pairs before discussing as a class.

Writing skill

Grammar note

We use the conjunction or linking word *but* to join two clauses. Often a comma is placed before *but*, especially when joining two long clauses. *But* shows a contrast between the two clauses.

3b Remind students that there must be a contrast when joining clauses with *but*.

3c Let students compare their answers in pairs before discussing as a class.

3C ANSWERS

1 *This tablet is great, but it's expensive.*
2 *Tablet screens aren't big, but they're good quality.*
4 *With this phone, you can watch videos, but you can't edit videos.*

Teaching notes

It is a good idea to support students by drawing a table on the board and eliciting words and phrases that they could use to describe bikes and motorcycles. It will mean introducing some new vocabulary. Use gestures to elicit some useful basic adjectives.

	Positive +	Negative −
Bikes	light	
	cheap	slow
Motorcycles	fast	
	great	expensive

4 Ask students to draw a table and write positive and negative words to describe bikes and motorcycles. Have them refer to the table in Exercise 2 as a model. Students work individually to write their replies. Ask them to check their writing for correct spelling, capital letters, and the use of *but*.

The Owl and the Pussycat

Videoscript

Narrator: In northern Spain, falconer Jordi Amenos regularly takes his young barn owl on training flights.

The owl, named Gebra, sharpens her flying skills, especially her takeoffs and landings.

Jordi's young cat begins to tag along on these walks. The cat watches the owl with interest.

And then, one day, Fum—meaning smoke in Catalan—goes airborne as well.

Most cats are agile, but Fum's moves belong in the Cirque du Soleil.

Fum leaps from his predatory instinct. But luckily, this is all in good fun.

Jordi Amenos Basora: In the beginning, I was not amused by the game because I saw that it could turn for the worst.

After a few days, I realized that the game was quite harmless and innocent.

And as it turns out, their games are really a sight to behold.

So, Jordi begins to capture the air show on tape for his own amusement.

When he edits the video and posts a link to his Facebook page the web traffic explodes.

His good friend, Ferran Marti, a web developer, remembers how surprised they both were.

Ferran Marti: On the seventh of May, Jordi put the video up on YouTube and I remember, one day, you put it on your Facebook profile and there were, like, a thousand visits, or something. I was surprised.

Technology can make some animals famous.

66

Jordi: Yes, I remember it that way, too. First it had one thousand visits, or something like that. And then, I went to sleep and the next day there were three hundred thousand visits. I thought, "What happened?"

After this, Ferran helps Jordi create a Fum and Gebra website where visitors post comments.

Ferran: They all love the story and want to find out more. That's why we had the idea of making the website to talk about Fum and Gebra's lives.

Before you watch

1 Read the list of objects and animals. Write what they can do.

fly	take photos and videos
climb trees	have information about things, people, etc.
make calls	take videos
connect to the Internet	have special pens

Cameras	*They can take photos and videos.*
Owls	They can fly.
Laptops	They can connect to the Internet.
Webcams	They can take videos.
Cats	They can climb trees.
Websites	(See below)
Cell phones	They can make calls.
Tablets	They can have special pens.

2 Look at the word box below. Listen and repeat the words after your instructor.

3 In the video, Jordi Amenos takes videos of his owl and cat. Which items from Exercise 1 do you think are in the video that you will see? What do you think Amenos does with the videos he takes?

While you watch

4 As you watch the video, match these items. One answer is used two times.
1 Gebra *a*   a owl
2 Fum and Gebra *e*   b web developer
3 Fum *c*   c cat
4 Facebook *d*   d website
5 Amenos and Marti *e* e friends
6 Marti *b*

5 Watch the video again. Put these items in order from 1–8.
- ☐2 Amenos edits the video.
- ☐8 Visitors to the website post comments.
- ☐6 300,000+ people see the video.
- ☐1 Jordi Amenos takes videos of Fum and Gebra.
- ☐3 Amenos puts the video on the Internet.
- ☐4 1,000 people see the video.
- ☐5 Amenos goes to bed.
- ☐7 Ferran Marti helps Amenos make a website about Fum and Gebra.

6 Choose the correct words to complete each sentence.
1 Fum is very _____, but he _____ fly.
   a big; can
   b heavy; likes to
   c agile; can't *(c circled)*
2 Jordi Amenos takes _____ and puts them on a _____.
   a videos; memory stick
   b photos; cell phone
   c videos; website *(c circled)*
3 Thousands of people _____ Amenos's _____.
   a visit; website *(a circled)*
   b visit; owl
   c post videos on; website

After you watch

7 What is your favorite piece of technology for watching videos? Why? Share your answers with a partner. Then describe the piece of technology to your partner.

8 Do you watch interesting or funny videos with animals? Where can you see them online? Get together with another pair and talk about the videos.

> I can see funny videos on…

agile (adj) /ˈædʒəl/ able to move quickly and easily

airborne (adj) /ˈeərˌbɔrn/ moving in the air

leap (v) /lip/ to jump

link (n) /lɪŋk/ a web address that you can click on

post (v) /poʊst/ to put something online

profile (n) /ˈproʊfaɪl/ information about someone

web developer (n) /ˈwɛb dɪˌvɛləpər/ someone who makes web pages

web traffic (n) /ˈwɛb ˌtræfɪk/ how many people visit a website

Before you watch

1 Read through the list as a class. Check the meaning of *owl* by using the photo and *cat* by making a simple drawing on the board. Then have students fill in the chart with sentences about what the objects and animals can do.

> **ANSWERS**
>
> websites: They can have information about things, people, etc.

2 Read through the words in the word box and have students repeat.

3 Have students place a check mark next to the objects and animals in Exercise 1 that they think they will see in the video. Discuss the second question as a class.

While you watch

4 Read through the items as a class. Play the video and ask students to match the items. Point out that one answer is used two times.

5 Play the video again. Then have students put the events in order. Guide students in identifying the first event in the sequence.

6 Tell students to read through the items carefully before selecting the answers. Check answers as a class.

After you watch

7 Survey the class to find out the most popular technology items for viewing videos.

8 If students make and/or post online their own interesting videos of animals, have them share a video with the class.

Grammar

1 Ask students to look at the photo. Ask: *What's her name?* Model one or two questions with *Can she…?* Then ask students to ask and answer questions in pairs.

> **ANSWERS**
> 1 Can she drive a car? Yes, she can.
> 2 Can she drive a motorbike? No, she can't.
> 3 Can she cook? Yes, she can.
> 4 Can she type? Yes, she can.
> 5 Can she speak Arabic? No, she can't.
> 6 Can she speak Russian? Yes, she can.
> 7 Can she write in Arabic? No, she can't.
> 8 Can she write in Russian? No, she can't.

2 Tell students to close their books then take turns to make sentences about Lynn using *can* and *can't*.

3 Students complete the text about the e-Reader.

Vocabulary

4 Students match the verbs and words.

5 Students write a check mark or an *X* next to each object.

6 Divide the class into pairs. Students tell their partner about the objects in Exercise 5.

7 Students take turns to say prices; their partner listens and points to the price tag.

Real life

8 Students complete the conversation with the words.

Speaking

9 Students practice the conversation in Exercise 8 in pairs. Remind them to change the objects and prices.

UNIT 5 REVIEW

Grammar

1 Work in pairs. Ask and answer questions about Lynn. Use *can*. Take turns.

1	drive a car ✓	5	speak Arabic ✗
2	drive a motorbike ✗	6	speak Russian ✓
3	cook ✓	7	write in Arabic ✗
4	type ✓	8	write in Russian ✗

2 Work in pairs. Make sentences about Lynn.

3 Complete the text with these words.

> 's   fantastic   has   invention   really

 This e-Reader has a ¹ _really_ big memory—it can store 1,400 books. It ² _'s_ small and light. It ³ _has_ a 15-hour battery and a keyboard on screen. E-readers are a ⁴_fantastic_ ⁵_invention_.

I CAN	
talk about ability (*can*)	☐
talk about possessions and features (*have*)	☐
describe objects (adjective + noun)	☐
use *very* and *really* correctly	☐

Vocabulary

4 Match the verbs from A with words from B.

A	B
drive	a bike
play	a car
play	the piano
ride	three languages
speak	tennis

---

5 Write ✓ or ✗ next to the objects.

1 You can listen to music with:
a phone ✓   headphones ✓ an MP3 player ✓

2 You can take a photo with:
speakers ✗   a phone ✓   a camera ✓

3 You can speak to people with:
a video camera ✗ a laptop ✓   a memory stick ✗

6 Work in pairs. Tell your partner about the objects in Exercise 5.

> *I have a phone. It's in my bag.*

7 Work in pairs. Take turns.

Student A: Choose a price tag and say the price.

Student B: Point to the price tag.

$14.99 $50 $71.40   £13.30
€17.50 $19.90   €90.95 $45.70

I CAN	
talk about abilities	☐
talk about technology	☐
talk about money	☐

Real life

8 Complete the conversation between a customer (C) and a salesperson (S) with these words.

> help   here   like   much   pay   that's   they're

S: Can I ¹ _help_ you?
C: How ² _much_ are these webcams?
S: ³ _They're_ 37 dollars.
C: OK. I'd ⁴ _like_ this webcam and a flash drive please.
S: ⁵ _Here_ you are. ⁶ _That's_ 47.50, please.
C: Can I ⁷ _pay_ with a card?
S: Yes, of course.

I CAN	
ask and talk about prices	☐
buy things in a store	☐

Speaking

9 Work in pairs. Practice the conversation in Exercise 8. Change the objects and the prices.

> **Extra activity**
>
> To review, play Bingo with prices. Draw a simple 5x5 Bingo grid on the board for students to copy. If needed, go over the rules of Bingo.
>
> Ask students to write a price in each box on their card. They can choose any price between (and including) $13 and $15 in multiples of five cents, e.g., *$13.10, $13.45, $14.50, $14.95*, etc.
>
> Read aloud prices between $13 and $15 at random. Students mark the prices they hear that are on their card. Verify the winner's numbers by having that student recite the numbers back to you.

Passionate sports fans in
Soweto, South Africa

FEATURES

70 A passion for vegetables
Giant vegetables

72 My favorite things
A profile of a scientist and
TV presenter

74 In love with speed
Racing with animals

78 At the market
A video about people at a
market

1 🔊 45 Look at the photo. What's the sport? Listen and check.

basketball	rugby	(soccer)	tennis

2 🔊 45 Look at these numbers. Then listen again and choose the correct option. Practice saying the numbers.

100 = one hundred	1,000,000 = one million
1,000 = one thousand	

1 About 270 *thousand* / (million) people play soccer around the world.
2 Soccer is popular in more than two (hundred) / *thousand* countries.
3 The World Cup prize is 30 *thousand* / (million) US dollars.

3 Work in pairs. Take turns to say the numbers. Then dictate three numbers to your partner.

300	9,000	20,000	800	70,000,000

4 Work in groups. Answer the questions.

1 Which sports are popular in your country?
2 What's the national sport in your country?
3 What sports can you play?

Passions

Warm-up

Introducing the theme: passions

Ask students to look at the photo in the Student Book. Ask: *Who are they? Where are they from? How do they feel?* Elicit any descriptive words that students already know, e.g., *happy, great, fantastic.*

Using the photo, pre-teach the words *fans* and *passion*, and the adjective *passionate* to show very strong feelings.

1 Ask students to look at the photo, and ask: *What's the sport?* Elicit guesses. If students don't know the sports in the box, use gestures to show meaning. Then play the audio.

PHOTO INFO

The 2010 FIFA World Cup was played in South Africa. Spain beat Holland in the final. Kaizer Chiefs, South Africa's most successful team, play at Soccer City stadium in Soweto, Johannesburg.

Rugby is another popular sport in South Africa. In 1995, the Rugby World Cup was hosted by South Africa and the national team won the trophy. The moment when president Nelson Mandela presented the trophy to the rugby team is remembered as an iconic moment in South African sport and politics, as it took place during the dismantlement of apartheid.

2 Give students a moment to read through the numbers. Read the numbers aloud and ask students to repeat them to practice pronunciation.

Play the audio again. Students listen and choose the correct answers.

Grammar and pronunciation notes

Note the stress on the first syllable: *hundred, thousand, million.*

When saying large numbers we include the word *and* after the word *hundred.*

350 = *three hundred AND fifty*

3,560 = *three thousand five hundred AND sixty*

Note that the singular form of *hundred, thousand,* and *million* is always used, e.g., *five thousand* NOT *five thousands.*

Teaching note

With stronger classes, introduce numbers with 50 and 500, e.g., 350 (*three hundred and fifty*) and 3,500 (*three thousand five hundred*).

4 Survey the class to find out the most popular answers. As needed, write vocabulary on the board.

A passion for vegetables

Warm-up

Test before you teach: food

Start the lesson by finding out how many food-related words students know. For example:

1 Bring in pictures of different types of basic foods, and use them to elicit words and write them on the board.

2 Draw a picture of a big, empty refrigerator on the board. Introduce the word *refrigerator*; then ask pairs of students to brainstorm foods that are in their refrigerators at home. Have students write the words in the refrigerator drawing on the board. As needed, provide the correct spelling and pronunciation.

3 Elicit and write the letters of the alphabet on the board. Then ask groups of students to think of one type of food for each letter, e.g., *A – apple*.

Reading

1 Ask students to look at the photo and the caption, and answer the question. Check comprehension of the words *giant* (= very, very big) and *pumpkin* (use the picture).

> **Extra activity**
>
> Ask: *What's a traditional vegetable dish in your country?*

Grammar

4 Look at the example as a class and elicit the negative form of *I like vegetables*. Then ask students to write whole sentences.

6a A passion for vegetables

Reading

1 Look at the photo and the caption. What is Steve Weston's passion? *vegetables*

2 Read about Steve Weston. Answer the questions.

1 Where is Steve Weston in the photo? *in his garden*
2 What's the name of this kind of vegetable? *pumpkin*
3 How much does the vegetable weigh? *1,500 pounds*
4 Can you eat this vegetable? *yes*

Grammar *like*

3 Look at the grammar box. <u>Underline</u> the sentences in the article with *like* and *don't like*.

▶ **LIKE**

I/You/We/You/They	like	pumpkins.
	don't like	pumpkin pie.
(don't = do not)		

For more information and practice, see page 164.

Competitions for giant vegetables are popular in the United States. This is my prize pumpkin!

A passion for vegetables
STEVE WESTON

Hi! My name's Steve Weston and I'm passionate about vegetables! Here I am in my garden with a giant pumpkin. <u>I like pumpkins a lot because they can grow big.</u> This pumpkin is about 1,500 pounds. <u>A lot of people like pumpkin pie, but I don't like it!</u>

pumpkin pie (n)
/ˈpʌmpkɪn ˈpaɪ/

70

Grammar notes

Here, students are being introduced to the affirmative and negative forms of simple present regular verbs.

Students may be pleasantly surprised to learn that there is no change in the singular *I* and *you* forms, and the plural *they, you,* and *we* forms. English does not differentiate between singular or plural *you*.

After *I, you, we,* and *they,* we use a form of *like* which is identical to the infinitive. To make the negative, add the negative form of the auxiliary verb *do* before the word *like*.

Watch out for common errors such as *I am like…* and *They not like….*

4 Look at the example. Then complete the sentences with *like* (☺) or *don't like* (☹).

Example:
I / vegetables. ☺
I like vegetables.

1 I / my garden. ☺ I like my garden.
2 I / competitions. ☹ I don't like competitions.
3 My friends / sports. ☺ My friends like sports.
4 I / soccer. ☹ I don't like soccer.
5 We / tennis. ☺ We like tennis.

5 Change the sentences in Exercise 4 so they are true for you. Read the sentences to your partner.

> *I don't like vegetables.*

Vocabulary **food**

6 Write these words with the photos.

> pasta chocolate vegetables salad

cheese

chocolate

eggs

fish

fruit

meat

pasta

rice

salad

vegetables

7 Work in pairs. Talk about the food in the photos.

> *I like cheese.*

> *I don't like cheese very much.*

Listening

8 🔊 46 Listen and mark the questions you hear.
① Do you like fruit? ③ Do you like meat?
② Do you like salad? ④ Do you like pasta?

9 🔊 46 Listen again and choose *like* (☺) or *don't like* (☹).

1 fruit   ☺ / ☹   3 meat   ☺ / ☹
2 salad   ☺ / ☹   4 pasta ☺ / ☹

Grammar *like* questions and short answers

10 Look at the grammar box. What's the question form of *like*?

▶ *LIKE* QUESTIONS and SHORT ANSWERS			
Do	I/you/we/you/they	**like**	fruit?
Yes, No,	I/you/we/you/they	**do.** **don't.**	

For more information and practice, see page 164.

11 Pronunciation *do you … ?*

a 🔊 47 Listen and repeat four questions from the interview.

b Work in pairs. Ask and answer the questions in Exercise 11a.

Speaking and writing

12 Prepare questions for a food survey. Write six questions with *Do you like … ?*

13 Work in groups. Ask and answer the questions.

> *Alex, do you like pizza?*

> *Yes, I do.*

> *Krish, do you like pizza?*

> *No, I don't.*

14 Which foods are popular? Write sentences about your results. Compare with other groups.

In our group, three people like pizza.

Vocabulary

6 Note that *eggs* and *vegetables* are the only count nouns here; all the other food words are noncount nouns.

Listening

8 Show the meaning of *fruit pie* by drawing a picture on the board.

Grammar

Pronunciation

11b Make sure students are using short answers with *do* and *don't.*

Speaking and writing

12 Tell students to use vocabulary from the unit or use their own food words (*pizza, ice cream, hamburgers,* etc.).

13 Divide the class into groups of four or five. Monitor to make sure that students are using questions and short answers correctly. Have groups keep track of the survey results, for use in Exercise 14.

My favorite things

Warm-up

Using words: likes and dislikes

Tell students that they have one minute to write down as many things that they like as they can think of, e.g., *coffee, chocolate, English, soccer, green*. Then have pairs of students compare lists. Find out what likes they have in common. What are some of the most popular "likes" for the class? And "dislikes"?

Vocabulary

1 Make sure that students understand all the words. Give examples, e.g., detective stories: Sherlock Holmes; reality shows: *Big Brother. Scuba diving* means diving with an oxygen tank, mask, and flippers.

Ask students to supply other words they know for each category.

> **ANSWERS**
>
> Music: *jazz, pop*
> Books: *detective stories, novels*
> Movies: *action movies, comedies*
> Animals: *birds, fish*
> TV: *reality shows, wildlife shows*
> Sports: *scuba diving, swimming*

2 Make sure students are using short answers correctly. Circulate the class to monitor and correct as necessary.

Reading

3 Introduce the reading by asking students to look at the photo of Zeb. Ask: *What can you see? Where is the man? What's his job? What does he like?*

6b My favorite things

Vocabulary **interests**

1 Match the categories in box A with the examples in box B. Check your answers with your instructor.

Example:
birds, fish – animals

A
animals   books   movies
music   sports   TV

B jazz   pop
    detective stories   novels
    action movies   comedies
    birds   fish
    reality shows   wildlife shows
    scuba diving   swimming

2 Work in pairs. Ask and answer questions about your favorite TV show, book, movie, and sport.

> Do you like TV?   Yes, I do.
>
> What's your favorite TV show?

Reading

3 Read the article about Zeb Hogan. Underline four interests from Exercise 1.

4 Read the article again. Are the sentences true (T) or false (F)?

1 Zeb Hogan has two jobs. T
2 He's a fisherman. F
3 He's from Botswana. F
4 His favorite sports are swimming and tennis.
                                            F

My favorite things | **Zeb Hogan**

Name: Zeb Hogan
Place of Birth: Arizona
Current City: Reno, Nevada
Job: Research Professor,
University of Nevada and
TV presenter: *Monster Fish*,
Nat Geo TV

72

Extra activity

Ask students to rewrite the false sentences in Exercise 4 so that they are true.

Background notes

Arizona and Nevada are states in the US Southwest, an area that is hot and dry.

The Okavango Delta, in the southern African country of Botswana, is a large, swampy area that attracts huge numbers of wild animals. It is home to over 70 species of fish.

Grammar *he/she* + *like*

5 Look at the grammar box. Then look at the article. What is the negative form of *likes*? *doesn't like*

> ▶ **HE/SHE + LIKE**
>
> | He/She | **likes**
doesn't like | fish.
cold places. |
> |---|---|---|
> | **Does** | he/she | **like** | coffee? |
> | Yes,
No, | he/she | **does.**
doesn't. |
> | (doesn't = does not) | | |
>
> For more information and practice, see page 165.

6 Look at the example. Write questions about Zeb Hogan.

Example:
like / fish? *Does he like fish?*

1 like / Botswana?
2 like / Arizona?
3 like / cold places?
4 like / hot places?
5 like / TV shows?

7 Work in pairs. Ask and answer the questions in Exercise 6 with *yes, no,* or *I don't know.*

Zeb Hogan likes <u>fish.</u> His passion is giant fish. He isn't a fisherman. He's a scientist. His job is to study and protect giant fish in different places around the world, like the Okavango Delta in Botswana. That's Zeb's favorite place. Zeb's from Arizona. It's a very hot, dry place. He doesn't like cold places, but he likes water. He loves <u>swimming and scuba diving.</u> Zeb's other passions are his friends, his family, and <u>wildlife shows on TV.</u>

8 Pronunciation *likes, doesn't like*

🔊 **48** Listen to five sentences about Zeb Hogan and repeat them.

Speaking

9 Work in pairs. Look at the table.

Student A: Choose a person.

Student B: Ask *Does she like … ?* to discover the identity.

Take turns.

> Does she like music?

> No, she doesn't.

> Does she like movies?

> Yes, she does.

> Is it Teresa?   Yes!

	Barbara	Diana	Stella	Teresa
🐾	✓	✓	✗	✗
📖	✗	✗	✓	✓
🎞	✗	✓	✗	✓
🎵	✓	✗	✓	✗
👟	✗	✓	✗	✓
🖥	✓	✗	✓	✗

Grammar

> **Grammar notes**
>
> Here, students are being introduced to the affirmative, negative, and question forms of simple present regular verbs in the third person.
>
> After *he, she,* and *it,* we use *like**s***. We add an *s* to the forms used with other pronouns. To make the negative, we add the negative form of the third person auxiliary verb *does* and change *likes* to *like.*
>
> Watch out for common errors such as *He like…* and *He doesn't likes….*

6 Ask students to look at the example, and elicit the extra words needed to form the questions from the prompts (*Does* and *he*). Add some extra items if students finish quickly.

6 like / swimming
7 like / scuba diving
8 like / family

> **ANSWERS**
>
> 1 Does he like Botswana?
> 2 Does he like Arizona?
> 3 Does he like cold places?
> 4 Does he like hot places?
> 5 Does he like TV shows?

Speaking

9 Warm up by asking students a few questions about the table to make sure that they understand the information. Remind students that the icons are labeled on page 72 in case they are not sure which category an icon represents.

> **HOMEWORK** Ask students to research a famous person. They should find out five of the person's likes and three dislikes and write a paragraph about them.

> **Extra activity**
>
> Write many different things students may like on the board, e.g., *tea, coffee, Chinese food, horror films, reality TV, basketball, soccer on TV.* Also take suggestions from the class.
>
> Divide the class into groups of four. Then split each group into two pairs. Each pair has three minutes to ask *Do you like…?* questions to find out as much information as they can about their partner. Tell them to remember as much as they can without taking notes.
>
> Within each group, change the pairs. Now, they must ask questions to find out what students have already discovered about their previous partner, e.g., *Does (Emma) like (basketball)?* Students take notes this time and check the answers as a group at the end.

In love with speed

Warm-up

Introducing the theme: sports events and races

Elicit as many famous sports events and races as you can from students and write them on the board. Ask students to say when they are, why they are important, and whether they like them.

Reading

1 Ask students to look at the photos. Model the words for pronunciation and ask students to repeat.

When checking answers, accept and discuss any answers as this will depend on the students' knowledge and cultural background.

SAMPLE ANSWERS

athletes: Olympics
motorcycles: MotoGP
cars: Formula 1 Grand Prix, Le Mans, Indy 500
boats: Americas Cup, Clipper Round the World Yacht Race
bicycles: Tour de France, Olympic road race

Pronunciation note

Note the stress: *bicycle*, *motorcycle*, *athlete*.

2 Ask students to work in pairs to answer the questions about the events they named in Exercise 1. Check answers as a class.

3 Give students two minutes to skim read the article and find the items.

ANSWERS

1 horse racing, camel racing, racing pigeons
2 China, Qatar, Belgium, Australia, UK
3 money, a special horse

Reading

1 Work in pairs. Look at the photos. Can you name famous sporting events with these things?

athletes   motorcycles   cars   boats   bicycles

2 Look at your answers from Exercise 1. Answer the questions for each event.

1 Which city or country is the race in?
2 What is the prize?
3 Can you name any famous winners of the event?

3 Read the article on page 75. Find:

1 three types of racing
2 five countries
3 two types of prizes

4 Read the article again. Complete the sentences.

1 _____ racing is popular in China.
2 _____ racing is popular in Europe.
3 People in Qatar love _____ racing.
4 _____ can run at 40 miles per hour.
5 _____ can fly 60 to 600 miles.

5 Match the comments from three people with the animal race.

1 "This sport is popular in Australia, but I don't like it."
2 "My birds are special to me. I like them a lot!"
3 "My brother is in this race. I can see him on his horse."

74

Grammar **object pronouns**

6 Look at the grammar box. Then look at the comments in Exercise 5. Find four object pronouns in the comments. *Circled in 5.*

▶ OBJECT PRONOUNS

Subject pronoun	Object pronoun
I	me
you	you
he	him
she	her
it	it
we	us
you	you
they	them

For more information and practice, see page 165.

7 Choose the correct option.

1 That's my horse. I love *them* / **it**.
2 He's fantastic. I like **him** / *her* a lot.
3 Australians are great. I like **them** / *him*.
4 Where's your sister? I can't see **her** / *you*.
5 The *Tour de France* is a great race. I like *her* / **it**.

8 Word focus *it*

a Match 1–5 with a–e. Then <u>underline</u> *it* in the sentences.

1 What time is <u>it</u>? b
2 Is <u>it</u> hot in your city today? e
3 What's your favorite place? a
4 What day is <u>it</u>? c
5 Hello? d

a Shanghai. I love <u>it</u>.
b <u>It</u>'s ten o'clock.
c <u>It</u>'s Monday.
d Hi, <u>it</u>'s Susan.
e No, <u>it</u>'s cold.

b Work in pairs. Ask and answer questions 1–4.

Speaking

9 Work in pairs. Ask and answer questions about international sporting events.

Student A: Turn to page 155.

Student B: Turn to page 159.

4 ANSWERS

1 Horse
2 Pigeon
3 camel
3 Camels
3 Pigeons

5 ANSWERS

1 camel
2 pigeon
3 horse

Grammar

6 As a follow-up, ask students to say what each pronoun refers to (*it*—sport; *me*—I; *them*—birds; *him*—brother).

IN LOVE WITH SPEED

People love speed, racing, and winning.
Read about our passion for races.

The Litang Horse Festival is in China. It's during the first week of August. The horses are small and fast. The races are over 180 miles. The prize is money or a special horse. People in China love this festival.

Camel racing is a popular sport in Qatar. A camel's top speed is about 40 miles per hour! They can run at 25 miles per hour over a long distance. Australians love camel racing too. One big race in Australia has prize money of $50,000.

Racing pigeons can fly from 60 to 600 miles. Pigeon races are popular in Belgium and in the United Kingdom. A racing pigeon's top speed is about 80 miles per hour. It was a sport at the Paris Olympic games in 1900!

festival (n) /ˈfestɪvəl/ a special day or celebration

Grammar notes

Object pronouns replace a noun when it is an object in a sentence. We often replace nouns to avoid repetition when we already know what is being referred to.

Word focus

8a When checking answers, point out the different uses of *it* (to give the time and day, to talk about the weather, to introduce yourself on the phone, and as a pronoun to replace a noun).

Speaking

HOMEWORK Tell students to research and write a short text about a famous sporting event.

Extra activity

Do students know any other animal races? Write these types and examples on the board: dogsled—Iditarod, horse racing—Kentucky Derby, bull running—Festival of San Fermín. Ask them what they know about these events. Split them into pairs or groups of three and have them research one to share with the class. Which races would students like to see or try?

Let's play ping pong

Vocabulary

1 Before playing the audio, ask students to look at the four adjectives and the illustrations and check that they understand the words. Play the audio twice if necessary.

> **Vocabulary notes**
>
> *Fantastic* and *great* both mean "very, very good." They are used to describe anything that gives you a very positive feeling.
>
> *Boring* and *horrible* have more specific meanings. *Boring* means "uninteresting." *Horrible* means "very bad" in a way that makes you feel disgusted, e.g., horrible food, weather, or experiences, but it would be unusual to describe a sport as "horrible."

Pronunciation

3 Encourage students to exaggerate the intonation pattern they hear.

4 You could turn this into a class survey. Have pairs of students create a three-column chart with the headings *Person/Thing, Fantastic, Boring,* and *Horrible.* They must fill in the first column with the items from Exercise 1 and four additional people or things. Then have them circulate and ask their classmates' opinions, e.g., *Do you like soccer? (Yes, I do. It's*

Vocabulary opinion adjectives

1 🔊 **49** Listen to three conversations (1–3). Match the words from the conversations with the four opinion adjectives.

a Emily Blunt   c pasta
b sports   d pizza

boring b

horrible
c

fantastic / great
a   d

2 Are the adjectives in Exercise 1 positive (+) or negative (–)? Write them in the table.

Positive +	Negative –
fantastic	horrible
great	boring

3 **Pronunciation** intonation

🔊 **50** Listen and repeat.

4 Work in pairs. Add the names of four people or things to the list in Exercise 1. Tell your partner your opinion.

> Basketball's boring.

76

Real life suggestions

5 🔊 **49** Complete the conversations with the expressions for making and responding to SUGGESTIONS. Then listen again and check.

1
A: Let's watch TV tonight.
B: _____ . What's on?
A: A movie with Emily Blunt is on at eight o'clock.
B: Oh, _____ . She's fantastic.
2
A: _____ .
B: _____ . I don't like ping pong.
A: OK. _____ ?
B: Sorry. Sports are boring.
3
A: Let's have spaghetti this weekend.
B: _____ . It's horrible.
A: _____ . How about pizza? Do you like pizza?
B: Yes, it's great.

> ▶ **SUGGESTIONS**
>
>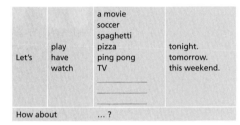
>
> Let's play ping pong tomorrow.
> That's a good idea.
> I love her.
> How about soccer?
>
> No, thanks.
> I don't like spaghetti.
> OK.

6 Add three ideas to the table below.

Let's	play have watch	a movie soccer spaghetti pizza ping pong TV _____ _____ _____	tonight. tomorrow. this weekend.
How about		… ?	

7 Work in pairs. Take turns to make suggestions and respond with opinions.

8 Work in a group. Make suggestions and agree on an activity for this weekend.

---

fantastic. / No, I don't. It's boring.). Have pairs share their results with the class.

Real life

> **5 ANSWERS**
>
> 1 B That's a good idea
>   B I love her
> 2 A Let's play ping pong tomorrow
>   B No, thanks
>   A How about soccer
> 3 B I don't like spaghetti
>   A OK

6 Tell students to be sure to add nouns that can be used with the verbs *play, have,* and *watch.*

> **Vocabulary notes**
>
> We use *Let's* + infinitive to make suggestions, e.g., *Let's watch TV.* We can also use the structure *How about* + noun, e.g., *How about tennis?*
>
> At this stage of students' learning, it's best to avoid using *How about* with a verb, since it requires the *-ing* form (*How about playing tennis?*).
>
> You might want to point out *What's on?* and *It's on (TV) at 9.* We use *on* to talk about movies and shows that appear on TV.
>
> Also, in English we tend to use *have* rather than *eat* with food when talking about meals (*Let's have pizza. Let's have lunch.*).

6e A fantastic film

Writing a review

1 Read the reviews (1 and 2). Match the reviews with two of the pictures (a–c).

a Black Hair by Hellen Vansen

b ERIN MONAHAN · SAILING ... ARGASSO

c BRUNO WILSON · DOUBLE AGENT

1 c ★★★★★ | review
This is a fantastic movie. I love it! The star is Bruno Wilson. I love him too! He's great in this film.
Peter Black (US)

2 a ★★★★★ | review
This is a great book. The writer is Helen Vansen. She's my favorite writer. I have all of her books. I really like them.
Eli (Argentina)

2 Read the reviews again. Complete the tables.

Movie title	Double Agent
Star	Bruno Wilson
Name of reviewer	Peter Black
Reviewer's opinion	fantastic movie

Book title	Black Hair
Writer	Helen Vansen
Name of reviewer	Eli
Reviewer's opinion	great book

3 Writing skill **pronouns**

a Use four of these pronouns to complete the review of movie b in Exercise 1.

he   her   him   it   she   she   them

This is a great movie. I love ¹ _it_ ! The star is Erin Monahan. I love ² _her_ . ³ _She_ 's my favorite movie star! ⁴ _She_ 's fantastic in this movie.

b Complete these sentences with the correct pronoun.

1 "Do you like Bruno Wilson's movies?"
  "Yes, I love _them_ ."
2 Russell Crowe is in this movie. _He_ 's great.
3 "Meryl Streep is my favorite movie star."
  "I don't like _her_ very much."
4 "I like Helen Vansen's books."
  "I like _them_ too."
4 "This movie is boring."
  "Oh! I like _it_ ."
5 This is a good book. _It_ 's fantastic.

4 Write a review for a book or movie you like.

5 Check your review. Check the pronouns and the spelling.

6 Work in pairs. Exchange your reviews. Do you agree with your partner's opinion?

A fantastic film

Warm-up

Introducing the theme: movies and books

Ask pairs of students to talk about what movies and books they like, particularly recent ones. Ask: *What movies do you like? What books do you like? Do you like the same things?*

Writing

1 Ask students to look at the pictures of the book and DVD covers. Ask: *What book/movie is it? Who is the writer? Who is in it? Does the reviewer like the book/movie?*

Writing skill

3a Draw stick figures for a man, a woman, and then a man and a woman together.

Ask students to say which pronouns go with the first picture (*he, him*), the second picture (*she, her*), and the third picture (*they, them*).

Then ask students to do the activity.

3b Model by completing item 1 as a class.

Grammar notes

Remind students that *he, she, it,* and *they* are subject pronouns, and *him, her, it,* and *them* are object pronouns. Notice that *they* and *them* are used regardless of the words they are replacing.

4 Tell students to use the reviews in the unit as a model.

6 Ask follow-up questions about the information in the reviews, e.g., *What movie/book is the review about? Who is the star/writer? What's the opinion of the reviewer?*

Extra activity

Bring in copies of a webpage or magazine page showing what's happening this weekend in your town or city, or find one that shows events in a big English-speaking city such as London or New York. Have students skim the page and choose activities they like. Then, in groups, have them make suggestions and agree on an activity to do.

At the market

Videoscript

Interviewer: Is this your local market?

Jan Szafranski: Yes, this is my local market and it's really great. You can buy a lot of things: fish, meat, fruit, vegetables, bread.

Amy Mills: Yes, it is. My house is in this street, so this is my local market.

Richard Lewis: Well, yes and no. I'm a teacher and my school is near this market.

Interviewer: Which stalls do you like?

Richard Lewis: Ah, my favorite stall is this cheese stall. I love cheese. That's my favorite— Brie—but I like Camembert, too. English cheese is good, but French cheese is great. I love it.

Amy Mills: Well, probably this fruit and vegetable stall. These peaches are from Spain … hmm, that's fantastic.

Jan Szafranski: I like the cheese stall. It has cheese from all around the world.

Interviewer: Tell us what you don't like.

Jan Szafranski: Fish, actually! My wife likes it but I don't. It has bones. I don't like them. And I can't cook it. No, I don't like fish very much.

Richard Lewis: Erm, I can't think. Maybe tomatoes. I don't like them very much.

Amy Mills: Well, I'm a vegetarian. I don't like meat. I like vegetables, rice, pasta, bread … but meat? No, I don't like it.

At the Covered Market in Oxford

78

Before you watch

1 Look at the photos. Write the names with the market stalls.

> a cheese stall 3   a fish stall 1
> a fruit and vegetable stall 2

2 Look at the word box. Find four things you can buy at the stalls in Exercise 1.

3 Work in pairs. Say things you can buy at a market. Take turns. How many things can you say in 30 seconds?

While you watch

4 Watch the video and write the number (1–3) next to the question.

  a Which stalls do you like? 2
  b Is this your local market? 1
  c Tell us what you don't like. 3

5 Work in pairs. What can you remember? How many things in your list from Exercise 3 are in the video?

6 Read the sentences. Then watch the video again and choose the correct option (a–c).

  1 Jan Szafranski … .
    a likes the fruit and vegetable stall
    ⓑ likes the cheese stall
    c likes the fish stall

  2 Amy Miller … .
    a doesn't like fruit
    b doesn't like vegetables
    ⓒ doesn't like meat

  3 Richard Lewis … .
    a loves English cheese
    ⓑ loves French cheese
    c loves tomatoes

7 Watch the video again. Are the sentences true (T) or false (F)?

  1 Richard's school is near the market. T
  2 Amy's favorite stall is the cheese stall. F
  3 Jan can cook fish. F

8 What can you remember? Who says these sentences? Write the name of the person.

  1 Yes, this is my local market. And it's really great.
  2 My wife likes it, but I don't. It has bones. I don't like them.
  3 I can't think—maybe tomatoes. I don't like them very much.
  4 I'm a vegetarian.

After you watch

9 Work in pairs. Take turns to buy things from your partner.

Student A: You are in the market. Write your shopping list.

Student B: You have a stall in the market. Decide what you sell and the prices.

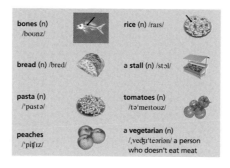

bones (n) /bəʊnz/
rice (n) /raɪs/
bread (n) /bred/
a stall (n) /stɔl/
pasta (n) /ˈpɑstə/
tomatoes (n) /təˈmeɪtoʊz/
peaches /ˈpitʃɪz/
a vegetarian (n) /ˌvedʒɪˈteəriən/ a person who doesn't eat meat

---

1 Ask students to find the word *stall* in the glossary. Ask them to look at the photos. Ask: *How many photos are there?* (3) *What are they?* (stalls) *Where are the stalls?*

2 Students look at the word box and find two things they can buy at the stalls in Exercise 1.

> **ANSWERS**
> *peaches, tomatoes, bread, bones*

3 Set this up as a quick competition in the class. Tell students they must find who can say the most words in 30 seconds. Check answers as a class.

While you watch

4 Students watch the video and write the numbers next to each question in the order they hear them.

5 Divide the class into pairs. Ask: *What can you remember? How many things in your list from Exercise 3 are in the video?* Check answers.

6 Give students time to read through the sentences. Then play the video again for students to choose the correct option. Check answers.

7 Give students some time to read the sentences and decide if they are true or false. Then play the video again for them to check and correct the false sentences.

8 Give students some time to read the sentences. Then ask students to write the name of the person next to each sentence. Check answers.

> **ANSWERS**
> **1** Jan
> **2** Jan
> **3** Richard
> **4** Amy

After you watch

> **Extra activity**
>
> Go through the words in the word list with the class. Then ask. *Do you like bread?* Elicit the answer *Yes. I like it very much.* Ask students to remember a negative response to this question from the video. Divide the class into pairs and have them ask and answer questions about what they like.

9 Review shopping expressions from lesson 5d. Students in pairs take turns to buy things from their partner. Extend the activity by having the room set up as a market with different stalls. Tell students that they will need signs for their stalls for a mingle activity. Students must walk around the class and ask for the food on their shopping list. The winner of the game is somebody who can buy everything on their list.

You could also role-play the three questions from the video with students in the classroom "market."

Grammar

1 Students complete the article about Kirk Allen with the correct form of *like*.

> **ANSWERS**
> **1** likes
> **2** *does he like*
> **3** *Does he like*
> **4** *like*
> **5** *Do you like*
> **6** *don't like*
> **7** *like*

2 Students complete the sentences with object pronouns.

Vocabulary

3 Students write the words. Then they look at the shopping basket and check the items that are in the basket.

4 Students underline the odd word in each group.

5 Students find examples for each category from Exercise 4.

> **ANSWERS**
> **1** pop, jazz
> **2** swimming, basketball
> **3** birds, camels, fish, horses
> **4** comedies, action movies
> **5** novels, detective stories

6 Students choose the correct option.

Real life

7 Students choose the correct option.

Speaking

8 Students work in pairs to practice the conversation in Exercise 7.

Grammar

1 Complete the article about Kirk Allen with the correct form of *like*.

Explore Travel

Kirk Allen is passionate about scuba diving. It's his job. He ¹_____ it very much. But ²_____ cold water? ³_____ boats? Read our interview with Kirk and find out.

Kirk, you are a professional scuba diver. Why?
Well, I ⁴_____ swimming and scuba diving. And I love the ocean.

⁵_____ the water?
Yes and no. I ⁶_____ cold water very much. It isn't very nice.

Is this your boat?
Yes, it is. I have three boats. I ⁷_____ big boats. They're fantastic!

2 Complete the sentences with object pronouns.

1 Read the interview with Kirk Allen. Read the interview with ___him___ .
2 Kirk Allen loves the ocean. He loves ___it___ .
3 Kirk Allen likes big boats. He likes ___them___ .
4 Kirk Allen doesn't like cold water. He doesn't like ___it___ .

I CAN	
talk about likes and dislikes (*like*)	
use object pronouns correctly	

Vocabulary

3 Add the vowels and write the words. Then look at the shopping basket and mark (✓) the things.

1 chs   cheese ✓
2 vgtbls   vegetables ✓
3 fsh   fish ✓
4 frt   fruit ✓
5 rc   rice ✓
6 ggs   eggs ✓
7 spghtt   spaghetti ✓
8 chclt   chocolate ✓

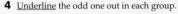

4 Underline the odd one out in each group.

Practice
1 <u>swimming</u> pop jazz
2 comedies <u>birds</u> action movies
3 camels <u>basketball</u> fish
4 <u>horses</u> novels detective stories

5 How many examples can you find in Exercise 4 for these words?

1 music   3 animals   5 books
2 sports   4 movies

6 Choose the correct option.

1 I like Adele. She's ⟨fantastic⟩/ horrible.
2 I don't like pigeons. They're great /⟨horrible.⟩
3 I love jazz. It's boring /⟨great.⟩
4 "Do you like reality shows?"
   "No, I don't. They're ⟨boring⟩/ fantastic."

I CAN	
talk about food	
talk about interests	
give positive and negative opinions (adjectives)	

Real life

7 Read the conversation. Choose the correct option.

A: Let's *have pizza /⟨watch a movie⟩/ play tennis* tonight.
B: That's a good idea. What's on?
A: A movie with Will Smith.
B: Oh, *it's horrible /⟨I don't like him⟩/ she's fantastic.*
A: How about Zoe Saldana? I have her new DVD.
B: *I don't like it. /⟨OK. Great.⟩/ Yes, it's great.*

I CAN	
give my opinion	
make and respond to suggestions	

Speaking

8 Work in pairs. Practice the conversation in Exercise 7 with the other two options.

> **Extra activity**
> Have students make plans for the weekend. In pairs, have them write a brief dialogue inviting and agreeing on a plan for a weekend afternoon or evening. Let them practice for a few minutes before asking them to perform from memory for the class.

Unit 7 Different lives

The festival of colors—the Holi festival—in Kolkata, India
Photo by Dibyangshu Sarkar

FEATURES

82 The Sami people
Life with reindeer

84 School life
An unusual school in Kenya

86 A year in British Columbia
Seasons of the year

90 The people of the reindeer
A video about the Sami people

1 Look at the photo and the caption. Answer the questions.

1 Where are the people? Kolkata, India
2 What is the celebration? the Holi Festival

2 🔊 **51** Work in pairs. Listen to information about the Holi festival. Choose the correct option.

1 The Holi festival is in *December /* (*March*)
2 It's a celebration of (*new life*) */ family life.*
3 The festival is one or two (*days*) */ weeks.*

3 The Holi festival is a celebration of spring. Look at these words for the four seasons. Listen and repeat them after your instructor.

spring   summer   fall/autumn   winter

4 Work in pairs. Which months are the seasons in your country?

> *I'm from Peru. Winter is June, July, and August.*

Different lives

Warm-up

Using words: reviewing colors, months, days, and countries

Divide the class into pairs to play *Write 7*. Write *colors* on the board. Tell pairs to write down seven color words and shout *Stop!* when they are done. The winners are the pair that finish first with all words spelled correctly. Repeat with *months, days,* and *countries.*

1 Ask students to look at the photo. Ask: *What colors do you see? How do the people feel? Are they happy? What country are they in?* Then ask them to read the caption and answer the questions.

2 Give students a moment to read through the sentences. Then play the audio. Ask students to listen and choose the correct option.

Vocabulary and pronunciation notes

Note the stress and pronunciation: summer, winter, autumn.

Point out that *fall* is a synonym for *autumn.*

Unlike days and months, seasons don't take a capital letter.

4 Divide the class into pairs or groups of four or five to say which months are in the different seasons in their countries. If you have a range of nationalities in your class, pair students from different parts of the world.

Extra activity

Get students to think about the fact that seasons are different in different parts of the world. Put a world map up. Point to a country and say a month; have students respond with a season. Point to a country in the opposite hemisphere (north or south) and say the same month; have students volunteer the season.

7a

The Sami people

Reading

Background notes

The Sami people number between 80,000 and 135,000 and traditionally live in the far north of Sweden, Norway, Finland, and the Kola Peninsula of Russia. Their ancestral lands cover a large area of the far north. They live in a traditional way by fur trapping, sheep herding, and reindeer herding.

3 ANSWERS

1 Norway, Sweden, Finland, Russia
2 reindeer
3 Sami

4 Point out that the words are all verbs.

5 Model the activity by reading aloud sentences about yourself (*I live in the US, I speak English, I have two children*, etc.). Then ask students to write their own sentences. Monitor and help with ideas, vocabulary, and spelling.

Extra activity

Ask students to prepare three sentences about themselves, two true and one false. They read aloud their sentences to their partner, who must guess which sentence is incorrect. Have them share the true and false sentences about themselves with the class.

Grammar

6 Point out that students have already used the simple present with the verb *like*. Elicit the affirmative and negative form of the verb.

7a The Sami people

Reading

1 Look at the two photos. What season is it? winter

2 Look at the photos and read the captions. Find:

snow   a sledge   reindeer

3 Read the article about the Sami people. Find:

1 four countries
2 an animal
3 a language

a Henrik Gaup and one of his reindeer

b Sami people at a winter camp

The Sami people

By Jessica Benko
Photos by Franz Aberham

Henrik Gaup and his family are Sami. The Sami people <u>live</u> in Norway, Sweden, Finland, and Russia. They are the "people of the reindeer." Henrik Gaup is a traditional Sami. "I <u>have</u> five children," he says. "I <u>teach</u> my children about the reindeer. They don't study with books." Henrik and his family <u>speak</u> Sami, but many Sami children don't understand it. Reindeer are very important to the Sami people. In the Sami language the word for "a group of reindeer" is *eallu* and the word for "life" is *eallin*.

82

Grammar notes

In Unit 6, students were introduced to the simple present with the verb *like*.

Students may be pleasantly surprised to learn that there is no change in the singular *I* and *you* forms, and the plural *they, you,* and *we* forms. English does not differentiate between singular or plural *you*.

After *I, you, we, and they*, English uses a form of the verb that is identical to the infinitive. To make the negative, English adds the negative form of the auxiliary verb *do* before the verb.

Watch out for common errors such as *I am live...* and *They not have...*

4 Underline these words in the article. Then complete the sentences with two of the words.

live	have	teach	speak

1 The Sami people ___live___ in Norway, Sweden, Finland, and Russia.
2 They ___speak___ the Sami language.

5 Use words from the box to write two sentences about yourself. Read your sentences to your partner.

Grammar simple present *I/you/we/they*

6 Look at the grammar box. Then look at this sentence. Choose the correct option. What is the negative form of the simple present?

Many Sami children *understand* /*don't understand* Sami.

> **SIMPLE PRESENT *I/YOU/WE/YOU/THEY***
>
> | I/You/We/You/They | **live** in Sweden. **don't study** with books. |
> |---|---|
>
> For more information and practice, see page 165.

7 Read about the Sami people. Choose the correct option. Check your answers with your instructor.

The traditional Sami ¹ *live* /*understand* reindeer. In the summer, they ² *have* /*live* in traditional tents. They ³ *have* / *study* tractors. Today many young Sami ⁴ *live* / *teach* in modern homes. They ⁵ *have* / *speak* television and the Internet. They ⁶ *don't speak* / *don't understand* traditional Sami life.

 a **tent** /tent/   a **tractor** /ˈtræktə/

---

8 Pronunciation *don't*

a 🔊 52 Listen and repeat four sentences.

b Are you different from the traditional Sami? Write three sentences with *don't*. Read your sentences to your partner.

> *I don't live in Sweden.*
> *They don't speak Spanish.*

9 Are these sentences true for you? Change them so they are true.

1 I don't live in a house.
2 I don't have three children.
3 I speak four languages.
4 I don't understand French.
5 I teach English.
6 I study with books.

Speaking and writing

10 Work in pairs. Find three things you have in common. Write sentences with *We*. You can use these verbs.

have	live	speak	study
teach	understand		

> *I live in a house.*

> *I live in an apartment.*

> *I speak English.*

> *I speak English too.*

We both speak English.

---

7 Ask students to look at the picture and use it to pre-teach *traditional*, *home*, and *tent*.

Pronunciation

8b Model the activity by referring students to the text about Sami lifestyles and eliciting a negative sentence, e.g., *I don't live in a tent.*

Ask students to write their own negative sentences and then read them aloud to a partner. Tell them to pay attention to the pronunciation of *don't*.

> **Pronunciation notes**
>
> Note that *don't* is strongly stressed. In spoken English we always use the shortened form *don't*.

9 Model changing the sentences in different ways, e.g., item 1 can change to *I live in a house* or *I don't live in a tent*. Check by asking students to read aloud sentences for the class.

> **Extra activity**
>
> Ask students to write five sentences about their partner, e.g., *I think you speak French.* Students read aloud the sentences to their partner, who confirms or denies the information.

Speaking and writing

10 Model the activity by saying sentences about yourself, e.g., *I have a sister, I speak French, I live in an apartment*, etc. Prompt a student to respond. Then divide the class into pairs. Tell them to make only affirmative sentences. Monitor students' use of the simple present.

> **HOMEWORK** Ask students to write a profile of a famous person. As another option, tell them not to mention the name of the person in the description; you can post the descriptions around the class for students to guess the identities.

> **Extra activity**
>
> Ask students to write a short personal profile. Collect the profiles and read them aloud, without revealing the names. The rest of the class must guess who it is.

7b

School life

Vocabulary

1 ANSWERS

The picture shows board, book, classmate, classroom, school, student, teacher

Vocabulary notes

The stress is on the first syllable of all these words except *university*.

Note that school usually connotes a place where people under 18 study; college (or a university) is where students study for a degree.

Reading and listening

Background notes

Kakenya Ntaiya was able to persuade a tribal elder to help pay for her education in the US. She has founded an academy for girls and is attempting to provide good primary education for girls in Kenya.

4 Ask students to correct the false information.

ANSWERS

1 No, she's a Maasai from Kenya.
2 No, she's a teacher.
3 No, she's a woman.

7b School life

Vocabulary education

1 Match seven of these words with things and people in the photo.

board	book	classmate	classroom	college	pen
pencil	school	student	teacher	university	

2 Work in pairs. Look at the photo. Use some words from Exercise 1 to make sentences.

> *It isn't a university.*

> *No, it's a school.*

Kakenya Ntaiya is from Kenya.
She's a Maasai. She is an unusual Maasai woman.
She has a PhD from an American university. Now Kakenya is back in Kenya. She's a teacher. This is her school.

Maasai (n) /mɑˈsaɪ/ people from a part of East Africa
unusual (adj) /ʌnˈjuːʒuəl/ different, not usual
village (n) /ˈvɪlɪdʒ/ a very small town

School life in Kenya

---

5 Ask students to read through the questions and answers. Elicit the answer to question 1 as a class. Then ask students to match the other questions and answers. Play the audio. Students listen and check.

Grammar

7 Read through the grammar box with the class. Ask students to underline the question forms in Exercise 5. Underline the verb forms in question 1 as a class. Refer students to page 165 for more information and practice.

ANSWERS

1 Do you work
2 Do boys study
3 Do the girls live
4 Do they go home
5 Do the girls learn

3 Use words from Exercise 1 to make true sentences.

1 I like my …   2 I have of lot of …
3 I study / don't study at a …

Reading and listening

4 Work in pairs. Read about Kakenya Ntaiya. Answer the questions.

1 Is she from America? No   2 Is she a girl? No
3 Is she a student? No

5 🔊 53 Listen to the interview with a teacher at the school. Match the questions (1–5) with the answers (a–e). Then listen again and check.

1 Do you work at Kakenya's school? e
2 Do boys study at the school? a
3 Do the girls live with their families? b
4 Do they go home in the summer? c
5 Do the girls learn English at the school? d

a No, they don't. The school is for girls.
b No, they don't. They live at the school.
c Yes, they do. They go home to their villages.
d Yes, they do. And in the summer we teach extra classes in English too.
e Yes, I do. I teach there. We have five teachers.

6 Work in pairs. Do you think this school is unusual? Why? / Why not?

Grammar simple present questions *I/you/we/they*

7 Look at the grammar box. Then look at the questions in Exercise 5. Underline the question forms.

▶ SIMPLE PRESENT QUESTIONS *I/YOU/WE/ YOU/THEY*		
Do	I/you/we/you/they	**study** English?
Yes, No,	I/you/we/you/they	**do.** **don't.**

For more information and practice, see page 165.

8 🔊 54 Put the words in order to make questions. Then listen to an interview with a student and check. Write (✔) or (✗) for his answers.

1 study / you / at a college / do / ?
2 classes / do / have / you / every day / ?
3 like / you / do / your classes / ?
4 you / do / live / near your university / ?
5 do / with your family / live / you / ?
6 you / go home / for the summer / do / ?

9 Pronunciation intonation in questions

🔊 55 Listen to the questions from Exercise 8.

Work in pairs.

Student A: You are the interviewer.

Student B: You are Carl.

Ask and answer the questions. Take turns.

Writing and speaking

10 Prepare questions for a survey. Use these verbs. Choose an option for each question.

have	like	live	study

1 _____ with friends? / with classmates?
2 _____ classes in the morning? / classes in the afternoon? / classes in the evening?
3 _____ near your school? / near your college?
4 _____ your book? / your classroom?

11 In pairs, ask and answer your questions.

Do you live with friends?

No, I don't. I live with my family.

---

8 Point out that, in item 2, *every day* goes at the end of the sentence.

ANSWERS
1 Do you study at a college? ✗
2 Do you have classes every day? ✗
3 Do you like your classes? ✔
4 Do you live near your university? ✔
5 Do you live with your family? ✗
6 Do you go home for the summer? ✔

Pronunciation

9 Students can use the audioscript on page 172 of the Student Book first, then practice with only the questions as prompts. The student playing Carl must remember his answers.

Pronunciation notes

In these questions, *Do you* is weakly stressed. The strong stress in the sentences is on the main verb and on the noun, e.g., *Do you study at a college?*

In *yes/no* questions, the intonation tends to rise at the end. Make sure students are attempting weak stress and rising intonation.

Extra activity

Ask students to close their books. Write these prompts on the board and ask students to improvise the conversation with Carl:

study / college	have / classes / every day
like / classes	live / family
live / near university	home / summer

Then have pairs repeat the conversation, giving their own personal information in the answers.

Writing and speaking

10 Ask students to complete the questions using *do you* + a verb from the box.

ANSWERS
1 Do you study
2 Do you have
3 Do you live
4 Do you like

HOMEWORK Ask students to write a summary of their survey results.

7c

A year in British Columbia

Warm-up

Using words: reviewing question forms

Divide the class into pairs and tell them they must find out five new things about you. Have them write questions using *Do you*, e.g., *Do you live near the town center? Do you like the color red?* Have pairs take turns asking you questions. You may want to answer *Yes, I do* or *No, I don't*, or add extra information.

Vocabulary

2 ANSWERS

1 snowy
2 sunny
3 rainy
4 cloudy / windy

Pronunciation notes

Note that these adjectives are stressed on the first syllable: *sunny*. You could point out that they all derive from nouns (*snow, sun*, etc.).

Extra activity

Write the names of different countries on the board. Ask students to say or guess what the current weather is like in those countries, e.g., *I think it's hot and sunny in Brazil.*

Reading

5 Pre-teach *ice, leaves, flowers,* and *trees* by drawing pictures on the board. Ask students to look at the photos and find the four items.

6 ANSWERS

a winter
b fall
c spring
d summer

Vocabulary **weather**

1 Repeat these words after your instructor.

cloudy   rainy   snowy

sunny   windy

2 🔊 **56** Listen to people from four places. Write the number (1–4) next to the weather word.

3 🔊 **56** Listen again. Match the speaker with the country and the season.

	Country	Season
1	Australia	autumn (fall)
2	Canada	spring
3	Great Britain	summer
4	South Africa	winter

4 Work in pairs. Describe the weather for seasons in your country.

> *I'm from India. Winter is the dry season. It's hot and sunny.*

Reading

5 Look at the photos on page 87 and find:

> flowers   ice   leaves   trees

6 Read the article on page 87. Match the paragraphs with the photos (a–d).

7 <u>Underline</u> the things people do in each season.

8 Do people in your country do the things in the article? Tell your partner.

> *We don't go skiing in the winter.*

9 Word focus *go*

a Look at these expressions with *go*. Find four of them in the article on page 87.

go to the beach	go to work	go home
go swimming	go for walks	

b <u>Underline</u> the option that is true for you.

1 I *go / don't go* to the beach in the summer.
2 I *go / don't go* swimming in the winter.
3 I *go / don't go* home in the evening.
4 I *go / don't go* to work every day.
5 I *go / don't go* for walks with my family.

Grammar **simple present with question words**

10 Look at the grammar box. Then look at the article. Find three of the question words from the grammar box in the article.

▶ SIMPLE PRESENT WITH QUESTION WORDS			
What			do?
Where			go?
Who	do	I/you/we/you/they/people	go with?
Why			go to the beach?
When			eat?

For more information and practice, see page 165.

11 Complete the questions with question words.

1 Where do you go in the summer?
2 What do you do in the fall?
3 When do flowers open?
4 Who do you go cycling with?
5 Why do you like winter?

Speaking

12 Work in pairs. Ask and answer questions like these.

- Why / like … ?
- What / do?
- When / do … ?
- Where / go?
- Who / go with?

> *Why do you like winter?*

> *I like cold weather.*

Background notes

British Columbia (BC) is Canada's westernmost province. Its capital is Victoria, but its largest city is Vancouver. BC is famous for its natural beauty and the mild climate along its coast.

7 The article contains a lot of vocabulary that may be new to students. Use gestures to check comprehension.

ANSWERS

Summer: People go to the beach.
Fall: Children go to school. Students go to college. People go to work.
Winter: A lot of people stay at home. They watch TV, read books, and cook winter food.
Spring: People go cycling and running. They go for walks.

Vocabulary notes

Point out that when describing sporting activities we use *go + -ing: go swimming, go skiing, go climbing.*

A YEAR IN BRITISH COLUMBIA

By Chuck Spender

S U M M E R

Where do people go in the summer?

Summer is a great time for a vacation here. The weather is hot and sunny. People go to the beach. I go to Vancouver Island with my family. We play summer sports and we go swimming in the lakes and rivers.

F A L L

What do people do in the fall?

In autumn, classes start. Children go to school. Students go to college. People go to work. It's cloudy and rainy. Trees change color from green to brown. I think it's a beautiful season.

W I N T E R

Where do people go in winter?

In winter, it's cold, rainy, and snowy, too. A lot of people stay at home. They watch TV, read books, and cook winter food. Winter is my favorite season. I like winter sports. I go to the mountains. I go skiing and climbing. It's very cold!

S P R I N G

Why do people like spring?

For a lot of people, spring is their favorite season. It's cloudy and rainy, but it isn't cold. Flowers open, birds sing, and trees are green. People go cycling and running. They go for walks. I play golf with my friends.

Extra activity

Ask students to close their books. Check that they remember the verb + noun collocations in the text. Write verbs on the board (e.g., *go, play, change, watch, read, cook*) and ask students to say what nouns they go with.

Word focus

Grammar notes

In English we omit the article with certain places: *go to school, go to work* (and also *go to college / church / prison / bed*).

With other places, we use the article: *go to the park, go to the beach, go to the shopping mall.*

Uniquely, we also omit *to* with *home: go home.*

With activities, we use *-ing: go swimming / skiing / shopping.*

9b Ask students to compare their sentences in pairs or small groups.

Grammar

10 Read through the grammar box with the class. Ask students to find question words in the article. Let them compare their answers in pairs. Refer students to page 165 for more information and practice.

Grammar notes

In English, we use these question words:

What (to ask about things, activities, events, etc.)

Where (to ask about places)

Who (to ask about people)

Why (to ask for a reason)

When (to ask about time)

In questions we use the following order:

Question word + auxiliary verb *do* + *I / you / we / they* + verb

Where   do   you   go?

Speaking

12 Tell students to choose a season and prepare questions and answers. They can look back at the text to find sentences to describe things they do. Then divide the class into pairs to ask and answer questions.

HOMEWORK Ask students to write a description about one season in their country. Tell them to include information about what other people do and what they do.

What's the matter?

Warm-up

Using words: feelings and activities

Divide the class into pairs. Write *I'm bored* on the board. Tell students that they have one minute to make a list of things to do. Ask the pair with the most suggestions to read them aloud. Write the suggestions on the board. Possible activities: *read a book, watch TV, go swimming, do your homework, take photos, write an email,* etc.

Vocabulary

1 Ask students to look at the pictures without looking at the words. Ask: *How do they feel?* Elicit words that students already know. Then play the audio.

Pronunciation notes

Note the strong stress and difficult pronunciation of some of these words: *thirsty, hungry, tired, bored.*

Extra activity

Act out the adjectives, e.g., wipe your forehead and look hot. Ask students to say how you feel. Then, in pairs, students take turns acting out the adjectives for their partners to guess.

Real life

4 Point out the meaning, use, and form of *What's the matter?* and *Why don't you…?*

Vocabulary notes

What's the matter? is a way of asking *What's the problem?*

In English, we use *Why don't you…?* to make a suggestion or give advice.

Note the form: *Why don't you* + verb. Although *don't* is a negative word, it is used here to make a positive suggestion.

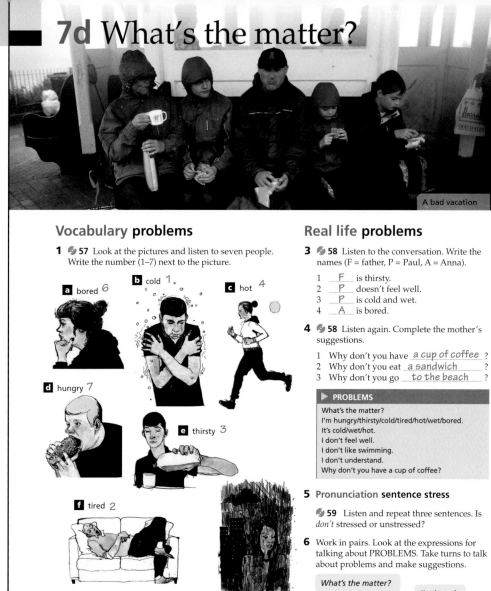

7d What's the matter?

A bad vacation

Vocabulary **problems**

1 🔊 **57** Look at the pictures and listen to seven people. Write the number (1–7) next to the picture.

a bored 6

b cold 1

c hot 4

d hungry 7

e thirsty 3

f tired 2

g wet 5

2 Work in pairs. Say how you feel right now.

> *I'm hungry!*

88

Real life **problems**

3 🔊 **58** Listen to the conversation. Write the names (F = father, P = Paul, A = Anna).

1 __F__ is thirsty.
2 __P__ doesn't feel well.
3 __P__ is cold and wet.
4 __A__ is bored.

4 🔊 **58** Listen again. Complete the mother's suggestions.

1 Why don't you have __a cup of coffee__ ?
2 Why don't you eat __a sandwich__ ?
3 Why don't you go __to the beach__ ?

> ▶ **PROBLEMS**
>
> What's the matter?
> I'm hungry/thirsty/cold/tired/hot/wet/bored.
> It's cold/wet/hot.
> I don't feel well.
> I don't like swimming.
> I don't understand.
> Why don't you have a cup of coffee?

5 Pronunciation **sentence stress**

🔊 **59** Listen and repeat three sentences. Is *don't* stressed or unstressed?

6 Work in pairs. Look at the expressions for talking about PROBLEMS. Take turns to talk about problems and make suggestions.

> *What's the matter?*
>
> *I'm bored.*
>
> *Why don't you read a book?*

Pronunciation

5 Discuss the question as a class.

ANSWER

The word *don't* is stressed in the sentences but not in the question.

6 Divide the class into pairs. Read aloud the model with a student. Then ask students to role-play conversations. Monitor carefully and make sure students are using the forms and stressing *don't* correctly.

With weaker classes, ask pairs to write a conversation and act it out for the class. With stronger classes, ask them to play different roles in their conversations, e.g., a mother and child, two friends, etc.

HOMEWORK Write this message on the board:

I'm bored in the evenings at home. I don't know what to do.

Dan

Tell students to write a response to Dan, suggesting what to do.

7e Photography club members

Writing a profile

1 Read Omar's profile. Are the sentences true (T) or false (F)?

1 Omar is a student. F
2 He's married. T
3 He's in a photography club. T

2 Writing skill **paragraphs**

a Read Omar's profile again. Write the number of the paragraph.

a interests: __3__
b profession: __1__
c family/friends: __2__

b Read the profile information for Jenna. Number the paragraphs (a–c) in the correct order (1–3).

c Read the notes for Luther. Organize them into three paragraphs. Then write sentences with them.

> Luther
> animals
> a teacher
> engineering
> my wife and children
> photos

3 Make notes about yourself for a profile.

- professional information
- family / friends
- interests / organizations

4 Use your notes and write three paragraphs.

5 Check your profile. Check the paragraph order, the spelling, and the punctuation.

6 Work in pairs. Exchange profiles. Find two things you and your partner have in common.

OMAR

PLT Photography club members

1 I'm an engineer. I work at PLT Engineering.
2 I'm married and I have three children. We live in a small town.
3 I like photography. I'm in the PLT photography club. In the winter, we meet on Sundays. We go out and take photos. In the summer, I go on vacation with my family. I take a lot of photos of my children and the places we go to.

JENNA

PLT Photography club members

a I live with three classmates. We live near our college. 2
b I like sports and photography. I take photos of sports people. 3
c I'm a student. I study engineering. In the summer, I work at PLT Engineering. 1

Unit 7 **Different lives** 89

Photography club members

Warm-up

Introducing the theme: photography

Bring in some of your own photos. Describe them or ask students to say what they see. Then ask: *Do you take photos? Are you in a photography club? Who and what do you take photos of?*

Writing skill

2b Ask students to read Jenna's profile and number the paragraphs so the information is in the same order as in Omar's profile. Let them compare their answers in pairs before discussing as a class.

Extra activity

Ask some questions to check the content of Jenna's profile, e.g., *Where does she work? What does she study? Where does she live? What does she like doing?*

With stronger classes, ask them to close their books and remember the information in the profile.

2c Tell students to organize the notes into the same three paragraphs as in Omar's profile. Review the paragraph sequence as a class, and then have students write the sentences.

SAMPLE ANSWER

I'm a teacher. I teach engineering at City College.
I'm married and I live with my wife and children near the college.
I like animals and photography. I take photos of animals.

---

3 Ask students if they are in a club. Elicit answers, and help students work out how to write in English the name of the club or organization that they are in. Tell students to prepare notes for their profile. Circulate and help students with ideas and vocabulary.

6 Check by having pairs tell the class the things they have in common. At this stage, you could also have students peer-edit each other's profiles.

Extra activity

Collect the profiles and post them around the classroom. Students circulate and read each others' profiles. Tell them to write a comment at the bottom of the profiles they read. Alternatively, ask students to find one thing that they have in common with each profile that they read.

HOMEWORK Ask students to write a profile about a friend or family member.

The people of the reindeer

Videoscript

Narrator: The Sami people's reindeer move in spring. The Sami people go with them.

These are Nils Peder Gaup's reindeer.

On the journey, the people live in tents.

These Sami people have traditional lives.

The children travel with the reindeer, too.

This snow is hard.

After snowy weather, it is soft.

Soft snow is good for the reindeer.

Well, that's all.

It's time to sleep.

A Sami man with his reindeer

90

Before you watch

1 Work in pairs. Look at the photo on page 90. Answer the questions.

1 What kind of animals are they?
2 Who are the "people of the reindeer"?
3 Where are they from?

2 Work in pairs. What can you remember about the Sami people's lives? Are these sentences true (T) or false (F)?

1 They live in big cities. F
2 They speak a traditional language. T
3 They have modern homes. F

While you watch

3 Watch the video and check your ideas from Exercise 1.

4 These things are in the video. Watch the video again and put the pictures in order.

a cup of coffee

a dog

a fire

snow 1

a tent

a woman

a young child

a young couple

5 Read these sentences about the Sami. Mark (✓) the things you can see in the video.

1 The Sami travel on tractors.
2 When they travel with the reindeer, the Sami ✓ cook their food on a fire.
3 Some young people wear traditional clothes. ✓
4 Reindeer meat is a traditional Sami food. ✓
5 Reindeer eat food under the snow.
6 The Sami people have dogs. ✓

After you watch

6 Complete the paragraph with verbs. You can use the same verb more than once.

The Sami ¹ _live_ in Norway, Sweden, Finland, and Russia. The reindeer ² _move_ in spring. The Sami people ³ _go_ with them. On the journey, the people ⁴ _live_ in tents. These Sami people ⁵ _have_ traditional lives.

7 Work in pairs. Ask and answer questions with *when, where, what, who,* and *why* about Sami life. Take turns.

Student A: You are from a Sami family. Choose your age—young or old.

Student B: You are a journalist.

a couple (n) /ˈkʌpəl/   sleep (v) /slip/

a fire (n) /faɪər/   snow (n) /snoʊ/

hard (adj) /hɑrd/   soft (adj) /sɔft/

a journey (n) /ˈdʒɜrni/ a trip from place A to place B   travel (v) /ˈtrævəl/ to go from place A to place B

1 Write *The people of the reindeer* on the board. Remind students about the topic of 7a and ask them what they remember about it.

ANSWERS

1 reindeer
2 the Sami people
3 Norway, Sweden, Finland, Russia

2 Give students some time to read the sentences and decide if they are true or false. Check answers. Encourage students to correct the false information.

While you watch

3 Students watch the video and check their ideas from Exercise 1. Have a few students share their answers with the class.

4 Play the video again. Students put the pictures in order. Check answers as a class.

ANSWERS

a	5	f	4
b	8	g	7
c	3	h	6
e	2		

5 Give students a moment to look at the sentences. Students mark the correct ones.

After you watch

6 Give students some time to read the paragraph. Students then complete the paragraph with the correct verbs. Play the video again for the students to check their answers.

7 Give students time to prepare for their roles.

UNIT 7 REVIEW

Grammar

1 Students read the text and underline two places and circle two languages in the article.

2 Students write the questions.

> **ANSWERS**
> 1 Where do Cathy and Albert live?
> 2 Do they have children?
> 3 Where do they teach?
> 4 Do they speak their parents' language?
> 5 Do their children speak Yirram?

3 In pairs, students prepare and roleplay the conversation. Point out that they must change their questions from *they* to *you*.

Vocabulary

4 Students complete the words about education.

> **ANSWERS**
> 1 student, teacher
> 2 university, school, classroom
> 3 book, pen

5 Students complete the sentences with the verbs.

> **ANSWERS**
> 1 study
> 2 live
> 3 speak
> 4 have
> 5 like

6 Students complete the sentences with weather words.

> **ANSWERS**
> 1 cloudy
> 2 sunny
> 3 snowy
> 4 windy
> 5 rainy

UNIT 7 REVIEW

Grammar

1 Read about Cathy Gulpilil. <u>Underline</u> two places and circle two languages in the article.

Cathy Gulpilil and her husband Albert are from the Northern Territory of Australia. Now they live in Sydney. They have two children. Cathy and Albert teach at a college. They speak English and Yirram – their parents' language. Cathy's and Albert's parents live in the Northern Territory. Cathy and Albert's children understand Yirram, but they don't speak it.

2 Write the questions.

1 where / Cathy and Albert / live?
2 they / have / children?
3 where / they / teach?
4 they / speak / their parents' language?
5 their children / speak Yirram?

3 Work in pairs. Take turns.

Student A: You are Cathy or Albert Gulpilil.

Student B: Interview your partner. Use **you** and the questions in Exercise 2.

> **I CAN**
> describe permanent states (simple present) ☐
> ask and answer questions about habits (simple present) ☐

Vocabulary

4 Complete the words about education.

1 People: classmate, st _ _ _ _ _, te _ _ _ _ _
2 Places: college, un _ _ _ _ _ _ _ _, sc _ _ _ _, cl _ _ _ _ _ _ _
3 Things: board, bo _ _, pe _

92

---

5 Complete the sentences with these verbs.

have	like	live	speak	study

1 My friends _____ engineering in college.
2 I _____ in a small town.
3 Do you _____ Arabic?
4 My parents don't _____ a TV.
5 I _____ summer.

6 Complete the sentences with weather words.

1 It's _____ in Panama City.

2 It's _____ in Dubai.

3 It's _____ in Stockholm.

4 It's _____ in Kyoto.

5 It's _____ in Shanghai.

> **I CAN**
> talk about education ☐
> talk about people's lives ☐
> talk about the weather ☐

Real life

7 Match words in A and B to make sentences. Then put the sentences in order to make a conversation.

	A	B	
1	I'm	No thanks, _____ cold.	4
2	it's	the matter?	1
3	What's	eat this pizza?	3
4	Why don't you	hungry.	2

> **I CAN**
> talk about problems ☐
> make suggestions ☐

Speaking

8 Work in pairs. Write a conversation with these ideas. Take turns to start.

1 thirsty / cup of coffee
2 hot / drink of water
3 don't understand / use a dictionary
4 bored / go for a walk

Real life

7 First, ask students to match the words in A to the words in B to make sentences. Then ask them to put the sentences in order to make a conversation.

Speaking

8 Read through the items as a class. Point out that each prompt contains a problem and a suggestion. Have pairs write and role-play the conversations.

Routines

Farmers and wild horses
Photo by Melissa Farlow

FEATURES

94 Day and night
Routines at home and at work

96 A typical day
Two National Geographic explorers

98 Cats in crisis
A job in tiger conservation

102 The elephants of Samburu
A video about wildlife in Africa

1 Work in pairs. Look at the photo. Where do you think this is?

2 🔊 **60** Read the sentences about the man in the photo. Which options are correct? Listen and check your ideas.

1 The job of the man in the photo is *in an office / outside.*
2 Farmers *use / don't use* cell phones.
3 They use *tractors / helicopters.*

3 Make true sentences about these jobs.

Artists Doctors Engineers Filmmakers Photographers Scientists Writers	work	outside. in laboratories. in offices. in studios. in hospitals. with people. with animals. with modern technology.

4 Work in pairs. Take turns choosing from Exercise 3.

I work in a hospital.

You're a doctor.

Warm-up
Introducing the theme: jobs
Play a guessing game. Tell students to imagine that you have a second job. They must ask you *Do you…?* questions to find out what your job is. Tell students that they can ask up to ten questions (e.g., *Do you work in an office?*) and you will only reply *Yes, I do* or *No, I don't.*

1 Ask students to look at the photo, and ask: *What can you see?* Elicit ideas. Then organize the class into pairs to discuss the question.

2 Students read the sentences and discuss the answers. Then play the audio. Students listen and check their ideas.

3 Give students a moment to read through the jobs. Tell them to make true sentences about each job. Let them compare their sentences in pairs.

If you have working students in your class, survey them for their own jobs. Write the jobs / professions on the board and brainstorm with students what people do in those jobs.

SAMPLE ANSWERS
Artists, engineers, filmmakers, and photographers work outside.
Scientists work in laboratories/ outside.
Writers work in offices.
Artists, filmmakers, and photographers work in studios.
Doctors work in hospitals.
Doctors, teachers, filmmakers, and photographers work with people.
Scientists, artists, filmmakers, and photographers work with animals.
They all work with modern technology.

Pronunciation notes
Note that the strong stress is on the first syllable of all these words except *engineer* and *photographer.*

4 In pairs, students take turns to choose a job and describe what they do. Their partner must guess the job.

Day and night

Vocabulary

1 Ask students to look at the pictures. Ask: *What can you see?* Elicit ideas and vocabulary. Ask students to match pictures and sentences. Check answers as a class.

Reading

4 Ask students to look at the photo. Ask: *What can you see?* Elicit ideas and vocabulary from the students. Ask the questions in the Student Book and elicit answers.

5 Call on a few students with similar routines to tell the class how they are similar.

> **6 ANSWERS**
> **1** gets up
> **2** doesn't eat
> **3** goes
> **4** It's
> **5** starts
> **6** finishes
> **7** has
> **8** starts
> **9** works
> **10** has
> **11** finishes
> **12** has
> **13** goes
> **14** doesn't work
> **15** goes

Vocabulary **routines**

1 Match the sentences (1–7) with the pictures (a–g).

1 I get up at ___six o'clock___ . _f_
2 I have breakfast at _____ . _g_
3 I start work at _____ . _b_
4 I have lunch in a _____ . _c_
5 I finish work at _____ . _a_
6 I have dinner at _____ . _e_
7 I go to bed at _____ . _d_

2 What time do you do the activities in Exercise 1? Fill in the information.

3 In pairs, discuss your daily routines.

> I get up at six o'clock.
> Wow, that's early! I get up at nine!

Reading

4 Look at the photo. Where is it? What kind of class is this?
morning exercise in Shanghai

5 Read about one of the women in the photo. Are your routines similar?

DAY AND NIGHT
A writer in China

Chen Hong is from Shanghai. She's a writer. She gets up at six o'clock. She doesn't eat breakfast. She goes to an exercise class. It's on the Bund, near the river. It starts at 7:15 and it finishes at 7:45. Then Chen has breakfast. She starts work at 8:30. She works at home. At noon, she has lunch. She finishes work at 6:30 in the evening. At eight o'clock, she has dinner with her family. She goes to bed at 10:30. Chen Hong doesn't work every day, but she goes to her exercise class every day.

A morning exercise class on the Bund (riverside) in Shanghai

Grammar

> ### Grammar notes
>
> Here, students are introduced to a wider range of regular verbs, using the third person (*he, she, it*) affirmative and negative forms of the simple present.
>
> After *he, she,* and *it*, we add *-s* (e.g., *starts*) or *-es* (e.g., *finishes*) to the verb. Note the irregular third person forms of *be* (*is*) and *have* (*has*).
>
> Watch out for common errors such as *He start…* and *She doesn't starts…*
>
> We often use the simple present to talk about routines and habits.

7 Ask students to look at the photo. Ask: *Where is he? What is his job?* Elicit and teach *astronomer*. Then ask students to complete the text. Check answers as a class.

> ### Extra activity
>
> Tell students that they are going to work in pairs to write a text about you (the teacher). First, they must prepare questions to ask you in order to get information they can use. After the class have asked you questions and made notes, they write a text similar to the one about Ronaldo.

Grammar simple present *he/she/it*

6 Look at the grammar box. Then <u>underline</u> the simple present verbs in the article about Chen Hong.

> **▶ SIMPLE PRESENT *HE/SHE/ IT***
>
> | | |
> |---|---|
> | He/She/It | **gets up** at 6:00. |
> | | **doesn't eat** breakfast. |
> | | **starts** at 7:15. |
>
> For more information and practice, see page 166.

7 Complete the text about an astronomer with the correct form of the verbs. Use some verbs more than once.

> finish   get up   go   have   not / work   start   work

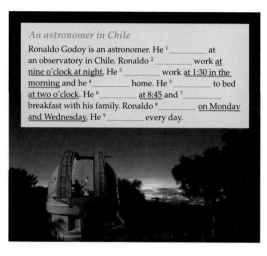

An astronomer in Chile

Ronaldo Godoy is an astronomer. He ¹_____ at an observatory in Chile. Ronaldo ²_____ work <u>at nine o'clock at night</u>. He ³_____ work <u>at 1:30 in the morning</u> and he ⁴_____ home. He ⁵_____ to bed <u>at two o'clock</u>. He ⁶_____ <u>at 8:45</u> and ⁷_____ breakfast with his family. Ronaldo ⁸_____ <u>on Monday and Wednesday</u>. He ⁹_____ every day.

Grammar prepositions of time

8 Look at the expressions in the grammar box. <u>Underline</u> similar expressions in the text in Exercise 7.

> **▶ PREPOSITIONS OF TIME**
>
>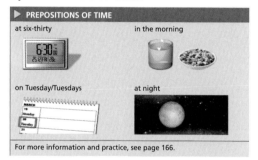
>
> at six-thirty   in the morning
>
> on Tuesday/Tuesdays   at night
>
> For more information and practice, see page 166.

---

9 Pronunciation *-s* and *-es* verbs

a 🔊 **61** Listen and repeat.

> works   starts   finishes   goes
> gets up

b 🔊 **61** Listen again. <u>Underline</u> the verb with an extra syllable.

> | work | start | finish | go | get up |
> |---|---|---|---|---|
> | works | starts | <u>finishes</u> | goes | gets up |

Speaking and writing

10 Work as a class. Ask questions. Find one name for each sentence. You have a time limit of five minutes.

> **Find a person in your class who ...**
>
> gets up at six o'clock.   _____
> doesn't work.   _____
> has eggs for breakfast.   _____
> works in the evening.   _____
> doesn't eat lunch.   _____
> goes to bed after midnight.   _____
> starts work at nine o'clock.   _____
> gets up late on the weekend.   _____

> Do you get up at six o'clock, Issa?

> No, I don't. I get up at 7:15.

> Do you get up at six o'clock, Leonardo?

> Yes, I do.

11 Write sentences with the names.

Leonardo gets up at six o'clock.

Grammar

8 Ask students to look at the expressions. Elicit when we say *in, at,* and *on.*

> **Grammar notes**
>
> We say *at* with times (*at 5:00*) and in the expression *at night.*
>
> We say *in the morning/ afternoon/evening.*
>
> We say *on* with days (*on Monday/ Tuesday*).

> **Extra activity 1**
>
> Ask students to think of two things that they do at 6:30, on Tuesday, in the morning, and at night.

> **Extra activity 2**
>
> Write unusual jobs on the board, e.g., *actor, president, nightclub manager, DJ on a breakfast radio show, nurse, soccer player.* Ask pairs of students to choose a job and write five sentences about their day. Have pairs read aloud their sentences for the class to guess the job.

Pronunciation

> **Pronunciation notes**
>
> The letter *s* is pronounced /s/ when it follows an unvoiced consonant (e.g., *works, starts, gets*).
>
> The letter *s* is pronounced /z/ when it follows a voiced consonant (e.g., *goes*).
>
> The letters *es* are pronounced /iz/, (e.g., *finishes*).

> **Extra activity**
>
> Elicit other verbs that students know (*like, do, play, watch,* etc.) and ask them to say whether they take *-s* or *-es* endings, and to say how they are pronounced.

Speaking and writing

10 Read through the items as a class. Then elicit question formation using *Do you…?*

Monitor conversations and make note of common errors with questions and short answers. At the end, write the errors on the board and correct them as a class.

> **HOMEWORK** Ask students to write a summary of their survey results.

8b A typical day

Warm-up

Introducing the theme: jobs and routines

Use the photos to pre-teach *archaeologist* and *geologist*. Then have pairs of students write questions for an archaeologist and a geologist about their jobs and daily routines (e.g., *Where do you work? What time do you get up?*).

After two minutes, ask two students to come to the front of the class. One is an archaeologist; the other is a geologist. They must improvise answers to their classmates's questions.

Reading

Pronunciation notes

Note the strong stress on the third-to-last syllable in each word: *archae<u>o</u>logist, ge<u>o</u>logist.*

Teaching notes

Check comprehension of difficult words from the reading. A good way of doing this is to tell students to underline all the words they don't know, and then guess their meaning from context. Tell students to share their guesses with a partner before looking up the word in a dictionary.

Grammar

Grammar notes

We use frequency adverbs to say how often we do routine things. They generally go between the subject and the main verb, e.g., *She never goes… .*

However, note that we often use *sometimes* at the start (or end) of a sentence, e.g., *Sometimes she eats with friends.*

The frequency adverb generally goes after the verb *be* and auxiliary verbs, e.g., *She doesn't often go out. She is usually late.*

Reading

1 Look at the photos (1 and 2) and the captions. Read the sentences and write A (archaeologists), G (geologists), or B (both).

1 They work on archaeological sites. A
2 They work outside. B
3 They study rocks. G
4 They study old objects. A

2 Work in pairs. What do you think is the daily routine of the people in the photos?

3 Read about a geologist and an archaeologist, and check your ideas from Exercise 2.

1 Archaeologists on a site in Canada

2 Geologists at work near the Azores, Atlantic Ocean

Cynthia Liutkus-Pierce
Geologist   `Location: US`

In the winter, Cynthia works in her university office in North Carolina. She gives lectures and she talks to her students every week. She <u>often</u> has meetings with other geologists. Every summer, she travels to Africa. She <u>usually</u> gets up and eats breakfast at six o'clock in the morning because it's very hot. She <u>never</u> works late. She goes to bed early, but she <u>sometimes</u> wakes up because the animals are noisy.

Julia Mayo Torne
Archaeologist   `Location: Panama`

Julia is from Panama. Her typical day changes with the seasons. In the dry season, Julia goes to her site. It's a good site and she <u>usually</u> finds objects every day. She <u>often</u> eats lunch there. In the evening, she <u>always</u> has coffee with her colleagues. They talk about their day. Then she reads before she goes to bed. In the rainy season, Julia returns to her laboratory. She studies the objects from the site, and writes articles and reports.

96

Pronunciation notes

Note the difficult pronunciation of *usually* and the silent /t/ in *often* (although some native speakers do pronounce the *t*).

5 ANSWERS

1 Julia sometimes gets up early.
2 Julia always has lunch with her colleagues.
3 Cynthia always goes to Africa in summer.
4 Julia usually reads novels.
5 Cynthia never travels in the winter.
6 Cynthia often writes reports.

6 Remind students that when the subject changes to *I*, the verb also changes, e.g., *gets* to *get*.

Listening

7 Ask students to read through the questions carefully. Ask: *Which questions are yes/no questions? Which questions have a question word?* Explain that *What does she do?* means *What's her job?*

8 After using the audioscript on page 172 to check their answers, have students role-play the conversation in pairs.

Grammar **frequency adverbs**

4 Look at the grammar box. Then look at the article. <u>Underline</u> the frequency adverbs.

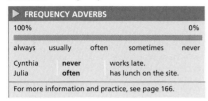

▶ FREQUENCY ADVERBS				
100%				0%
always	usually	often	sometimes	never
Cynthia	**never**		works late.	
Julia	**often**		has lunch on the site.	

For more information and practice, see page 166.

5 Rewrite the sentences with the adverb in the correct position.

1 Julia gets up early. (sometimes)
2 Julia has lunch with her colleagues. (always)
3 Cynthia goes to Africa in the summer. (always)
4 Julia reads novels. (usually)
5 Cynthia travels in the winter. (never)
6 Cynthia writes reports. (often)

6 Make the sentences in Exercise 5 true for you. Tell your partner.

Listening

7 🔘 **62** Listen and number the questions (1–6).

a Does she go to Africa every year? 5
b Does she work at this university? 1
c What does she do? 3
d Does she give lectures? 4
e Where does Cynthia go? 6
f Does she teach languages? 2

8 🔘 **62** Listen again and answer the questions.

Grammar **simple present questions** *he/she*

9 Look at the grammar box. Find two questions from Exercise 7.

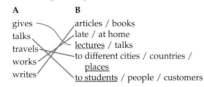

▶ SIMPLE PRESENT QUESTIONS *HE/SHE*				
What Where	**does**	he/she	**do?** **work?**	He/She's a geologist. He/She **works** in Africa.
	Does	he/she	**work** at this university?	
	Yes, No,	he/she	**does.** **doesn't.**	

For more information and practice, see page 166.

10 Put the words in order to make questions.

1 Julia / does / where / work / ?
2 meet / does / who / Cynthia / ?
3 Cynthia / children / teach / does / ?
4 Julia / like / does / coffee / ?
5 does / have lunch / where / Julia / ?
6 Cynthia / does / what time / get up / ?

11 Work in pairs. Ask and answer the questions.

Vocabulary **job activities**

12 Match a verb in A with words in B. Then <u>underline</u> three things that Cynthia does.

A   **B**

gives   articles / books
talks   late / at home
travels   <u>lectures</u> / talks
works   to different cities / countries / <u>places</u>
writes   <u>to students</u> / people / customers

13 Look at these jobs. Write sentences with the expressions in Exercise 12.

a journalist   a waiter   a businesswoman

a nurse   a receptionist   a salesperson

Speaking

14 Work in pairs. Tell your partner about your friends and family. Use the words in Exercise 13.

> *My brother travels for his job.*
> *He's a businessman.*

15 Work in pairs. Ask your partner five questions about one of the people in Exercise 14.

> *Does your brother*
> *travel every week?*

> *No, he doesn't. He*
> *travels every month.*

Grammar

Grammar notes

In the third person, the auxiliary verb *do* changes to *does*. The main verb takes the infinitive form (*go*, *work*, etc.), not the third person form. Note the word order in questions:

Question word	+ auxiliary verb
What	*does*

+ subject	+ verb
she	*do?*

Watch out for errors such as: *What she does? Does she gives lectures?*

10 ANSWERS

1 *Where does Julia work?*
2 *Who does Cynthia meet?*
3 *Does Cynthia teach children?*
4 *Does Julia like coffee?*
5 *Where does Julia have lunch?*
6 *What time does Cynthia get up?*

11 Remind students that they can find answers in the article on page 96.

Vocabulary

12 Read through the example as a class. Students may need to refer back to the article to find out what Cynthia does.

13 Tell students to write at least one sentence for each job; fast finishers could do more.

SAMPLE ANSWERS

A journalist writes articles.
A waiter talks to customers.
A businesswoman travels to different places.
A nurse talks to patients.
A receptionist talks to people.
A salesperson talks to customers.

Extra activity

Write on the board some other jobs and ask students to write a sentence for each one.

Speaking

HOMEWORK Ask students to write about the job and routine of a family member or a famous person.

Cats in crisis

Warm-up

Introducing the theme: cats

Write *cats* on the board and then write *facts* and *opinions*. Ask pairs of students to think of three facts (e.g., *they eat meat; they like fish*) and three opinions (e.g., *they're beautiful*) about cats. Write students' ideas under each category.

Reading

1 Ask students to look at the pictures. Ask: *What are they?* Say the names and ask students to repeat. Ask students to match the types of cat to the places.

2 Read through the sentences as a class. If needed, act out *sleep* and *hunt*.

3 Ask students to correct the false sentences.

ANSWERS

1 T
2 F. They hunt at night.
3 F. They hunt other animals.
4 T
5 T

4 Ask students to read the article again and find the information.

ANSWERS

1 hunts
2 goes into the forest
3 checks the cameras
4 Writes reports, meets with colleagues

5 Tell students to look at the article again to find answers.

ANSWERS

1 3,500
2 170
3 automatic cameras and radio collars
4 8
5 every month

8c Cats in crisis

Reading

1 Work in pairs. Match the animals in the photos (1–4) with the places (a–d).

a Africa and Asia 2
b Asia 4
c South America 1
d Africa 3

1 a jaguar

2 a leopard

3 a lion

4 a tiger

2 Mark the sentences as true (T) or false (F).

1 Tigers eat animals. T
2 They sleep at night. F
3 They hunt people. F
4 Thailand has a lot of tigers. T
5 Tigers live in forests. T

3 Read the article and check your answers from Exercise 2.

4 Read the article again. Find these things.

1 one thing a tiger does at night
2 one thing Saksit Simcharoen does at night
3 two things Saksit Simcharoen does every month
4 one other thing he does in his job

5 Answer the questions.

1 How many wild tigers are in Asia today?
2 How many people work in the wildlife park?
3 How does Saksit study the tigers in the park?
4 How many tigers in the park have radio collars?
5 How often does Saksit write a report?

Grammar *How … ?*

6 Look at the grammar box. Choose the correct option.

We use "how" to ask for <u>information</u> / *a "yes" or "no" answer.*

> ▶ **HOW … ?**
>
> **How** does Saksit study the tigers in the park?
> **How many** people does Saksit work with?
> **How often** does Saksit write a report?
>
> For more information and practice, see page 166.

7 Put the words in order to make questions with *how*. Then work in pairs. Ask and answer the questions with your partner.

1 tigers / how many / in the park / are / ?
2 in the park / cameras / are / how many / ?
3 have / how often / a meeting / Saksit / does / ?
4 help / we / can / tiger conservation / how / ?

8 Word focus *every*

a Look at the sentences. Which words can follow *every*? Time words

1 Every month Saksit writes reports.
2 Does she go to Africa every year?
3 Does he travel every week?
4 Rosanna doesn't work every day.
5 I have a meeting every Tuesday.

b Write five sentences about yourself using *every*. Read your sentences to your partner. What do you have in common?

Speaking

9 Tigers are night animals. What about you? Are you a "morning person" or an "evening person"? Take a quiz.

Student A: Turn to page 155.

Student B: Turn to page 159.

Extra activity

Ask students to get together in groups of three and research roadblocks to big cat conservation. What are some of the challenges these animals are facing in their survival? Give them some ideas: hunting, poaching, habitat destruction, medicinal uses on black market.

CATS IN CRISIS

TIGERS, LIONS, LEOPARDS, AND JAGUARS ARE ALL "BIG CATS"... AND THEY ARE IN CRISIS!

A tiger in the forest at night in Sumatra, Indonesia
Photo by Steve Winter

Tigers

number of wild tigers
in 1900 – 100,000
in 2010 – 3,500

Tigers live in many places in Asia, from very cold mountains in the Himalayas to very hot areas. They usually live in places without people. Tigers eat other animals. They hunt at night. In places without people, tigers also hunt in the day. They usually kill wild animals, but they sometimes kill domestic animals. Tigers are in crisis because people move into their areas and sometimes kill them.

Tiger conservation

tigers in Huai Kha Khaeng
Wildlife Park
in 1980 – 20
in 2010 – 60

Saksit Simcharoen works at the Huai Kha Khaeng Wildlife Park in Thailand. The park is a tiger conservation area. About sixty tigers live there. Saksit works with 170 people in the park. He goes into the forest at night. He doesn't see many tigers, but the park has 180 automatic cameras. They take photos of tigers. Saksit checks the cameras. About eight of the tigers in the park have radio collars. Every month Saksit writes reports about the tigers in the area and meets with his colleagues. Saksit loves his job because the tigers in the park are not in crisis.

A team in Thailand studies a tiger.

automatic (adj) /ˌɔtəˈmætɪk/ without a human operator
conservation (n) /ˌkɑnsərˈveɪʃən/ protection
crisis (n) /ˈkraɪsɪs/ a difficult or dangerous time
domestic (adj) /dəˈmestɪk/ not wild

a radio collar (n) /ˈreɪdioʊ ˌkɑlər/

Unit 8 **Routines** 99

Grammar

7 Remind students that the answers to the first three questions are in the article.

ANSWERS

1 How many tigers are in the park? (about 60)
2 How many cameras are in the park? (180)
3 How often does Saksit have a meeting? (every month)
4 How can we help tiger conservation?

Extra activity

Discuss question 4 in Exercise 7 as a class. Elicit ideas from the class. Ideas might include: protect the tigers' habitats, establish new national forests, use radio collars and automatic cameras to protect tigers, donate money to conservation.

Word focus

8b Model the activity by reading aloud a few sentences about yourself (e.g., *I teach English every day, I have coffee every morning*).

Tell students to make sure they put the expression with *every* at the beginning or end of the sentence.

Speaking

9 Pre-teach *alarm clock* (with a gesture or drawing) and *it depends* (*maybe yes / maybe no*).

Give students time to prepare questions from the prompts. Circulate and help students to form the questions accurately.

After students ask and answer the questions, tell them to check the results on page 157 in the Student Book.

ANSWERS

1 Do you wake up before your alarm clock?
2 Do you always have breakfast?
3 Where are you?
4 What time do you get up on the weekend?
5 What is the main meal of the day for you?
6 Do you fall asleep in front of the TV at night?

Extra activity

Refer students to National Geographic's website, where they can learn more about big cat conservation. Ask them to look for information on Beverly and Dereck Joubert, who specialize in big cat conservation.

One moment, please

Warm-up

Test before you teach: phone calls

Divide the class into pairs and have them sit back-to-back. Tell them that they are going to take turns calling each other. Give a situation and have students act out the conversation, using any language they have.

1 It's your partner's birthday.

2 You're at a movie theater, and your partner is late.

3 You want to speak to your colleague's wife or husband.

4 You have no money; your partner is rich.

Real life

2 Ask students to look at the photos. Ask: *What do you see? Where are the people?* Elicit ideas and vocabulary from students, and make sure they understand the words in the captions.

3 Ask students to look at the expressions in the box and decide whether they are said by a caller or by a receptionist.

Vocabulary notes

When English speakers answer the phone, they say *Hello* or, in formal situations, *Good morning, Good afternoon,* or *Good evening.*

Note the use of *Can I...?* to ask for permission. *May I...?* and *Could I...?* are other, more polite expressions.

I'll call back later means *I will call again at a later time.*

Pronunciation

5 Model the soft, unvoiced /s/ sound and the voiced /z/ sound. Tell students to cover their ears and repeat the sounds. They should be able to feel the vibration when making the /z/ sound.

8d One moment, please

Real life **on the phone**

1 🔊 **63** Listen to three phone calls (1–3). Match the number of the conversation to the person.

a Mrs. Jackson 3
b Ed Carr 1
c Mr. Watts 2

2 🔊 **64** Look at the photos. Then listen to two of the phone calls again. Mark (✓) the reasons the callers can't speak to the persons.

3 Look at the expressions for ON THE PHONE. Write caller (C) or receptionist (R).

> ▶ **ON THE PHONE**
> Good morning, / Hello, PJ International. R
> May I help you? R
> Yes, can I speak to Ed Carr, please? C
> Yes, one moment, please. R
> I'm sorry. He's/She's in a meeting. R
> OK. Thank you. / Thanks. C/R
> I'll call back later. C

4 Complete the conversation with the expressions.

R: _Good morning_ , City College. _May I help you?_ ?
C: Yes, _Can I speak to_ Mrs. Jackson, please?
R: _I'm sorry._ . She's out of the office at the moment.
C: OK, thank you. _I'll call back later_ .
_____ .

5 Pronunciation /s/ and /z/

🔊 **65** Listen to these words. Is the s like *this* or *is*? Listen again and repeat.

pleaṣe	he'ṣ	yeṣ	Fridayṣ
workṣ	thankṣ		

6 Work in pairs. Practice phone calls. Use the ideas in the photos.

works from home on Fridays   out of the office ✓

on vacation   with a customer

doesn't work in the afternoons   in a meeting ✓

ANSWERS

/s/: yes, works, thanks
/z/: please, he's, Fridays

Pronunciation notes

Both /s/ and /z/ are produced in the same way. The tongue is pressed gently against the upper palate, thus allowing air through as the sound is made. The difference is that /z/ is voiced (the voicebox vibrates as the sound is made), while /s/ is unvoiced.

Extra activity

Write conversation prompts on the board (e.g., ... *morning ... help you ... sorry ... meeting ... back later ... bye*). Have pairs of students improvise conversations.

8e My new job

Writing an email

1 Read Vijay's email about his new job in a call center.
Complete the email with seven of these words.

classmates	colleagues	evening	job
morning	office	phone calls	tasks

2 Who do you think the email is to?

a his boss   **b** his friend   c his colleague

> Hi!
> Here I am at my new ¹ _job_ ! It's <u>good</u>!
> The ² <u>office</u> opens at 8:00 a.m. I <u>usually</u>
> <u>arrive</u> at about 7:45 and I have <u>coffee</u> with my
> ³<u>colleagues</u>. They're great. We have a <u>meeting</u> every
> ⁴<u>morning</u> and the <u>boss</u> gives us our ⁵ _tasks_
> for the day. I <u>usually</u> make about 40 ⁶<u>phone calls</u> a
> day. I finish early on Fridays. Let's <u>meet</u> for lunch.
> How about next <u>week</u>?
> Vijay

3 Writing skill **spelling: double letters**

a Look at the email again. <u>Underline</u> the words with
double letters.

b Complete the words with the letter. How many
words have double letters? 9

1 ar _t_ ist (t)   6 di _ff_ icult (f)
2 busine _ss_ man (s)   7 di _nn_ er (n)
3 cla _ss_ es (s)   8 m _ee_ t (e)
4 co _ll_ ege (l)   9 su _mm_ er (m)
5 di _ff_ erent (f)   10 w _ee_ kend (e)

c Complete the email from a student with words from
Exercises 1 and 3b.

> Hi!
> Here I am at my new ¹_____ ! It's good! I have
> ²_____ every day except Wednesday. My courses
> aren't ³_____ . I usually write about two essays
> a week. I often go out with my ⁴_____ in the
> evenings. Let's ⁵_____ and play tennis. How
> about next ⁶_____ ?
> Jim

4 Write an email to a friend. Include a
suggestion to meet.

5 Work in pairs. Exchange emails. Check the
spelling. Reply to your partner's email.

My new job

Warm-up

Introducing the theme: emails

Write *emails* on the board and
ask: *How often do you write
emails? Who do you often write
to? With friends, what do you
write about? In your job, what
do you write about?*

Writing

1 Go through the word bank
as a class. Check *classmates* and
colleagues by asking: *Which are
people at school/work?* Check *tasks*
by writing a job on the board (e.g.,
waiter) and asking: *What tasks does
he do?* (He takes orders, he clears
tables, etc.) Then ask students
to read the email and complete
it with the words, working out
the meaning of new words from
the context.

> **Vocabulary notes**
>
> Emails to friends are written in
> informal English. We often start
> with *Hi* or *Hello* and sign off with
> *See you later* or similarly informal
> phrases. We use abbreviated
> forms (*they're*, *What's*) and
> often use emoticons (☺) and
> exclamations (*Wow!*).

Writing skill

3a Introduce the concept of
double letters by writing *letters*
on the board and asking: *How
many "t"s?*

> **Pronunciation notes**
>
> Many English words have double
> consonants. They often affect
> the pronunciation of the vowel
> sound that precedes them, e.g.,
> *diner* (with one "n") and *dinner*
> (with two "n"s).

3c Ask students to read the email
quickly. Ask: *Who is it from?* (Jim)
Who is it to? (a friend) *Where is
Jim?* (at school). Then ask students
to complete the email.

> **SAMPLE ANSWERS**
>
> 1 college
> 2 classes
> 3 difficult
> 4 classmates
> 5 meet
> 6 weekend

4 You may want to begin by
brainstorming routines-related
vocabulary as a class and writing it on
the board. Ask questions like: *What do
you usually do in your job? What do you
do in the evenings and on weekends?* Then
ask students to write the email. Tell
them to write about their actual job or

a class, using the two emails on the page
as models. Circulate and look at their
emails, pointing out or correcting any
errors as you see them.

5 Check the activity by asking students
to say where and when they will meet
and what they will do.

> **HOMEWORK** If your students know
> and trust each other, ask them to
> exchange email addresses, and give
> them your email address. Ask students
> to write emails in English to each other.
> Tell them to write about the English
> course they are taking.

The elephants of Samburu

Videoscript

Narrator: Nick Nichols takes photos of the elephants in their family groups, and of individual elephants, too.

Nick takes a lot of photos, about 10,000 in total.

Daniel Lentipo works for *Save the Elephants*.

He can identify individual elephants in Samburu Reserve.

Daniel teaches Nick how to identify individual elephants.

Nick and Daniel follow the elephants for ten hours every day.

The elephants drink.

They have a bath.

They eat.

Elephants are gentle and intelligent.

Nick explains that Daniel sometimes puts his hand up to the elephants.

The elephants put their trunks up.

It's a greeting—like "hello."

This ten-year-old elephant greets Nick.

The Samburu Reserve is a very good place for these elephants.

The elephants greet their family members with their trunks … and by calling.

At night, the elephants lie down to sleep.

In the morning, Nick and Daniel get up early and start work again.

An elephant at night in Samburu National Reserve

102

Before you watch

1 Work in pairs. Look at the photo and the caption. Where does this elephant live?

Samburu National Reserve

2 Read about Samburu. Answer the questions.

1 Where is the Samburu National Reserve?
2 What does the organization Save the Elephants do?
3 How does Google Earth help Save the Elephants?

The Samburu National Reserve is in Kenya. Lions, leopards, elephants, and buffalo live in the reserve. The reserve is the home of the elephant conservation organization Save the Elephants. It works in four African countries: Kenya, Mali, Gabon, and South Africa. Save the Elephants works with Google Earth to follow elephants with GPS collars.

3 Work in pairs. How much do you know about elephants? Choose the option you think is correct.

1 Elephants live *in family groups* / *alone*.
2 Elephants *like* / *don't like* water.
3 Elephants eat *plants* / *animals*.
4 Elephants *hunt* / *sleep* at night.

While you watch

4 Watch the video. Check your answers above.

5 Choose the correct option (a–c).

1 Nick Nichols
   a is a photographer for National Geographic.
   b is a student.
   c works for Save the Elephants.

2 Daniel Lentipo
   a is a photographer for National Geographic.
   b is a student.
   c works for Save the Elephants.

3 Daniel teaches Nick how to
   a take photos of the elephants.
   b identify individual elephants.
   c follow elephants.

4 Nick and Daniel follow the elephants for
   a four hours a day.
   b eight hours a day.
   c ten hours a day.

5 Elephants put their trunks up
   a at night.
   b to greet other elephants.
   c when they are thirsty.

6 Watch the video again. Write three things:

1 the elephants do every day.
2 Nick and Daniel do every day.

After you watch

7 Read about Nick and Daniel's work routine. Complete the text with these verbs.

drive	get up	start	study
work	work	take	

Nick Nichols [1] _____ for National Geographic. Daniel Lentipo is the Chief Research Assistant at the Samburu National Reserve. Nick and Daniel [2] _____ early every day. They [3] _____ work early. Daniel [4] _____ the jeep and he [5] _____ the elephants. Nick [6] _____ photos of the elephants. Nick and Daniel sometimes [7] _____ at night. Nick's photos of sleeping elephants are very unusual.

8 Work in pairs.

Student A: You are a photographer.

Student B. You are a journalist.

Prepare answers to these questions. Then take turns to ask and answer the questions.

- Who do you work for?
- Where do you work?
- Where do you travel to in your job?
- What do you take photos of / write about?
- What's a typical day like in your job?

call (v) /kɔl/ to make a noise	**identify** (v) /aɪˈdentɪˌfaɪ/ to find
follow (v) /ˈfɒloʊ/ to travel behind a person or animal	**an individual** (n) /ˌɪndɪˈvɪdʒuəl/ one person or animal
gentle (adj) /ˈdʒent(ə)l/ kind	**a jeep** (n) /dʒip/
greet (v) /grit/ to say "hello"	**lie down** (v) /ˈlaɪ ˈdaʊn/
a hand (n) /ˈhænd/	**sleep** (v) /slip/
a bath (n) /ˈbæθ/	**a trunk** (n) /trʌŋk/

Before you watch

1 Ask students to look at the photo and the caption. Ask: *Where does this elephant live?*

2 Tell students that the video is about elephants in the Samburu National Reserve. Students read the text and answer the questions.

ANSWERS

1 The Samburu National Reserve is in Kenya.
2 Save the Elephants works with Google Earth / is an elephant conservation organization.
3 Google Earth follows elephants with GPS collars.

3 Put students in pairs. Give students some time to go through the sentences and choose the correct option. Elicit ideas from the class. Don't check the answers at this stage.

While you watch

4 Play the video. Students check their answers from Exercise 3.

5 Give students some time to read the items. Play the video again. Students choose the correct option to complete the sentences.

6 Put students in pairs. Play the video again for students to write down their answers. Accept any correct answers.

ANSWERS

1 Drink, take a bath, eat
2 Follow elephants for 10 hours, take photos, wake up early to start work

After you watch

7 Give students some time to read the paragraph. Students complete the text with the correct form of the verbs.

ANSWERS

1 works
2 get up
3 start
4 drives
5 studies
6 takes
7 work

8 Give students time to read the list of questions and prepare answers. Then divide the class into pairs and have them take turns to ask and answer the questions.

UNIT 8 REVIEW

Grammar

1 Students write sentences with the underlined words.

> **ANSWERS**
> 1 He has a new job.
> 2 He drives from New Mexico to Arizona.
> 3 He works Monday to Friday.
> 4 He starts work at 6 o'clock.
> 5 He doesn't have breakfast.
> 6 He eats a snack.
> 7 He has lunch in a restaurant.
> 8 He works late.

2 Students rewrite sentences 3, 6, and 8 with the adverbs.

> **ANSWERS**
> 3 I usually work Mon. to Fri.
> 6 I sometimes eat a snack in my truck. (Sometimes I...)
> 8 I often work late.

3 Students complete the sentences with prepositions.

4 Students complete the questions and write answers.

Vocabulary

5 Students match a verb from A with a word from B.

6 Students work in pairs to ask and answer questions. If necessary, review the word pairs and elicit the question word that is used with each one and model question formation.

7 Students complete the sentences with the verbs.

Real life

8 Students put the phone conversation in order.

Speaking

9 Students ask and answer questions in pairs.

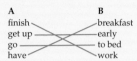
Grammar

1 Read about Joel Murray. Write eight sentences with the <u>underlined</u> words. Use *he*.

Hi. I'm Joel. I'm 46. I'm a truck driver. [1] I have a new <u>job</u>. In my new job, [2] I drive <u>from New Mexico to Arizona</u> every week. That's about 1,500 miles. [3] I work <u>Monday to Friday</u>. [4] I start work at <u>six o'clock</u>. [5] I don't have <u>breakfast</u>, but [6] I eat <u>a snack</u> in my truck. [7] I have lunch in <u>a restaurant</u> with other drivers. [8] I work <u>late</u>.

2 Rewrite sentences 3, 6, and 8 with these adverbs:

   3 usually   6 sometimes   8 often

3 Complete the sentences with prepositions.

1 Joel drives to Arizona ___*on*___ Mondays.
2 He doesn't work ___*in*___ the evening.
3 He finishes work ___*at*___ 4:30 p.m.
4 He takes a vacation ___*in*___ August.

4 Complete the questions with three of these expressions. Then answer the questions.

How many	How much	How often	How old

1 ___How old___ is Joel? *46*
2 ___How many___ miles does he drive every week? *1,500*
3 ___How often___ does Joel work late? *often*

> **I CAN**
> say what people do every day (simple present) ☐
> say when people do things (prepositions of time) ☐
> say how often people do things (frequency adverbs) ☐
> use *how* correctly ☐

Vocabulary

5 Match a verb from A with a word from B.

A	B
finish	breakfast
get up	early
go	to bed
have	work

6 Work in pairs. Ask and answer questions about your day with the expressions from Exercise 5.

7 Complete the sentences with these verbs.

talk	travel	work	write

1 Journalists ___*write*___ articles.
2 Businessmen ___*travel*___ to different countries.
3 Salespeople ___*talk*___ to customers.
4 Waiters ___*work*___ late.

> **I CAN**
> talk about routines ☐
> talk about job activities ☐

Real life

8 Put the phone conversation in order.

a Hello. 2
b Oh. Well, can I speak to her assistant? 6
c Yes, can I speak to Ms. Becker, please? 4
d Can I help you? 3
e I'm sorry. She's on vacation this week. 5
f Good morning, Sports Unlimited. 1
g OK. Thank you. 8
h Yes, one moment please. 7

> **I CAN**
> say why people can't answer a phone call ☐
> make phone calls ☐

Speaking

9 Work in pairs. Take turns.

Student A: You have a new job as a driver.

Student B: Ask your friend about his/her new job. Use the ideas below.

what / do?	what time / start?
where / work?	how often / work late?
how many days / work?	you / like the job?

> **Extra activity**
>
> Take note of any pronunciation issues students have had during this unit. To review, play a game. For example, write on the board tongue twisters using /s/ and /z/, e.g. *On Saturdays, Miss Wise sits and sings.* Have students practice saying them aloud. Then ask students to write and practice their own tongue twisters.

A passenger shows her passport and train ticket at Ollantaytambo station near Machu Picchu, Peru.
Photo by Michael S. Lewis

FEATURES

1 Work in pairs. Look at the photo. Who does the woman work for (a–c)? Who are the other people?

a   a bus company   ⓑ a train company   c   an airline

2 🔊 66 Listen to four people talk about travel. Write the number of the speaker (1–4) next to the picture.

by boat 4   by bus 2   by plane 3   by train 1

3 🔊 66 Listen again and complete the table.

	Where do they go?	When?
1	New York	every week
2	Asia	in the summer
3	No where	never
4	Mallorca	in the summer

4 Work in pairs. Ask and answer questions about travel with *where*, *when*, and *how*?

Where do you go?

I travel to Cairo.

Travel

Warm-up

Personal response

Ask students questions about travel, e.g., *How do you come to school? How do you travel to work? Where do you go on weekends, and how do you travel there? Where do you go on vacation, and how do you get there?*

1 Ask students to look at the photo, and ask: *What can you see?* Elicit ideas and vocabulary (*people, man, woman, train, tickets, passports*). Then divide the class into pairs to discuss the questions.

2 Ask students to look at the pictures and the words. Then play the audio. Students listen and write the number of the speaker next to the type of travel they talk about.

3 Play the audio again. Students listen and complete the table. Let them compare answers in pairs before discussing as a class.

4 Write *Where? When?* and *How?* on the board and elicit questions about travel using these question words. Students then work in pairs to ask and answer the questions. Ask individuals to share what they found out about their partner.

Extra activity 1

Ask students where they can get to from their hometown(s) via the modes of transportation presented.

Extra activity 2

If you have a map in your classroom, get students to practice transportation vocabulary by pointing to two destinations and asking how to get from one to the other. Tell students they can suggest more than one option. For example: New York to Paris (by plane); Rome to Athens (by plane or by boat); Moscow to Shanghai (by plane or by train).

Travel essentials

9a Travel essentials

Warm-up

Test before you teach: clothes

Stand in front of the class and ask: *What am I wearing?* Ask students to say or guess what the clothes you have on are called. Don't confirm or deny the words, just find out what students know. Ask two students (one male, one female) to stand up, and ask the class to say what they are wearing.

Then ask pairs of students to write down as many clothing-related words as they can in two minutes. Find out who has the longest list.

Vocabulary

Vocabulary notes

A pair of (meaning *two*) is used not only with *shoes, boots, socks,* etc. but also with items of clothing with two legs (*pants, shorts, jeans,* etc.).

A top is used as a general word, usually by women, to describe many things worn on the top half of the body, including *T-shirts, shirts,* and light *sweaters.*

Sweater is a common general word for a warm top made from wool or similar material.

2 Begin this activity by reviewing colors. Point to items of clothing around the class and ask: *What color is it?* If necessary, write the colors on the board. Then model the activity by describing a student's clothing and asking the rest of the class who it is.

Extra activity

Bring in magazine pictures of people and ask students to describe what they are wearing. Alternatively, post the pictures around the room and describe a person; ask students to walk around the class until they find the person.

Vocabulary clothes

1 Look at the photos. Repeat the words after your instructor.

a pair of boots

a hat

a T-shirt

a pair of sandals

a coat

a jacket

a skirt

a pair of jeans

a blouse

a dress

a pair of shoes

a shirt

a pair of pants

a scarf

a pair of shorts

a sweater

2 Work in pairs. Look at the people in your class. Match clothes with names.

A white shirt and a jacket.

Ramon?

Yes.

3 Work in pairs. Talk about your clothes. What do you usually wear … ?
- to work
- to class
- on the weekend
- on vacation

Reading

4 Read the article. <u>Underline</u> the clothes.

5 Read the article again. What does Kate always take with her? What about her sister and her husband?

6 What do you always take? Tell your partner.

By Kate Renshaw

TRAVEL *essentials*

I'm a travel writer. I usually travel alone, but my family sometimes comes with me. It's difficult because they always have a lot of bags. Look at this photo of our trip to Ecuador. <u>There are</u> eight people and <u>there are</u> about fifteen bags! In my sister's bags <u>there are</u> three <u>jackets</u>, four or five <u>sweaters</u>, seven pairs of <u>pants</u>, and two <u>dresses</u>. <u>There are</u> six or seven books, too. She never travels without books. In my husband's bag <u>there's a</u> pair of <u>boots</u>, a pair of <u>shoes</u>, and a pair of <u>sandals</u>! And his maps. My husband loves maps and he always takes them on trips.

When I travel alone, I take a very small suitcase. <u>There's a</u> pocket for my travel documents and inside <u>there are</u> two parts, one for clothes and one for my laptop. I never travel without my laptop! That's it!

3 Model the activity by telling students what you wear for work and on the weekend.

Ask students to prepare sentences about their clothes, then tell a partner.

Reading

4 Ask students to skim the article and underline the clothes.

5 Point out that *without* is the opposite of *with*.

ANSWERS

Kate: laptop
Sister: books
Husband: maps

6 List students' responses on the board.

Grammar *there is/are*

7 Look at the grammar box. Then look at the article. <u>Underline</u> the sentences with *there's* and *there are*.

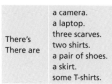

▶ **THERE IS/ARE**			
There's	a	laptop	
There are	two some	parts clothes	in my suitcase.
(there's = there is)			

For more information and practice, see page 166.

8 Make sentences about things in Kate's bags in the photo. Use the words below.

There's There are	a camera. a laptop. three scarves. two shirts. a pair of shoes. a skirt. some T-shirts.

9 Pronunciation *there is/are*

🔊 **67** Listen and repeat the sentences from Exercise 8. Pay attention to the stress.

Speaking and writing

10 Imagine you travel a lot. Choose three countries to complete the sentences. Write a list of the things you pack in your suitcase for each trip.

1 I travel to _____ for my job.
2 I go to _____ on my vacation.
3 I go to _____ to visit my family.

11 Work in pairs. Tell your partner where you go and what's in your suitcase.

> *I often travel to Singapore. In my suitcase today, there's a pair of shoes …*

Grammar

Grammar notes

Here, *there* is a pronoun that is used to express that someone or something exists or happens.

We use *there's* (*there is*) when it is followed by singular or noncount nouns.

We use *there are* when it is followed by plural nouns. Note that we say *There are some shoes* but *There's a pair of shoes.*

Pronunciation

Pronunciation notes

In natural spoken English, both *there's* and *there are* are reduced.

Be sure to correct pronunciation, especially the *th* sound, early and often, asking students to rpeat after you, so that they have the pronunciation correct early on and don't take pronunciation issues with them to higher levels.

Speaking and writing

10 Ask students to think of three countries first, and then complete the sentences. Then have them create their packing lists. Monitor and help with ideas, spelling, and pronunciation.

11 Invite volunteers to share their destinations and their list with the class.

Extra activity 1

Divide the class into groups of four. Give each group a very different travel destination, e.g., the North Pole, Mount Everest, Hawaii, the Amazon, etc. Tell the groups that they have five minutes to write a list of things to take. The winner is the team with the longest list of items that are appropriate for their destination.

Extra activity 2

Tell students that they are taking a weekend trip to New York City. Elicit things to take in their suitcase and write them on the board. Then, in small groups, have students decide which are the five most important items in their suitcases.

9b

Places to stay

Listening

Vocabulary note

A couple is used to describe two people who are in a romantic relationship (e.g., *husband and wife, boyfriend and girlfriend*).

PHOTO INFO

Cape Town is a large city on the coast of South Africa. It is Africa's most popular destination for international tourists, and is famous for Table Mountain National Park, beaches, Robben Island (where Nelson Mandela was imprisoned), and other historical areas.

1 ANSWERS

Hostel: young couples, students
Hotel: families, business travelers

2 Give students a moment to read through the questions. Then play the audio.

Grammar

Grammar notes

We use *there isn't* with singular or noncount nouns. We use *there aren't* with plural nouns.

We use *any* with plural nouns (and noncount nouns) in negative and question forms.

9b Places to stay

Listening

There are cheap rooms at this youth hostel in Cape Town.

An expensive, but very comfortable, hotel in Cape Town.

1 Look at the photos. Which people stay in these two places?

> business travelers   families
> students   young couples

2 **68** Listen. Then read Luke's questions and <u>underline</u> the words he uses.

1   Are there any hotels near the *airport* / *beach*?
2   Is there a youth hostel *downtown* / *near the airport*?
3   Is there *a bus* / *a train* to downtown?

3 **68** Listen again. Are the sentences true (T) or false (F)?

1   There's a youth hostel near the airport. F
2   There are some cheap hotels near the airport. F
3   There's a train to downtown. F

108

Grammar *there is/are* negative and question forms

4 Look at the sentences and questions in the grammar box. When do we use *any*? With plural objects

▶ THERE IS/ARE NEGATIVE AND QUESTION FORMS		
There **isn't**	a train.	
There **aren't**	**any** cheap hotels.	
Is there	a youth hostel?	Yes, there **is**. No, there **isn't**.
Are there	**any** hotels?	Yes, there **are**. No, there **aren't**.
For more information and practice, see page 166.		

5 Work in pairs. Tell your partner the name of your hometown or a place you know. Write questions about your partner's town. Use *Is there a/an ... ? / Are there any ... ?*

airport nice beach cheap restaurants good hotels tourist attractions youth hostels	in near	the city/town downtown

---

5 If students are from or live in the same town, tell them to think of other towns that they know well. Give them two minutes to prepare questions using the prompts.

6 Check by asking students to tell the class about their partner's town.

Vocabulary

Pronunciation notes

Point out the stress and pronunciation of the more unusual words: *armchair* and *sofa*.

Extra activity

Ask students to categorize the words by room, e.g., *What is in the bedroom?* (*bed, closet, etc.*).

Alternatively, act out using the furniture items (e.g., sitting on a chair, watching TV, etc.) for students to guess.

6 Work in pairs. Ask and answer your questions from Exercise 5.

> Are there any good hotels near downtown?

> No, there aren't.

Vocabulary furniture

7 🔊 69 Look at the photos (1–12). Then listen and repeat the words. Write the words with the photos.

armchair	bathtub	bed chair desk fridge
lamp	shower	sofa table TV closet

1 _____

2 _____

3 _____

4 _____

5 _____

6 _____

7 _____

8 _____

9 _____

10 _____

11 _____

12 _____

8 Work in pairs. Which things are there usually in a hotel room?

> There's a bed, …

9 🔊 70 Listen to the conversation. Mark (✓) the furniture in Exercise 7 that you hear.
TV, bed, fridge, lamp, sofa

10 🔊 70 Listen again. Which room (a or b) is it? *a*

Speaking

11 Work in pairs. You are in a hotel. Ask and answer questions about your hotel room.

Student A: Turn to page 156.

Student B: Turn to page 160.

---

7 ANSWERS

1 TV
2 bathtub
3 bed
4 chair
5 table
6 lamp
7 desk
8 sofa
9 closet
10 armchair
11 shower
12 fridge

8 SAMPLE ANSWERS

There's usually a TV, a shower, a bed, a chair, a desk, a lamp, a small table, and a closet. Also possible: a bathtub, a fridge, a sofa, and an armchair.

Speaking

Extra activity 1

In pairs, have students take turns describing their bedroom to a partner, who will draw a simple floor plan of the furniture. Students should then check the drawings for accuracy.

Extra activity 2

Have students take a moment to write a brief description of the other room in image B.

HOMEWORK Ask students to write a description of their bedroom or the perfect hotel room.

Extra activity 3

Divide students into pairs. Separately, prepare a set of pieces of paper with prices on them, one for each pair. The prices should range from very high – enough for a very swanky hotel room – to very low – maybe only enough for a really low-budget place. Tell students they are going to stay in a hotel in a glamorous location this weekend.

Have the pick a piece of paper without seeing the price. When they turn it over, explain to them that that is how much money they have to spend on the hotel. Have them prepare a description of the hotel room they can afford with this money. Then have them share their budget and their projected accommodations with the class.

Across a continent

Warm-up

Using words: reviewing places

Divide the class into pairs. Write these word pairs on the board and ask students to say how they are different: *town/city; country/ continent; road/street; hotel/ hostel.*

Reading

1 Ask students to look at the map and the photos. Ask: *What can you see? Where are they?* Elicit ideas. Use the pictures to pre-teach *truck, hitchhike,* and *trip.* If any students are Russian or know Russia, ask them to tell the class about the pictures. Then have students answer the question individually.

2 ANSWERS

Places mentioned: Moscow, Novosibirsk, Kungur Ice Cave, Perm, Irkutsk, Ulan-Ude, Lake Baikal, Vladivostock

Extra activity

Ask students to look in the text and find two things about traveling across Russia that they like and two things that they don't like. Tell them to discuss their ideas with a partner, then tell the class.

Vocabulary

5 Ask students to draw a line from the verb in column A to the corresponding words in column B. Then ask them to read the article to check their answers.

Reading

1 Work in pairs. Look at the map and the photos on page 111. What things do you think you can see or do on a trip across Russia?

2 Read the article on page 111 and check your ideas from Exercise 1. Then find the places in the article on the map.

3 Are the sentences true (T) or false (F)?

1   There's a road from Moscow to Vladivostok. T
2   There are two trains every day from Moscow to Vladivostok. F
3   You can't sleep on the train. F
4   You can leave the train and stay in hotels. T
5   There aren't any towns near Lake Baikal. F
6   The Trans-Siberian Highway is only for trucks. F

4 Work in pairs. Is this the kind of trip you like? What do you like?

> I love trips to different countries.

> I like to vacation on the beach.

Vocabulary travel

5 Match a verb in A with words in B. Check your answers in the article.

A	B
travel	a bus
leave	an ice cave
book	from east to west
use	home
stay	in hotels
visit	in Vladivostock
take	Moscow
drive	your tickets
arrive	a travel agent
fly	your car

6 Complete the sentences with verbs from Exercise 5.

1   "What time does your plane _____?"
    "At 8:40 in the morning."
2   We don't _____ in expensive hotels.
3   I usually _____ my tickets with a travel agent.
4   A boat _____ Vladivostok for Japan every week.
5   Let's _____ a bus from the airport.
6   "Is there an airport in Irkutsk? Can you _____ there?"
    "Yes, there is."

7 Word focus *take*

a Look at these expressions with *take.* Find one of the expressions in the article on page 111.

take a bus   take a photo   take a suitcase

b Work in pairs. Ask and answer the questions.

1   How many suitcases do you take when you travel?
2   Do you usually take photos when you are on vacation?
3   Do you often take a taxi / a bus / a train / a plane? Where to?

Grammar imperative forms

8 Look at these sentences from the article. Are the words in **bold** nouns or verbs? Verbs

> ▶ IMPERATIVE FORMS
>
> **Book** your tickets in advance.
> **Don't wait** until you arrive.
> (don't = do not)
>
> For more information and practice, see page 167.

9 Complete these sentences from the article with the missing verb.

1   _Travel_ non-stop in seven days.
2   _Stay_ in hotels.
3   _Go_ sightseeing in the big cities.
4   _Take_ the new Trans-Siberian Highway.
5   _Drive_ your car.

Writing and speaking

10 Work in pairs. Write five tips for travelers in your country or a country you know. Think of reasons for the tips.

> *Don't travel by bus.*

11 Work in groups of four. Discuss your travel tips. Ask follow-up questions.

> *Don't travel by bus.*

> *Why?*

> *The buses are very slow.*

ANSWERS

leave	Moscow
book	your ticket
use	a travel agent
stay	in hotels
visit	an ice cave
take	a bus
drive	your car
arrive	in Vladivostock
fly	home

6 ANSWERS

1   arrive/leave
2   stay
3   book
4   leaves
5   take
6   drive/fly

Across a continent *by rail* and *by road*

Russia is a very large country. There are eight time zones between Moscow in the west and Vladivostok in the east. It's 5,600 miles and there are two ways to travel: by rail and by road.

BY RAIL: **THE TRANS-SIBERIAN RAILWAY**

Trains leave Moscow almost every day. Book your tickets in advance—don't wait until you arrive in Moscow. You can book online or use a travel agent. There are two options:

Travel non-stop in seven days. You sleep and eat on the train. You can talk to other passengers, learn some words in Russian, and enjoy the views. The train travels through amazing mountains, beautiful forests, and strange deserts.

Stop on the way and stay in hotels. Go sightseeing in the big cities. In Novosibirsk, the main city in Siberia, there are museums, art galleries, theaters, and a famous opera house. Or visit the Kungur Ice Cave near Perm. From the towns of Irkutsk or Ulan-Ude, you can <u>take a bus or train</u> to Lake Baikal, a UNESCO World Heritage site. Lake Baikal is 395 miles long and there are only four or five towns near it. The lake is a great place for sports activities. Diving, hiking, and horseback riding are all popular.

BY ROAD: **THE TRANS-SIBERIAN HIGHWAY**

Are you adventurous? Then take the new Trans-Siberian Highway. Drive your car or, for the trip of a lifetime, hitchhike with Russian drivers in their cars and trucks.

And when you finally arrive in Vladivostock, you can fly home or continue your trip. There's a boat to Japan every week.

adventurous (adj) /əd'ventʃərəs/ an *adventurous* person likes danger
(do it) in advance (exp) /ɪn əd'væns/ to do one thing before another thing
hitchhike (v) /'hɪtʃ,haɪk/ to ask a stranger for a ride
lifetime (n) /'laɪf,taɪm/ all of your life

A truck passes hitchhikers in Tuva, in central Russia.

Extra activity

Divide the class into groups according to the country that they wrote tips about in Exercise 10. Have each group create a poster for the tips. Display the posters in different areas of the classroom. Tell some group members to stay with their poster and tell others to walk around the room and "visit" the other posters. The "visiting" students must ask questions about the posters; their classmates standing with the posters answer them.

Vocabulary notes

Point out some of the collocations involving prepositions, e.g., *arrive in* + a city; *travel from* + place; *travel to* + place.

Word focus

Vocabulary notes

Take has many meanings. Here, it means *travel on* (*take a bus*), *photograph* (*take a photo*), and *carry with you* (*take a suitcase*).

Grammar

8 Ask students to look at the sentences in the grammar box. Discuss the question as a class. Refer students to the information and practice on page 167.

Grammar notes

The imperative in English is exactly the same form as the infinitive without *to*. The negative imperative is formed with *don't* + infinitive without *to*.

Writing and speaking

10 Model by providing two or three tips for your own country and reasons for them.

11 Check by asking which tips were most helpful.

HOMEWORK Ask students to do research online about a country that they would like to visit, and write a set of tips for visiting that country.

9d

At the hotel

Vocabulary

Real life

Pronunciation

9d At the hotel

Vocabulary hotel services

1 Match the hotel services (1–5) in the brochure with the explanations (a–e).

Guest services – numbers

1	room service	101
2	wake-up call	110
3	business center	109
4	laundry	111
5	medical service	112

THE MARLIN HOTEL

a a doctor or nurse 5
b something to eat in your hotel room 1
c a service to wash or clean your clothes 4
d a room with computers, printers, and Internet 3
e a telephone call to wake you 2

2 Which services do you think business travelers use? And tourists?

Real life requests

3 🔊 71 Read part of a conversation between a hotel guest and a receptionist. Match a guest's requests (1–4) with the receptionist's responses (a–d). Then listen and check your answers.

1 I'd like a wake-up call at 7:30, please. b
2 I'd like to have dinner in my room this evening. d
3 I'd like to use the Internet. c
4 Is there a bank near the hotel? a

a Yes, there's one on this street.
b In the morning? Certainly, sir.
c No problem, sir. There's wi-fi in all the rooms.
d Of course. There's a menu in your room.

4 🔊 71 Listen again and answer the questions.

1 What's the guest's room number? 327
2 Where's the menu? on the desk
3 Where's the bank? on this street, next to the movie theater

112

> **REQUESTS**
>
> **I'd like a** wake-up call at 7:30, please.
> **I'd like to** get room service.
> **I'd like to** book a taxi.
> **Certainly,** sir/ma'am.
> **Of course.**

5 Pronunciation *I'd like*

a 🔊 72 Listen and repeat three of the sentences.

b Work in pairs. Practice these requests. Use *I'd like a …* or *I'd like to … .*

breakfast in my room	use the Internet
a wake-up call	see a doctor

I'd like breakfast in my room.   *Certainly.*

6 Work in pairs.

Student A: You are a hotel guest. Make two requests and/or ask for information.

Student B: You are the hotel receptionist. Respond to the requests and/or answer the questions.

Take turns. Use the ideas in Exercise 5b and those below.

room service
book a table in the restaurant
stay an extra night
make an international phone call
a bus stop / subway station near the hotel

5b Make sure that pairs take turns being the guest and the receptionist. If needed, brainstorm possible responses for the receptionist (*Certainly, No problem, Of course,* etc.).

You may want to extend the activity by giving students these additional prompts: *call a taxi, some sandwiches, a map of the city, see the manager, a bottle of water, change my room.*

ANSWERS

I'd like breakfast in my room.
I'd like a wake-up call.
I'd like to use the Internet.
I'd like to see a doctor.

6 Give students time to prepare for their roles. Check by having several pairs role-play their conversations for the class.

9e A great place for a weekend

Writing travel advice

1 Read the advice and answer the questions.

1. What's the name of the city?
2. How can you travel there?
3. Where can you eat?
4. What can you eat?
5. What can you see?
6. What can you do?

2 Read the advice again. <u>Underline</u> four tips.

3 Writing skill **because**

a Look at the sentence from the text. Find more sentences with *because*.

*Lisbon is a great place for a vacation **because** there is a lot to see and do.*

b Rewrite these sentences with *because*.

1. Go in spring. It's very hot in summer.
2. Travel by bus. It's cheap.
3. Book your hotel in advance. It's a very popular place.

4 Make notes about a place you know. Use the questions in Exercise 1. Then write two or three paragraphs of advice for travelers to the place. Include at least one tip.

5 Check your advice. Check the spelling, the punctuation, and the verbs.

6 Work in pairs. Exchange advice. Is your partner's place a good place to travel to?

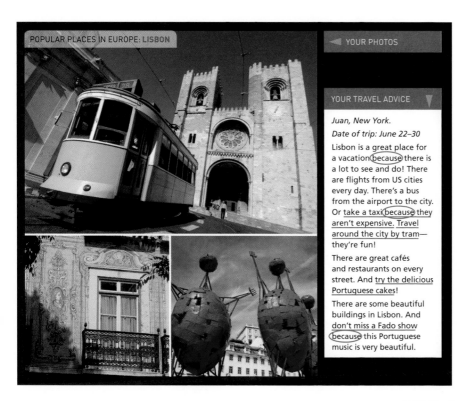

POPULAR PLACES IN EUROPE: **LISBON**

◀ YOUR PHOTOS

YOUR TRAVEL ADVICE ▼

Juan, New York.
Date of trip: June 22–30

Lisbon is a great place for a vacation(because)there is a lot to see and do! There are flights from US cities every day. There's a bus from the airport to the city. Or take a taxi(because)they aren't expensive. Travel around the city by tram—they're fun!

There are great cafés and restaurants on every street. And try the delicious Portuguese cakes!

There are some beautiful buildings in Lisbon. And don't miss a Fado show(because)this Portuguese music is very beautiful.

---

4 If students come from different places, they could write about their home city. If they come from the same place, ask them to write about a city they have visited or a city that they used to live in.

Give students three or four minutes to make notes to answer the questions. Monitor and help with ideas.

HOMEWORK Ask students to write travel advice for a visitor who wants to come to their home town.

A great place for a weekend

Warm-up

Introducing the theme: Lisbon

Write *Lisbon* on the board and tell students to write anything they know about the place on the board. They can write facts or opinions, e.g., *It's a city. It's in Portugal. It's beautiful. There is a castle.* Read aloud the sentences, and ask any students who know the city to tell the class about it.

Writing

Background notes

Lisbon (or *Lisboa* in Portuguese) is the capital city of Portugal. It is on the Tagus River on the Atlantic coast. Its most famous sites include the Belem Tower, the Jeronimos Monastery, and elegant squares. It is a major international port.

Fado is a melancholy type of music that dates back to the early nineteenth century. It is Portugal's national music.

1 ANSWERS

1. Lisbon
2. flights, bus, taxi, tram
3. cafés and restaurants
4. Portuguese cakes
5. beautiful buildings, Fado music show
6. take the tram, listen to Fado

2 Remind students that we use the imperative to give advice.

Writing skill

3a Read the example as a class. Point out how *because* joins two clauses and gives a reason.

3B ANSWERS

1. *Go in spring because it's very hot in summer.*
2. *Travel by bus because it's cheap.*
3. *Book your hotel in advance because it's a very popular place.*

Along the Inca Road

Videoscript

Narrator: Karin Muller is in South America. She's in a village in Ecuador and there's a market today.

Karin buys some food before she starts her trip.

It's day one on Karin's trip. They walk along the mountain track. There's something unusual. Two helicopters fly above them.

Then there's a very loud bang. One of the helicopters crashes.

The men are OK.

Karin helps them with their things.

There are many ways to travel through South America: by canoe, hitchhiking, by truck, on foot.

And there are many people to meet with their donkeys, horses, and of course, llamas.

The Inca Road takes Karin from Ecuador to Chile on one long adventure.

A woman walks along an ancient Inca road.

114

Before you watch

1 The Inca road goes through Ecuador, Peru, Bolivia, Chile, and Argentina. How old is it? Choose the correct option (a–c).

a 50 years old   ⓑ 500 years old
c 5,000 years old

2 Work in pairs. Read the introduction to the video. What things do you think you can see or do on a trip along the Inca Road?

Along the Inca Road

Karin Muller is an American adventurer and writer. She is on a trip through South America to explore the cultures and people along the Inca Road. She travels more than 3,000 miles through four countries. Her adventure begins in Ecuador.

While you watch

3 Watch the video and mark (✓) what you see.

a plane	a truck ✓
a donkey ✓	a bus ✓
a camel	a sheep ✓
a helicopter ✓	a horse ✓
a bicycle	a llama ✓
a canoe ✓	a train

4 Watch the video again. Choose the correct option or options (a–c).

1 Where does Karin start her trip?
   a in the United States
   b in Peru
   ⓒ in Ecuador

2 What can you buy at the village market?
   ⓐ animals   ⓑ snacks   ⓒ vegetables

3 Where does Karin walk on day 1?
   a across a desert
   b along a beach
   ⓒ through mountains

4 How does Karin travel?
   ⓐ hitchhiking   b by train   ⓒ on foot

5 Who does Karin meet?
   ⓐ farmers   ⓑ passengers   ⓒ tourists

5 Watch the video again. Mark these sentences true (T) or false (F).

1 There's a young boy at the market. T
2 There are three fish on Karin's plate. F
3 The tent is orange and blue. T
4 There's a woman on the road when Karin hitchhikes. T
5 There's a man in a blue shirt at the bus stop. T
6 On the beach, Karin wears a hat. T

After you watch

6 Match the two parts of the sentences about Karin.

1 She goes canoeing   a a lot of people.
2 She rides   b across sand dunes.
3 She walks   c in a river.
4 She meets   d in the back of a truck.

7 Work in pairs. Have two conversations:

1 At the market food stall

Student A: You are Karin. Ask about the food.

Student B: You are the stall holder.

> What's this?   It's fish.

2 Meeting people on a trip

Student A: You are the helicopter pilot.

Student B: You are Karin.

> Hi. I'm ... . Nice to meet you.   Hello. ...

ancient (adj) /ˈeɪnʃənt/ very very old

a bang (n) /bæŋ/ very loud noise

a canoe (n) /kəˈnuː/

crash (v) /kræʃ/

a donkey (n) /ˈdɒŋki/

gold (n) /ɡoʊld/ a metal in jewelry

a goldmine (n) /ˈɡoʊldˌmaɪn/ a place to find gold

a landmine (n) /ˈlændˌmaɪn/ a type of bomb

a llama (n) /ˈlɑːmə/

loud (adj) /laʊd/ very noisy

a plate (n) /pleɪt/

a sand dune (n) /ˈsænd ˌduːn/

a sheep (n) /ʃiːp/

a track (n) /træk/

Before you watch

1 Ask students to look at the photo. Ask: *What can you see? Where is she?* You may also want to find the countries which the Inca road system goes through, on a map.

Ask students: *How old is this road?* Put students in pairs to make predictions. Check answer as a class.

2 Put students in pairs. Give them some time to read the introduction to the video and answer the question. Accept all possible answers.

While you watch

3 Play the entire video without sound. Students watch and mark the things they see. Check answers as a class.

4 Give students some time to read the questions. Play the video with the sound. Students watch, listen, and choose the correct option or options. Point out that there might be more than one answer.

5 Give students some time to read the sentences and decide if they are true or false. Then play the video again for them to check their answers. You may want to have them correct the false information.

After you watch

6 Students match the two parts of the sentences. You may want to check the answers in the form of a game. Demonstrate the game by asking one of the students to read the first part of the first sentence. Elicit the second part of the first sentence. Students in pairs take turns to finish the sentences.

You may also want to set this activity as a chain game or put students in groups of three or four.

7 Put students in pairs. Give them some time to prepare the conversations. Check by asking a few pairs to role-play the conversations.

Grammar

1 Ask students to look at the photo and complete the questions with *is there / are there*.

> **ANSWERS**
> **1** Is there
> **2** Are there
> **3** Are there
> **4** Is there

2 Divide the class into pairs. Students take turns to ask and answer the questions in Exercise 1.

3 Students read the sentences and look at the photo. They change the false sentences so that they are true.

> **ANSWERS**
> **1** F, There is a map.
> **2** T
> **3** T
> **4** F, There is a pair of boots.

4 Students put the words in order to form complete sentences.

> **ANSWERS**
> **1** Don't be late.
> **2** Wait a moment.
> **3** Don't travel at night.
> **4** Try the local cafés.
> **5** Don't stay in this hotel.

Vocabulary

5 Students read the sentences and decide which options are not logical.

6 Students match the two parts to make sentences about a hotel room.

7 Students complete the sentences with the verbs.

> **ANSWERS**
> **1** book
> **2** arrives
> **3** take
> **4** leaves
> **5** stay
> **6** visit

UNIT 9 REVIEW

Grammar

1 Look at the photo. Write questions with *is there / are there*?

1 _____ a map?
2 _____ books?
3 _____ tickets?
4 _____ a passport?

2 Work in pairs. Ask and answer the questions in Exercise 1. Take turns.

3 Are these sentences true (T) or false (F)? Change the false sentences so they are true.

1 There isn't a map.
2 There's a bottle of water.
3 There are some books.
4 There isn't a pair of boots.

4 Put the words in order.

1 late / be / don't
2 moment / a / wait
3 night / travel / don't / at
4 cafés / try / local / the
5 stay / hotel / this / don't / in

> **I CAN**
> use *there is* and *there are* correctly ☐
> give instructions (imperative forms) ☐

Vocabulary

5 Read the sentences. Which item doesn't belong?

1 In cold weather, I wear ⟨a pair of sandals⟩ / a coat / a pair of boots / a hat.
2 In hot weather, I wear a T-shirt / a pair of sandals / a skirt / ⟨a jacket⟩.
3 At home, I wear a sweater / ⟨a scarf⟩ / a pair of jeans / a top.
4 In the office, I wear a pair of pants / ⟨a T-shirt⟩ / a shirt / a pair of shoes.

 116

---

6 Match the two columns to make sentences.

1 There's a tourist information brochure *a*
2 Is there one bed *b*
3 You can put these bottles *d*
4 There's an armchair, *e*
5 Is there a shower *c*

a on the table.
b or two?
c in the bathroom.
d in the fridge.
e but there isn't a sofa.

7 Complete the sentences with the verbs.

arrives	book	leaves	stay	take	visit

1 We usually _____ our tickets online.
2 The train _____ in Kyoto at midnight.
3 We can _____ a bus to the airport.
4 Our plane _____ Kyoto at 10:20.
5 We often _____ in cheap hotels.
6 We usually _____ the museums.

> **I CAN**
> talk about clothes ☐
> talk about furniture ☐
> talk about travel ☐
> talk about hotel services ☐

Real life

8 Complete the requests (1–4) in a hotel. Then match the requests with the responses (a–d).

breakfast	room service	stay	use

1 I'd like to ___use___ the Internet. *d*
2 I'd like _breakfast_ at 7:30 a.m., please. *a*
3 I'd like to ___stay___ an extra night. *c*
4 I'd like _room service_ *b*

a The restaurant opens at 7:00 a.m.
b Of course. The number is 101.
c Certainly, sir. What's your name?
d Of course. There's wi-fi in your room.

> **I CAN**
> make and respond to requests ☐
> ask for and give information ☐

Speaking

9 Work in groups. You work in your town's tourist information center. What is there for visitors to do and to see? List at least six things and say where they are.

Real life

8 Students complete the requests (1–4) in a hotel. Then they match the requests with the responses (a–d).

Speaking

9 Divide the class into groups. Tell each group to prepare a list of at least six things to do in the town and say where they are. Ask each group to give a short presentation to the class.

Invention of color television.
Photo by Willard Culver

FEATURES

118 Explorers

"Firsts" in exploration

120 Heroes

Who was your hero?

122 The first Americans

The first people on the American continents

126 The space race

A video about the history of space exploration

1 Work in pairs. Do you know this invention? What does it do?

2 🔊 73 Can you match the invention with the years? Listen and check your answers.

Year	Invention
1950	Blu-ray discs
1963	color television
1973	digital cameras
1975	digital television
1993	cell phones
1995	MP3 players
2006	video recorders

3 Work in pairs. Choose and write five years in a list. Dictate them to your partner. Then compare your lists.

History

Warm-up

Using words: review of numbers 0–1,000

Write between ten and fifteen numbers in random order on the board. Choose some that are often confused, e.g., 15 and 50, 13 and 30, 100 and 1,000, etc. Divide the class into two teams and ask a student from each team to come up to the board. Call out a number. The first student to touch the correct number wins a point for their team.

1 Ask students to look at the photo and ask: *Who are they? Where are they?* Elicit ideas. Check comprehension of *invention*. Then divide the class into pairs to answer the questions.

SAMPLE ANSWERS

television; It gets images and sounds that are sent by television.

2 Have students read through the lists and try to match the items. Then play the audio so that they can check their answers.

Vocabulary notes

With the years up to 1999 and from 2010, the year is read as pairs of digits:

1996 = nineteen ninety-six

1806 = eighteen "oh" six

2012 = twenty twelve

From 2000 to 2009, years are pronounced like ordinary cardinal numbers:

2000 = two thousand

2003 = two thousand three

3 Students choose and write five years, then dictate them to a partner. Then students compare their lists.

Extra activity

For additional practice saying years aloud, write a list of important years on the board and call on volunteers to say the year and why it is famous. Examples: 1969, man goes to the Moon; 1492, Columbus arrives in America; etc.

Follow up by asking students important years in their own lives that they will likely need practice reciting; their years of birth, graduation, etc.

This topic may need periodic reinforcement for students to master.

Explorers

Warm-up

Introducing the theme

Write *explorers* on the board and explain or elicit the meaning (people who travel and study new lands). Ask: *What can you explore?* and write the students' ideas on the board, e.g., *mountains, new countries, space.* Ask the students if they know any famous explorers from their country.

Reading and listening

1 Ask students to look at the photo while they cover the caption with one hand. Ask: *What can you see? Where are they?* and elicit ideas. Then ask students to read the caption and check their answers.

2 Begin by reading through the names of the explorers with students. Then complete the first sentence as a class.

ANSWERS

Ferdinand Magellan

Roald Amundsen

Yuri Gagarin

Valentina Tereshkova

Junko Tabei

Ann Bancroft

3 Pre-teach *was born* and *king.* Have students read through the items, and then play the audio.

ANSWERS

1 Junko Tabei
2 Ferdinand Magellan
3 Ann Bancroft
4 Roald Amundsen

The first American expedition on Everest in 1963
Photo by National Geographic expedition photographer and writer Barry Bishop

Reading and listening

1 Look at the photo of the mountaineers. Where are they? Read the caption and check your answer. Everest

2 Complete the quiz. Check your answers with your instructor.

captain (n) /'kæptɪn/ a leader or commander
expedition (n) /ˌekspə'dɪʃən/ a trip with scientists and/or explorers

North Pole (n) /'nɔrθ 'poʊl/
South Pole (n) /'saʊθ 'poʊl/
around the world (exp) /ə'raʊnd ðə 'wɜrld/
space (n) /speɪs/

Explorers Quiz: historical moments

Do you know these famous explorers?

- The first expedition around the world was from 1519 to 1522. The expedition captain was _____ .
- The first successful South Pole expedition was in 1911. The expedition leader was _____ .
- The first man in space was _____ . The first woman in space was _____ . They were both from Russia.
- On May 16, 1975, _____ was the first woman to reach the top of Everest.
- The first woman to reach the North Pole was _____ on May 1, 1986.

Ferdinand Magellan   Yuri Gagarin   Roald Amundsen

Junko Tabei   Ann Bancroft   Valentina Tereshkova

118

Grammar

Grammar notes

Was and *were* are the past forms of *am, is,* and *are,* and are used to describe permanent and temporary states in the past: *He was an explorer. / She was born in 1955.*

The negative forms are *wasn't* and *weren't* (full forms are *was not* and *were not*).

The question forms are *was he/she…?* or *were they/we…?* The short answers are *Yes, he/she was. No, he/she wasn't. Yes, they were. / No, they weren't.*

When we talk about when things happened, we don't use an article with the year: *in 1679.*

To talk about the year when something happened, we use *in,* e.g., *Yuri Gagarin was born in 1934.*

To talk about the dates when something happened, we use *on,* e.g., *I was born on April 12, 1961.*

3 🔊 **74** Listen. Then match the texts with four of the people from the quiz.

1 She <u>was</u> born in 1939. She <u>was</u> in a team of Japanese mountaineers. They <u>were</u> all women.

2 He <u>was</u> born in 1480. He <u>was</u> Portuguese, but he <u>was</u> an explorer for the Spanish King Carlos I.

3 She <u>was</u> born in the United States on September 29, 1955. She <u>was</u> the leader of an expedition to the South Pole in 1993. The expedition <u>was</u> all women.

4 He <u>was</u> from Norway and he <u>was</u> born on July 16, 1872. His father <u>was</u> a sea captain.

Grammar *was/were*

4 Look at the past forms of *be* in the grammar box. <u>Underline</u> these forms in the texts in Exercise 3.

▶ WAS/WERE		
I/He/She/It	**was**	born in 1480. an explorer.
You/We/You/They	**were**	explorers. from Russia.

For more information and practice, see page 167.

5 Pronunciation *was/were* weak forms

a 🔊 **75** Listen and repeat.

b Complete the sentences. Read them to your partner. What do you have in common?

1 I _____ born in _____ [place].
2 My father _____ born in _____ [year].
3 My mother _____ born in _____ [year].

6 Complete the paragraphs with *was* and *were*.

Yuri Gagarin ¹ _was_ born in 1934. His parents ² _were_ farmers. From 1955 to 1961, he ³ _was_ a pilot. The first space rockets ⁴ _were_ small and so the first people in space ⁵ _were_ small too. Gagarin ⁶ _was_ a small man—five foot and one inch (1.57 m).

Valentina Tereshkova ⁷ _was_ born in 1937 in central Russia. Her parents ⁸ _were_ from Belarus. She ⁹ _was_ a factory worker. After their trips into space, on April 12, 1961, and June 16, 1963, Gagarin and Tereshkova ¹⁰ _were_ famous all over the world.

Vocabulary dates

7 Look at the table. Complete it with information from the quiz.

Important dates in exploration	
May 1st, 1986	first woman at the North Pole
June 2nd, 1953	news of first men on Everest
November 3rd, 1957	Sputnik II into space
October 4th, 1957	Sputnik I into space
5th / 6th / 7th / 8th / 9th / 10th / 11th	
April 12th, 1961	first man in space
December 13th, 1972	last man on the Moon
December 14th, 1911	first people at the South Pole
15th	
May 16th, 1975	first woman on Everest
17th / 18th / 19th	
July 20th, 1969	first men on the Moon

8 🔊 **76** Listen and repeat the ordinal numbers.

9 🔊 **77** Say these ordinal numbers. Then listen and check.

21st	22nd	23rd	24th	25th	26th
27th	28th	29th	30th	31st	

Speaking

10 Work in pairs. What are three important dates in your country?

> *September 16th is Independence Day.*

11 Work in pairs.

Student A: Dictate five important dates from your past to your partner.

Student B: Say the dates.

Student A: Say why the dates are important.

> *the first of September 1990*

> *It was my first day of school.*

Unit 10 History 119

Pronunciation

Pronunciation notes

Was and *were* have weak pronunciation in affirmative sentences and are pronounced with *schwa* sounds.

5b Model the activity by doing the first sentence yourself, e.g., *I was born in 1978 in the US.*

Extra activity

Do a chain activity. Have a student read aloud their completed item 1 from Exercise 5b. The next person repeats the sentence and adds their own, e.g., *Carlos was born in Spain, and I was born in Italy.* Continue the chain. At the end, you may want to sum up the information in one sentence and write it on board, e.g., *Eight people were born in Spain, two people were born in France...*

Vocabulary

Vocabulary notes

Ordinal numbers in English are so called because they tell us the order of events. They are also used to say dates.

First, second, third are ordinal numbers for numbers one, two, three. After that, the ordinal numbers are formed with number + *th*. Also, we say *twenty-first, twenty-second, twenty-third,* and NOT *twenty-oneth,* etc.

We use *last* at the end of a sequence of things. It means the final one, and it's not an ordinal number.

8 Ask students to look at the table in Exercise 7 again. Explain that 1st is short for *first*, and 16th is short for *sixteenth*. Play the audio; students listen and repeat. Play the audio again pausing after problem numbers, e.g., fourth, fifth, sixth, eighth, twelfth, and drill the pronunciation.

Pronunciation notes

In ordinal numbers, *th* is pronounced like /θ/ and is unvoiced. Ordinal numbers are often preceded by the article *the*.

Vocabulary notes

Students may encounter other ways of saying and writing dates, e.g., *the twenty-second of September* or *September the twenty-second*.

Speaking

Extra activity

Use Exercise 11 to play a memory game. Ask students to read aloud the important dates; write them on the board in random order. Then call out any date. The students try to remember who said this date and why it was important.

HOMEWORK Ask students to prepare a quiz on important dates in the history of their country.

▬ 10b Heroes

Warm-up

Using words: review of job-related vocabulary

Write three questions on the board: *What do you do? What does your father/mother do? What does your best friend do?* and have students ask and answer them in pairs. Write all the answers on the board. Produce a "top 5" list of popular professions in the class.

Reading and listening

1 Ask students to look at the photos, and write on the board: *Who are they? Where are they?* Role-play the example conversation with a student.

2 Check the meaning of *hero* by talking about one or two of your heroes. Ask: *Who was your hero when you were young?*

> **ANSWERS**
>
> 1 March 13–18 7:30 PM
> 2 their heroes
> 3 Aneta, Joe, Clare
> 4 Aneta: Michael Johnson; Joe: David Attenborough; Clare: her teachers, Peter and Rose Harvey

5 After checking answers, ask students what else they remember from the audio.

Grammar

> **Grammar notes**
>
> The verb *be* is sometimes an auxiliary verb (*He was born in…* ; *He wasn't playing…*) and sometimes a linking verb (*He was world champion*).
>
> It's irregular and conjugates differently from other verbs. Make it's important to make sure students are confident when manipulating these forms before moving on to *did* and *didn't* and regular past forms.
>
> Note that with short answers, we just use the linking verb. Students may make the mistake of saying, for example, *Yes, I happy*.

Reading and listening

1 Work in pairs. Look at the photos of the people. What do you know about them?

> Who's this?
>
> I'm not sure. I think he's an athlete.

2 Read the information about the radio show *Heroes*. Answer the questions.

1 When is the show on the radio?
2 What do the people on the show talk about?
3 Who is on the show today?
4 Who were their heroes?

David Attenborough

107.1 WFNX 7:30 p.m. March 13–18

Peter and Rose Harvey

Michael Johnson

Heroes

Who is a hero?

In this program, we talk to people about their heroes. Today we hear about Aneta's hero, the Olympic champion Michael Johnson. Joe's hero wasn't happy in his first job, but is now the television star David Attenborough. We also talk to Clare. Her heroes weren't famous, but they were important to her. They were her teachers at college.

> **ANSWERS**
>
> We make the negative form by adding the contracted form of not (wasn't, weren't). We make the question form by inverting was or were and the subject (Was he…? Were they…?).

Pronunciation

7a Ask students to look through the sentences and think about how the strong forms might be pronounced. Then play the audio.

> **Pronunciation notes**
>
> Note that, while the stress on these words is weak in the affirmative form, it is strong in the negative, question, and short answer form.

3 🔊 **78** Complete the sentences with these words. Then listen to the show and check.

> art   eight   first   funny   great   interesting

1 He was a _great_ athlete.
2 He was the world champion _eight_ times.
3 His _first_ job was with books.
4 All his shows were really _interesting_
5 Mrs. Harvey was my _art_ teacher.
6 She was very _funny_ .

4 🔊 **78** Listen again. Choose the correct answer.

1 Was he the Olympic champion?
   (Yes, he was.)/ No, he wasn't.
2 Were you good at sports in school?
   (Yes, I was.)/ No, I wasn't.
3 Was it his first job?
   Yes, it was. /(No, it wasn't.)
4 Were you born then?
   Yes, I was. /(No, I wasn't.)
5 Were they good teachers?
   (Yes, they were.)/ No, they weren't.

5 What can you remember? Write Aneta, Joe, or Clare.

1 _Clare_ 's heroes weren't famous.
2 _Aneta_ was on the basketball team at school.
3 _Joe_ 's favorite show was *Life on Earth*.

Grammar *was/were* negative and question forms

6 Look at the grammar box. How do we make the negative and question forms of *was* and *were*?

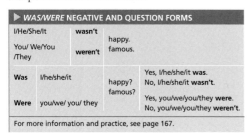

> ▶ **WAS/WERE NEGATIVE AND QUESTION FORMS**

I/He/She/It	**wasn't**	happy.
You/ We/You /They	**weren't**	famous.

Was	I/he/she/it	happy? famous?	Yes, I/he/she/it **was**. No, I/he/she/it **wasn't**.
Were	you/we/ you/ they		Yes, you/we/you/they **were**. No, you/we/you/they **weren't**.

For more information and practice, see page 167.

7 **Pronunciation strong forms**

a 🔊 **79** Listen and repeat.

1 <u>Was</u> he the Olympic champion?
   Yes, he <u>was</u>.
2 <u>Was</u> it his first job?
   No, it <u>wasn't</u>.
3 <u>Were</u> they good teachers?
   Yes, they <u>were</u>.

b 🔊 **79** Listen again. Are the <u>underlined</u> words weak or strong? _strong_

8 Write questions with *was* or *were*.

1 Michael Johnson / on TV / ?
2 your hero / David Attenborough / ?
3 your parents / famous / ?
4 you / happy at school / ?
5 your teachers / friendly / ?
6 you / good at sports / ?

9 Work in pairs. Think about when you were young. Ask and answer the questions in Exercise 8.

Vocabulary **describing people**

10 Work in pairs. Think of a person you both know for each word.

> famous   friendly   good
> happy   interesting nice

Speaking

11 Write the answers to these questions about two heroes from your past.

- Who was he/she?
- Was he/she on television? famous? a teacher? a … ?
- Why was he/she your hero?

12 Work in groups. Write the names from Exercise 11 on pieces of paper. Mix them. Take turns to read a name. Ask and answer the questions about the names.

> Who was Jill Roberts?

> She was my first boss.

8 ANSWERS

1 Was Michael Johnson on TV?
2 Was your hero David Attenborough?
3 Were your parents famous?
4 Were you happy at school?
5 Were your teachers friendly?
6 Were you good at sports?

9 Monitor and check that students are using the questions and short forms correctly.

Vocabulary

Pronunciation notes

Note the strong stress: *famous, friendly, interesting.*

Speaking

11 Ask students to prepare answers to the questions individually. Students might not realize at first that heroes do not necessarily need to be historical or famous people; they can be friends, family members, teachers, etc. Model the activity by giving them two heroes of your own: one famous, and one whom you know personally. Supply additional vocabulary as needed, e.g., *boss, neighbor, best friend*, etc.

12 Encourage students to ask follow-up questions.

HOMEWORK Ask students to write about their childhood hero.

The first Americans

Warm-up

Introducing the theme: native peoples and native Americans

Bring in a few pictures of objects related to the theme, e.g., feathers, a wigwam, wooden carvings, baskets, etc. Have pairs of students talk about what they are (in their own words) and what connects them. Elicit ideas and elicit the theme of the lesson.

Reading

1 Accept and discuss any answers at this stage.

Extra activity

If your students come from a variety of countries, have them prepare short presentations on important leaders of native cultures from their countries. Have them use these sentence starters:

… was important because…

He/She was born in…

He/She was a war/political hero because…

3 ANSWERS

1 Last Inca leader
2 west and south N America
3 June 16, 1829
4 Apache war hero

Vocabulary

5 ANSWERS

Present: today, now
Past: ago, at that time

Grammar notes

These expressions are used at the start or end of sentences.

Ago is used with a period of time (e.g., *ten minutes ago, a thousand years ago*).

10c The first Americans

Reading

1 Mark these sentences as true (T) or false (F).

1 The Inca Empire was in North America. F
2 The Maya people were from Central America. T
3 The Aztecs were from Peru. F
4 The Sioux people were from South America. F

2 Read the first paragraph of the article. Check your answers from Exercise 1.

3 Read the rest of the article. Answer the questions.

1 Who was Tupac Amaru?
2 Where were the Apache people from?
3 When was Geronimo born?
4 Why was Geronimo famous?

4 Who were the leaders in your country's history?

Vocabulary **time expressions**

5 <u>Underline</u> these words and expressions in the article. Do they use verbs in the present or past form?

today	ago	at that time	now

6 Complete the sentences with words and expressions from Exercise 5. In two sentences, more than one word is possible.

1 About two hundred years ___ago___ Geronimo was born.
2 _Today/Now_ people know the name "Geronimo."
3 _Today/Now_ the Maya people live in Mexico.
4 _At that time_, the Native Americans and the US were at war.

7 Word focus *first*

a Look at the sentences. Is *first* a date (D) or a number (N)?

1 The first man in space was Yuri Gagarin. N
2 Why was the first of May 1986 important? D
3 The first American expedition to Everest was in 1963. N

b Work in pairs. Ask and answer the questions.

1 Who was your first best friend?
2 When was your first day of school?
3 Where was your first job?
4 Who was your first boss?

Speaking

8 Look at these people. Are they from North America or South America?

George Washington N   Tupac Amaru S

Hillary Clinton N   Pocahontas N

Simón Bolívar S   Robert E. Lee N

9 Now work in two pairs in a group of four. Talk about famous Americans.

Pair A: Turn to page 156.

Pair B: Turn to page 160.

Extra activity

Write the following on the board:

1 Today, … but in the past, …

2 Years ago, … but now, …

Ask students to think of two differences between now and the past, and to write complete sentences using the prompts. Ask them to read aloud their sentences.

Word focus

Extra activity

Ask students to write sentences about other firsts: CD, book, job, word in English, etc.

THE FIRST AMERICANS

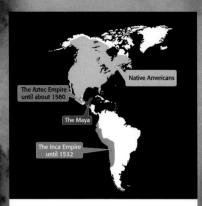

The Aztec Empire until about 1580
Native Americans
The Maya
The Inca Empire until 1532

Geronimo: Apache hero
June 16, 1829 – February 17, 1909

Today there are 23 countries in North, Central, and South America. But five hundred years ago, a large area of South America, including Peru, was part of the Inca Empire. In Central America and Mexico, the Maya people were important. The Aztec empire also ruled in Mexico. In North America, there were different groups in different areas, for example, the Apache, Navajo, and Sioux. Today the name for these different groups is Native Americans. The leaders of these people are still famous today; for example, the last Inca leader Tupac Amaru, the Aztec emperor Moctezuma, and the Apache war hero, Geronimo.

The Apache people were from the south and west of North America. Geronimo was the grandson of an important Apache leader. He was born on June 16, 1829. When Geronimo was a young man, there was a war between Mexico and the US, and the Native Americans. At that time, his family's land was part of Mexico. Now, it's part of the US.

Geronimo was an Apache war hero. From 1886 until 1909 he was a prisoner of war. But he was also a famous celebrity. He was with President Theodore Roosevelt on March 4, 1905, his first day as president.

celebrity (n) /sɪˈlebrɪti/ a person famous in their lifetime
land (n) /lænd/ area or nation
war (n) /wɔr/ conflict. For example: World War I, 1914–1918.

Speaking

Background notes

George Washington (1732–1799) was the first president of the US.

Hillary Clinton is a Democratic politician, the wife of former president Bill Clinton, and was Secretary of State during the first Obama administration.

Pocahontas (1595–1617) was the daughter of a Native American chief in Virginia during the early years of British colonization. She married an English settler and traveled to England.

Simón Bolívar (1783–1830) was a military and political leader who played a key role in the Latin American struggle for independence from Spain. He led Venezuela, Colombia, Ecuador, Peru, and Bolivia to independence. He was president of Venezuela, and remains a national hero there.

Robert E. Lee (1807–1870) was a general who commanded the Confederate Army during the US Civil War.

HOMEWORK Tell students to write a description of a famous person from the American continents that they know and admire.

Language notes

Take a few moments to clear up the naming conventions surrounding the Americas and the people from them.

Point out to the students that the word *American* has multiple accepted meanings. With respect to a person, it is most commonly understood to mean a person was born in or is a citizen of the United States of America. However, it can also refer to a person from anywhere in North, Central, or South America, including indigenous people (Native Americans). This second definition may already be familiar to Spanish speakers.

Students may hear the term *America* used as a synonym for the United States of America. However, this usage is not correct. *America* is actually a geographical term that can refer to either North or South America. The two continents and their associate islands are collectively known as *the Americas*. The United States of America can be referred to by its full name, the *US*, the *USA*, or, more informally, as *the States*, but not as *America*.

10d

I'm sorry

Vocabulary

1 Drill the words for pronunciation, pointing out the stress in *asleep* and *busy*.

2 Monitor and check that students are using the forms correctly.

Real life

Pronunciation

5b Have pairs role-play the conversations in Exercise 4. Tell them to pay attention to word stress.

6 If needed, allow students to write new conversations first before role-playing.

10d I'm sorry

Vocabulary activities

1 Match the photos (a–f) with the words.

At nine o'clock yesterday I was … .

1	asleep *b*	4	in traffic *e*
2	at home *f*	5	sick *d*
3	busy *c*	6	on the phone *a*

2 Work in pairs. Ask and answer questions.

> Were you at home at nine o'clock yesterday?

> Yes, I was.

Real life apologizing

3 🔊 80 Listen to three conversations. Write the number of the conversation (1–3) next to the places.

a in a café 3   b in a classroom 1   c in an office 2

4 🔊 80 Listen again. Complete the conversations with expressions for APOLOGIZING.

1
S: Hi, I'm sorry I'm late. ¹ _The bus was late._
T: That's OK. Take a seat.

2
R: Umm, the meeting was at 2:30. Where were you?
C: Oh, I'm sorry. ² _I was very busy._
R: ³ _It's OK._ It wasn't an important meeting.

3
A: So, what about yesterday? We were at your house at ten o'clock. Where were you?
B: I'm very sorry. ⁴ _We weren't at home._ We were at my sister's house!
A: It's OK. ⁵ _Don't worry._

> **▶ APOLOGIZING**
>
> | | |
> |---|---|
> | I'm (very) sorry. | We weren't at home. |
> | I'm sorry I'm late. | It's OK. |
> | The bus was late. | That's OK. |
> | I was (very) busy. | Don't worry. |

5 Pronunciation sentence stress

a 🔊 81 Listen and repeat these sentences. Underline the word with the main stress.

1 I'm <u>sorry</u> I'm late.   3 I was <u>very</u> busy.
2 The <u>bus</u> was late.   4 We <u>weren't</u> at <u>home</u>.

b Work in pairs. Practice the conversations.

6 Work in pairs. Practice the conversations again. Use the vocabulary in Exercise 1.

> Hello.

> Hi, I'm sorry I'm late. I was in traffic.

> That's OK.

10e Childhood memories

Writing a blog

1 Work in pairs. Ask and answer the questions.

1 Do you read blogs? What about?
2 Do you write a blog? What about?

2 Answer the questions.

1 When and where was Tyler born?
2 Where was his family's house?
3 What was his favorite toy?
4 Who were his friends?

3 What information does he give about these things?

1 his parents and family
2 his house
3 his toys
4 his friends

4 Writing skill *when*

a Complete these sentences from the blog.

1 When I was a child, <u>we weren't rich.</u>
2 When I was ten, <u>my best friends were Jack and Nathan.</u>

b Find two more sentences with *when*.

c Rewrite these sentences as one sentence with *when*. Don't forget the comma.

1 My parents were young. They weren't rich.
2 My father was a student. He was poor.
3 I was a child. I was happy.
4 I was three. My sister was born.

5 Make notes about your childhood. Answer the questions in Exercise 2 for yourself. Make notes about the things in Exercise 3.

6 Use your notes and write two or three paragraphs about your childhood memories. Include a sentence with *When*.

7 Check your blog. Check the spelling, the punctuation, and the verbs.

8 Work in pairs. Exchange blogs. Find one surprising thing in your partner's blog. Ask two questions about his or her childhood.

MY CHILDHOOD MEMORIES

Tyler Sanford

I was born on July 4, 1990, in Texas. My parents were teachers. When I was a child, we weren't rich. Our house was in a small town. It wasn't a big house. My family was small: me, my parents, and my grandfather. My grandfather was old. He was kind and funny. <u>But when he wasn't well, he wasn't happy.</u>

I remember my favorite toy. It was a helicopter. It was a present from my grandfather. And I remember my first bicycle. It was red and it was fantastic. My friend Jack's bike was blue. When I was ten, my best friends were Jack and Nathan. They were in my class at school. We were bored at school. <u>But when we were on vacation, it was great.</u> We were typical boys!

---

3 ANSWERS

1 small family, old grandfather, kind, funny, not rich
2 in a small town, not big
3 favorite is a helicopter, remembers first bicycle
4 best friends were Nathan and Jack, bored at school, fun on vacation

Writing skill

4C ANSWERS

1 When my parents were young, they weren't rich.
2 When my father was a student, he was poor.
3 When I was a child, I was happy.
4 When I was three, my sister was born.

Extra activity

Put students' blogs on the classroom walls. Ask students to walk around, read each other's blogs, and write comments.

HOMEWORK Ask students to write a short biography of their favorite historical character.

Childhood memories

Warm-up

Introducing the theme: blogs

Bring in a large sheet of paper and have a class blog for the day. Write the first post:

CLASS BLOG

Well, here I am in class. I love teaching! And it's time for a lesson about blogs.

(Carla)

Hold up the paper and tell students to pass it around and contribute to it during the lesson. They can write a comment on the class or about learning English, and must put their name. At the end of the lesson, put the blog on the wall for students to read.

Writing

Background notes

A blog (short for *web log*) is a discussion site or information site on the web on which the blogger writes entries (called *posts*) which are displayed in reverse order. Blogs can be written by individuals in the form of a series of diary entries, or they can be multi-author blogs; often these are professionally edited.

2 Ask students to look at the photo of Tyler. Ask: *Where is he from? How old is he?* Elicit ideas. Ask students to say what they want to find out about his life and his family. Students read the blog and answer the questions.

ANSWERS

1 July 4, 1990, in Texas
2 small town in Texas
3 helicopter
4 Jack and Nathan

The space race

Videoscript

Narrator: <u>John F. Kennedy, the president of the United States,</u> in 1961.

In the 1950s and 1960s, there was a race between the United States and the Soviet Union—the space race.

Kennedy's famous speech about space was on May 25th, 1961. <u>Alan Shepard was the first American in space</u>, on May 5th, 1961.

But he wasn't the first person in space. That was the Russian, Yuri Gagarin.

<u>Sputnik was the first satellite.</u> It was part of the Soviet Union's space program in 1957.

On April 12th, 1961, the Soviet Union was the first country to send a person into space.

In the United States, Alan Shepard, John Glenn, Gus Grissom, and four more astronauts were part of the <u>Mercury program</u>.

<u>John Glenn was the first American to orbit the Earth</u>, on February 20th, 1962.

The next goal was <u>to put a man on the Moon. This was the Apollo program</u>.

There was a tragedy on January 27th, 1967, when there was a fire on Apollo 1. Three astronauts, including Gus Grissom, died.

On July 20th, 1969, there was success for Apollo 11.

For the first time in history, there were men on the Moon. The first man was Neil Armstrong and the second was Buzz Aldrin.

The next American space program was the Shuttle program.

There were also tragedies on this program, in 1986 with the <u>Challenger shuttle and in 2003 with the Columbia shuttle</u>. The

The first American in space

126

shuttle was also part of the International Space Station program. <u>This is a program by the United States, Russia, Canada, Japan, and Europe</u>.

Before you watch

1 Work in pairs. What do you know about the space race? Discuss.

2 Work in pairs. How many astronauts can you name? Where were they from?

While you watch

3 Watch the video without sound. How many times do you see these things?
a: more than 10   b: about 6

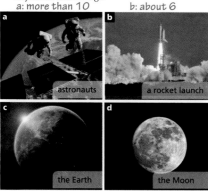
a   astronauts
b   a rocket launch
c   the Earth
d   the Moon

c: 3   d: 2

4 Watch the video. Check your answers from Exercise 1.

5 Work in pairs. Match the dates with the events.

Date	Event
1957	fire on Apollo 1
April 12, 1961	men on the Moon
May 5, 1961	Sputnik in space
February 20, 1962	the first American in space
January 27, 1967	the first person in space
July 20, 1969	the first American to orbit the Earth

6 Watch the first part of the video again and check your answers from Exercise 5.

7 Work in pairs. Check your memory. Take turns to ask and answer these questions.

1 Who was president of the United States in 1961?
2 Who was Alan Shepard?
3 What was Sputnik?
4 What was the Mercury program?
5 Who was John Glenn?
6 What was the Apollo program?

8 Watch the second part of the video. Answer the questions.

1 What were *Challenger* and *Columbia*?
2 Which countries send astronauts to the International Space Station?

After you watch

9 Complete the sentences with *was, wasn't, were,* or *weren't.*
1 The Soviet Union and the United States __were__ in a space race.
2 Sputnik __was__ part of the Soviet Union's space program.
3 Alan Shepard, John Glenn, and Gus Grissom __were__ part of the Mercury program.
4 On January 27, 1967, there __was__ a fire on Apollo 1.
5 The first men on the Moon __weren't__ Russian.

10 Work in groups. Write a list of five important events in the last ten years. Ask and answer the questions about the events.

• What was the date of the event?
• Where were you?
• Who were you with?

die (v) /daɪ/ Yuri Gagarin (1934–1968)—He was born in 1934. He died in 1968.

a fire (n) /faɪər/

a goal (n) /goʊl/ an aim

Mercury (n) /ˈmɜrkjəri/ the first planet from the Sun

orbit (v) /ˈɔrbɪt/ to travel around a planet

a program (n) /ˈproʊɡræm/ work or tasks connected to a goal

a satellite (n) /ˈsæt(ə)l.aɪt/

a shuttle (n) /ˈʃʌt(ə)l/

the Soviet Union (n) /ðə ˈsoʊviət ˈjunjən/ the USSR

a speech (n) /spitʃ/ a person makes a speech when they speak at a public event

Sputnik (n) /ˈsputnɪk/ Soviet satellite

a success (n) /sək'ses/ a very good result

a tragedy (n) /ˈtrædʒədi/ a terrible event

Before you watch

1 Put students in pairs to answer the question. Accept any correct answers.

While you watch

3 Play the video without sound. Students watch the video and mark the things as they see them. The task helps them to focus on the video, but it is not too important whether they have the same answers or not.

4 Play the video again. Students check their answers from Exercise 1.

> **ANSWER**
> It was a race between the United States and the Soviet Union (in the 1950s and 1960s).

5 Students in pairs match the dates with the events.

> **ANSWERS**
> April 12, 1961: the first person in space
> May 5, 1961: the first American in space
> February 20, 1962: the first American to orbit the Earth
> January 27, 1967: fire on Apollo 1
> July 20, 1969: men on the Moon

6 Play the first part of the video (00:00–02:00) again for students to check their answers from Exercise 5.

7 Give students a moment to go through the sentences. In pairs, students take turns to ask and answer the questions to check their memory. Don't give them the answers at this stage.

> **ANSWERS**
> 1 JFK
> 2 First American in space
> 3 Russian satellite
> 4 Put a man in space
> 5 Astronaut in Mercury program, first to orbit earth
> 6 Put a man on the moon

---

8 Play the entire video again for students to check their answers from Exercise 7.

> **ANSWERS**
> 1 Two space shuttles that experienced tragedies (Challenger: 1986, Columbia: 2003)
> 2 United States, Russia, Canada, Japan, and Europe

After you watch

9 Give students some time to go through the sentences to complete them. Check answers.

10 You may want to elicit the ideas first and write them on the board. Divide the class into groups of three or four. Students take turns to ask and answer the questions about the events. Monitor conversations and help with any difficult vocabulary. Ask several students to tell you what they found out about their partners.

UNIT 10 REVIEW

Grammar

1 Students complete the article with *was* or *wasn't*.

ANSWERS
1 was
2 wasn't
3 was
4 was
5 wasn't
6 was
7 was
8 was
9 was

2 Students complete the sentences with *was* or *were*.

ANSWERS
1 was
2 were
3 was
4 were
5 was

3 and 4 Students complete the questions with *was* or *were*. Then, in pairs, they ask and answer the questions.

Extra activity

Have students pick another athlete (winner of the Tour de France or another Olympian). They should research the person and write a brief biography, using the paragraph on Bradley Wiggins as a model.

Vocabulary

5 Students complete the sentences with ordinal numbers.

ANSWERS
1 first
2 third
3 fifth
4 eighth
5 tenth
6 thirty-first

6 Students complete the sentences.

7 Students choose the correct option.

Real life

8 Students put the conversation in order.

Speaking

9 and 10 In pairs, students choose two famous people and take turns asking and answering questions.

UNIT 10 REVIEW

Grammar

1 Complete the article about Bradley Wiggins with *was* or *wasn't*.

Bradley Wiggins: the first British winner of the *Tour de France*

Bradley Wiggins ¹ _____ the first British winner of the *Tour de France*, but he ² _____ born in Great Britain. He ³ _____ born in Belgium. His mother ⁴ _____ English, but his father ⁵ _____ ; he ⁶ _____ Australian. His father ⁷ _____ a professional cyclist. Wiggins won his first medal at the Olympic Games in 2000 when he ⁸ _____ 20 years old. He ⁹ _____ the winner of the 2012 *Tour de France*.

2 Complete the sentences about the *Tour de France* with *was* or *were*.

1 The first race _____ in 1903.
2 The cyclists in 1903 _____ from France, Italy, Germany, and Belgium.
3 The first winner five times in a row (1991–1995) _____ Miguel Indurain, a Spanish cyclist.
4 From 2006 to 2009, the winners _____ from Spain.
5 In 2011, the winner _____ Australian.

3 Complete the questions about Bradley Wiggins with *was* or *were*.

1 Where and when / he born? was
2 Where / his parents from? were
3 What / his father's job? was
4 How old / Wiggins in 2000? was

4 Work in pairs. Ask and answer the questions in Exercise 3. Take turns.

I CAN	
talk about the past (*was/were*)	☐
say when people did things (time expressions)	☐

128

Vocabulary

5 Complete the sentences with ordinal numbers.

1 The _____ person in a race is the winner.
2 The person in _____ place gets a bronze medal.
3 May is the _____ month of the year.
4 August is the _____ month of the year.
5 October is the _____ month of the year.
6 The year ends on the _____ of December.

6 Complete the sentences with these words.

in	in	of	on	the

1 I was born _on_ the third _of_ June.
2 My sister was born _in_ 1987.
3 My wife was born on _the_ 27th of September.
4 My son was born _in_ April.

7 Choose the correct option.

1 My first boss was very (nice) / great.
2 My sister is always (happy) / famous.
3 This TV presenter is very great / (interesting).
4 Bradley Wiggins is a (famous) / interesting cyclist.
5 I wasn't always (good) / nice at sports.
6 My math teacher at school was nice and fantastic / (friendly).

I CAN	
say dates	☐
describe people (adjectives)	☐
talk about activities	☐

Real life

8 Put the conversation in order.

a Don't worry. Are you OK now? 6
b Hello, Carolyn. 1
c Hi. Where were you this morning? 2
d Oh! I'm sorry. I was sick. 5
e The boss was here at nine o'clock. 4
f Why? 3
g Yes, thank you. 7

I CAN	
say where I was at different times	☐
make and accept apologies	☐

Speaking

9 Work in pairs. Choose two famous people. Prepare questions for an interview with these people.

10 Ask and answer your questions. Take turns.

Extra activity

For additional practice with ordinal numbers and years, have students share their birthdays from their seats. They should take notes on each other's dates of birth. Then, have them stand up and put themselves in a line according to order of birth (oldest at one end, youngest at the other). They should confirm each other's birthdays with the people they stand next to.

Unit 11 Discovery

Photo by Tim Laman

FEATURES

130 The mystery of "Ötzi the Iceman"

An unusual discovery

132 Adventurers in action

Discover your local area

134 Discovering Madagascar

An accident in Madagascar

138 Perfumes from Madagascar

A video about two scientists in Madagascar

1 Work in pairs. Look at the photo. What can you name?

2 Work in pairs. Which of the captions (a–c) matches the photo? Why?

    a An unusual campsite in the forests of Papua New Guinea.
    b Police find a mystery object in a river in Papua New Guinea.
    ⓒ A scientist discovers new plants in the forests of Papua New Guinea.

3 🔊 **82** Listen and check your ideas from Exercise 2.

4 🔊 **82** Listen again and complete the sentences.

    1 A large _number_ of these discoveries are in Indonesia.
    2 Scientists in Papua New Guinea usually find about two new plants or animals every _week_ .
    3 Scientists sometimes arrive and leave by _helicopter_

5 Work in pairs. Can you name six animals and plants from your country?

Discovery

Warm-up

Personal response

Write *Papua New Guinea* on the board and ask students to brainstorm as many words as they can connected to the topic, and come and write them on the board. If students know facts about the place, they might write *island, country, forests,* etc. If they know little or nothing, they might write *unusual, beautiful, what is it*? etc. At the end, comment on or explain any interesting words. Students will find out more facts in the lesson.

1 Ask students to look at the photo. Ask: *Where is the man? What is he doing?* Organize the class into pairs to name the things they see in the picture.

> **ANSWERS**
>
> jungle, man, trees, plants, sky, tent

2 Give students time to read the captions, and check any unknown words. Students discuss the captions in pairs.

3 Play the audio. Students listen and check their ideas.

4 Play the audio again. Students listen and complete the sentences.

5 Elicit one or two animals and plants to get students started, and then ask pairs of students to write their lists.

The mystery of "Ötzi the Iceman"

Warm-up

Using words

Write these words from the text about "Ötzi" on the board: *body, ice, mystery, investigation, old*.

Tell students to look up any words they don't know. Then, in pairs, have them think of how the words go together in a story. Ask a few pairs to share their ideas with the class.

Reading

Background notes

Ötzi the Iceman (pronounced /'œtsi/) is a natural mummy of a man who lived in about 3300 BC. He is Europe's oldest natural human mummy. Today, his body and the artifacts found with him can be seen in the South Tyrol Museum of Archaeology in Bolzano in South Tyrol, Italy.

1 ANSWERS

1 Germany
2 Austrian Alps
3 in the ice
4 scientific

Grammar

Grammar notes

Many of the most common verbs in English take an irregular past form. Often, the change in form involves a change in one sound between the present and past (*get – got, take – took, find – found, have – had*, etc.). Sometimes, the past form is very unlike the present form (*be – was, go – went*). There is no easy way to learn these forms; students must simply memorize them.

11a The mystery of "Ötzi the Iceman"

Reading

1 Read the article about an unusual discovery. Answer the questions.

1 Where were the tourists from?
2 Where were they in September 1991?
3 Where was the body?
4 What kind of investigation was it?

2 Read the article again. <u>Underline</u> the past forms in the article. Then write the verbs next to the past forms.

1	was/were	*be*		be
2	went	*go*		find
3	found	*find*		go
4	took	*take*		have
5	had	*have*		take

Grammar **irregular simple past verbs**

3 Look at the grammar box. Then choose the correct option.

There is *only one* / more than one simple past form for each verb.

▶ IRREGULAR SIMPLE PAST VERBS
I/You He/She/It We/You/They   **went** for a walk. **found** a body.
For more information and practice, see page 167.

4 Complete the sentences with these irregular simple past verbs.

found	had	took	went

1 The German tourists ___*went*___ to the police station.
2 The police ___*found*___ some arrows near the body.
3 The person ___*had*___ unusual shoes.
4 Scientists ___*took*___ the body to a museum of archaeology in Italy.

PART 1: THE DISCOVERY

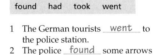

The mystery of "Ötzi the Iceman"

THE DISCOVERY In September 1991, two German tourists <u>were</u> on vacation in the Austrian Alps.

They <u>went</u> for a walk and they <u>found</u> a body in the ice. The body <u>was</u> very old. It <u>wasn't</u> the body of a mountaineer. The police <u>took</u> it to the University of Innsbruck in Austria.

This body <u>was</u> a mystery. <u>Was</u> it a man or a woman? Who <u>was</u> he or she? The person <u>had</u> an unusual knife and a bag with arrows. Where <u>was</u> he or she from? How old <u>was</u> the body? There <u>were</u> many questions. But this <u>wasn't</u> a police investigation. It <u>was</u> a scientific investigation.

Listening

5 🔊 83 Listen to part 2 of the Iceman's story: the investigation. <u>Underline</u> any information that is different.

1 The <u>police</u> started their investigation.
2 Scientists called the body "Ötzi."
3 He was about <u>65</u> years old.
4 He lived <u>10,000</u> years ago.

6 🔊 83 Match the sentence parts. Then listen again and check.

1 The scientists studied   from the north of Italy.
2 They finished   Ötzi.
3 Ötzi was   the body.
4 He walked   their report.
5 An arrow killed   to the mountains.

Listening

5 Ask students to read through the sentences carefully. Tell students to guess which sentences are true. Then play the audio.

Extra activity

Write on the board: *Ötzi, small, 45, the north of Italy, 5,000 years ago, walked, mountains, died, spring, arrow, killed*. Ask pairs of students to tell or write the story of Ötzi from the prompts.

Grammar

Grammar notes

There are some slight exceptions to the usual *-ed* ending. If a verb ends with e, only *d* needs to be added (*lived, died*, etc.). If a verb ends with consonant + *y* (*study, carry*, etc.), the *y* changes to *i* (*studied, carried*). Note, however, that if it ends with vowel + *y*, there is no change (*stayed, played*). Watch out for common spelling errors: *studyed, plaied*, etc.

The Iceman at the South Tyrol Museum of Archaeology in Bolzano, Italy

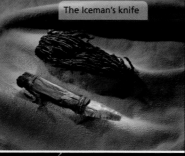

The Iceman's knife

The Iceman's arrows and a bag for the arrows

Grammar regular simple past verbs

7 Look at the grammar box. What do we add to verbs to make the regular simple past form? -ed

► REGULAR SIMPLE PAST VERBS	
I/You	**studied** the body.
He/She/It	**called** him Ötzi.
We/You/They	**finished** their report.

For more information and practice, see page 167.

8 Pronunciation *-ed* verbs

🔊 **84** Listen and repeat the infinitive and simple past form of these verbs. Which verb has an extra syllable?

1	call	called	5	kill	killed
2	die	died	6	live	lived
3	discover	discovered	7	start	(started)
4	finish	finished	8	study	studied

9 Write true sentences with this information.

Albert Einstein	died	from Germany.
Dian Fossey	lived	gorillas in Africa.
John Lennon	studied	in 1980.
Marie Curie	was	in North America.
The Apache people	went	to the university in Paris.

10 Complete the sentences. Use the simple past form of the verb.

1 My grandmother __had__ (have) six children.
2 She __died__ (die) in 1998.
3 My grandfather __studied__ (study) with Albert Einstein.
4 My father __went__ (go) to Cuba.
5 I __lived__ (live) in Italy last year.

Writing and speaking

11 Write sentences about you and your family with the verbs in Exercise 10. Write one false sentence.

My parents went to the South Pole in 2009.

12 Read your sentences to your partner. Can you guess the false sentence?

> My parents went to the South Pole in 2009.
>
> I think that's false!

Pronunciation

8 Give students a moment to look through the verb forms and think about how they are pronounced. Check the meaning of *syllable* by asking how many syllables are in *discover*. When checking, point out the /t/, /d/, and /ɪd/ endings.

Pronunciation notes

The *-ed* ending in regular verbs is only pronounced /ɪd/ when it follows a /t/ or a /d/ sound at the end of a verb, (e.g., *waited, started*). Students at this level often overuse the /ɪd/ pronunciation (e.g., *walk-ed, finish-ed*, etc.).

After verbs that end with a voiced consonant sound or a vowel sound, *-ed* is pronounced /d/ (e.g., *killed*). After verbs that end with an unvoiced consonant sound, *-ed* is pronounced /t/ (e.g., *walked*).

9 Emphasize that there are many possible answers.

SAMPLE ANSWERS

Albert Einstein was from Germany.
Dian Fossey studied gorillas in Africa.
John Lennon died in 1980.
Marie Curie went to the university in Paris.
The Apache people lived in North America.

Extra activity

Ask students to write their own sentences about two famous people from their country.

Writing and speaking

Extra activity

Write on the board: *Last weekend, I…* and 10–15 past forms (*went, had, took, found*, etc.). Ask students to choose five verbs and use them to tell the story of something they did last weekend.

Background notes

Albert Einstein (1879–1955) was the most brilliant physicist of the twentieth century. He developed the theory of relativity. He was born in Germany but lived in the US from 1933 until he died in 1955.

Dian Fossey (1932–1985) was an American zoologist who spent her career studying the behavior of gorillas. She was murdered in Rwanda in 1985.

John Lennon (1940–1980) was one of the Beatles, the famous sixties pop band. He was living in New York City when he was murdered.

Marie Curie (1867–1934) was born in Poland but spent her career in Paris. She carried out research into radioactivity and won two Nobel prizes.

Adventurers in action

Warm-up

Introducing the theme: adventure

Write *adventure sports and activities* on the board and ask students to tell you some sports or activities in their area that people can do. Write them on the board and pre-teach some vocabulary. Ask students which activities are adventurous or dangerous, easy or difficult, interesting or boring.

Reading and listening

Background notes

Alastair Humphreys was born in 1977. His cycling trip covered 46,000 miles over four years and three months. He cycled through Europe and Africa to Cape Town, crossed to South America by boat, then cycled to Alaska, and crossed Russia and China on the way home. In 2011, he won the National Geographic Adventurer of the Year award for his "local adventures."

The **Marathon des Sables** is a grueling 150-mile marathon run held annually across the sands of the Sahara desert.

The **M25** is a busy highway that goes around greater London. It is 117 miles (188 kilometers) long.

3 Ask students: *Do you follow people on Twitter?* Elicit students' experiences. Then ask students to read the sentences carefully. Play the audio. Students listen and put the sentences in order.

Background notes

Twitter is an online social networking and microblogging service. Users send and receive "tweets," which are text-based messages of up to 140 characters. Celebrities often have thousands of "followers"—other users who read the celebrity's tweets.

Reading and listening

1 Read the article and answer the questions.

1 How old is Alastair Humphreys? 35
2 Where does he live? London
3 What's his job? writer and adventurer
4 How does he travel on his adventures? walking and biking

2 Underline the simple past forms of these verbs in the article.

| have | go | leave | see | meet | make |

3 🔊 85 Listen to an interview with Jamie, a Twitter follower of Alastair. Put the sentences in order.

a His friend made a video. 4
b He went swimming. 3
c They posted the video online. 5
d He watched a video. 1
e He drove to a lake. 2

4 🔊 85 Can you remember? Why did Jamie go to the lake? Listen again and check.

He saw a video about swimming in the River Thames.

ADVENTURERS
IN ACTION!

132

Extra activity

Point out the verb-noun collocations in the listening. Write *make, watch, see, send, go, drive,* and *stay* on one side of the board, and *a video, home, to a lake,* and *at home* on the other. Ask students to match the collocations (*make, watch, see, send a video; go, drive home / to a lake; stay at home*).

Pronunciation

5 Make sure that students attempt the linking and weak stress in the words, and the rising intonation.

Pronunciation notes

Did you…? is pronounced with the strong stress on the main verb. In *yes/no* questions, there is rising intonation at the end.

Grammar

7 ANSWERS

1 Did he run a marathon in 2008?
2 Did he walk across India in 2009?
3 Did he go to Iceland last year?
4 Did he drive around the M25 last year?
5 Did he make videos in 2006?

5 Pronunciation *did you ... ?*

🔊 86 Listen and repeat these questions from the interview.

1 Did you watch Alastair's videos?
2 Did you like it?
3 Did you make a video too?

Grammar simple past negative and question forms

6 Look at the grammar box. Which auxiliary verb do we use to make questions and negatives in the simple past? *do*

▶ SIMPLE PAST NEGATIVE AND QUESTION FORMS		
I/You/He/She/It We/You/They	**didn't**	**leave** the UK.
Did	I/you/he/she/it we/you/they	**walk?** Yes, I/you/he/she/it/we/you/they **did**. No, I/you/he/she/it/we/you/they **didn't**.

For more information and practice, see page 168.

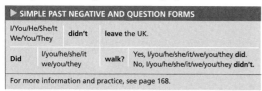

After ten years of international adventures, last year Alastair Humphreys stayed in the UK. He **had** a different kind of adventure: a "local adventure." We asked him about it.

Tell us about your last adventure. Did you go to a dangerous place?

No, I didn't. I <u>went</u> around London on the M25 highway.

Did you drive?

No, I walked. I <u>left</u> my house in London in January. It was cold and it was snowy. It wasn't easy, but I <u>saw</u> some beautiful new places. And I <u>met</u> interesting people. It was a local adventure.

And then what did you do?

I had one or two more local adventures and I <u>made</u> videos about them. People around the world watched the videos. They liked my ideas and they went on local adventures too.

> **DISCOVER YOUR LOCAL AREA**
> Age: 35
> Home: London
> Profession: Writer and adventurer
>
> **ADVENTURES:**
> 2001–2005: bike trip around the world
> 2008: *Marathon des Sables*
> 2009: walking trip across India
> 2010: walking trip across Iceland
>
> ALASTAIR HUMPHREYS

7 Look at the example. Then write questions about Alastair.

Example:
bike / around the world two years ago?

Did he bike around the world two years ago?

1 run / a marathon in 2008?
2 walk across India / in 2009?
3 go to Iceland / last year?
4 drive around the M25 / last year?
5 make videos / in 2006?

8 Work in pairs. Ask and answer the questions in Exercise 7.

> *Did he bike around the world two years ago?*

> *No, he didn't.*

9 Write sentences about Alastair with the information in Exercise 7.

He walked across Iceland in 2010.

Writing and speaking

10 Prepare a survey about last year. Write questions with these ideas.

- go on vacation
Did you go on vacation last year?
- stay in a hotel
- make a video
- leave your job
- drive to an interesting place
- meet an old friend
- send a message on Twitter

11 Work as a class. Find one name for each question.

> *Did you go on vacation last year?*

> *Yes, I did. I went to Cairo.*

12 Write sentences with the names.

José went to Cairo last year.

Grammar note

Simple past negative form: subject + *didn't* + infinitive verb

Note that after the auxiliary *didn't*, the infinitive is used. Watch out for errors such as *They didn't left* and *He not went*.

Simple past question form: *Did* + subject + infinitive verb

Again, the infinitive is used. Watch out for errors such as *Did you walked? Went she home?*

Short answer forms use the auxiliary, e.g., *Yes, I did* and *No, I didn't*. Students often feel a need to use the main verb, which is incorrect: *Yes, I walked.*

8 Divide the class into pairs. Ask students to find the answers in the article first. Then ask students to take turns to ask and answer questions.

ANSWERS

1 Yes, he did.
2 Yes, he did.
3 No, he didn't.
4 No, he didn't.
5 No, he didn't.

9 ANSWERS

He biked around the world from 2001 to 2005.

He ran a marathon in 2008.

He walked across India in 2009.

He didn't go to Iceland last year.

He didn't drive around the M25 last year.

He didn't make videos in 2006.

Writing and speaking

10 Model question formation. With a strong class, tell them not to write questions. With a weaker class, ask them to write out the questions.

---

11 Model the activity by having the class ask you a few questions. Answer *Yes, I did* or *No, I didn't*, and give extra information (e.g., *I went to Casablanca; I stayed in the Grand Hotel*).

HOMEWORK As a class, brainstorm vacation-related vocabulary, e.g., *stay in a hotel, meet friends, swim in the ocean, lie in the sun, walk in the mountains, go to the beach, go dancing, go on a boat, take photos, buy souvenirs*. Then ask students to write about where they went and what they did on their last vacation.

Discovering Madagascar

11c Discovering Madagascar

Warm-up

Introducing the theme: Madagascar

Write *Madagascar* in the middle of the board and ask students: *What is it?* They may tell you that it is a place in Africa, a children's movie, or they may not know at all.

Elicit questions that students would like to ask about Madagascar and write them at random on the board, e.g., *Where is it? How big is it? What can you see there? What can you do there?*

Explain that it is an island off the east coast of Africa with animals and plants that you won't find anywhere else in the world. Invite students who know more to share any details with the class.

Reading

1 Use the photos to pre-teach some key words: *sharp (rocks); deep (cut); lemur; species* (a group of a particular type of animals or plants).

2 Review these adjectives by asking students to think of synonyms (*attractive, wonderful, amazing, different*) or antonyms (*safe, terrible, boring, similar*) to explain the words. With a weaker class, give synonyms or antonyms and ask students to match them to the adjectives. Then have pairs do the activity. Explain that there are no incorrect answers.

Pronunciation notes

Note that the strong stress in these words is on the first syllable, except for *fantastic* and *unusual*.

3 ANSWERS

1 March
2 biologist and photographer
3 find new species
4 tsingy, lemurs, animals, plants, birds

Reading

1 Look at the photos on page 135 and find:

an animal	a plant	rocks

2 Work in pairs. Which things in the photos do these adjectives describe?

beautiful	dangerous	fantastic
interesting	unusual	

3 Read the article and answer the questions.

1 When did the writer go to Madagascar?
2 Who did he go with?
3 Why did they go to Madagascar?
4 What did they see there?

4 Read the last paragraph of the article again. Complete the sentences.

1 The writer fell on a ___rock___ .
2 He cut his ___leg___ .
3 He went to the hospital
4 A nurse cleaned his ___leg___ .
5 She asked him a ___question___ .

5 Work in pairs. What did the nurse think about the trip? Do you agree with her?

Grammar simple past with question words

6 Look at the grammar box. Which question words are in Exercise 3? what when, why, who

▶ SIMPLE PAST WITH QUESTION WORDS			
What			do?
Where			go?
When	did	I/you/he/she/it we/you/they	arrive?
Why			fall?
Who			meet?
For more information and practice, see page 168.			

7 Complete the questions with the correct *wh-* word.

1 ___What___ did he cut?
2 ___Where___ did he go?
3 ___What___ did he see there?
4 ___What___ did she say?

8 Work in pairs. Ask and answer the questions in Exercise 7.

9 Word focus *with*

a Look at the pictures. Find and complete these two sentences from the article.

1 I was with a ___biologist and photographer___

2 We saw unusual white lemurs with ___red eyes___ .

b Match the two parts of the sentences.

1 I booked my tickets with — a animals.
2 You can hitchhike with — b a travel agent.
3 Vets work with — c my friends.
4 We saw a bird with — d Russian drivers.
5 I had lunch with — e unusual colors.

Speaking

10 Work in pairs. Tell Neil Shea's story with these verbs. Take turns to say a sentence. You can use some verbs more than once.

arrived	cleaned	cut	fell
saw	traveled	walked	went

5 When checking, point out that "a little crazy" is very informal (sometimes offensive).

ANSWER

She thought it was dangerous and "a little crazy."

Background notes

The Republic of Madagascar is a large island country in the Indian Ocean off the southeastern coast of Africa. It split from India about 88 million years ago and its animals and plants have evolved in isolation. Twenty-two million people live there. It's a poor country, dependent on ecotourism and agriculture.

There are officially 101 species or sub-species of lemurs, a type of primitive primate that has evolved successfully in the absence of competition from monkeys.

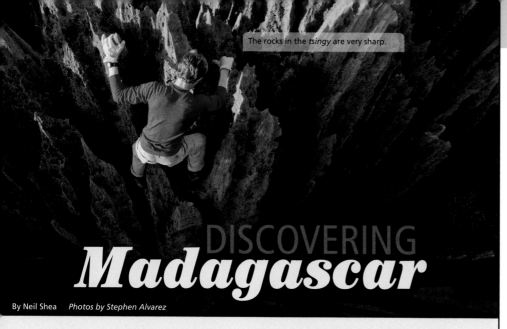

The rocks in the *tsingy* are very sharp.

DISCOVERING
Madagascar

By Neil Shea   *Photos by Stephen Alvarez*

I arrived in Madagascar in March, at the end of the rainy season. I was with a biologist and a photographer. We wanted to find some new species. We traveled to the park with our guide and after five days, we finally arrived there.

We walked through the *tsingy*. The rocks cut our clothes and our shoes. It was dangerous, but we saw hundreds of animals and plants. We saw beautiful birds and unusual white lemurs with red eyes. They didn't have any problems on the *tsingy* rocks!

Madagascar is a fantastic place. About 90 percent of the animals and plants there live only in Madagascar. Scientists love it! There are some very unusual animals and plants in Madagascar's Tsingy de Bemaraha national park, but it's a dangerous place. The rocks— the "tsingy"—in the park are very sharp. Neil Shea reports.

One afternoon, I fell on a rock. I cut my leg. The cut was very deep. It took two days to reach the hospital. The nurse cleaned my leg. "I have a question. Why did you go to the *tsingy*?" she asked. Then she said, "It's very dangerous. I think you are a little crazy." She didn't understand us. The *tsingy* is a natural paradise.

crazy (adj) /'kreɪzi/ not sensible

There are twenty-three types of this plant in the world. Eighteen of them are only in Madagascar.

This lemur lives only in Madagascar.

---

7 Point out to students that some items may have several possible correct answers (for example, item 2 might also be *why* or *when*). However *where* is probably the most logical.

> **Grammar notes**
>
> Note that *cut* is the same in the infinitive and past form. It is also used as a noun in the text.

Grammar

> **Grammar notes**
>
> *Wh-* questions in the simple past use this structure:
>
> Question word + *did* + subject + verb in the infinitive form
>
> *What   did   you   do?*
>
> Note what the question words refer to: *When* (a time), *Who* (a person), *Why* (a reason), *What* (a thing), *Where* (a place).
>
> Note also that *What did you do?* is an open question which is usually answered with another verb, <u>not</u> *do*, e.g., *I went to a party, I had some lunch, I played tennis.*

8 Point out the past simple forms of *cut, go, see,* and *say*.

Word focus

> **Vocabulary notes**
>
> The preposition *with* is used to describe when people are together (*I was with a biologist*), sharing things (*I had lunch with my colleagues*), and to describe characteristics (*a lemur with red eyes*).

> **Extra activity**
>
> Write these sentence starters on the board and ask students to finish them with their information:
>
> *I live with…*
>
> *I often play sports with…*
>
> *My best friend is a man/woman with…*

Speaking

10 Divide the class into pairs. Give them time to look at the verbs and decide which order they appear in the text. They then take turns to say sentences about the story from memory, using the verbs in the correct order.

Did you have a good time?

Warm-up

Personal response

Write on the board: *Where did you go last weekend? What did you do? Who did you go with?* Put students into pairs to ask the questions. Check by asking individuals to tell the class about their partner's weekend.

Real life

1 Use the photo to teach the word *shark*.

> **SAMPLE ANSWER**
>
> You can see an island with palm trees, white sand, and very clear ocean water. There is a shark in the ocean.

> **3 ANSWER**
>
> 1 Yes, they did.
> 2 No, they didn't.
> 3 No, they didn't.

Vocabulary

> **5 ANSWER**
>
> last week, last year, last night

6 Begin the activity by asking students: *What did you do on Friday / last night / last week?* etc. Elicit sentences and write some prompts on the board, if necessary.

8 Read through the example dialogue and elicit other examples from the prompts. Refer students to the examples in the *Talking about the past* box. Monitor conversations and make note of common errors that you can go over as a class.

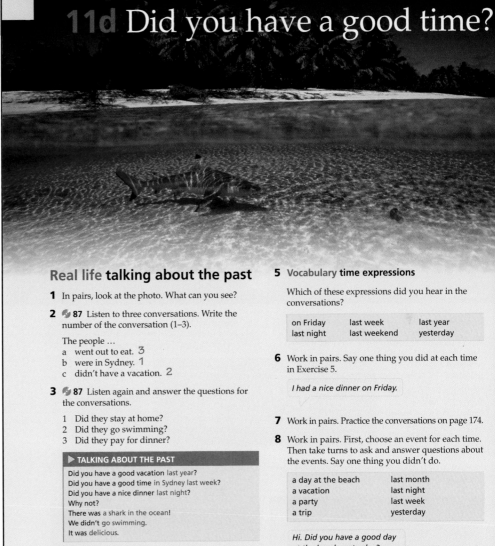

Real life **talking about the past**

1 In pairs, look at the photo. What can you see?

2 **87** Listen to three conversations. Write the number of the conversation (1–3).

The people …
a went out to eat. 3
b were in Sydney. 1
c didn't have a vacation. 2

3 **87** Listen again and answer the questions for the conversations.

1 Did they stay at home?
2 Did they go swimming?
3 Did they pay for dinner?

> ▶ **TALKING ABOUT THE PAST**
>
> Did you have a good vacation last year?
> Did you have a good time in Sydney last week?
> Did you have a nice dinner last night?
> Why not?
> There was a shark in the ocean!
> We didn't go swimming.
> It was delicious.

4 Pronunciation *didn't*

88 Listen to three sentences from the conversations and repeat them.

5 Vocabulary **time expressions**

Which of these expressions did you hear in the conversations?

| on Friday | last week | last year |
| last night | last weekend | yesterday |

6 Work in pairs. Say one thing you did at each time in Exercise 5.

> *I had a nice dinner on Friday.*

7 Work in pairs. Practice the conversations on page 174.

8 Work in pairs. First, choose an event for each time. Then take turns to ask and answer questions about the events. Say one thing you didn't do.

a day at the beach	last month
a vacation	last night
a party	last week
a trip	yesterday

> *Hi. Did you have a good day at the beach yesterday?*
>
> *No, I didn't go.*
>
> *Why not?*
>
> *It was very cold!*

Extra activity

Play *two truths and a lie*. Have students write three sentences about their lives, two true and one false, using the expressions in Exercise 5. Have them take turns reading their sentences (all three) to the class. The class can then ask questions about the details of each of the three statements to figure out which ones are true and which is false.

HOMEWORK Tell students to write one of their conversations from Exercise 8.

11e Thank you!

Writing an email

1 Work in pairs. Look at the photo. What's the situation?

2 Read the email. Choose the correct option (a–c).

a Lili, Bibia, and Mark went on vacation together.
ⓑ Bibia and Mark visited Lili.
c Lili visited Bibia and Mark.

> Dear Lili,
>
> Thank you for a fantastic weekend! It was great to see you and we had a fantastic time.
>
> On the way home we had a little adventure (see photo)! We got home late, but it was OK.
>
> Thanks again. Talk to you soon!
>
> Love,
> Bibia and Mark

3 Read the parts of an email (a–c). Which part completes the email to Lili?

a We missed the plane (!), but we found a hotel and stayed there for the night.

b We got lost! We didn't have a map so we went on the wrong road!

ⓒ We had a problem with the car! We called my dad. After an hour, he came and helped us.

4 Writing skill expressions in emails

a Write S or E next to the expressions we use to start (S) or end (E) an email.

All the best, E	Hi S
Best wishes, E	Love, E
Dear S	Regards, E

b Complete this email from Toni to Celia with expressions from Exercise 4a.

> ¹ Hi/Dear Celia
>
> Thanks for your help yesterday. I found my car keys when I got home!
>
> See you soon.
> ² All the best,/Regards,/Love, Toni

5 Work in pairs. Each person choose one of these situations. Tell your partner how you helped him/her.

- You helped him/her when he/she lost his/her phone.
- You helped him/her when he/she didn't have any money.
- You sent him/her some photos.
- He/She had dinner at your house.

6 Write a "thank you" email to your friend for his/her help in the situation in Exercise 5.

7 Exchange emails with your friend. Ask a follow-up question about your friend's email.

Thank you!

Warm-up

Introducing the theme: thank you

Write *Thank you for…* on the board. Ask students in pairs to think of three recent situations when somebody did something that they could thank them for. Provide examples, e.g., *Simon bought me lunch.* (You may want to introduce the expression *Thank you for + -ing*, e.g., *Thank you for buying me lunch*).

Writing

1 Possible explanations for the picture include: *they got lost, they had an accident, they had a problem with the car.*

3 You may need to explain *miss* (not get on a plane, train, etc. because you are late), *get lost* (not know where you are), and *map* (act out unfolding a map and finding a place on it with your finger).

Extra activity

Ask students to find the past forms in the email and excerpts, and categorize them as regular forms (*missed, stayed, called, helped*) and irregular forms (*was, had, got, found, went, came*).

Writing skill

4a Point out that these expressions are used in informal emails to friends and family. *Dear* and *Regards* can also be used in formal emails.

Vocabulary notes

In informal emails, people write in a friendlier more casual way than in formal letters. So *Hi Celia* is more common than *Dear Celia*, and using spoken expressions such as *Bye for now* and *See you soon* is as common as informal written expressions such as *All the best* and *Best wishes*. Similarly, using abbreviations (*Thanks*) and contractions (*I'm*) is standard.

may need, e.g., *find / phone; lend / some money; look at / photos; cook / dinner.*

6 Tell students to write their emails on a separate piece of paper so that they can exchange it with their partner later. Tell students to check their emails carefully for simple past tense errors.

> **HOMEWORK** Ask students to write an email to you. Tell them to include the phrase *Thanks for…*

5 Make sure that students choose a different situation from their partner. Once they have chosen their situations, elicit verb-noun collocations that they

Perfumes from Madagascar

Videoscript

Narrator: Madagascar is a fantastic island. There are some very unusual plants in the forests.

It's a very interesting place for scientists.

<u>These scientists are from Switzerland</u>.

They went to Madagascar last year.

They wanted to find <u>plants for perfumes</u>.

Some plants and flowers have fantastic scents.

The scientists traveled into the forest by boat.

Then they flew in a balloon. They looked for interesting flowers and fruit.

When they were back <u>in Switzerland, they studied the new scents in the laboratory</u>.

Roman Kaiser I'm quite happy. It's already very close to this beautiful stephanotis scent as I experienced it on the Tampolo River.

Narrator: There are many natural and man-made scents in this laboratory.

Last year, this scientist found two new plants.

<u>One plant had green fruit.</u>

<u>The second plant had red fruit.</u>

They cut the fruits and they tasted them.

<u>But they didn't like them.</u>

There are many things to discover in Madagascar.

It's a natural paradise.

An unusual plant in the Madagascan forest

138

Before you watch

1 Work in pairs. Answer the questions.

  1 What perfumes do you know or use?
  2 Where do perfumes come from?

2 Work in pairs. Do you think these sentences about Madagascar are true (T) or false (F)?

  1 Madagascar is an island. T
  2 There are some unusual plants in the forests. T
  3 It's an interesting place for scientists. T
  4 It's easy to travel into the forests by car. F

While you watch

3 Watch the video without sound. Mark (✓) the things you see.

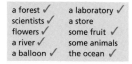

a forest ✓	a laboratory ✓
scientists ✓	a store
flowers ✓	some fruit ✓
a river ✓	some animals
a balloon ✓	the ocean ✓

4 Watch the video with sound. Then choose the correct summary (a or b).

  a Some scientists discovered a new flower.
     They made a new perfume.
     They sold the perfume in Madagascar.

  (b) Some scientists went to Madagascar.
     They looked for plants and flowers.
     One of the scientists found two new plants.

5 Read the sentences. Then watch the video again. Are the sentences true (T) or false (F)?

  1 The scientists are from Switzerland. T
  2 They make perfumes. T
  3 Their laboratory is in Madagascar. F
  4 They found plants with black fruit. F
  5 Willi Grab didn't like the taste of the fruit. T

6 Work in pairs. Which option(s) (a–c) are true?

  1 The scientists went to Madagascar…
    (a) because there are a lot of interesting plants.
    b because they go there every year.
    (c) because they wanted to find new plants.

  2 They saw…
    a some interesting animals.
    b some beautiful flowers.
    (c) some unusual fruits.

After you watch

7 Match the two parts of the sentences.

  1 The scientists went to Madagascar
  2 They traveled into
  3 Then they flew in
  4 They looked for
  5 They cut the fruits and
  6 They studied the new scents
  7 Last year, this scientist found two

  a a balloon.
  b in the laboratory.
  c interesting flowers and fruits.
  d the forest by boat.
  e they tasted them.
  f last year.
  g new plants.

8 Work in pairs. Take turns. Read the sentences in Exercise 7.

Student A: Read the first part of the first sentence.

Student B: Read the second part of the first sentence.

9 Work in pairs. Take turns.

Student A: You are a scientist. You went to Madagascar.

Student B: You are a journalist.

Ask and answer questions with *when*, *where*, *what*, *who*, and *why* about the trip to Madagascar.

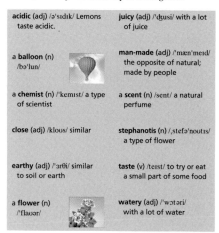

acidic (adj) /əˈsɪdɪk/ Lemons taste acidic.

a balloon (n) /bəˈlun/

a chemist (n) /ˈkemɪst/ a type of scientist

close (adj) /kloʊs/ similar

earthy (adj) /ˈɜrθi/ similar to soil or earth

a flower (n) /ˈflaʊər/

juicy (adj) /ˈdʒusi/ with a lot of juice

man-made (adj) /ˈmænˈmeɪd/ the opposite of natural; made by people

a scent (n) /sent/ a natural perfume

stephanotis (n) /ˌstefəˈnoʊtɪs/ a type of flower

taste (v) /teɪst/ to try or eat a small part of some food

watery (adj) /ˈwɔtəri/ with a lot of water

---

8 Model the activity by asking some of the students to read the first part of the first sentence in Exercise 7. Have another student read aloud the second part of the sentence.

9 In pairs, students take turns to interview each other.

Note: Weaker students can base the interview on the video, and the stronger students can make up their own details.

Before you watch

1 Pre-teach *scents* and *balloon* with gestures and drawings. Drill the pronunciation.

2 Give students some time to read the sentences and decide if they are true or false. Don't give the correct answers at this stage.

While you watch

3 Play the video without sound. Students mark the things they see.

4 Give students some time to read two summaries of the video. Then play the video with sound for students to choose the correct summary.

5 Give students some time to read the sentences and decide if they are true or false. Then play the video again for them to check.

6 Give students a moment to go through the sentences. Then divide the class into pairs to complete the items. Check answers.

After you watch

7 Students match the two parts of the sentences. Don't check the answers at this stage.

> **ANSWER**
> **1** last year. (f)
> **2** the forest by boat. (d)
> **3** a balloon. (a)
> **4** interesting flowers and fruits. (c)
> **5** they tasted them. (e)
> **6** in the laboratory. (b)
> **7** new plants. (g)

UNIT 11 REVIEW

Grammar

1 Students complete the blog with the simple past forms of the verbs.

> **ANSWER**
>
> **1** were
> **2** was
> **3** had
> **4** took
> **5** sent
> **6** saw
> **7** talked
> **8** asked

2 Students decide if the sentences are true or false, and then turn the false sentences negative in order to make them true.

> **ANSWERS**
>
> **1** F, Carly didn't go to Canada.
> **2** F, She wasn't on a bus.
> **3** T
> **4** T

3 Students read Carly's answers and write the questions.

> **ANSWERS**
>
> **1** Did you go in the water?
> **2** Did you have a good time?
> **3** Did you take any photos?
> **4** Who did you go with?

4 Tell students to prepare questions from the prompts then take turns asking and answering the questions.

> **ANSWERS**
>
> **1** Where did you go?
> **2** When did you get there?
> **3** What did you see?
> **4** Who did you talk to?
> **5** Why did you go?

Vocabulary

5 Students complete the sentences with six of the verbs. Some items have more than one possible answer.

UNIT 11 REVIEW

Grammar

1 Complete the blog with the simple past forms of the verbs.

Field notes

A blog by National Geographic Expeditions

Last month, I was with a group of people on a boat. We ¹_____ (be) in Alaska. Justin Hofman, a scuba diver, ²_____ (be) in the water. He ³_____ (have) a camera. He ⁴_____ (take) pictures underwater. He ⁵_____ (send) video pictures to us on the boat. It was very exciting! We ⁶_____ (see) beautiful animals and plants. There was an audio connection too. Justin ⁷_____ (talk) about the animals and plants and we ⁸_____ (ask) him questions. It was a great experience.

Posted by Carly

2 Read the blog again. Are the sentences true (T) or false (F)? Change the verb to the negative form to make the false sentences true.

1 Carly went to Canada.
2 She was on a bus.
3 Justin Hofman took photos.
4 Carly saw interesting things.

3 Read Carly's answers. Write the questions.

1 No, I didn't go in the water.
2 Yes, I had a great time.
3 No, I didn't take any photos.
4 I went with my friends.

4 Work in pairs. You were on the boat in the photo. Ask and answer questions with these words.

1 Where / go?   4 Who / talk to?
2 When / get there?   5 Why / go?
3 What / see?

140

> **ANSWER**
>
> **1** made
> **2** cleaned
> **3** drove
> **4** met
> **5** took
> **6** paid

6 Students write true personal sentences with six of the verbs from Exercise 5 and the time expressions.

> **I CAN**
>
> talk about the past (irregular and regular simple past verbs)
>
> ask and answer questions about the past (question words)

Vocabulary

5 Complete the sentences with six of these verbs.

| cleaned | cut | drove | fell | finished | found |
| made | met | paid | sent | swam | took |

Yesterday

1 I _____ breakfast.
2 I _____ my room.
3 I _____ to a café.
4 I _____ my friend Alex.
5 He _____ a photo of us.
6 I _____ for lunch.

6 Write true sentences for you with six of the verbs from Exercise 5 and time expressions.

> Last night / weekend / week / month / year
> On Monday / Tuesday, etc.

7 Work in pairs. Read your sentences.

> **I CAN**
>
> talk about people's lives
>
> say when people did things

Real life

8 Read the conversation and choose the best option.

A: Did you have *a good day at the beach /* *a nice dinner / a good vacation* last night?
B: No, I didn't.
A: Oh? Why not?
B: The food was delicious, but my friend *missed the plane / saw a shark in the water /* *cut her hand with her knife!*
A: Oh no!

> **I CAN**
>
> talk about the past
>
> give reasons for events in the past

Speaking

9 Work in pairs. Practice the conversation in Exercise 8 with the other two options.

---

7 Students take turns to read aloud their sentences to their partner.

Real life

8 Students choose the best options to complete the conversation.

Speaking

9 In pairs, students practice the conversation, using the other two options.

Unit 12 The weekend

A group of women in Chengdu, China
Photo by Cary Wolinsky

FEATURES

142 At home

A family in Indonesia

144 Next weekend

Weekend activities

146 A different kind of weekend

Helping people on the weekend

150 Saturday morning in São Tomé

A video about artists and musicians in São Tomé

1 Work in pairs. Look at the photo of women on their day off work. What days do you work or study?

2 🔊 89 Work in pairs. Look at the photo again and discuss the questions. Then listen and check your ideas.

1 Which day of the week do you think is the women's day off?
2 What do you think they usually do on their day off?
3 Which days do you think are the weekend in China?

3 🔊 89 Listen again. Write the weekend days for these countries. What about your country?

Oman: <u>Thursday</u>, <u>Friday</u>
Egypt: <u>Friday</u>, <u>Saturday</u>

4 Work in pairs. What do you do on the weekend? Do you stay at home, do you go out, or do you work?

> *I work on Saturday, and on Sunday I stay home.*

Unit 12

The weekend

The weekend

Warm-up

Using words and introducing the theme: the weekend

On the board, write *weekend*, and *verbs, nouns,* and *adjectives*. Ask students to think of verbs, nouns, or adjectives that go with the word *weekend*. Start them off by suggesting *play* and *sleep* (verbs), *fun* and *vacations* (noun), *happy* and *relaxing* (adjectives). Then, in pairs, ask them to think of more words. Have students fill in the verbs, nouns, and adjectives categories.

1 Ask students to look at the photo first. Ask: *What can you see? Who are they? Where are they? Are they happy? Why?* Then ask them to discuss the question in pairs.

2 Give students a moment to guess answers to the questions in pairs. Review days of the week if necessary. Then play the audio. Ask students to listen and check their guesses.

> ### ANSWERS
>
> 1 Sunday
> 2 They usually meet and go out for the day (to stores, museums, and movie theaters).
> 3 Since 1995, Saturday and Sunday are days off for office workers, but only Sunday for factory workers.

4 Open the activity by telling students what you do on the weekend. Review weekend activities (*stay at home, go shopping, play soccer,* etc.). Write a list of verb-noun collocations on the board. Then ask students to discuss the questions in pairs.

At home

Warm-up

Test before you teach: activities at home and the present continuous

Tell students that you are at home and it's 7 a.m. Act out getting up, taking a shower, getting dressed, and eating breakfast. Then tell students it's 7 p.m. and act out eating dinner, watching TV, and reading a book. Tell students to call out the activities you are doing.

Vocabulary

Pronunciation notes

Note that the stress is on the first syllable of all these words: fridge, oven, sofa.

2 Model the activity by describing one thing about each room in your house.

Extra activity

Have a class quiz to check the words from Exercise 1. Ask: *What do you cook food in? What do you put milk and cheese in? Where do you eat? Where do you take a shower? What do you put your clothes in? What do you sit on when you eat? Where do you watch TV?*

Divide the class into teams. The first team that shouts out the correct answer to each question gets a point.

Listening

3 Write the rooms on the board, and remind students of the stress and pronunciation. Ask: *What are they doing?* Use the pictures to pre-teach key words from the listening (*bathing, mats, ironing, smiling*).

Vocabulary **rooms in a house**

1 Look at the things (1–5) there are in different rooms. Write the rooms next to the things. Check your answers with your instructor.

| bathroom | bedroom | dining room | ~~kitchen~~ |
| living room | | | |

1 a fridge, an oven   *kitchen*
2 a chair, a table   *dining room*
3 an armchair, a sofa   *living room*
4 a bed, a closet   *bedroom*
5 a bathtub, a shower, a toilet *bathroom*

2 Work in pairs. Tell your partner one thing about each room in your home.

> *We don't have a dining room. We eat in the kitchen.*

> *My kitchen is very small.*

HOME LIFE
PHOTO PROJECT

We asked our readers to take photos of the important things in their homes. This week, we show Ayu Malik's photos. It's Saturday at her home in Sumatra, Indonesia.

ANSWERS

1 kitchen	4 living room
2 bathroom	5 bedroom
3 outside / on a porch	6 outside

5 ANSWERS

a Ayu's father and his friend
b Amir's brother and his son
c Ayu's husband (Amir)
d Ayu's brother and his friend
e Ayu's mother
f Ayu's sister

Listening

3 Look at the photos (1–6) of a family at home in Indonesia. Which rooms are the people in?

4 🔊 **90** Match the sentences with the photos. Then listen and check.

a They're drinking coffee. 3
b He's playing a computer game with his son. 4
c He's bathing his daughter. 2
d They're washing their bikes. 6
e She's making lunch. 1
f She's ironing. 5

5 🔊 **90** Listen again and say who the people are. Write next to the sentences in Exercise 4.

Example:
a They're drinking coffee.
   Ayu's father and his friend

Grammar present continuous

6 Look at the grammar box. Then look at the sentences in Exercise 4. Which auxiliary verb do we use to make the present continuous? *to be*

▶ **PRESENT CONTINUOUS AFFIRMATIVE and NEGATIVE**

I	am (not)	**sitting** on the floor.
You/We/They	are (not)	**making** lunch.
He/She/It	is (not)	**ironing**.

For more information and practice, see page 168.

7 Complete the sentences about the photos on page 142.

1 _Ayu's mother_ is cooking.
2 _____ are smiling.
3 _____ are sitting on mats.
4 _____ is lying on the sofa.
5 _____ is standing alone.
6 _____ is wearing shorts.

8 Write true sentences about the photos. Use the negative form when necessary.

1 Ayu's mother /eat
   Ayu's mother isn't eating.
2 Amir / play with his daughter
3 Ayu's father and his friend / read a book
4 Amir's brother / watch TV
5 Ayu's sister / do homework
6 Ayu's brother / wash his cars

9 Look at these questions from the conversation with Ayu Malik. Which photos are the questions about?

a What's she making? 1
b Are they sitting outside or inside? 3, 4
c What are they doing? 2, 3, 4, 6
d Are they reading? 3, 4

10 Work in pairs. Ask and answer the questions in Exercise 9.

▶ **PRESENT CONTINUOUS QUESTIONS and SHORT ANSWERS**

	Am	I	
(What)	Are	you/we/you/they	**reading? doing?**
	Is	he/she/it	

Yes, I am. No, I'm not.
Yes, he/she/it is. No, he/she/it isn't.
Yes, you/we/you/they are.
No, you/we/you/they aren't.

For more information and practice, see page 168.

11 Look at the photo below. Write questions. Then ask and answer the questions with your partner.

Example:
children / watch TV?
Are the children watching TV?

1 boy / lie on the sofa?   3 women / wear scarves?
2 man / sit on a chair?   4 girls/ sit on the floor?

Speaking

12 Work in groups. Show some of your photos to the group. Take turns to ask and answer questions.

Who's that?
That's my cousin and her husband.
What are they doing?
They're singing.

Unit 12 **The weekend** 143

Grammar

7 ANSWERS

1 Ayu's mother
2 Ayu's husband and daughter
3 Ayu's father and his friend
4 Amir's brother
5 Ayu's sister
6 Ayu's brother

Grammar notes

In English, we form the present continuous with the auxiliary verb *be* and the *-ing* form of the main verb (or present participle).

Remind students that the *be* form is usually contracted in spoken English (*I'm sitting, She's going*), and in the negative form, *not* is usually contracted (*She isn't going* but *I'm not sitting*).

The present participle is formed by adding *-ing* to the infinitive of the main verb. Note the irregular forms:

sit, run, get become *sitting, running, getting* (because the verbs end with consonant + vowel + consonant)

come, live lose the e and become *coming, living*, etc.

lie, die become *lying, dying*, etc.

8 ANSWERS

2 Amir is playing with his daughter.
3 Ayu's father and his friend aren't reading a book.
4 Amir's brother isn't watching TV.
5 Ayu's sister isn't doing homework.
6 Ayu's brother isn't washing his cars.

9 Point out the form in the grammar box or write question c on the board and label the form if necessary (see Grammar notes).

Grammar notes

Present continuous question forms are made by inverting the subject and the *be* verb form:

Question word + *be* + subject + verb in *-ing* form

What   are   they   doing?

---

11 ANSWERS

Example Yes, they are.

1 Is the boy lying on the sofa? No, he isn't.
2 Is the man sitting on a chair? Yes, he is.
3 Are the women wearing scarves? Yes, they are.
4 Are the girls sitting on the floor? No, they aren't.

Extra activity

Students take turns choosing a person in the class, and their partner asks questions to guess the person, e.g., *Is this person sitting near the door?* Start by eliciting some ideas for questions and write some prompts on the board.

Speaking

12 Model the activity by showing some photos on your phone, and describing the people. Then put students in small groups to take turns asking and answering questions.

Unit 12 **The weekend** 143

12b Next weekend

Warm-up

Using words: activities

Write *Activities* in the middle of the board. Then write the verbs *go, play, read,* and *meet* on the board. In pairs, have students write down as many activities as they can in two minutes, using the verbs.

Vocabulary

1 ANSWERS

They are in a shopping mall.
They are shopping and walking around.

3 Ask students to complete the *me* column for themselves by writing *always, sometimes,* or *never* next to each activity. After interviewing their partner, have students tell the class about the similarities and differences.

Listening

4 Ask students to look at the information. Ask: *What are the events? Where can you see them?* Ask some follow-up questions, e.g., *How long is the sale? Where is the folk music concert? When is the evening with Helen Skelton? How much is it?* Then play the audio.

5 ANSWERS

1 She is going shopping tomorrow/ on Saturday.

2 She is going shopping because *Sports Gear* is having a sale.

3 Helen Skelton is giving a talk at the museum.

4 Alex is going to see Helen Skelton.

Vocabulary weekend activities

1 Look at the photo. Where are the people? What are they doing?

2 Read the *On the weekend* questionnaire. Are the activities at home (H) or out of the home (O)?

3 Work in pairs. Complete the questionnaire. Are your weekends similar or different?

> I never get up late on the weekend.

> I sometimes get up late.

On the **weekend**	How often do you do these weekend activities? Always? Sometimes? Never?	
	me	my partner
get up late H		
go out to eat O		
go for a walk O		
go shopping O		
go to the movies O		
go to a museum O		
meet friends O		
play soccer O		
read the newspaper H		
visit family O		

A busy shopping center on a typical Saturday

144

Vocabulary notes

To talk about future plans we can use *next* with a day or other time word to talk about a future time period, e.g., *next Wednesday, next July, next week. Next Tuesday* usually means the Tuesday of the following week.

When we are talking about the time period we are in now, we use *this,* e.g., *this week, this Tuesday.* So on Monday we might say *this Wednesday* to mean the day after tomorrow, and *next Wednesday* to mean the Wednesday of next week.

Near the end of the week we would use *this weekend,* not *next weekend.*

Listening

4 🔊 **91** Look at the information about three events. Then listen to a conversation between friends. Mark (✓) the events they talk about.

5 🔊 **91** Listen again. Answer the questions.

1 When is Lauren going shopping?
2 Why is she going shopping?
3 Who is giving a talk at the museum?
4 What is Alex doing on Sunday?

6 Pronunciation *going* and *doing*

🔊 **92** Listen to five sentences from the conversation. Notice the /w/ sound in *going* and *doing*. Repeat the sentences.

Grammar present continuous with future time expressions

7 Look at the sentences from the conversation in Exercise 4 in the grammar box. Are the speakers talking about now or a time in the future?

A time in the future

> ▶ **PRESENT CONTINUOUS WITH FUTURE TIME EXPRESSIONS**
>
> What are you doing **this weekend**?
> Sports Gear is having a sale **tomorrow**.
> She's giving a talk about her trip **on Sunday evening**.
>
> For more information and practice, see page 168.

8 Look at the information for City Hall in Exercise 4. Write the conversation between Alex and Oscar.

A: What / you / do / this weekend?
O: *I'm not sure.*   My sister / come / tomorrow.
A: she / stay the weekend?
O: *Yes, she is.*   We / go / to a party on Saturday.
A: *Does she like music?*   The West Country Folk Band / play at City Hall on Sunday.
O: *OK. Great!*

Speaking

9 Write activities for this weekend.

Saturday	
MORNING	
AFTERNOON	
EVENING	

Sunday	
MORNING	
AFTERNOON	
EVENING	

10 Work in pairs. Ask and answer questions about next weekend. Are you doing the same things?

> What are you doing on Saturday morning?

> I'm going shopping with my sister. What about you?

Grammar

> **Grammar notes**
> In English, we use the present continuous to talk about arrangements that we have already made for the future.

8 Ask students to write present continuous sentences from the prompts.

> **ANSWERS**
> A: What are you doing this weekend?
> O: I'm not sure. My sister is coming tomorrow.
> A: Is she staying the weekend?
> O: Yes, she is. We are going to a party on Saturday.
> A: Does she like music? The West Country Folk Band is playing at City Hall on Sunday.
> O: OK. Great!

Speaking

9 Have students share their plans with the class. What are the most popular types of plans?

> **Extra activity**
> Tell students you are going to give them an amount of money to spend this weekend. Divide them into pairs; hand out one slip of paper with an amount of money written on it to each pair. The amounts should range from very little to quite a lot. Have students make their plans in accordance with their assigned budgets, and then share their budget and plans with the class.

> **HOMEWORK** Ask students to write a description of their plans for next weekend.

A different kind of weekend

12c A different kind of weekend

Warm-up

Personal response

Write *volunteer work* on the board and ask what it means (work for no money that you do to help other people or because you like doing it). Ask: *What volunteer work do people do? Why do they do it? Why is it important that people do volunteer work? What volunteer work do you do?*

Reading

1 Accept any answers at this stage. When checking, elicit ideas and use the opportunity to pre-teach *tornado, build, panel, wall,* and *roof.*

2 ANSWERS

1 They are doing volunteer work. They are helping to build a house.
2 They are in Greensburg, Kansas.
3 They are volunteers and "weekend builders."

4 ANSWERS

1 blue panel
2 His friends
3 her new house
4 the new wall

Grammar

Grammar notes

We use the simple present to talk about habits, routines, and things that are always true.

We use the simple past to talk about finished past actions and states.

We use the present continuous to talk about things happening now or these days, or to talk about arrangements for the future.

Reading

1 Look at the photos on page 147. Answer the questions.

1 What do you think the people are doing?
2 Where do you think they are?
3 Is there anything unusual about them?

2 Read the article and check your ideas from Exercise 1.

3 Read the article again. Are the sentences true (T) or false (F)?

1 Joel Connor works for free on the weekend. T
2 He's a builder. F
3 He's building a house for his family. F
4 He works with his friends. T
5 He's coming to Greensburg next weekend. F

4 Look at the photos on page 147. Complete the sentences.

1 Joel is moving a large _____ .
2 _____ are working on the roof.
3 Jill Eller is standing near _____ .
4 Jill's holding a part of _____ .

5 Match a verb in A with words in B. Check your answers in the article.

A	B
build	people
help	a house
know	a project
start	people
work	in an office

Grammar **tense review**

6 Look at these four sentences from the article. Underline the verbs. Then write past (P), present (PR), or future (F) next to the sentences.

1 Joel Connor <u>works</u> in an office in Kansas. PR
2 The community <u>started</u> a project. P
3 Jill <u>is standing</u> near her new house. PR
4 Next weekend, Joel <u>is moving</u> to a different project. F

---

7 Add these expressions to the sentences.

In this photo
From Monday to Friday
Last year

1 _____ , Joel Connor works in an office.
2 _____ , the community started a project.
3 _____ , Jill is standing near her new house.

8 Word focus *do*

a Match the questions (1–5) with the answers (a–e).

1 What (do) you *do*? b
2 What (are) you *doing*? d
3 What (do) you usually *do* on the weekend? e
4 What (did) you *do* on the weekend? c
5 What (are) you *doing* on the weekend? a

a I'm going to a concert with a friend.
b I'm a builder.
c I visited my cousin in Miami.
d I'm making lunch.
e I meet my friends.

b The verb *do* is a main verb and an auxiliary verb. Look at the questions. <u>Underline</u> the main verbs and circle the auxiliary verbs.

c Work in pairs. Ask and answer the questions in Exercise 8a.

> What do you do?
>
> I'm a …

Speaking

9 Work in groups. Plan a special weekend for a person you all know. Then tell the class.

> Next weekend is our special weekend for Tracey. On Saturday morning, we're all going shopping. Then Tracey is having a beauty makeover.

Extra activity

Write these phrases on the board: *At the moment, Next Tuesday, Last Friday, Every weekend, Right now, Tomorrow, Two weeks ago, On Mondays.* In pairs, have students say which tenses are usually used with each phrase. Then ask them to write true sentences using the phrases, e.g., *At the moment, I'm sitting in class. Next Tuesday, I'm playing tennis with Mark.*

7 ANSWERS

1 From Monday to Friday
2 Last year
3 In this photo

Joel Connor works in an office in Kansas. His job is a typical nine-to-five, Monday-to-Friday job, but on the weekend, he does something different. He does volunteer work. He helps different organizations and people for free. Every weekend, there's a new project. This weekend, Joel is helping to build a house. You can see him in the photo. He's moving a large blue panel. It's part of a wall. Joel isn't a professional builder, but the other people are volunteers too.

These "weekend builders" are from the small town of Greensburg in Kansas. A year ago, a tornado hit their town. After the tornado, the community started a project to build new homes. The project is for 30 new homes. They have help from a building company and the volunteers.

"I heard about the tornado and the new project. I knew some people in Greensburg so I wanted to help," Joel says. His friends are here this weekend too. They're on the roof. They're working with Jill and Scott Eller. Jill and Scott are building their new house. Jill (right) is standing near her new house. She's holding a part of the new wall. They're making the house "tornado-resistant." That's why it has an unusual shape.

The Ellers' house is almost ready, so next weekend, Joel is moving to a different project. Why does he volunteer? "I have time, I can help people, I make friends, and it's fun! So why not?" he says.

tornado /n/ /tɔrˈneɪdoʊ/ a very windy storm
tornado-resistant /n/ /tɔrˈneɪdoʊ rɪˌzɪstənt/ a tornado can't hurt this

Word focus

8a Start by reading through the questions and having the class say which tense is used in each one (*Answers: simple present, present continuous, simple present, simple past, present continuous for future*). Then ask students to match the questions to the answers.

8b Point out to students that do is not the only auxiliary verb in Exercise 8a.

8c Drill the questions in 8a for pronunciation first. Model each question, showing the weak stress of *do,* the auxiliary verb, and the strong stress on the question word and *do,* the main verb.

Speaking

9 Read through the example description as a class, and point out that *we're all* is used to emphasize that you are doing an activity together. Give groups five minutes to plan their weekend. Then ask a spokesperson from each group to present their plan. Note how well students use present continuous forms and correct common errors at the end.

Would you like a brochure?

12d Would you like a brochure?

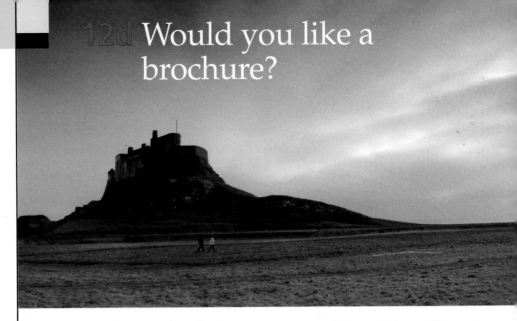

Warm-up

Personal response

Write *weekend trips* on the board, and check the meaning (*trips* are short journeys to go and visit places). Ask: *What trips do people do on the weekend in your country? What trips do you enjoy doing? What weekend trips did you often do when you were a child? Are you going on a weekend trip soon? Where are you going?*

Vocabulary

1 ANSWERS

1 museum/exhibition
2 court
3 brochure
4 round-trip ticket

Vocabulary notes

An exhibition is a show of paintings, photos, or objects in a museum or a gallery.

A brochure is a small, thin book that has pictures and information about places, products, events, etc.

PHOTO INFO

Lindisfarne is a low-lying island off the northeast coast of England. It is a popular tourist destination because of its historic monuments and nearby nature reserve. This castle was built in the 16th century.

Real life

3 Give students a moment to read the sentences.

Vocabulary weekend trips

1 Complete the sentences. There is one extra word.

| brochure | court | exhibition | museum | round-trip ticket |

1 You look at pictures in an _____ .
2 You play tennis on a _____ .
3 You read a _____ .
4 You buy a _____ to go to a place and come back.

Real life **buying tickets**

2 **93** Listen to three conversations (a–c). Match the number of tickets with the place and the price.

Number of tickets	Place	Price
a four	a castle	16 dollars
b three	a museum	10 dollars
c two	a tennis court	34 dollars

3 🔊 **93** Listen again. Are the sentences true (T) or false (F)?

a 1 There are four children. F
  2 They get a brochure in French. T

b 3 They buy one-way tickets. F
  4 They are going to the castle and gardens. T

c 5 People are playing on all the tennis courts. F
  6 They buy a ticket for two hours. F

148

---

4 Pronunciation *would you … ?*

a 🔊 **94** Look at the expressions for BUYING TICKETS. Listen and repeat.

b Work in pairs. Ask and answer questions with *Would you like … ?*

| a single ticket |
| to play soccer |
| a drink |
| to go to the museum |

▶ **BUYING TICKETS**

Four tickets to the museum, please.
Three round-trip tickets to Lindisfarne, please.
Would you like a brochure?
Would you like it in English?
Would you like to buy the tickets now?

5 Work in pairs. Look at the audioscript on page 174. Practice the conversations.

6 Work in pairs. Buy and sell tickets.

Student A: Turn to page 156.

Student B: Turn to page 160.

Pronunciation

Grammar notes

We use the form *Would you like* + noun to ask politely if somebody wants something.

We use the form *Would you like to* + infinitive to ask politely if somebody wants to do something.

4b Monitor carefully and make sure students are using the forms correctly.

6 For the first role-play, Students A have information about ticket prices. They must think about how to give that information, and how to ask questions with *Would you like…?* Students B are in charge of a group. They must look at the missing information and think about how to ask for it. Give students plenty of time to prepare and support as they think of things to say.

HOMEWORK Ask students to write about a place that they would like to visit for the weekend. Tell them to include what is interesting about the place and why they would like to go.

12e Join us for lunch

Writing an invitation

1 Read the invitation. Answer the questions.

1 Why are Estefania and Tim celebrating?
2 How are they celebrating?
3 When and where is it?
4 What do you think *RSVP* means?

2 Read the replies to the invitation. How many people are coming to the party? 4

1
> Estefania, thank you for the lunch invitation. My sister is arriving from Canada that day, so I can't come! Yoko

2
> Today at 6:51 PM   Pete:
>
> Hi Tim. Thanks for the invitation. I'm coming!

3
> Hi Estefania. We'd like to come to lunch, but Bill has swim class. Can we come late? Is that OK?
> Maya and Steve

4
> Dear Estefania and Tim
>
> Thank you very much for your invitation. We had a great time when we saw you last year. We are traveling on April 4, so we can't make it this time. Sorry!
>
> Dani and Eve

5
> Hi Stef and Tim
> Thank you for the invitation. I'd like to come. Why don't I bring a cake? See you on April 4!
> Gabi

ESTEFANIA AND TIM ARE MOVING!

PLEASE JOIN US FOR LUNCH

ON SUNDAY APRIL 4 AT 2 P.M.

OUR NEW ADDRESS IS 3 FORD STREET

CHULA VISTA

RSVP STEF@ROUNDHOUSE.NET

---

3 Writing skill **spelling: verb endings**

a Read the invitation and the replies again. Write the forms of the verbs.

1 move   moving
2 arrive   arriving
3 come   coming
4 swim   swimming
5 travel   traveling

b How does the spelling of these verbs change in the present continuous?

c Complete the table. Spell the verbs correctly.

	Present continuous	Simple present (he/she/it)	Simple past
do	doing	does	did
drive	driving	drives	drove
fly	flying	flies	flew
lie	lying	lies	lied
make	making	makes	made
see	seeing	sees	saw
sit	sitting	sits	sat
smile	smiling	smiles	smiled
study	studying	studies	studied

4 Write an invitation to an event like a party. Check the spelling.

5 Exchange invitations with somone in your class. Read your classmate's invitation. Can you go to this event? Write a reply. If you can't go, give a reason. Give the reply to your classmate.

Join us for lunch

Introducing the theme: invitations

Ask students: *When did you last send an invitation to friends? What event was it for? What did you write in the invitation? How many people came?*

Writing

1 ANSWERS

1 new house
2 lunch
3 Sunday, April 4, 2 PM at
4 répondez s'il vous plaît = please respond to this invitation

Writing skills

Grammar notes

When forming the present participle, we add -*ing* to the verb.

If a verb ends with *e*, we drop the *e* before adding -*ing*.

If a verb ends with consonant + vowel + consonant, the final consonant is doubled when the final syllable is stressed (*swimming, beginning,* etc.). When the final syllable is not stressed, we do not double the consonant (e.g., *opening*).

When verbs end with *ie*, we change the *ie* to *y* before adding -*ing* (*die – dying, lie – lying*).

3b ANSWERS

Adds -ing, drops the final -e or doubles the final consonant, if applicable.

Extra activity

Ask students to think of other verbs that have irregular -*ing* endings (*live, die, put, get,* etc.).

HOMEWORK Ask students to write an invitation to a special event that they are having in the coming year.

4 Ask students to decide what event to plan before writing their invitation. They should use the invitation in Exercise 1 as a model. You may want to have them write the invitations on index cards.

Saturday morning in São Tomé

Videoscript

Narrator: It's early on Saturday morning in São Tomé. Children are playing. Some people are resting.

The main beach near the city of São Tomé is very busy. Boats are arriving with fish. There are a lot of flying fish today.

In the mountains, people are taking vegetables to market.

Oswaldo Santos is from São Tomé. He's usually at home on Saturdays. Oswaldo is a musician. He's in a group called Grupo Tempo. He plays the guitar, he sings, and he writes music.

This Saturday morning, Oswaldo is visiting his friends, Guillerme and Nezo.

Oswaldo and Guillerme are driving to the south of the island.

Nezo lives in a small town here.

Oswaldo, Guillerme, and Nezo are playing a new song. They're giving a concert next week. Today they're preparing for the concert.

Guillerme and Nezo are painters, too. They paint things from local life: the people, the colors, and the animals.

Their music and art is about life in São Tomé.

12f Saturday morning in São Tomé
Video

This fisherman doesn't work on Saturdays.

150

Before you watch

1 Work in pairs. Ask and answer these questions.

1 Can you play a musical instrument?
2 Can you paint or draw?
3 Do you go fishing?
4 Can you swim?

2 Work in pairs. What do these people do on the weekend? Write true sentences.

People	Activities
	do homework.
Children	give concerts.
Farmers	go to school.
Fishermen	go to the market.
Musicians	meet friends.
Salespeople	play music.
	rest.

3 Work in pairs. What do the people in Exercise 2 do on the weekend in your country?

4 São Tomé is the captial of São Tomé and Principe. How many islands are there in the country? 2

While you watch

5 These things are in the video. Watch the video again and put the pictures in order.

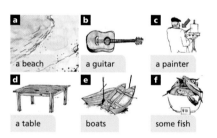

a a beach
b a guitar
c a painter
d a table
e boats
f some fish

1 and 2: Boats and beach (same time)
3 fish
4 guitar
5 table
6 painter

6 Watch the video again and write down one thing about each person.

1 Oswaldo Santos   2 Guillerme   3 Nezo

7 Work in pairs. Compare your answers from Exercise 6.

8 Watch the video again and answer the questions.
1 Who is playing in the water? The children are playing in the water.
2 Who is resting in a boat? A man is resting in a boat.
3 Who is buying fish? Women are buying fish.
4 Who is playing the guitar? Oswaldo is playing the guitar.
5 Who is singing? Oswaldo and Guillerme are singing.
6 Who is painting? Guillerme and Nezo are painting.

9 Work in pairs. Ask and answer the questions in Exercise 8. Do you agree?

After you watch

10 Complete the text with these words.

art   colors   concert   guitar   life   music
musician   painters   people   song

Oswaldo is a ¹ musician. He's in a group called *Grupo Tempo*. He plays the ² guitar , he sings, and he writes ³ music .

Oswaldo, Guillerme, and Nezo are playing a new ⁴ song . They're giving a ⁵ concert next week.

Guillerme and Nezo are ⁶ painters too. They paint things from local life: the ⁷ people , the ⁸ colors , and the animals. Their music and ⁹ art is about ¹⁰ life in São Tomé.

11 Work in pairs. Make notes about musicians or artists you like. Tell your partner about them.

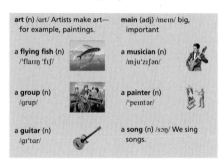

art (n) /ɑrt/ Artists make art— for example, paintings.

a flying fish (n) /'flaɪŋ 'fɪʃ/

a group (n) /grup/

a guitar (n) /gɪ'tɑr/

main (adj) /meɪn/ big, important

a musician (n) /mju'zɪʃən/

a painter (n) /'peɪntər/

a song (n) /sɔŋ/ We sing songs.

Before you watch

1 Ask students to look at the photo. Ask: *What can you see? Where are they?* Then divide the class into pairs to take turns to ask and answer the questions. Check answers to find out what abilities and interests your students share.

2 In pairs, students make true sentences about the people. Accept any logical matches.

SAMPLE ANSWERS

Children do homework, meet friends, and play with friends.

Farmers go to the market, meet friends, and rest.

Fishermen go to the market, meet friends, and rest.

Musicians give concerts, play music, sing songs, and meet friends.

Salespeople go to the market, meet friends, and rest.

3 In pairs, students look at the people in Exercise 2 again and take turns asking and answering the questions.

4 Students look at the map and answer the question.

While you watch

5 Play the entire video. Students watch and put the pictures in order.

6 Play the video again, pausing where necessary. Students watch and write one thing about each person.

SAMPLE ANSWERS

1 Oswaldo Santos is from São Tomé. He is a musician. He's in a group called Grupo Tempo. He plays the guitar, he sings, and he writes music.

2 Guillerme is a painter. He paints things from local life. He is giving a concert next week.

3 Nezo is a painter. He lives in a small town here. He is giving a concert next week.

7 Put students in pairs to compare their answers from Exercise 6. Check answers as a class.

8 Give students some time to go through the questions. Note the singular verb in the questions even if the answer is plural, e.g., *Children are playing…* Play the video again. Students watch, listen, and answer the questions.

9 In pairs, students take turns to ask and answer the questions in Exercise 8. Ask: *Do you agree? Why / Why not?* Check answers.

After you watch

10 Give students some time to read the text and complete the text with the words. Check answers.

11 Write the name of a musician you like on the board. Encourage students to ask you questions about him/her. Then ask students to make short notes about musicians or artists they like.

Grammar

1 Ask students to look at the photo. Ask: *Where are they? What are they doing?* Students match the words (1–5) with the people (a–d). Then they write sentences with the present continuous.

> **ANSWERS**
> **1** He is wearing a brown jacket.
> **2** She is holding some books.
> **3** She is talking to her friend.
> **4** He is walking to the bus stop.

2 Students complete the paragraph with the correct form of the present continuous.

> **ANSWERS**
> **1** are standing
> **2** are opening
> **3** are not getting
> **4** are waiting
> **5** are going
> **6** are thinking
> **7** are not going
> **8** are taking

3 Students put the words in the conversation in order.

> **ANSWERS**
> A What are you doing?
> B I am leaving the office.
> A It is late.
> B We are working late this week.
> A Are you coming to the beach tomorrow?
> B What time are you going?
> A We are leaving at eleven o'clock.
> B Is your friend coming?

Vocabulary

4 Divide the class into pairs. Give students time to prepare questions. Students take turns to ask and answer questions about rooms with the words.

UNIT 12 REVIEW

Grammar

1 Look at the photo of people at a bus stop in Santiago, Chile. Match the words (1–4) with the people (a–d) in the photo. Then write sentences with the present continuous.

c 1 wear / a brown jacket
b 2 hold / some books
d 3 talk / to her friend
a 4 walk / to the bus stop

2 Complete the paragraph about the photo with the correct form of the present continuous.

It's Friday evening in Santiago. These people ¹_____ (stand) at a bus stop. There's a bus and its doors ²_____ (open), but the people ³_____ (not get) on it. They ⁴_____ (wait) for different buses. Some of the people ⁵_____ (go) home. They ⁶_____ (think) about the weekend. Some ⁷_____ (not go) home. They ⁸_____ (take) the bus to work.

3 Put the words in the conversation in order.

A: *Oh hello.* you / what / doing /are / ?
B: office / I / leaving / the / am / .
A: *Really?* late / is / it / .
B: *I know.* this / working / we / late / are / week / .
A: *OK.* to / coming / you / tomorrow / the beach / are / ?
B: *I don't know.* are / going / time / you / what / ?
A: leaving / at /are /eleven o'clock / we / .
B: friend / is / coming / your / ?
A: *Yes, he is.*
B: *OK. Great.*

I CAN
talk about now (present continuous)
talk about the future (present continuous with future time expressions)
use the simple present, present continuous, and simple past correctly

Vocabulary

4 Work in pairs. Ask and answer questions about the rooms where people do these things. Use these words.

1 cook?   4 watch TV?
2 sleep?   5 eat?
3 take a shower?   6 read?

5 Match a verb from A with words from B.

A	B
get up	to a concert
go	family
have	soccer
meet	friends
play	late
read	the newspaper
visit	a party

6 Work in pairs. Tell your partner what you usually do on the weekend. Do you do similar things?

> I CAN
> talk about rooms in a house
> talk about weekend activities

Real life

7 Match the requests (1–4) with the responses (a–d).

1 A round-trip ticket to Oxford. c
2 Three tickets for the concert, please. d
3 Two tickets for Cinema One, please. a
4 Two tickets for the museum, please. b

a Two adults? That's twenty-four dollars, please.
b Here you are. Would you like an audio guide?
c Are you coming back today?
d Would you like to sit upstairs or downstairs?

> I CAN
> buy tickets
> talk about weekend trips

Speaking

8 Work in pairs. Tell your partner about your plans. What are you doing next weekend/week/month?

> **ANSWERS**
> **1** Where do people cook? (in a kitchen)
> **2** Where do people sleep? (in a bedroom)
> **3** Where do people take a shower? (in a bathroom)
> **4** Where do people watch TV? (in a living room)
> **5** Where do people eat? (in a dining room)
> **6** Where do people read? (in a living room / bedroom)

5 Students match a verb from A with words from B.

6 Divide the class into pairs. Students take turns to tell their partner about the

things they usually do on the weekend. When checking, find out if the students do similar things.

Real life

7 Students match the requests (1–4) with the responses (a–d).

Speaking

8 Give students time to think about their plans. Then organize the class into pairs. Students tell their partner about their plans.

Communication activities

UNIT 1a, Exercise 15, page 11

Student A

1 Listen to your partner. Write the jobs.

a .... b ....
c .... d ....

2 Spell these jobs to your partner.

e   driver

f   artist

g   photographer

h   writer

UNIT 2b, Exercise 13, page 25

Student A

1 Look at the photo. You are on vacation in Oman. Look at the sentences (1–4) and choose an option. Then have a telephone conversation with your friend (Student B) about your vacation.

1   You're *OK* / *happy*.
2   It's *hot* / *cold*.
3   The beach is *nice* / *beautiful*.
4   Your hotel is *nice* / *OK*.

2 Your friend (Student B) is on vacation. Prepare questions with these words. Then have a telephone conversation with Student B.

1 where?	4 city / beautiful?
2 OK?	5 hotel / nice?
3 cold?	

UNIT 3b, Exercise 9, page 37

Student A

1 Look at the information about photo A. Answer your partner's questions about this photo.

Ivan
Miroslava
in Russia
Miroslava's sister
Ivan's 23 and Miroslava's 21

2 Look at photo B. Ask your partner about this photo. Ask questions with *who, where, what,* and *how old*.

UNIT 4b, Exercise 10, page 49

Student A

1 Look at the information about photo A. Answer your partner's questions about this tower.

2 Look at photo B. Ask your partner about this tower. Ask the questions on page 49.

- The Space Needle tower
- It's in Seattle in the United States.
- It's open every day of the year.
- It's a symbol of Seattle. It's in Hollywood movies, for example, *Sleepless in Seattle*.

UNIT 5c, Exercise 7, page 62

Student A

1 Tell your partner about this microwave oven. Use *can* and *has*.

shopping_online.com

EasyCook Microwave

Product features:
cook and heat food ✓
3 power options ✓
make cakes ✗
digital clock ✓
buy online ✓

2 Listen to your partner. Make notes (1–5) about this microwave oven.

ProfessionalChef Microwave

1 ....
2 ....
3 ....
4 ....
5 ....

3 Look at the two microwave ovens. Do you think they are cheap or expensive?

UNIT 6c, Exercise 9, page 74

Student A

1 Look at the photos and the information about sports events 1 and 3. Ask your partner five questions about events 2 and 4. Complete the information. You get 5 points if you identify the event after one question, 4 points if you ask two questions, etc.

	1 Wimbledon	2	3 the Dakar Rally	4
1 **Where?**	London		South America	
2 **When?**	June and July		January	
3 **What kind of event?**	a competition		a race	
4 **Prize?**	money		–	
5 **Sport?**	tennis		racing	

2 Look at the information about Wimbledon and the Dakar Rally. Answer your partner's questions.

UNIT 8c, Exercise 9, page 98

Student A

Write the questions (1–3) and choose your answers.

Then ask your partner the questions. Write your partner's answers and check the results on page 157.

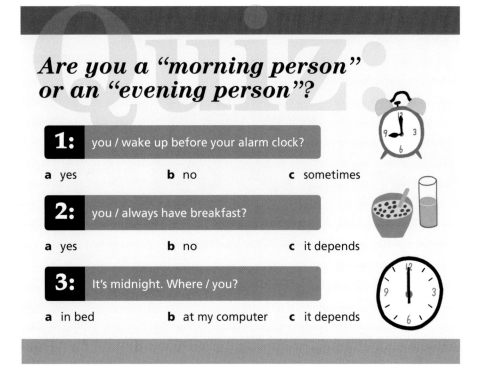

Are you a "morning person" or an "evening person"?

1: you / wake up before your alarm clock?

a yes   **b** no   **c** sometimes

2: you / always have breakfast?

a yes   **b** no   **c** it depends

3: It's midnight. Where / you?

a in bed   **b** at my computer   **c** it depends

UNIT 9b, Exercise 11, page 109

Student A

1 Look at this room. Answer Student B's questions.

2 Look at these two rooms. Student B has one of these rooms. Ask questions to find out which one. Use *Is there a...?* and *Are there any...?*

UNIT 10c, Exercise 9, page 122

Pair A

1 Listen to Pair B. Who are the people?

2 Look at the notes. Tell Pair B about these two people. Don't say the names.

Date of birth	1595
Place of birth	Virginia, North America
Biographical information	a prisoner of the English married to an English farmer, John Rolfe
Name	Pocahontas

Date of birth	January 19, 1807
Place of birth	Virginia, North America
Biographical information	leader, the Army of Northern Virginia, Confederacy, American Civil War also was in war between Mexico and the US
Name	Robert E. Lee

UNIT 12d, Exercise 6, page 148

Student A

1 You work in a museum's ticket office. Look at this information and answer Student B's questions.

> ## Great Explorers Exhibition
>
> Tickets: adults $2.50; children $1.50
>
> Brochures: $2.00
>
> Audio program: English, French, German, Spanish

2 You are a group of two adults and four children. You are going to Bambridge Castle. Ask Student B questions to find out when the last bus leaves and how much the tickets cost.

> *Buses to Bambridge Castle*
> *Every hour 9:15 – _____*
> *Tickets: one-way $ _____ ; round-trip $ _____*
> *Round-trip ticket + admission to castle $ _____*

UNIT 1a, Exercise 15, page 11

Student B

1 Spell these jobs to your partner.

a filmmaker

b engineer

c doctor

d teacher

2 Listen to your partner. Write the jobs.

e _____ f _____

g _____ h _____

UNIT 2b, Exercise 13, page 25

Student B

1 Your friend (Student A) is on vacation. Prepare questions with these words. Then have a telephone conversation with Student A.

1 where?   4 beach / beautiful?
2 OK?   5 hotel / nice?
3 cold?

2 Look at the photo. You are on vacation in New York. Look at the sentences (1–4) and choose an option. Then have a telephone conversation with your friend (Student A) about your vacation.

1 You're *OK / happy*.
2 It's *hot / cold*.
3 The city is *nice / beautiful*.
4 Your hotel is *nice / OK*.

UNIT 3b, Exercise 9, page 37

Student B

1 Look at photo A. Ask your partner questions about the photo with *who, where, what,* and *how old*.

2 Look at the information about photo B. Answer your partner's questions about this photo.

John
Anna
in Alaska, US
the officiant (person marrying the couple)
John's 28 and Anna's 27

UNIT 8c, Exercise 9, page 98: answers

Are you a "morning person" or an "evening person"?

Results

Mostly A: You are a morning person. Evening activities are hard for you. Office jobs are good for you.

Mostly B: You are an evening person. Morning activities are difficult for you. Good jobs for you are jobs in hospitals, the arts, and the media.

Mostly C: You are not a morning person or an evening person. Most people are this way.

UNIT 4b, Exercise 10, page 49

Student B

1 Look at photo A. Use the questions on page 49 to ask your partner about this tower.

2 Look at the information about photo B. Answer your partner's questions about this tower.

- The Minaret of the Samarra Mosque
- It's in Samarra in Iraq.
- It's not open to tourists at the moment.
- The spiral shape is famous. Samarra is a UNESCO World Heritage Site.

UNIT 5c, Exercise 7, page 62

Student B

1 Listen to your partner. Make notes (1–5) about this microwave oven.

EasyCook Microwave

1 ....
2 ....
3 ....
4 ....
5 ....

2 Tell your partner about this microwave oven. Use *can* and *has*.

shopping_online.com

ProfessionalChef Microwave

Product features:
memory (100 options) ✓
10 power options ✓
cook and heat food ✓
make cakes ✓
buy online ✓

3 Look at the two microwave ovens. Do you think they are cheap or expensive?

UNIT 6c, Exercise 9, page 74

Student B

1 Look at the information about the New York Marathon and the Masters. Answer your partner's questions.

	1 _____	2 the New York Marathon	3 _____	4 the Masters
1 **Where?**		New York		Georgia, USA
2 **When?**		November		April
3 **What kind of event?**		a race		a competition
4 **Prize?**		money		money, a green jacket
5 **Sport?**		running		golf

2 Look at the photos and the information about sports events 2 and 4. Ask your partner five questions about events 1 and 3. Complete the information. You get 5 points if you identify the event after one question, 4 points if you ask two questions, etc.

UNIT 8c, Exercise 9, page 98

Student B

Write the questions (4–6) and choose your answers.

Then ask your partner the questions. Write your partner's answers and check the results on page 157.

Quiz!

Are you a "morning person" or an "evening person"?

4: What time / you / get up on the weekend?

a early   **b** late   **c** the same time as usual

5: What / the main meal of the day for you?

a lunch   **b** dinner   **c** it depends

6: you / fall asleep in front of the TV at night?

a yes   **b** no   **c** sometimes

UNIT 9b, Exercise 11, page 109

Student B

1 Look at these two rooms. Student A has one of these rooms. Ask questions to find out which one. Use *Is there a...?* and *Are there any...?*

2 Look at this room. Answer Student A's questions.

UNIT 10c, Exercise 9, page 122

Pair B

1 Look at the notes. Tell Pair A about these two people. Don't say the names.

Date of birth	July 24, 1783
Place of birth	Caracas, South America
Biographical information	married to a Spanish woman: Maria Teresa
	leader of four countries: Colombia, Venezuela, Ecuador, and Bolivia
	first president of Venezuela
Name	Simón Bolívar

Date of birth	February 22, 1732
Place of birth	Virginia, North America
Biographical information	leader, the American army, War of Independence
	first president, US
Name	George Washington

2 Listen to Pair A. Who are the people?

UNIT 12d, Exercise 6, page 148

Student B

1 You are a group of two adults and three children. You are American and one of the children is German. Visit the Great Explorers Exhibition at a museum. Ask Student A questions to find out about tickets, brochures, and the audio program.

Great Explorers Exhibition

Tickets: adults $_____ ; children $_____

Brochures: $_____

Audio program: English, _____ , _____ , Spanish

2 You work in the ticket office of a bus company. Look at this information and answer Student A's questions.

Buses to Bambridge Castle

Every hour 9:15 – 6:15

Tickets: one-way $4.25; round-trip $7.00

Round-trip ticket + admission to castle $8.50

Grammar summary

UNIT 1

a/an (articles)

a + single noun with consonants: *b, c, d, f,* etc.
a <u>driver</u>, **a** <u>filmmaker</u>
an + single noun with vowels: *a, e, i, o, u*
an <u>artist</u>, **an** <u>engineer</u>

Practice

1 Complete the sentences with *a* or *an*.

1 I'm <u>a</u> scientist.
2 I'm <u>a</u> writer.
3 I'm <u>an</u> explorer.
4 I'm <u>an</u> artist.
5 I'm <u>a</u> photographer.

I + am, you + are

I	am ('m)	John.
You	are ('re)	a student.

Practice

2 Complete the sentences with *I'm* or *You're*.

1 ALEX: <u>I'm</u> Alex.
  MIREYA: Hi, Alex.
2 ROBERT: <u>You're</u> Mattias Klum.
  MATTIAS: Yes, I am.
3 CAROLYN: Hi!
  ALEX: <u>You're</u> Carolyn.
4 MIREYA: Hello.
  ROBERT: Hi! <u>I'm</u> Robert Ballard.
5 ALEX: I'm a photographer.
  ROBERT: <u>You're</u> Alex Treadway.

he/she/it + is

He	is ('s)	Brazilian
She	is ('s)	from Japan.
It	is ('s)	in Italy.

Practice

3 Write sentences with *He's*, *She's*, and *It's*.

1 Dechen (f) / from Ladakh She's from Ladakh.
2 Manu (m)/ Nepalese He's Nepalese.
3 Dechen / Indian She's Indian.
4 Jagat / in Nepal It's in Nepal.
5 Manu / from Jagat He's from Jagat.

I + am, you + are, he/she/it + is (be)

I	am ('m)	John.
You	are ('re)	a student.
He	is ('s)	Brazilian.
She	is ('s)	from Japan.
It	is ('s)	in Italy.

Practice

4 Complete the sentences with *am*, *are*, and *is*.

1 Hi! I <u>am</u> Elena.
2 Paul <u>is</u> an engineer.
3 He <u>is</u> from Hong Kong.
4 It <u>is</u> in China.
5 You <u>are</u> English.

my, your

I'm Jared. **My** name's Jared.
You're Maria. **Your** name's Maria.

Practice

5 Complete the sentences with *my* and *your*.

1 <u>My</u> name's Lisa. I'm from Peru.
2 Hello! You're my teacher. <u>Your</u> name's Mr. Jones. I'm Tomas.
3 Hello! <u>My</u> name's Paolo.
4 Hi. I'm Juan. What's <u>your</u> name?
5 <u>My</u> cell number is 695-555-7362.
6 John, what's <u>your</u> home number?

UNIT 2

we/they + are

We	are ('re)	in Canada.
They	are ('re)	from Brazil.
		Italian.

Practice

1 Complete the sentences.

1 This is Jack. This is Bill. <u>They</u> are Canadian.
2 France and Spain <u>are</u> in Europe.
3 Bruno and Paola are from Italy. <u>They're</u> Italian.
4 I'm with my teacher. <u>We</u> 're in a classroom.
5 Jane and Barry are American. <u>They</u> 're from the United States.

be

I	am ('m)	
You	are ('re)	
He		
She	is ('s)	in Canada.
It		from Brazil.
		Italian.
We		
You	are ('re)	
They		

Practice

2 Choose the correct option.

1 My name is Carlos and I (am) / is / are a student.
2 Toshiba am / (is) / are Japanese.
3 You am / is / (are) a student.
4 My teacher am / (is) / are from Chicago.
5 I'm with my friend. We am / is / (are) in China.

be negative forms

I	am not ('m not)	
You	are not (aren't)	a teacher.
He		from Europe.
She	is not (isn't)	in China.
It		
We		from Europe.
You	are not (aren't)	in China.
They		

Practice

3 Rewrite the sentences with the verb in the negative form.

1 Jack's a student. *Jack isn't a student.*
2 We are Spanish. *We aren't Spanish.*
3 I'm happy. *I'm not happy.*
4 Susana and Gina are from Peru. *Susana and Gina aren't from Peru.*
5 You're a writer. *You aren't a writer.*

be questions and short answers

Am I		Yes, I **am**.
		No, I'**m not**.
Are you	in a hotel?	Yes, she/he/it **is**.
	nice?	No, she/he/it **isn't**.
Is she/he/it	from Peru?	Yes, we/you/they **are**.
		No, we/you/they **aren't**.
Are we/you/they		

Practice

4 Write questions with the correct form of *be*. Then answer each question with *yes* and *no*.

1 Simona / from Bolivia? *Is Simona from Bolivia? Yes, she is. / No, she isn't.*
2 John / a teacher? *Is John a teacher? Yes, he is. / No, he isn't.*
3 you / on vacation? *Are you on vacation? Yes, I am. / No, I'm not.*
4 your hotel / nice? *Is your hotel nice? Yes, it is. / No, it isn't.*
5 Susana and Gina / in Paris? *Are Susana and Gina in Paris? Yes, they are. / No, they aren't.*

plural nouns

Add *-s*.
a friend → friends

Change *-y* to *-ies*.
a city → cities

Add *-es* to nouns that end in *-s*, *-ch*, and *-ss*.
a bus → buses

Practice

5 Write the plural of these nouns.

1 a lake   4 an airport   7 a mountain
2 a country   5 a beach   8 a tent
3 a car   6 a photo   9 a student

1 lakes   5 beaches
2 countries   6 photos
3 cars   7 mountains
4 airports   8 tents
*   9 students*

UNIT 3

possessive *'s*

Alexandra is Philippe's daughter.
Simone and Jacques are Alexandra's grandparents.

Note: The possessive *'s* is not a contraction of *is*.
Who's Fabien? = Who is Fabien?
He's my brother. = He is my brother.
He's Jean-Michel's son. = He is Jean-Michel's son.

Practice

1 Look at the family tree. Write sentences.

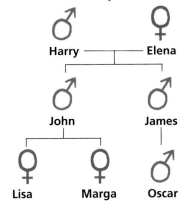

1 James / Oscar / father
2 John and James / Elena / sons
3 Lisa and Marga / Harry / granddaughters
4 Lisa / Marga / sister
5 Elena / Oscar / grandmother

his, her, our, their

This is	my your his her our their	friend.

Practice

2 Choose the correct option.

1 This is a photo of my brother at *her* / (*his*) wedding.
2 My wife is Russian. (*Her*) / *My* name is Olga.
3 We are happy. It's *his* / (*our*) daughter's wedding.
4 Hi, Zara. Is it *her* / (*your*) birthday today?
5 My parents are on vacation. It's *his* / (*their*) wedding anniversary.

1 1 James is Oscar's father.
   2 John and James are Elena's sons.
   3 Lisa and Marga are Harry's granddaughters.
   4 Lisa is Marga's sister.
   5 Elena is Oscar's grandmother.

irregular plural nouns

a child → **children**
a man → **men**
a woman → **women**
a person → **people**

Remember: Add -s or -es and change -y to -ies to make regular plural nouns.

Practice

3 Complete the singular and plural nouns.

1 How old are the wom___ _en_ in the photo?
2 Who are the pe___ _ople_ at the wedding?
3 This chil___ _d_ is three years old.
4 Who is the pe___ _rson_ in this photo?
5 James and Eliza are my chil___ _dren_ .

UNIT 4

prepositions of place

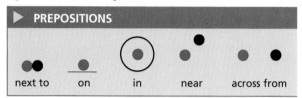

The museum is **next to** the market.
The market is **in** a building.
The movie theater is **near** the bank.
The café is **across from** the bus station.

Practice

1 Look at the picture. Complete the sentences.

1 The bank is ___ _next to_ ___ the hotel.
2 The bank is ___ _across from_ ___ the Tourist Information Center.
3 Two people are ___ _in_ ___ the park.
4 The parking lot is ___ _near_ ___ the hotel.
5 The Science Museum is ___ _next to_ ___ the parking lot.
6 Three people are ___ _near_ ___ the movie theater.

this, that

This book is in Portuguese.

That's Big Ben!

Use *this* for things that are near you but *that* for things that aren't near you.

Practice

2 Look at the picture in Exercise 1. Read the words of the people in the park. Choose the correct option.

1 "(This) / That park is nice."
2 "This /(That) is my bank."
3 "Is (this)/ that your book?"

question words

What's that?
Where's the bank?
When's the park open?

Why's the Statue of Liberty famous?
Who's this?
How old is he?

Practice

3 Match the questions (1–5) with the answers (a–e).

1 Where's O'Hare airport? _b_
2 What's your address? _c_
3 How old is your brother? _e_
4 Who's that in the park? _d_
5 When are banks open in your country? _a_

a From Monday to Friday.
b It's in Chicago.
c It's 36 Oxford Street.
d My sister and her children.
e He's 27.

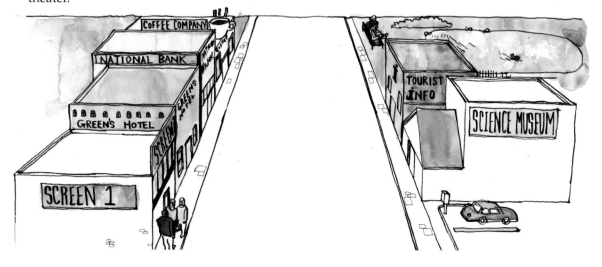

UNIT 5

can/can't

Affirmative		Negative	
I/You		I/You	
He/She/It	**can** cook.	He/She/It	**can't** cook.
We/You/They		We/You/They	

can't = cannot

Practice

1 Choose the correct option.

1 Babies *can / (can't)* run.
2 Children *(can) / can't* see.
3 Cars *can / (can't)* fly.
4 Animals *can / (can't)* speak.

can questions and short answers

Questions			Short answers		
Can	I/you he/she/it we/you/they	cook?	Yes, No,	I/you he/she/it we/you/they	**can.** **can't.**

Practice

2 Write questions and answers.

1 he / sing ✓ Can he sing? Yes, he can.
2 you / drive a car ✓ Can you drive a car? Yes, I can.
3 they / play table tennis ✗ Can they play table tennis? No, they can't.
4 she / cook ✗ Can she cook? No, she can't.
5 we / speak English ✓ Can we speak English? Yes, we / you can.

have/has

I/You We/You/They	**have**	a cell phone. batteries.
He/She/It	**has**	

Practice

3 Complete the sentences with *have* and *has*.

1 I ___have___ two cameras.
2 My laptop ___has___ a webcam.
3 My friends ___have___ three children.
4 My sister ___has___ a great job.

adjective + noun

My headphones are new.
I have new headphones.
Note: Adjectives have only one form: *I have ~~news~~ headphones.*
The word order is adjective + noun, NOT noun + adjective: *I have ~~headphones new~~.*

Practice

4 Put the words in order to make sentences.

1 is / camera / this / Japanese / a   This is a Japanese camera.
2 fantastic / phone / my / a / memory / has   My phone has a fantastic memory.
3 MP3 player / you / great / a / have   You have a great MP3 player.
4 is / Jack's / man / an / grandfather / old   Jack's grandfather is an old man.

very, really

	This camera is It's	expensive. great/fantastic.
	This camera is It's	**really** **very** really ~~very~~	expensive. great/fantastic.

Practice

5 Rewrite the sentences with *very* or *really* where possible.

1 This laptop is light. (really) This laptop is really light.
2 Their house is big. (very) Their house is very big.
3 My friend's new phone is fantastic. (really) My friend's new phone is really fantastic.
4 That microwave is great. (very) (not possible)
5 We have an old car. (very) We have a very old car.

UNIT 6

like

Affirmative
I/You/We/You/They **like** fruit.

Negative
I/You/We/You/They **don't like** vegetables.
(don't = do not)

Practice

1 Write sentences with the correct form of *like*.

1 I / basketball ☹   I don't like basketball.
2 We / tennis ☺   We like tennis.
3 I / coffee ☺   I like coffee.
4 They / cake ☹   They don't like cake.

like questions and short answers

Questions				Short answers
Do	I you we you they	**like**	pizza?	Yes, I/you/we/you/they **do.** No, I/you/we/you/they **don't.**

Note: "*Do you like pizza?*" "*Yes, I do.*" NOT "*Yes, I ~~like~~.*"

Practice

2 Write questions with the words. Then answer the questions.

1 cheese / they ✓   Do they like cheese? Yes, they do.
2 fruit / you ✗   Do you like fruit? No, I don't.
3 fish / they ✓   Do they like fish? Yes, they do.
4 rice / they ✗   Do they like rice? No, they don't.

he/she + like

Affirmative		Negative	
He She	**likes** books.	He She	**doesn't like** music.

Questions			Short answers
Does	he she	**like** fish?	Yes, he/she **does**. No, he/she **doesn't**.

(doesn't = does not)

Practice

3 Three of these sentences are missing *does* or *doesn't*. Rewrite them with the missing word.

1 Zeb likes Arizona.
2 Joanna like action movies. *Joanna doesn't like action movies.*
3 your teacher like music? *Does your teacher like music?*
4 Ryan like swimming. *Ryan doesn't like swimming.*

object pronouns

Diana likes	me. you. him. her. it. us. you. them.

Practice

4 Look at the underlined nouns. Complete the sentences with an object pronoun.

1 I like <u>birds</u>, but my friend doesn't like ___them___ .
2 <u>We</u> can't see you. Can you see ___us___ ?
3 <u>She</u>'s a popular writer, but I don't like ___her___ .
4 Do you like <u>pop music</u>? Yes, I love ___it___ .
5 <u>Matt Damon</u> is fantastic in the *Bourne* movies. I love ___him___ .

UNIT 7

simple present *I/you/we/you/they*

Affirmative			Negative		
I You We You They	**speak**	Sami.	I You We You They	**don't speak**	Sami.

(don't = do not)

Practice

1 Rewrite the sentences using the form in parentheses.

1 I live near a beach. (negative) *I don't live near a beach.*
2 You don't have a car. (affirmative) *You have a car.*
3 My friends speak English. (negative) *My friends don't speak English.*
4 We study on vacation. (negative) *We don't study on vacation.*

simple present questions *I/you/we/you/they*

Questions				Short answers
Do	I you we you they	**live**	in Sweden?	Yes, I/you/we/you/they **do**. No, I/you/we/you/they **don't**.

Practice

2 Write questions with the words. Then write the answers.

1 in Egypt (you / live) ✓ *Do you live in Egypt? Yes, I do.*
2 to college (they / go) ✗ *Do they go to college? No, they don't.*
3 Spanish (I / study) ✓ *Do I study Spanish? Yes, I / you do.*
4 friends in this class (we / have) ✓ *Do we have friends in this class? Yes, we / you do.*
5 at this school (you / teach) ✗ *Do you teach at this school? No, I don't.*

simple present with question words

What Where Who Why When	**do**	I/you/we/you/they/people	do? go? meet?

Practice

3 Read the questions and answers. Complete the questions with a question word.

1 " ___What___ do you do?"
"I work in a school."
2 " ___When___ do you go on vacation?"
"In the summer."
3 " ___What___ do you do on summer vacation?"
"I play golf."
4 " ___Who___ do you play golf with?"
"I play golf with my brothers."
5 " ___Where___ do your brothers live?"
"They live near me."
6 " ___Why___ do you play golf?"
"I like it."

UNIT 8

simple present *he/she/it*

Affirmative		Negative	
He/She/It	**gets up** at 7:30	He/She/It	**doesn't work**.

(doesn't = does not)

Add -s.
get up → *gets up*

Add -es to verbs that end in -ch and -sh.
teach → *teaches*, *finish* → *finishes*

The verbs *go, do,* and *have* are irregular.
go → *goes, do* → *does, have* → *has*

Practice

1 Write the correct form of the verb in parentheses.
1 Kristen ___doesn't go___ (not / go) to work during the day.
2 She ___works___ (work) in the evening.
3 She ___doesn't work___ (not / work) in a school.
4 She ___teaches___ (teach) adults at a college.
5 She ___starts___ (start) work at 5:30 and she ___doesn't finish___ (not / finish) until ten o'clock.

prepositions of time

at + time	**at** 6:30
on + day	**on** Tuesday/Tuesdays
in (the) + part of day, month, season	**in** the morning, **in** July, **in** the summer

Note: *at night*

Practice

2 Complete the text with the correct preposition.

Alan works in the city. He gets home ¹ ___at___ seven o'clock ² ___in___ the evening. He has dinner ³ ___at___ 8:30 and ⁴ ___in___ winter he watches TV. He goes out for dinner ⁵ ___on___ Fridays. He can go to bed late because he doesn't work ⁶ ___on___ Saturdays.

frequency adverbs

100%

*I **always** have breakfast.*
*We **usually** get up early.*
*My friend **often** works late.*
*I **sometimes** travel for my job.*
*My friend **never** writes emails.*

0%

Note: The word order is adverb + verb, except with *be*: *I am never late*, NOT *I ~~never am~~ late*.

Practice

3 Put the words in order to make sentences.
I usually have coffee in the morning.
1 in the morning / coffee / have / usually / I
2 travels / colleague / my / for her job / often
3 homework / never / our / gives / teacher / us
4 always / I / at night / read *I always read at night.*
5 studies / my / at home / friend / sometimes
2 My colleague often travels for her job.
3 Our teacher never gives us homework.
5 My friend sometimes studies at home.

simple present questions *he/she*

Questions			Short answers
Does	he she	**teach**?	Yes, he/she **does**. No, he/she **doesn't**.
Questions with question words			

What does he/she **do**?
Where does he/she **go** in the summer?

Practice

4 Read the sentence. Then write a question with the words in parentheses.
Does he have breakfast at 8:30?
1 Carl doesn't have breakfast at 7:30. (8:30 ?)
2 Anna doesn't finish work at 6:30. (what time ?)
What time does she finish work?
3 Julia doesn't go to bed late. (early ?) *Does she go to bed early?*
4 Michael doesn't work in an office. (where ?)
Where does he work?
5 My brother doesn't read novels. (what ?)
What does he read?

How … ?

How does he take photos?
***How many** people do you work with?*
***How often** does your friend call you?*
***How old** is that tiger?*
***How much** is this book?*

Practice

5 Read the sentence. Then write a question with the words in parentheses and an expression with *How….*
How many friends do you have?
1 I have 200 friends on Facebook. (you ?)
2 I'm 23. (you ?) *How old are you?*
3 This camera is $99. (that camera ?) *How much is that camera?*
4 I call my sister every day. (your sister ?) *How often do you call your sister?*
5 I take videos with my phone. (you ?)
How do you take videos?

UNIT 9

there is/are

Singular	Plural
There's a book in my bag. (There is)	**There are** some books in my bag.

Practice

1 What's in my suitcase? Write sentences.
1 a map ✓ *There's a map.*
2 clothes ✓ *There are some clothes.*
3 a camera ✓ *There's a camera.*
4 a pair of sandals ✓ *There's a pair of sandals.*

there is/are negative and question forms

Negative singular	Negative plural
There isn't a bus. (There is not)	**There aren't** any hotels. (There are not)
Questions and short answers singular	**Questions and short answers plural**
Is there a sofa? Yes, **there is**. No, **there isn't**.	**Are there** any trains today? Yes, **there are**. No, **there aren't**.

Practice

2 What's in my suitcase? Write questions. Then answer them.

1 a hat ✗ *Is there a hat?*
No, there isn't.
2 a passport ✓
Is there a passport? Yes, there is.
3 pairs of shoes ✓ *Are there any pairs of shoes? Yes, there are.*
4 tickets ✗ *Are there any tickets? No, there aren't.*

imperative forms

***Book** the hotel online.*
***Don't travel** by bus.*
(don't = do not)

Practice

3 Read the instructions from a travel guide for some tourists. Choose the best option.

1 (Don't forget)/ Forget your passports.
2 Don't arrive /(Arrive) at the airport on time.
3 (Don't be)/ Be late.
4 Don't wait /(Wait) a moment, please.

UNIT 10

was/were

Affirmative
I/He/She/It **was** Korean.
You/We/You/They **were** Korean.

Practice

1 Complete the paragraph with *was* or *were*.

Sally Ride [1] _was_ the first American woman in space. She [2] _was_ born in 1951. Her first space flight [3] _was_ in 1983. She [4] _was_ the writer of five books for children. They [5] _were_ about space and science.

was/were negative and question forms

Negative
I/He/She/It **wasn't** famous.
You/We/You/They **weren't** famous.
(wasn't = was not, weren't = were not)

Questions			Short answers
Was	I he she it	happy at school?	Yes, I/he/she/it **was**. No, I/he/she/it **wasn't**.
Were	you we you they		Yes, you/we/you/they **were**. No, you/we/you/they **weren't**.

Practice

2 Complete the sentences with *was, wasn't, were,* and *weren't*.

1 "_Was_ Neil Armstrong the first man in space?"
"No, he _wasn't_ ."
2 My parents are from Hong Kong. They _weren't_ born in Europe.
3 "_Were_ you born in 1986?"
"Yes, I _was_ ."
4 "_Were_ the first televisions in color?"
"No, they _weren't_ ."
5 I _wasn't_ very good at music in school and I can't play a musical instrument.

UNIT 11

irregular simple past verbs

Affirmative	
I/You/He/She/It/We/You/They	**went** to the Alps. **had** a good vacation.

do → did; find → found; go → went; have → had;
leave → left; make → made; see → saw; take → took

Practice

1 Complete the sentences with the simple past form of the verb.

1 We _took_ (take) a lot of photos.
2 The tourists _went_ (go) for a walk.
3 I _had_ (have) lunch at home yesterday.
4 We _saw_ (see) a great movie last week.
5 I _made_ (make) dinner last night.
6 My father _left_ (leave) for work.

regular simple past verbs

Affirmative
I/You/He/She/It/We/You/They **walked** in the mountains.

Add *-ed* or *-d*.
start → started, live → lived

Change *-y* to *-ied*.
study → studied

Practice

2 Complete the sentences with the simple past form of the verbs in parentheses.

Last weekend we [1] _went_ (go) for a walk in the mountains. We [2] _started_ (start) early in the morning. We [3] _walked_ (walk) for two hours. Then we [4] _had_ (have) a snack. We [5] _found_ (find) a bag on the walk. We [6] _took_ (take) the bag to the police station. They [7] _found_ (find) a lot of money in the bag.

simple past negative and question forms

Negative
I/You/He/She/It/We/You/They **didn't take** a vacation last year.

Questions
Did I/you/he/she/it/we/you/they **drive**?

Short answers
Yes, I/you/he/she/it/we/you/they **did**.
No, I/you/he/she/it/we/you/they **didn't**.

(didn't = did not)

Note: In the negative and in question forms, we use the simple past of *do* (*did*) + verb (*go*, *drive*, etc.), NOT
They didn't ~~took~~ a vacation last year.
Did they ~~took~~ a vacation last year?

Practice

3 Complete the interview with an explorer.

Q: ¹ _Did you travel_ (you / travel) a lot last year?
A: Yes, I ² _did_ . I went to 17 countries.
Q: Wow! ³ _Did you go_ (you / go) to South America?
A: Yes, we did. We went to Ecuador, Peru, and Chile.
Q: ⁴ _Did you write_ (you / write) a blog about your trip?
A: No, I ⁵ _didn't_ , but I made a website.

simple past with question words

Questions with question words			
What Who Where When Why	**did**	I/you/he/she/it/we/you/they	see? go?

Practice

4 Write questions for these answers. Use a question word and the correct form of the underlined verb.

1 We <u>met</u> lots of interesting people. _Who did you meet?_
2 They <u>went</u> to Cancun in Mexico. _Where did they go?_
3 She <u>saw</u> some beautiful buildings. _What did she see?_
4 We <u>arrived</u> at the hotel at night. _When did you arrive at the hotel?_
5 I <u>went</u> there because I like the food. _Why did you go there?_

UNIT 12

present continuous

Affirmative / Negative		
I	am / 'm not	cooking. eating. reading.
He/She/It	is / isn't	
You/We/You/They	are / aren't	

We use the present continuous for activities in progress at the time of speaking.

Practice

1 Complete the sentences with the present continuous of the verb in parentheses.

1 The teacher _is talking_ (talk).
2 Javier and Cheng _aren't writing_ (not write).
3 I _am listening_ (listen).
4 Juan and Paolo _are reading_ (read).
5 Tomas _isn't watching_ (not watch) a video.

Questions			Short answers		
Am	I		Yes,	I he/she/it you/we/you/they	am. is. are.
Is	he/she/it	cooking?			
Are	you/we/you/they		No,	I he/she/it you/ we/you/they	'm not. isn't. aren't.

Practice

2 Write questions with these words. Use the information in Exercise 1 to answer the questions.
1 Tomas / watch a video _Is Tomas watching a video? No, he isn't._
2 I / listen _Am I listening? Yes, I am._
3 Javier and Cheng / write _Are Javier and Cheng writing? No, they aren't._
4 the teacher / talk _Is the teacher talking? Yes, he / she is._
5 Juan and Paolo / read _Are Juan and Pablo reading? Yes, they are._

present continuous with future time expressions

I'm meeting my friends	tomorrow. on Saturday (morning). this/next weekend. on June 8.

We use the present continuous + future time expressions for future plans.

Practice

3 Read each sentence. Does it refer to now (N) or the future (F)?

1 I'm playing tennis on Sunday. F
2 We aren't watching this TV show. N
3 My friends are coming this weekend. F
4 Is your family having a party tonight? F
5 What are you doing in June? F
6 My sister is staying with us. N

Audioscripts

Unit 1

🎵 **1**

Hi! I'm Mike.

🎵 **2**

M: Hi. I'm Mattias. I'm a filmmaker.
C: Hi. I'm Carolyn. I'm a writer.
R: Hello. I'm Robert. I'm an explorer.
M: Hi. I'm Mireya. I'm a scientist.
A: Hello. I'm Alex. I'm a photographer.

🎵 **3**

explorer   filmmaker

photographer   scientist

writer

🎵 **4**

A: Hello.
C: Hi.
A: I'm Alex Treadway.
C: Oh, you're a photographer!
A: Yes.

🎵 **5**

Y: Hi.
M: Hello. I'm Mattias Klum.
Y: Oh, you're a filmmaker!
M: Yes, for National Geographic.

🎵 **6**

a b c d e f g h i j k l m n o p q r s t
u v w x y z

🎵 **7**

1 **P:** I'm Paola.
   Q: Can you spell that?
   P: Yes. P–A–O–L–A.
2 **B:** I'm Bryan.
   Q: Can you spell that?
   B: Yes. B–R–Y–A–N.
3 **S:** I'm Sean.
   Q: Can you spell that?
   S: Yes. S–E–A–N.
4 **A:** I'm Ana.
   Q: Can you spell that?
   A: Yes. A–N–A.

🎵 **8**

Brazil	Brazilian
Canada	Canadian
China	Chinese
Egypt	Egyptian
France	French
Germany	German
Great Britain	British
Italy	Italian
Japan	Japanese
Mexico	Mexican
Oman	Omani
Spain	Spanish
the United States	American

🎵 **9**

zero	one
two	three
four	five
six	seven
eight	nine
ten	

🎵 **10**

A: What's your phone number?
B: My cell phone number is 619 408 7132.
A: 6–1–9 4–0–8 7–1–3–2. OK! And what's your work number?
B: It's 661 467 9285.
A: 6–6–1…
B: …4–6–7 9–2–8–5.
A: Great. Thanks.

🎵 **11**

R: Good morning. What's your name, please?
L: Hi. My name's Schultz.
R: Can you spell that?
L: Yes. S–C–H–U–L–T–Z: Schultz.
R: What's your first name?
L: Liam: L–I–A–M.
R: Thank you. What's your job?
L: I'm a photographer. I'm from *Today* magazine.
R: OK. Sign here, please.
L: OK. Thanks. Bye.
R: Goodbye.

🎵 **12**

R: What's your name, please?
R: What's your first name?
R: What's your job?

🎵 **13**

Y: Hi, Katya. How are you?
K: Fine, thanks. And you?
Y: I'm OK. This is Silvia. She's from Madrid.
K: Nice to meet you, Silvia.
S: Nice to meet you too.

Unit 2

🎵 **14**

the ocean

an island

a beach

a mountain

a city

a lake

🎵 **15**

We're in Egypt.

We're from India.

We're happy.

They're on vacation.

They're Australian.

They're French.

🎵 **16**

1 We aren't in Tunisia.
2 It isn't a beach.
3 Brad isn't on the camel trek.
4 I'm not in this photo.

🎵 **17**

a It's twelve degrees in London today.
b Phew! It's cold! It's thirty-five degrees today.
c It isn't hot. It's eighteen degrees.
d It's twenty-seven degrees here.
e Wow! It's eighty degrees in Sydney today.
f It's nice out. It's sixty-five degrees.

🎵 **18**

G: Hi! Where are you now? Are you in France?
L: Yes, I am. I'm in the Alps. It's beautiful!
G: Are you OK?
L: No, I'm not. It's two degrees!
G: Wow! Is it cold in your hotel?
L: No, it isn't. The hotel is nice.
G: It's eighty-six degrees in Sydney today.
L: Oh! That's hot!
G: Are Kara and Ona in France?
L: No, they aren't. They're on a beach in Morocco!

🎵 **19**

1 **Q:** Are you OK?
   A: Yes, I am.
2 **Q:** Is Kara in France?
   A: No, she isn't.
3 **Q:** Are you and Paul in Sydney?
   A: Yes, we are.
4 **Q:** Is Greg in London?
   A: No, he isn't.
5 **Q:** Are Kara and Ona in Morocco?
   A: Yes, they are.
6 **Q:** Is your hotel nice?
   A: Yes, it is.

🎵 **20**

lakes	airports
cars	countries
beaches	buses

🎵 **21**

cities	doctors
friends	hotels
mountains	offices
phones	students
tents	

🎵 **22**

A: Good evening.
S: Good evening. My name's Sato. This is my ID.
A: Thank you. Where are you from, Mr. Sato?
S: I'm from Tokyo.
A: Ah! Is this your address?
S: Yes, it is.
A: What's the zip code?
S: It's 170–3293.
A: OK. Are you on vacation here?
S: No, I'm not. I'm on business.
A: What's your telephone number in the US?
S: It's 718 157 0963.
A: Thanks. Is this your email address?
S: Yes, it is: e p sato at hotmail dot com.
A: OK. Sign here, please. Here are your keys.
S: Thanks. What's the license plate number?
A: It's with your keys—BD6 ATR.
S: Thanks.

🎵 **23**

vacation	address
car	email
key	number
telephone	

Unit 3

 24

Danvir and Mohan are brothers. Ravi and Danvir are father and son. Ravi and Mohan are father and son.

 25

Alexandra Cousteau is part of a famous family. She's Jacques Cousteau's granddaughter. Jean-Michel Cousteau is Jacques Cousteau's son. He's a filmmaker. Jean-Michel's children are Fabien and Celine. Fabien's a marine explorer. Celine's an explorer. Jean-Michel's brother Philippe is dead. Philippe's children are Alexandra and Philippe Jr. Alexandra's an environmentalist. Her brother is an environmentalist too. And Alexandra's grandmother Simone was the first woman scuba diver.

 26

1 Simone is Philippe's mother.
2 Celine is Jean-Michel's daughter.
3 Alexandra is Jacques's granddaughter.
4 Simone is Fabien's grandmother.

 27

1 They're at a wedding.
2 He's at a meeting.

 28

A: Congratulations!
B: Thank you. We're very happy.
A: Ah, she's lovely. What's her name?
B: It's Juba.
A: Hello, Juba.

 29

1 **A:** Emma and I are engaged.
   B: Wow! Congratulations!
   A: Thanks very much.
   B: I'm very happy for you. When's the wedding?
   A: We're not sure…maybe in August.

2 **C:** Hello!
   D: Hello, come in.
   C: Happy anniversary!
   D: Oh, thanks!
   C: How long is it?
   D: Twenty-five.
   C: Wow! Twenty-five years.

3 **E:** Happy birthday, Freya!
   F: Thank you.
   E: How old are you? Nineteen or twenty?
   F: Actually, I'm twenty-one.
   E: Oh, great!

 30

Congratulations!

Happy anniversary!

Happy birthday!

Unit 4

 31

Shanghai is a city in China. Shanghai is big, but it isn't the capital city—Beijing is the capital of China. Shanghai is a rich city. A lot of the buildings in Shanghai are new. The Pearl TV tower is in Shanghai. It's famous in China. Tourists from around the world visit Shanghai. They visit the river and the Pearl TV tower.

 32

1 **A:** Excuse me?
   B: Yes?
   A: Where's the train station?
   B: It's on Exeter Street.
   A: Is it near here?
   B: Yes, it is.
   A: OK. Thanks.

2 **C:** Excuse me?
   D: Yes?
   C: Is the information center near here?
   D: Yes, it is. It's near the park.
   C: OK. Thanks.

3 **E:** Excuse me?
   F: Yes?
   E: Is the parking lot on this street?
   F: No, it isn't. This is Exeter Street. The parking lot's on Milk Street. It's next to the park.
   E: Thank you very much.

4 **G:** Excuse me?
   H: Yes?
   G: Where's the bank?
   H: I'm not sure. Oh! It's across from the market.
   G: Is it near here?
   H: Yes, it is.
   G: OK. Thanks.

 33

T: Hi.
A: Good morning.
T: Is this a map of the city?
A: No, it isn't. That's a map of the city.
T: OK. And where's Tokyo Tower?
A: It's near the Prince Park…here it is.
T: Oh yes. Is it open on Sunday?
A: Yes, it is.

 34

1 **A:** Excuse me. Is that a map of Tokyo?
   B: Yes, it is.

2 **A:** Is this a train schedule?
   B: No, it's a bus schedule.

3 **A:** Is that guidebook in English?
   B: Where?
   A: The book next to you.
   B: No, it isn't. It's in Spanish.

 35

T: Are museums open on Monday?
A: Yes, they are. They're open every day of the week.
T: OK. Are stores open every day?
A: Yes, they are. They're open every day of the week too.
T: Are banks open on Sunday?
A: No, they aren't. They're open Monday to Friday in the morning and afternoon. And they're open on Saturday morning.

36

1 Q: What time is it?
 A: It's five o'clock.
2 Q: What time is it?
 A: It's one thirty.
3 Q: What time is it?
 A: It's seven fifteen.
4 Q: What time is it?
 A: It's nine forty-five.
5 Q: What time is it?
 A: It's two twenty.
6 Q: What time is it?
 A: It's six o'clock.

37

1 A: Hi. Can I help you?
 C: Two coffees, please.
 A: Large or small?
 C: Small.
 A: Anything else?
 C: No, thanks.
2 A: Hi. Can I help you?
 C: Can I have a bottle of water, please?
 A: Anything else?
 C: Yes. A salad.
 A: OK. Four dollars, please.
3 A: Can I help you?
 C: A tea and a fruit juice, please.
 A: Anything else?
 C: Yes. Two pastries, please.
 A: OK. Here you are. Seven dollars, please.
 C: Here you are.

38

1 Can I help you?
2 Can I have a water, please?

Unit 5

39

Look at this fantastic photo. It's not a toy or a robot—this is a man. His name's Yves Rossy—or Jetman—and he can fly. Rossy is from Switzerland. Here, Rossy is above the Swiss Alps. He's in the air for a short time—only five minutes. But it's fantastic!

40

1 Robots can speak.
2 Robots can carry things.
3 People can't fly.
4 I can speak English.
5 My grandfather can't run.

41

L: Hi. Welcome to "Technology Today." I'm Lewis Jones and this morning I'm in a university technology department. I'm here with Christine Black and Tomo, a Japanese robot. Hi, Christine.
C: Hi, Lewis.
L: Christine, tell me about this robot.
C: Well, Tomo is from Japan. She's from a new generation of robots. They can do things that people can do.
L: "She"? Or "it"?
C: Aha! We say "she." She's a robot.
L: OK. So, she's from Japan. Can she speak Japanese?
C: Oh yes, she can speak Japanese and English.
L: OK. Can she sing?
C: Yes, she can.
L: And can she play the piano?
C: Yes, she can.
L: Wow! I can't sing or play the piano. Can she swim?
C: Well, Tomo can't swim, but some robots can swim.
L: OK. Well, my last question is about the name. What does "Tomo" mean?
C: It means "intelligent" in Japanese.
L: OK, Christine, thanks very much.
C: Thanks!

42

a two dollars and thirty cents
b thirteen pounds fifty
c fifteen euros
d three euros seventy-five cents
e seventeen dollars eighty cents
f eighteen dollars

43

1 It's thirty dollars.
2 It's forty dollars.
3 It's fifteen dollars.
4 It's sixteen dollars.
5 It's seventy dollars.
6 It's eighteen dollars.

44

1 A: Can I help you?
 C: How much is this alarm clock?
 A: This is a clock radio. It's fifty dollars.
 C: Hmm, that's a little expensive. Thanks.
 A: That's OK. No problem.
2 A: Can I help you?
 C: Yes, I'd like this video camera, please.
 A: Certainly.
 C: Is it HD?
 A: Yes, it is. The image quality is fantastic.
 C: Great.
 A: OK, that's ninety-five dollars and fifty cents, please.
 C: Here you go.
3 C: Excuse me.
 A: Yes, can I help you?
 C: How much are these flash drives?
 A: They're five ninety-nine each.
 C: Can I pay with euros?
 A: Yes, of course.

Unit 6

45

These fans are passionate about soccer. Their team is the Kaizer Chiefs. Soccer and rugby are big sports in South Africa today. Soccer is an international sport—about 270 million people play soccer in more than 200 countries. The soccer World Cup is every four years. The World Cup prize is millions of dollars—$30 million for the World Cup in South Africa! Many international soccer players are millionaires. Soccer is a sport of passion and money!

46

I: Hi, Steve. Congratulations on your prize.
S: Thank you very much.
I: So, you are passionate about vegetables. But do you like fruit?
S: Yes, I do. I like fruit. I have a lot of fruit in my garden.
I: We know you don't like pumpkin pie. Do you like fruit pie?
S: No, I don't. But people in my family like fruit pie a lot.
I: So, giant vegetables are very important to you. But what about other food? What do you like?

47

I: Do you like fruit?
I: Do you like fruit pie?
I: Do you like meat?
I: Do you like pasta?
S: Oh well, I like salad.
I: Do you like meat?
S: No, I don't—but I like fish.
I: And pasta? Do you like pasta?
S: Yes, I do. I like spaghetti and I like macaroni too.
I: OK, thanks very much, Steve.
S: Thank you!

48

1 He likes fish.
2 He likes Botswana.
3 He doesn't like cold places.
4 He likes water.
5 He likes coffee.

49

1 A: Let's watch TV tonight.
 B: That's a good idea. What's on?
 A: A movie with Emily Blunt is on at eight o'clock.
 B: Oh, I love her. She's fantastic.
2 C: Let's play ping-pong tomorrow.
 D: No, thanks. I don't like ping-pong.
 C: OK. How about soccer?
 D: Sorry. Sports are boring.
3 E: Let's have spaghetti this weekend.
 F: No, don't like pasta. It's horrible.
 E: OK. How about pizza? Do you like pizza?
 F: Yes, it's great.

50

She's fantastic.

Sports are boring.

It's horrible.

It's great.

Unit 7

💿 **51**

The Holi festival—or festival of colors—is in March. It's a very happy festival. It's a celebration of spring and new life. People say "goodbye" to winter and "hello" to spring. In India, the winter months are December, January, and February. The Holi festival is one or two days. It's a big celebration in parts of India and in other parts of the world.

💿 **52**

They don't understand traditional Sami life.

They don't live in France.

We don't study Sami.

I don't have a car.

💿 **53**

I: Hello, Miriam. Nice to meet you.
M: Hello.
I: Do you work at Kakenya's school?
M: Yes, I do. I teach there. We have five teachers.
I: Do you like it?
M: Yes, I do.
I: Do boys study at the school?
M: No, they don't. The school is for girls.
I: Only girls?
M: Yes, only girls.
I: That's unusual!
M: Yes, it is.
I: Do the girls live with their families?
M: No, they don't. They live at the school.
I: OK. And do they go home in summer?
M: Yes, they do. They go home to their villages.
I: Do the girls learn English at the school?
M: Yes, they do. And in the summer we teach extra classes in English too.
I: OK. Thank you, Miriam.
M: Thank you.

💿 **54**

I: Hi, Carl.
C: Hi.
I: Do you study at a college?
C: No, I don't. I'm at a university.
I: Do you have classes every day?
C: No, I don't. I have classes on Monday, Wednesday, Thursday, and Friday.
I: Do you like your classes?
C: Yes, I do.
I: Do you live near your university?
C: Yes, I do.
I: Do you live with your family?
C: No, I don't. I live in a dorm.
I: Do you go home for the summer?
C: Yes, I do. I go home for the summer and in December.

💿 **55**

1 Do you study at a college?
2 Do you have classes every day?
3 Do you like your classes?
4 Do you live near your university?
5 Do you live with your family?
6 Do you go home for the summer?

💿 **56**

1 I live in Canada. My favorite time of year is winter. It's cold and snowy.
2 I'm studying in South Africa. I like spring. It's sunny and it isn't cold.
3 I'm studying in Australia. Summer is the wet season. It's hot and rainy. I don't like it!
4 I live in Great Britain. In autumn here, it's cloudy. It's windy too, but I like it. We don't have a dry season!

💿 **57**

1 Ooh, I'm cold.
2 I'm tired.
3 I'm thirsty.
4 Uff, I'm hot.
5 Ugh, I'm wet.
6 Oh, I'm bored.
7 Mmm, I'm hungry.

💿 **58**

M: What's the matter?
F: It's cold and I'm thirsty.
M: Why don't you have a cup of coffee? Here you are.
F: Thanks.
M: Paul, are you OK?
P: No, I'm not. I don't feel well.
M: Why don't you eat a sandwich? Here.
P: No, thanks. I'm not hungry. I'm cold and I'm wet.
M: What's the matter, Anna?
A: I'm bored.
M: Why don't you go to the beach? Go swimming.
A: In the rain? Mom!
M: I don't understand you all. We're on vacation!

💿 **59**

Why don't you have a cup of coffee?

I don't feel well.

I don't understand you all.

Unit 8

💿 **60**

I: Do you like your job?
M: Yes, I love my job. I'm a farmer. I don't work in an office. I work outside. I work in Nevada, in the United States. Every day is different in my job.
I: What do you do?
M: We work with animals. Today farmers use modern technology. We have cell phones and computers. We don't use tractors—we use helicopters!

💿 **61**

1 He works in Chile.
2 He starts work at nine o'clock.
3 He finishes work at 1:30.
4 He goes to bed at two o'clock.
5 He gets up at 8:45.

💿 **62**

M: Who's Cynthia Liutkus-Pierce? Does she work at this university?
W: Yes, she does.
M: I don't know her. Does she teach languages?
W: No, she doesn't.
M: What does she do?
W: She's a geologist.
M: Oh, OK. Does she give lectures?
W: Yes, she does. And she works in Africa.
M: Oh, does she go to Africa every year?
W: Yes, she does. She goes in the summer.
M: I know some geologists in Africa. Where does Cynthia go?
W: I don't know. I think she goes to Tanzania.
M: Oh, my friends are in Angola.

💿 **63**

1 R: Good morning, PJ International. Can I help you?
  C: Yes, can I speak to Ed Carr, please?
  R: I'm sorry. He's in a meeting.
  C: OK, thank you. I'll call back later. Goodbye.
  R: Goodbye.

2 R: Hello, Green Wildlife Park. Can I help you?
  C: Good morning. Can I speak to Mr. Watts, please?
  R: Yes, one moment, please.
  C: Thank you.

3 R: Good morning, City College. Can I help you?
  C: Yes, can I speak to Mrs. Jackson, please?
  R: I'm sorry. She's out of the office at the moment.
  C: OK, thank you. I'll call back later. Goodbye.
  R: Goodbye.

💿 **64**

1 R: Good morning, PJ International. Can I help you?
  C: Yes, can I speak to Ed Carr, please?
  R: I'm sorry. He's in a meeting.
  C: OK, thank you. I'll call back later. Goodbye.
  R: Goodbye.

3 R: Good morning, City College. Can I help you?
  C: Yes, can I speak to Mrs. Jackson, please?
  R: I'm sorry. She's out of the office at the moment.
  C: OK, thank you. I'll call back later. Goodbye.
  R: Goodbye.

💿 **65**

please he's yes Fridays works thanks

Unit 9

💿 **66**

1 I travel from Boston to New York for my job. I go every week. I usually go by train because I can work on the train.
2 I'm studying in Australia and I travel in the summer. I love Asia! I travel by bus. It's really interesting. You meet a lot of people.
3 I live in San Francisco. I don't like flying, so I never travel by plane. I don't really travel.
4 I'm from Barcelona, but my parents live in Mallorca. I visit them every summer. I usually go by boat.

67

There's a camera.

There's a laptop.

There are three scarves.

There are two shirts.

There's a pair of shoes.

There's a skirt.

There are some T-shirts.

68

S: OK, that's the flight. Let's look for a hotel now. Is it for two nights or three?

L: Three nights: Friday, Saturday, and Sunday. Are there any hotels near the airport?

S: Yes, there are. But they're expensive. Just a minute…no, there aren't any cheap hotels near the airport. They're all expensive. This one is four hundred dollars a night!

L: Wow! Well, what about a youth hostel? Is there a youth hostel near the airport?

S: OK, let's see. I don't think so…no, there isn't. I don't like youth hostels. They aren't very comfortable.

L: OK. Let's look downtown. Are there any cheap hotels there?

S: Yes, of course there are.

L: Well, that's good. And is there a bus to downtown?

S: A bus from the airport? Yes, there is. There's a bus every twenty minutes from the airport to downtown. There isn't a train, but that's OK.

L: And there are taxis, too.

S: I think the bus is fine. OK, let's look at these hotels.

69

1 TV
2 bathtub
3 bed
4 chair
5 table
6 lamp
7 desk
8 sofa
9 closet
10 armchair
11 shower
12 fridge

70

L: Wow, this room is really big! Oh, it's two rooms! The bed is in here, look!

S: It's fantastic!

L: I know. And it isn't really expensive…

S: Are you sure?

L: Yes. Oh, I like these lamps!

S: Yes, they're really unusual!

L: This sofa is very comfortable. And what's this? Oh, it's a fridge.

S: Are there any drinks in it? I'm really thirsty.

L: Yes, there are some bottles of water. Here.

S: Thanks.

S: Where's the TV?

L: I don't know. There isn't one.

S: What? There isn't a TV!

71

R: Good afternoon, sir. Can I help you?

G: Hello. Yes, I'd like a wake-up call at 7:30, please.

R: In the morning? Certainly, sir. What's your room number?

G: 327.

R: OK, 327…wake-up call for 7:30.

G: And I'd like to have dinner in my room this evening.

R: Of course. There's a menu in your room. It's on the desk.

G: Oh, yes!

R: Call 101 for room service.

G: Fine. I'd like to use the Internet too.

R: No problem, sir. There's wi-fi in all the rooms.

G: Great. Oh, and is there a bank near the hotel?

R: Yes, there's one on this street. It's next to the movie theater.

G: OK, thanks a lot.

72

I'd like a wake-up call at 7:30, please.

I'd like breakfast in my room.

I'd like to use the Internet, too.

Unit 10

73

1950 color television
1963 video recorders
1973 cell phones
1975 digital cameras
1993 MP3 players
1995 digital television
2006 Blu-ray discs

74

1 She was born in 1939. She was in a team of Japanese mountaineers. They were all women.

2 He was born in 1480. He was Portuguese, but he was an explorer for the Spanish king Carlos I.

3 She was born in the United States on September 29, 1955. She was the leader of an expedition to the South Pole in 1993. The expedition was all women.

4 He was from Norway and he was born on July 16, 1872. His father was a sea captain.

75

He was born in 1480.

He was an explorer.

He was Portuguese.

They were explorers.

They were from Russia.

76

first, second, third, fourth, fifth, sixth, seventh, eighth, ninth, tenth, eleventh, twelfth, thirteenth, fourteenth, fifteenth, sixteenth, seventeenth, eighteenth, nineteenth, twentieth

77

twenty-first, twenty-second, twenty-third, twenty-fourth, twenty-fifth, twenty-sixth, twenty-seventh, twenty-eighth, twenty-ninth, thirtieth, thirty-first

78

I: Aneta, who was your hero when you were young?

A: When I was about ten years old, my hero was Michael Johnson. He was a great athlete.

I: Was he the Olympic champion?

A: Yes, he was. And he was the world champion eight times.

I: Were you good at sports at school?

A: Well…yes, I was. I was on the basketball team at school.

I: Joe, who was your hero when you were young?

J: When I was young, my hero was David Attenborough. He was on television. His shows about animals and nature were fantastic.

I: Was it his first job?

J: No, it wasn't. His first job was with books, but he wasn't happy in that job.

I: Which is your favorite David Attenborough show?

J: I think it's *Life on Earth*. But all his shows were really interesting.

I: That was in 1979…were you born then?

J: No, I wasn't! But I have the DVD.

I: Clare, who was your hero when you were young?

C: My heroes weren't famous. They were my teachers at my school. The teachers were really nice and friendly. Mrs. Harvey was my art teacher. She was very funny. And she was married to my English teacher, Mr. Harvey.

I: Were they good teachers?

C: Yes, they were. They were fantastic.

79

1 Was he the Olympic champion? Yes, he was.
2 Was it his first job? No, it wasn't.
3 Were they good teachers? Yes, they were.

80

1 **T:** Hello!
   S: Hi, I'm sorry I'm late. The bus was late.
   T: That's OK. Take a seat.

2 **C:** Oh, hi Ravi.
   R: Hi Clare.
   C: Umm, the meeting was at 2:30. Where were you?
   R: Oh, I'm sorry. I was very busy.
   C: It's OK. It wasn't an important meeting.

3 **A:** Mmm, this coffee is good!
   B: Yes, it is.
   A: So, what about yesterday? We were at your house at ten o'clock. Where were you?
   B: I'm very sorry. We weren't at home. We were at my sister's house!
   A: It's OK. Don't worry.

81

1 I'm <u>sorry</u> I'm late.
2 The <u>bus</u> was late.
3 I was very <u>busy</u>.
4 We weren't at <u>home</u>.

Unit 11

🔊 82

Scientists discover hundreds of new plants and animals every year. A large number of these discoveries are in Indonesia. In fact, scientists in Papua New Guinea usually find about two new plants or animals every week. It's a fantastic place. There aren't many people in the area and it isn't easy to get there. Scientists sometimes arrive and leave by helicopter!

🔊 83

The scientists at the University of Innsbruck started their investigation. They took photos and they studied the body. They discovered the body was a man. They called him "Ötzi" because the body was in the Ötztal mountains in the Alps. The scientists finished their report. It was very interesting.

Ötzi was a small man. He was about 45 years old when he died. He was from the north of Italy and he lived about 5,000 years ago. The scientists think he walked to the mountains. The scientists think he died in spring. They also think an arrow killed him.

🔊 84

1	call called	5	kill killed
2	die died	6	live lived
3	discover discovered	7	start started
4	finish finished	8	study studied

🔊 85

I: Hi, Jamie.
J: Hello.
I: Did you watch Alastair's videos?
J: Well, I didn't see the first or second video, but I saw a video about swimming in the River Thames.
I: Did you like it?
J: Yes, I did. I liked it a lot. The next weekend, I didn't stay at home. I drove to a lake near my house and went swimming.
I: Was that an adventure?
J: Yes, because usually I go to the swimming pool. It was very different in the lake.
I: Did you make a video too?
J: Yes, my friend went with me. He filmed me on his phone and we sent the video to Alastair online.

🔊 86

1 Did you watch Alastair's videos?
2 Did you like it?
3 Did you make a video too?

🔊 87

1 A: Did you and Sonia have a good time in Sydney last week?
   B: Yes, we did, thanks. But we didn't go swimming.
   A: Oh? Why not?
   B: There was a shark in the water!
2 C: Did you and Jack have a good vacation last year?
   D: No, we didn't.
   C: Oh? Why not?
   D: Well, we stayed at home. We didn't have any money!
3 E: Did you and Alice have a nice dinner last night?
   F: Yes, we did. It was delicious. And we didn't pay!
   E: Oh? Why not?
   F: My boss paid!

🔊 88

We didn't go swimming.

We didn't have any money.

We didn't pay!

Unit 12

🔊 89

The young women in this photo work in a factory from Monday to Saturday. But today is Sunday—it's the weekend. On Sunday, they usually meet and go out for the day. Most stores, museums, and movie theaters are open, so there are a lot of things to do. In different countries, the weekend is on different days. In some countries—for example, Oman—the weekend is Thursday and Friday. In Algeria, Egypt, and Qatar, the weekend is Friday and Saturday. These Chinese factory workers have one day off, but office workers have Saturday off too. The Saturday and Sunday weekend is quite new in China—it started in 1995.

🔊 90

I: Ayu, tell us about these photos.
A: Well, this is my mother. She's in the kitchen. She's cooking.
I: What's she making?
A: She's making lunch. We have a big family lunch every Saturday.
I: And who's this?
A: That's my husband, Amir, in the bathroom. He's bathing our daughter.
I: How old is your daughter?
A: She's eighteen months old. And this is my father with his friend. They're talking and drinking coffee.
I: What are they sitting on?
A: They're sitting on the mats we use in Indonesia. And then this photo is Amir's brother with his son.
I: What are they doing? Are they reading?
A: No, they aren't. They're playing a game on Amir's computer. This is my sister. She's in the bedroom. She's ironing. I usually help her.
I: And what about this last one?
A: This is my brother. He's wearing shorts. He and his friend are washing their bikes. They do that every Saturday.
I: Which is your favorite photo?
A: Oh, I think it's the one of my husband and my daughter because they're both smiling and happy.

🔊 91

A: Hi Lauren, it's Alex.
L: Oh, hi! Where are you?
A: I'm on the bus. I'm going home from work. So, what are you doing this weekend?
L: Well, I'm going shopping tomorrow.
A: Of course. You always go shopping on Saturdays.
L: No, I don't! Anyway, Sports Gear is having a sale tomorrow.
A: Really?
L: Yes, they're selling all the winter sports stuff at half price.
A: Wow! And what about on Sunday?
L: I don't know. What are you doing?
A: Well, do you remember Helen Skelton? She went down the Amazon River last year.
L: Oh yes.
A: She's giving a talk about her trip on Sunday evening. I'm going with my brother. Would you like to come?
L: Where is it?
A: At the Natural Science Museum. Tickets are free.
L: OK! Why not?

🔊 92

I'm going home from work.

What are you doing this weekend?

I'm going shopping tomorrow.

What are you doing?

I'm going with my brother.

🔊 93

a C: Four tickets to the museum, please.
  S: Four adults?
  C: Oh sorry, no. Two adults and two children.
  S: OK. That's ten dollars, please. Would you like a brochure for the Home Life exhibition?
  C: Yes, please.
  S: Would you like it in English? We have brochures in French, German, and Japanese, too.
  C: Oh, French, please.
  S: Here you are.
  C: Thanks.
b C: Three round-trip tickets to Lindisfarne, please.
  S: Are you coming back today?
  C: Yes, we are. Is there a bus after six o'clock?
  S: Yes, there is. There's a bus every hour. The last one is at nine o'clock.
  C: OK.
  S: Are you going to the castle and gardens? Would you like to buy the tickets now?
  C: Oh, yes. Great.
  S: It's a special weekend ticket. That's thirty-four dollars, please.
  C: Here you are.
  S: Thank you.
c S: Good morning.
  C: Hi. It's busy today! Are there any free tennis courts?
  S: Yes, there are. The people on court 4 are finishing now.
  C: OK, great. A ticket for two people, please.
  S: Would you like it for one hour or two hours?
  C: Umm, just a minute…Ellen, do you want to play for one hour or two?
  E: One is fine.
  C: OK. So just one hour, please.
  S: That's sixteen dollars.
  C: Thanks.

🔊 94

Would you like a brochure for the Home Life exhibition?

Would you like it in English?

Would you like to buy the tickets now?

Grammar summary: answer key

UNIT 1

1

1 a   2 a   3 an   4 an   5 a

2

1 I'm   3 You're   5 You're
2 You're   4 I'm

3

1 She's from Ladakh.   4 It's in Nepal.
2 He's Nepalese.   5 He's from Jagat.
3 She's Indian.

4

1 am   2 is   3 is   4 is   5 are

5

1 My   2 Your   3 My   4 your   5 My   6 your

UNIT 2

1

1 They   3 They're   5 They
2 are   4 We

2

1 am   2 is   3 are   4 is   5 are

3

1 Jack isn't a student.
2 We aren't Spanish.
3 I'm not happy.
4 Susanna and Gina aren't from Peru.
5 You aren't a writer.

4

1 Is Simona from Bolivia? Yes, she is. / No, she isn't.
2 Is John a teacher? Yes, he is. / No, he isn't.
3 Are you on vacation? Yes, I am. / No, I'm not.
4 Is your hotel nice? Yes, it is. / No, it isn't.
5 Are Susana and Gina in Paris? Yes, they are. / No,
   they aren't.

5

1 lakes   4 airports   7 mountains
2 countries   5 beaches   8 tents
3 cars   6 photos   9 students

UNIT 3

1

1 James is Oscar's father.
2 John and James are Elena's sons.
3 Lisa and Marga are Harry's granddaughters.
4 Lisa is Marga's sister.
5 Elena is Oscar's grandmother.

2

1 his   2 Her   3 our   4 your   5 their

3

1 women   3 child   5 children
2 people   4 person

UNIT 4

1

1 next to   3 in   5 next to
2 across from   4 near   6 near

2

1 This   2 That   3 this / that

3

1 b   2 c   3 e   4 d   5 a

UNIT 5

1

1 can't 3 can't

2 can 4 can't

2

1 Can he sing? Yes, he can.

2 Can you drive a car? Yes, I can.

3 Can they play table tennis? No, they can't.

4 Can she cook? No, she can't.

5 Can we speak English? Yes, we / you can.

3

1 have 2 has 3 have 4 has

4

1 This is a Japanese camera.

2 My phone has a fantastic memory.

3 You have a great MP3 player.

4 Jack's grandfather is an old man.

5

1 This laptop is really light.

2 Their house is very big.

3 My friend's new phone is really fantastic.

4 (not possible)

5 We have a very old car.

UNIT 6

1

1 I don't like basketball. 3 I like coffee.

2 We like tennis. 4 They don't like cake.

2

1 Do they like cheese? Yes, they do.

2 Do you like fruit? No, I don't.

3 Do they like fish? Yes, they do.

4 Do they like rice? No, they don't.

3

2 Joanna doesn't like action movies.

3 Does your teacher like music?

4 Ryan doesn't like swimming.

4

1 them 2 us 3 her 4 it 5 him

UNIT 7

1

1 I don't live near a beach.

2 You have a car.

3 My friends don't speak English.

4 We don't study on vacation.

2

1 Do you live in Egypt? Yes, I do.

2 Do they go to college? No, they don't.

3 Do I study Spanish? Yes, I / you do.

4 Do we have friends in this class? Yes, we / you do.

5 Do you teach at this school? No, I don't.

3

1 What 3 What 5 Where

2 When 4 Who 6 Why

UNIT 8

1

1 doesn't go 3 doesn't work 5 starts, doesn't finish

2 works 4 teaches

2

1 at 2 in 3 at 4 in 5 on 6 on

3

1 I usually have coffee in the morning.

2 My colleague often travels for her job.

3 Our teacher never gives us homework.

4 I always read at night.

5 My friend sometimes studies at home.

4

1 Does he have breakfast at 8:30?

2 What time does she finish work?

3 Does she go to bed early?

4 Where does he work?

5 What does he read?

5

1 How many friends do you have?

2 How old are you?

3 How much is that camera?

4 How often do you call your sister?

5 How do you take videos?

UNIT 9

1

1 There's a map.
2 There are some clothes.
3 There's a camera.
4 There's a pair of sandals.

2

1 Is there a hat? No, there isn't.
2 Is there a passport? Yes, there is.
3 Are there any pairs of shoes? Yes, there are.
4 Are there any tickets? No, there aren't.

3

1 Don't forget	3 Don't be
2 Arrive	4 Wait

UNIT 10

1

1 was	3 was	5 were
2 was	4 was	

2

1 Was, wasn't	3 Were, was	5 wasn't
2 weren't	4 Were, weren't	

UNIT 11

1

1 took	3 had	5 made
2 went	4 saw	6 left

2

1 went	4 had	6 took
2 started	5 found	7 found
3 walked		

3

1 Did you travel	3 Did you go	5 didn't
2 did	4 Did you write	

4

1 Who did you meet?
2 Where did they go?
3 What did she see?
4 When did you arrive at the hotel?
5 Why did you go there?

UNIT 12

1

1 is talking	3 am listening	5 isn't watching
2 aren't writing	4 are reading	

2

2 Is Tomas watching a video? No, he isn't.
3 Am I listening? Yes, I am.
4 Are Javier and Cheng writing? No, they aren't.
5 Is the teacher talking? Yes, he / she is.
6 Are Juan and Paolo reading? Yes, they are.

3

1 F	2 N	3 F	4 F	5 F	6 N

Photocopiable communicative activities

Unit 1 Communicative activity

My name is...

1
Name: Mary
Last name: Johnson
Job: writer
Nationality: English

5
Name: Louise
Last name: Hurst
Job: artist
Nationality: Canadian

2
Name: Jack
Last name: Robinson
Job: explorer
Nationality: American

6
Name: Nick
Last name: Clarke
Job: engineer
Nationality: Scottish

3
Name: Robert
Last name: Marriott
Job: filmmaker
Nationality: Australian

7
Name: Michael
Last name: Taylor
Job: teacher
Nationality: South African

4
Name: Anna
Last name: Flynn
Job: doctor
Nationality: Irish

8
Name: Pauline
Last name: Smith
Job: photographer
Nationality: New Zealander

Find out information to complete the table.

First name	Last name	Job	Nationality
Mary			
Jack			
Robert			
Anna			
Louise			
Nick			
Michael			
Pauline			

Unit 2 Communicative activity
Where are you?

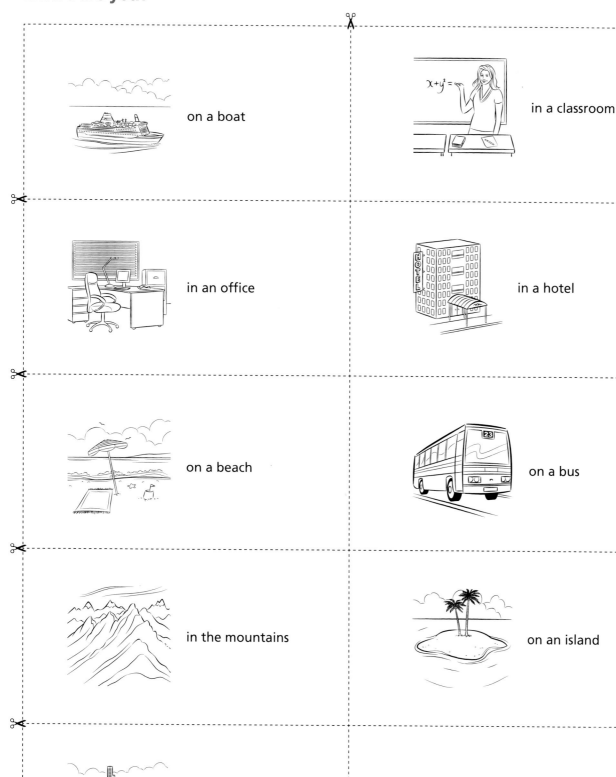

on a boat

in a classroom

in an office

in a hotel

on a beach

on a bus

in the mountains

on an island

in a city

in a car

Unit 3 Communicative activity

Who's Patrick's brother?

Student A: Family tree

Ask your partner questions (e.g., *Who's Patrick's brother? Who's Patrick's dad?*) and complete your family tree.

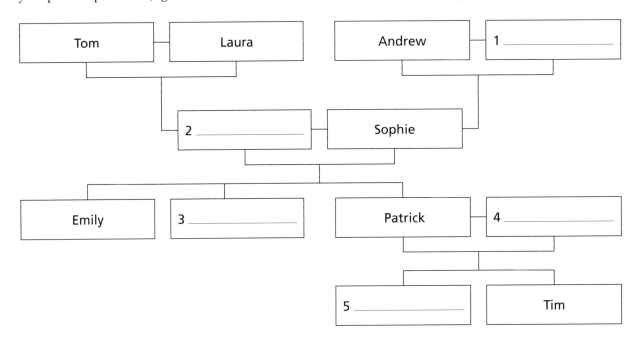

✂ -

Student B: Family tree

Ask your partner questions (e.g., *Who's Patrick's sister? Who's Patrick's mom?*) and complete your family tree.

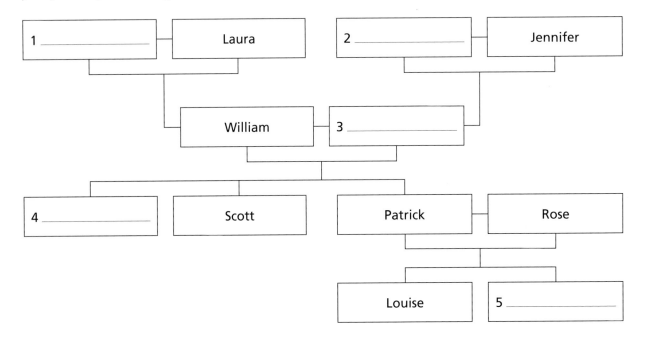

Unit 4 Communicative activity

Find the differences

Ask your partner questions about his or her town map (e.g., *Where's the book store?*) and answer your partner's questions (e.g., *The book store is opposite the café and next to the museum.*). Check the things that are the same. Find two differences.

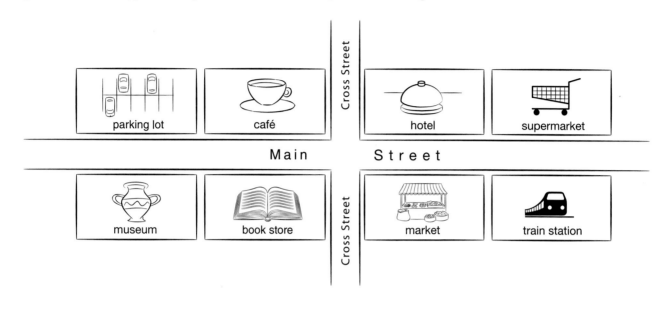

Ask your partner questions about his or her town map (e.g., *Where's the book store?*) and answer your partner's questions (e.g., *The book store is opposite the café and next to the bank.*). Check the things that are the same. Find two differences.

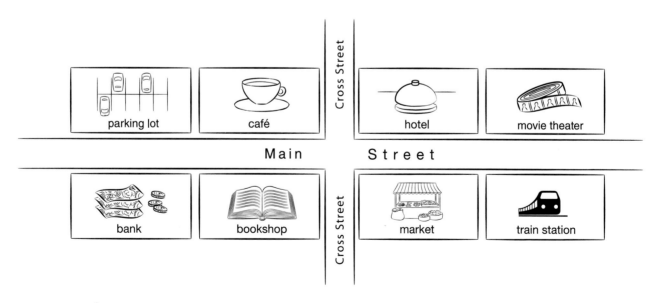

Unit 5 Communicative activity

Find someone who...

Find someone who...

1 ...can play a musical instrument.

2 ...can say "hello" in three different languages.

3 ...can sing a song in English.

4 ...can write with their left hand.

5 ...can dance salsa.

6 ...can ride a horse.

7 ...can make a cake.

8 ...can repair a computer.

	Name	Extra information
1		
2		
3		
4		
5		
6		
7		
8		

Unit 6 Communicative activity

Perfect partner

Which men and women would make perfect partners? Discuss in groups.

Amy Spink

likes: detective stories

dislikes: fast food

favorite things: reality TV shows

Tony Green

likes: good music

dislikes: reading

favorite thing: my pet cat

Sharon Bell

likes: blues songs

dislikes: diving

favorite things: animals

Darren Park

likes: scuba diving

dislikes: sweet things

favorite thing: music

Diana Pratt

likes: sports

dislikes: fruit pie

favorite things: comedy movies

Tom Frazer

likes: books

dislikes: hamburgers

favorite things: reality TV shows

Unit 7 Communicative activity

Quiz

What's your favorite season? Take the quiz and find out.

1 Which sports do you like?

  a cycling
  b swimming
  c soccer
  d skiing

2 Which food or drink do you prefer?

  a green salad
  b ice cream
  c pumpkin pie
  d hot tea

3 What is a good place for a vacation?

  a New Jersey's green countryside
  b Mexico's beautiful beaches
  c Washington's forests
  d the north of Canada

4 On the weekend, you …

  a work in the garden
  b go to the beach
  c read a book
  d stay in bed and sleep

5 What is the perfect place to live?

  a an apartment in Atlanta
  b a tent on a beach
  c a small house by the lake
  d a big house in a forest in Canada

6 What is your favorite color?

  a green
  b yellow
  c orange
  d white

 -

ANSWERS

More a answers: Everything is new, green, and happy. You are happy, too, because you're a spring person.
More b answers: You are a very nice person and have a lot of friends. You're summer!
More c answers: You're an fall person. You're intelligent and know a lot.
More d answers: You're a winter person. A big cup of hot tea and a good book make you happy.

Unit 8 Communicative activity

A day in the life of a doctor

Read the text and ask your partner for information. Use the words in parentheses to help you. Then answer your partner's questions.

A doctor's day

My name is Maria. I'm _____ (how old?) and I'm a doctor. I get up at _____ (what time?).

I never have breakfast, only a small cup of coffee. At 8 o'clock, I go to work by bus.

I _____ (how often?) help patients from 8:30 to 12:00. At _____ (what time?) I have lunch

with the other doctors.

I finish work at 8 o'clock in the evening. At home, I help my _____ (who?) with their homework,

and my husband cooks _____ (what?). We go to bed at 11 o'clock. We are usually very tired.

✂ -

Read the text and answer your partner's questions. Then ask your partner for information. Use the words in parentheses to help you.

A doctor's day

My name is Maria. I'm 30 and I'm a _____ (what?). I get up at 7 o'clock. I _____ (how often?)

have breakfast, only a small cup of coffee. I go to work at _____ (what time?) by bus.

I usually help patients _____ (when?). At 12:30 I have lunch with the other doctors.

I finish work at _____ (what time?) in the evening. At home, I help my daughters with their

homework, and my husband cooks a big dinner. We go to bed at _____ (what time?). We are

usually very tired.

Unit 9 Communicative activity

Four suitcases

Student A

Who has your suitcase? Call your friends and ask questions to find out (e.g., *Is there a laptop in the suitcase? Are there any shoes?*). Answer their questions. Get your suitcase back!

You have your friend's suitcase!

Contents: a skirt, a laptop, a pair of shoes, two dresses, a camera

You want to find your suitcase!

Contents: a laptop, a pair of shoes, a dress, a scarf, a coat

Student C

Who has your suitcase? Call your friends and ask questions to find out (e.g., *Is there a laptop in the suitcase? Are there any shoes?*). Answer their questions. Get your suitcase back!

You have your friend's suitcase!

Contents: a camera, a pair of pants, a book, a pair of glasses, a laptop

You want to find your suitcase!

Contents: a skirt, a camera, a pair of shoes, two dresses, a laptop

Student B

Who has your suitcase? Phone your friends and ask questions to find out (e.g., *Is there a laptop in the suitcase? Are there any pants?*). Answer their questions. Get your suitcase back!

You have your friend's suitcase!

Contents: a pair of pants, a camera, a scarf, a pair of shoes, a pair of glasses

You want to find your suitcase!

Contents: a camera, a pair of pants, a book, a pair of glasses, a laptop

Student D

Who has your suitcase? Phone your friends and ask questions to find out (e.g., *Is there a camera in the suitcase? Are there any shoes?*). Answer their questions. Get your suitcase back!

You have your friend's suitcase!

Contents: a laptop, a pair of shoes, a dress, a scarf, a coat

You want to find your suitcase!

Contents: a pair of pants, a camera, a scarf, a pair of shoes, a pair of glasses

Unit 10 Communicative activity

Where were you yesterday?

Where were you yesterday at these times? Write your answers. Ask your partner questions and write the answers in the table.

Example:　　A: *Where were you at 6 a.m. yesterday?*

　　　　　　B: *I was in bed.*

Part 2

Answer your partner's questions. When were you in the same place?

Where were you ...	You	Your partner
at 6 a.m. yesterday?		
at 8 a.m. yesterday?		
at 9 a.m. yesterday?		
at 11 a.m. yesterday?		
at 1 p.m. yesterday?		
at 3 p.m. yesterday?		
at 5 p.m. yesterday?		
at 7 p.m. yesterday?		
at 10 p.m. yesterday?		
at 1 a.m. yesterday?		

Unit 11 Communicative activity

I know what you did last summer

You traveled to Antarctica.

You helped your grandmother in the garden.

You had Chinese food and didn't like it.

You took photographs of animals in a forest.

You spoke French.

You found $10,000.

You studied for your English test.

You called your friends.

You walked in the mountains.

You got married.

You ate a grilled chicken sandwich in a famous American restaurant.

You went on a boat trip.

Unit 12 Communicative activity

How much do you remember? Take the quiz.

1 What's Alex Treadway's job?   _____

2 Where is Loch Ness?   _____

3 On what island in the Pacific are the beaches black?   _____

4 In what country can you find hot lakes?   _____

5 What was Jacques Cousteau's wife's name?   _____

6 What is Jetman's real name?   _____

7 What does the robot Tomo's name mean in Japanese?   _____

8 What animal can you see at the Litang Festival in China every August?   _____

9 Name a traditional dish in the United States made of pumpkin.   _____

10 What is the name of traditional Portuguese music?   _____

11 What did two men in New Jersey invent in 1950?   _____

12 Where did Roald Amundsen go to in 1911?   _____

13 In what country can you see a festival of colors?   _____

14 What animal do the Sami people understand?   _____

15 Name three types of "Big Cats."   _____

16 How tall was Yuri Gagarin?   _____

17 How did "Ötzi the Iceman" die?   _____

18 Who was the first woman in space?   _____

19 Why are the rocks in Madagascar's national park dangerous for people?   _____

20 What day is always a day off for people in China?   _____

Photocopiable communicative activities: Teacher's notes

Unit 1

GOAL: To practice talking about names, jobs, and nationalities

MATERIALS: A photocopy of the information table for each student in the class (or to save paper, copy the table on to the board and ask students to copy it). A photocopy of the ID cards for every eight students, cut into eight cards.

METHOD: Hand out one ID card to each student in the class. If you have more than eight students, use a second sheet of ID cards. Some students will have the same card, but that's OK. Ask students to stand up, walk around, and ask and answer questions to find out each other's names, jobs, and nationalities. Students note the answers in the information table. When checking, ask students to tell the class what information they found.

Unit 2

GOAL: To practice questions with *be* and the vocabulary of places

MATERIALS: One photocopy (cut into ten cards) for each group of four or five students

METHOD: Divide the class into groups of four or five. Hand out a set of ten cards to each group. Student A turns over a card and mimes being in the location on the card. The other students in the group must guess where the student performing the mime is. Remind students of the *yes / no* questions *Are you in / on a…?* and the responses *Yes, I am* and *No, I'm not*. Students must use the questions to make guesses.

The student who guesses correctly gets a point. Then Student B turns over a card and acts out being in the next location. Students guess where he or she is. Continue until all the cards have been used.

Unit 3

GOAL: To practice possessive *'s* and the vocabulary of family members

MATERIALS: One photocopy for each pair of A and B students (cut in half)

METHOD: Organize the class into pairs and give the students in each pair an A or B part of the worksheet. Tell students not to look at each other's card. Model the activities by asking one or two questions. For example, *Who's Patrick's brother? Who's Patrick's mother?* Once students have the idea, they must ask and answer questions until they have both completed their family trees. When checking, ask some questions and elicit answers.

Unit 4

GOAL: To practice prepositions of place and the vocabulary of stores and other places

MATERIALS: One photocopy for each pair of A and B students (cut in half)

METHOD: Organize the class into pairs and give the students in each pair an A or B part of the worksheet. Tell students not to look at each other's map. Model the activities by asking one or two questions, e.g., *Where's the book store?* Elicit answers and make sure students can use *in, next to, near,* and *opposite*. Once students have the idea, they must ask and answer questions until they have found two differences between their maps. When checking, elicit the differences.

Unit 5

GOAL: To practice asking and answering questions with *can* and *can't*

MATERIALS: One photocopy for each student in the class

METHOD: Hand out a photocopy of the worksheet to each student. Tell them to think about which activities in the list they can do. Model the activity by asking one or two *Can you…?* questions. Students then stand up, walk around, and ask different people questions. When they find someone who says *Yes, I can* to a question, they must write the name in the table and add extra information (for example, which musical instrument, which three languages). In a large class, tell students to find a different person for each question.

Unit 6

GOAL: To practice *likes* and *doesn't like*

MATERIALS: One photocopy for each group of four or five students

METHOD: Hand out a photocopy of the worksheet to each group. Tell them to read the information about the three women and the three men. Then tell them that they are in a dating agency. They must talk together and decide which man is the perfect partner for which woman. Model the activity by saying: *"What does Amy like?" "Oh, she likes detective stories." "What about Darren?" "Oh, he doesn't like stories. He likes music."* Once students have the idea, give them five minutes to ask questions and discuss ideas. Then ask each group to say who is the perfect partner for who, and why.

Unit 7

GOAL: To practice present simple question forms, seasons, and general vocabulary from the unit

MATERIALS: One photocopy for each student

METHOD: Hand out a photocopy of the quiz to each student. Tell them to read the quiz and choose answers that are true for them. Then ask students to compare their answers with a partner and read the answer key together.

Alternatively, ask students in pairs to take turns to ask and answer the questions first, to note their partner's answers, then to tell their partner which season suits them.

Unit 8

GOAL: To practice simple present question forms and frequency adverbs

MATERIALS: One photocopy for each pair of A and B students (cut in half)

METHOD: Organize the class into pairs and give the students in each pair an A or B part of the worksheet. Tell them not to look at their partner's copy. Give students time to think of the questions they need to ask to find out the missing information. Go around and help students with question forming. When students are ready, ask them to take turns to ask and answer questions with their partner to find the information. At the end, ask students to look at each other's texts to check their answers.

> **ANSWER**
>
> My name is Maria. I'm 30 and I'm a doctor. I get up at 7 o'clock. I never have breakfast, only a small cup of coffee. At 8 o'clock, I go to work by bus.
> I usually help patients from 8:30 to 12:00. At 12:30 I have lunch with the other doctors.
> I finish work at 8 o'clock in the evening. At home, I help my daughters with their homework, and my husband cooks a big dinner. We go to bed at 11 o'clock. We are usually very tired.

Unit 9

GOAL: To practice simple present question forms and frequency adverbs

MATERIALS: One photocopy for each group of students (cut in four)

METHOD: Read out the following situation:

You travel with four friends by train. You all take the wrong suitcase home by mistake! Who has your suitcase now? Call your friends and ask questions to find out. Answer their questions. Get your suitcase back!

Divide the class into groups of four. Hand out a different card to each student (A, B, C, and D). Tell students to "call" their friends in their group and ask questions to find their suitcase, e.g., *Is there a laptop in the suitcase? Are there any shoes?*

> **ANSWERS**
>
> **a.**-has C's suitcase, **b.**-has D's suitcase, **c.**-has B's suitcase, **d.**-has A's suitcase.

Unit 10

GOAL: To practice *was* and *were* and times

MATERIALS: One photocopy for each student

METHOD: Hand out a photocopy of the worksheet to each student. Tell them to think about each time and write where they were at that time yesterday. Model the question and answer in the example. Then organize the class into pairs and ask them to take turns asking and answering questions. Students write down their partner's answers. In feedback, ask, *Where was Jaime / Anna / Ivan*, etc.?

Unit 11

GOAL: To practice simple past forms

MATERIALS: One photocopy for each group or for the class

METHOD: Divide the class into groups of four or five. Make one photocopy of the worksheet for each group. Cut up the statements and hand out each set to each group, in a pile face down. Each student in the group takes a card and thinks about how to mime the sentence on the card. When they are ready, one student mimes their sentence. The rest of the group must shout out what the student did until they get the sentence exactly right. Then it is another student's turn.

Alternatively, do this as a class activity. One student comes to the front of the class. Give him or her a card. The student acts out the sentence and the class must guess and shout out what it is.

Unit 12

GOAL: To remember / revise information from the Student Book in a quiz

MATERIALS: One photocopy for each student

METHOD: Divide the class into pairs to do the quiz. You could ask students to do it in one of two ways. You could ask them to do it without looking at the Student Book—find out what they remember. Or you could do it as a research task—students look through the Student Book in pairs to find the answers.

> **ANSWERS**
>
> 1 He's a photographer.
> 2 In Scotland
> 3 Hawaii
> 4 Iceland
> 5 Simone
> 6 Yves Roissy
> 7 intelligent
> 8 horse
> 9 pumpkin pie
> 10 fado
> 11 color TV
> 12 South Pole
> 13 India
> 14 reindeer
> 15 tiger, lion, leopard, jaguar
> 16 5 foot and one inch
> 17 an arrow killed him
> 18 Valentina Tereshkova
> 19 They are sharp
> 20 Sunday

Workbook answer key

Unit 1

1a (page 4)

1 2 explorer 3 photographer 4 student
5 writer 6 scientist

2 1 an 2 a 3 a 4 an 5 a 6 a

3 I'm, I'm

4 1 I'm 2 I'm 3 you're

5 1 I'm 2 You're 3 I'm 4 I'm

1b (page 5)

1 2 France 4 Brazil 6 Canada 8 Mexico
3 Egypt 5 Japan 7 United States

2 2 Egyptian, Egypt 5 Brazil, Brazilian
3 Germany, German 6 Japan, Japanese
4 Italian, Italy

3 2 He's Japanese.
3 He's Brazilian.
4 It's Italian.
5 It's French.
6 He's Egyptian.

1c (page 6)

1 1 Africa – b 3 Asia – d
2 North America – c 4 South America – a

2 a nine b three c eight d five
e two f seven g six h four

3 1 your 2 My 3 My 4 your 5 My
6 your 7 My 8 your 9 My

4 2 Joana is <u>from</u> Madrid.
4 This phone call is <u>from</u> Boris.
6 He's <u>from</u> Germany.

1d (page 7)

1 1 morning 2 afternoon 3 evening 4 night

2 1 b Good afternoon. What's your name, please?
2 a Can you spell that?
3 f What's your last name?
4 e Thank you. What's your job?
5 d OK. Thanks.
6 c Goodbye.

3 1 How are you?
2 This is Kara.
3 Nice to meet you, Kara.
4 Nice to meet you too.

4 Students' own answers

1e (page 8)

1a 2 I'm from the United States.
3 Gabrielle is from Brazil.
4 Portugal is in Europe.
5 Chris Anthony is a photographer.
6 Jakarta is in Indonesia.

Answers will vary.

1b a city – Jakarta
a continent – South America
a country – Brazil
a language – French
a name – Chris Anthony
a nationality – Portuguese

2b 1 ? 2 . 3 . 4 ? 5 . 6 . 7 ? 8 ?

2c 1 What's your name? 5 My name's Marcus Garcia.
4 Can you spell that? 6 Yes. G-A-R-C-I-A.
7 How are you? 3 I'm fine.
8 What's your phone number? 2 It's 916-555-3290.

3 First name – Greta
Last name – Lessard
Nationality – Canadian
Job – writer

Learning skills / Check! (page 9)

1 jobs: artist, doctor, engineer, explorer, filmmaker, teacher
countries: China, Great Britain, India, Italy, Oman,
the United States
numbers: eight, five, four, nine, one, seven, six, ten,
three, two

2 Students' own answers

3 1 student 2 photo 3 English 4 three 5 phone 6 seven

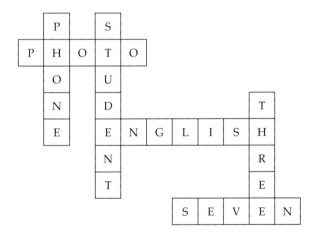

Unit 2

2a (page 10)

1 2 lake   2 city   4 island   5 beach   6 mountain

2 b

3 2 They're   3 They're   4 We're   5 We're   6 They're

4 2 'm not   3 aren't   4 isn't   5 aren't   6 aren't

2b (page 11)

1 2 twenty-four   4 sixty-three   6 eighty-one
3 forty-seven   5 seventy-six

2 2 seventy-nine
3 seventy
4 seventy-two
5 ninety-nine
6 sixty-three
7 sixty-four
8 eighty-four

3 2 Yes, it is.   4 Yes, it is.   6 Yes, it is.
3 No, it isn't.   5 No, it isn't.

4 2 ✓   3 ?   4 ?   5 ✓   6 ?

5 2 Are John and Jane in Rome?
3 She's on the beach.
4 Paul and Meera are in Santiago.
5 Is your name Andy?
6 You're OK.

2c (page 12)

1 1 black   4 red   7 gray   10 pink
2 orange   5 blue   8 white
3 brown   6 green   9 yellow

2 1 What's this color in English?
2 Are you in a hotel?
3 Are they in Tokyo?
1 b   2 a   3 c

3 1 cold/freezing   3 blue   5 hotel
2 white   4 gray   6 friend/sister

4 1 buses   4 cities   7 countries   10 friends
2 tents   5 offices   8 classes
3 cars   6 photos   9 addresses

5 1 friends   3 countries   5 hotel
2 island   4 Mountains   6 beaches

2d (page 13)

1 1 a, d   2 c, e   3 b, g   4 f, h

2 1 Where   2 What   3 What   4 Is   5 What

3 Address – 17 North Street
Zip code – 33550
Email address – julia21@gmail.com
Phone number – 202-555-2255

2e (page 14)

1 1 233 South Wacker Drive, Chicago – c
2 221b Baker Street, London – d
3 350 Fifth Avenue, New York – a
4 1600 Pennsylvania Avenue, Washington, DC – b

2 Burton Creek Inn
Bliss Road
Lake Tahoe, Utah
96158

3 First name – David
Last name – Smith
Address – 64 Atlantic Avenue
City, State – Brooklyn, New York
Zip code – 11201
Country – USA

4 First name – Diana
Last name – Black
Address – 26 Elm Street
City – Brooklyn
Zip Code – 11021
Country – USA
Email address – d.black@gmail.com

Learning skills / Check! (page 15)

1 1 b   2 c   3 a   4 d

4 Charles de Gaulle, John F. Kennedy, and John Lennon
are airports.
Cuba, Fiji, and Hawaii are islands.
Loch Ness and Titicaca are lakes.

Unit 3

3a (page 16)

1 1 brother 2 sister 3 mother 4 father

2 1 daughter 2 sons 3 parents

3 2 grandmother and granddaughter
3 grandmother and grandson
4 grandfather and grandson
5 mother and daughter

4 1 granddaughter 4 mother
2 father 5 grandfather
3 daughter 6 parents

5 2 Liam is my brother's son.
3 Who's Anne's sister?
4 What's Moira's phone number?
5 Is this Jerry's car?
6 Are you Liam's brother?

3b (page 17)

1 1 January 4 April 7 July 10 October
2 February 5 May 8 August 11 November
3 March 6 June 9 September 12 December

2 1 sister 3 father, mother
2 grandfather, grandmother 4 sister

4 1 Their, Their, their
2 Our, Our, our
3 His, His, Her

5 1 What 2 Who 3 Who was 4 Where

3c (page 18)

1 1 b 2 c 3 a

2 1 old 2 rich 3 poor 4 big 5 small 6 young

3 1 British 2 French 3 young 4 age 5 five 6 old

4 1 children – I 3 families – R 5 people – I
2 countries – R 4 men – I 6 women – I

5 1 in 2 at 3 at 4 at 5 in

3d (page 19)

1 1 a wedding 3 a new baby
2 an engagement 4 a wedding anniversary

2 1 c Happy Anniversary! *or* a Congratulations!
2 a Congratulations!
3 b Happy Birthday!
4 a Congratulations!

3 1 c a b 2 c d b a

3e (page 20)

1 1 are not 5 they are 9 who is
2 he is 6 we are 10 you are
3 I am 7 what is
4 is not 8 when is

2 1 What's his address?
2 It isn't their wedding anniversary.
4 They're engaged.
6 What's your sister's name?
8 It's in March.
9 I'm thirty.
11 He's getting married.

3 To Laura and George,
Happy Anniversary!
Best wishes from Sandra

4 To Martina and Jeff,
Congratulations on your new son!
Love from Alex

Learning skills / Check! (page 21)

1 1 cousins 4 grandson
2 old 5 present
3 wedding anniversary 6 men

3 1 artist 3 tennis player
2 politician

4 1 family 3 woman 5 poor
2 cousins 4 wedding 6 grandmother

5

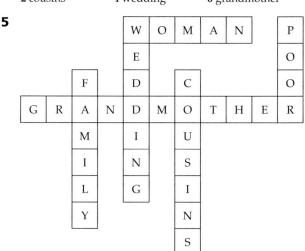

Unit 4

4a (page 22)

1
1 bank	5 market
2 café	6 museum
3 park	7 parking lot
4 movie theater	8 bus station

2 1 park 2 movie theater 3 museum
4 parking lot

3 2 The bus station is on Norfolk Street.
3 The Express Café is next to the museum.
4 The market is near the Express Café.
5 The information center is next to the bank.
6 The movie theater is opposite the bank.

4b (page 23)

1 1 this 2 that

2
1 Saturday	4 Friday	7 Sunday
2 Wednesday	5 Thursday	
3 Tuesday	6 Monday	

3 Monday, Tuesday, Wednesday, Thursday, Friday, Saturday

4 a Where is that?
b When is it open?
c Is it open today?
d Is it on the map?
e What is the name of this street?

5 1 What / is this building?
2 Where / are we?
3 When / is the market open?
4 Why / is this building famous?

4c (page 24)

1 2 It's ten fifteen.
3 It's twelve thirty.
4 It's five twenty.
5 It's six ten.
6 It's eight forty-five.

2 1 What's the name of this building?
2 What's the capital of France?
3 Is that a map of the city center?
4 This is a photo of my family.
5 I'm from the United States of America.
6 It's made of plastic.

3 1 a scientist
2 Addis Ababa
3 London
4 Ethiopia
5 East Africa Time, traditional Ethiopian time

4 b traditional Ethiopian time c East Africa Time

5 1 It's seven fifteen.
2 It's seven minutes past four.
3 It's eleven o'clock.

4d (page 25)

1
1 coffee	4 water	7 salad
2 tea	5 pastry	
3 fruit juice	6 sandwich	

2

1 1 Yes, two pastries, please. 2 No, thanks.

2 1 Can I have a cup of coffee, please?
2 Large.
3 No, thanks.

3 1 Can I help you?
2 Anything else?
3 OK, here you are. Thirteen dollars, please.

3 1 Yes, I'd like a sandwich.
2 One, please.
3 Yes, I'd like some fruit juice.
3 Yes, that's it.

4e (page 26)

1 2 Our hotel is near the old city and the ocean.
3 The Grand Bazaar is old and famous.
4 The coffee and the food are great.
5 The people are nice and friendly.
6 The Topkapi Palace museum and the Hagia Sophia museum are great.

2 1 The stores are great.
2 The museum is famous.
3 The city is beautiful.
4 The markets are big.
5 The hotel is new.
6 The people are friendly.

3 1 Hello 2 in 3 near 4 and 5 is 6 here 7 great 8 you

Learning skills / Check! (page 27)

2
1 here	3 name	5 open	7 please
2 this	4 near	6 time	8 help

V	E	Y	P	L	E	A	S	E	E
O	T	L	E	N	E	B	X	Q	Y
N	H	Q	B	T	P	C	O	G	T
A	I	W	I	H	L	V	P	W	N
M	S	H	E	L	P	M	E	G	E
E	O	R	W	J	S	K	N	P	A
W	O	Y	I	J	D	O	S	L	R
B	I	U	O	Q	H	E	R	E	V
Y	T	I	M	E	V	L	T	A	I
O	A	Z	E	O	C	S	R	I	A

Unit 5

5a (page 28)

1   1 can   2 can't   3 can't   4 can   5 can   6 can

2   1 play   3 play   5 cook   7 swim
        2 drive   4 sing   6 ride   8 speak

Possible answers

3   2 Can you drive a car?
        3 Can your father play table tennis?
        4 Can your sister sing?
        5 Can your mother cook?
        6 Can you ride a bike?
        7 Can your brother swim?
        8 Can your friends speak English?

5b (page 29)

1   1 a camera   4 a video camera
        2 a laptop   5 a webcam
        3 a cell phone   6 headphones

2   1 F   2 T   3 F   4 T

3   2 Alvaro has a cell phone and a video camera.
        3 Linzi and Jay have a laptop and headphones.
        4 Boris has a cell phone and headphones.

4   2 light   3 young   4 friendly   5 young   6 friendly

Possible answers

5   1 It's a new backpack.
        2 It's a famous family. It's a fantastic family.
        3 They're new batteries. They're small batteries.
        4 It's a nice bag. It's a light bag.
        5 They're famous robots. They're new robots.
        6 It's a big photo. It's an old photo.

5c (page 30)

1   c

2   1 T   2 T   3 F   4 T   5 F

3   4 These bikes are a very good idea.
        6 The water is very clean.

4   1 d   2 c   3 a   4 b

5d (page 31)

1   1 an alarm clock   2 flash drives   3 speakers   4 a video camera

2   1 Can I help you?
        2 How much are these speakers?
        3 And how much is this alarm clock?
        4 Can I pay with cash?
        5 Here you are.

5e (page 32)

1a 3 4 6

1b 2 My computer is new, but it is very slow.
        3 This phone is very basic, but it is cheap.
        4 This store is big, but it isn't very good.
        5 I can ride a motorcycle, but I can't drive a car.
        6 She can speak Russian, but she can't write in Russian.

2   phone, laptop, computer

3   1 d   2 c   3 a   4 b

4   Example answer:

Hi Pascal,

Laptops are cheap, but you can't carry a laptop in your pocket. New phones are expensive, but Skype is cheap.

Good luck in your new job!

Mike

Learning skills / Check! (page 33)

1   1 piano   2 swim   3 alarm clock

4   1 Singapore   3 dollar   5 Yves Rossy
        2 solar   4 digital   6 Kyoto

5   gadget

Unit 6

6a (page 34)

1 1 tennis   2 basketball   3 rugby   4 soccer   5 ping pong

2 2 I don't like soccer.
3 I don't like rugby.
4 I like tennis.
5 I like ping pong.

Possible answers

3 2 Do you like soccer? No, I don't.
3 Do you like rugby? No, I don't.
4 Do you like tennis? Yes, I do.
5 Do you like ping pong? Yes, I do.

4 a five hundred   e thirteen thousand
b nine million   f eighty-eight thousand
c seven thousand   g ten million
d twenty-five million

5 1 cheese   5 fruit   9 salad
2 chocolate   6 meat   10 vegetables
3 eggs   7 pasta
4 fish   8 rice

6b (page 35)

1 1 books   3 action movies   5 TV shows
2 swimming   4 music   6 birds

2 1 birds   3 action movies   5 swimming
2 TV shows   4 music   6 books

3 2 Andrew's friend doesn't like jazz.
3 Does Emile like scuba diving?
4 Emile doesn't like novels.
5 Frances doesn't like pop music.
6 Does Frances like tennis?

4b 1 a lot   2 very much

4c 1 Andrew likes jazz a lot.
2 He doesn't like pop music very much.
3 I don't like tea very much.
4 We like sports a lot.
5 My friend doesn't like TV very much.
6 My friends like movies a lot.

6c (page 36)

1 1 international sports   2 four   3 Great Britain
4 an artificial leg   5 100 meter race

2 1 it   2 him   3 them   4 her   5 you   6 me   7 it   8 it

3 1 What time is it?   4 Is it hot?
2 How much is it?   5 Do you like cheese?
3 What day is it?

6d (page 37)

1 1 ☹   2 ☺   3 ☺   4 ☹

4 1 play   3 like   5 love   7 don't like
2 don't like   4 watch   6 have

6e (page 38)

1 1 c   2 e   3 a

2 1   1 b The star is Joaquin Phoenix.
2 d He's my favorite actor.
3 e He's really good in this movie.
4 h I have all of his movies on DVD.
2   1 f The food is great and it isn't expensive.
3   1 a The music is from countries around the world.
2 c The singers are fantastic!
3 g They have beautiful voices.

4 1 It   2 it   3 They   4 them   5 They   6 We

5 2 A: This movie is boring!
2 B: Oh! I think it's very good.
3 B: Yes, I do. She's fantastic!

Learning skills / Check! (page 39)

1 You can find out all this information from a dictionary.

5 basketball, cheese, eggs, pasta, rugby, salad, tennis, vegetables

B	I	H	T	F	U	I	F	O	J	X
L	C	H	E	E	S	E	I	O	Y	P
O	E	P	N	Q	E	P	R	Q	Q	E
E	Y	A	N	A	R	O	U	D	S	K
E	T	P	I	W	L	W	G	I	A	A
T	B	A	S	K	E	T	B	A	L	L
I	O	S	A	U	G	A	Y	A	A	R
V	I	T	R	I	G	S	W	X	D	I
S	S	A	M	D	S	G	G	E	E	F
D	E	T	N	F	Z	H	I	B	T	L
V	E	G	E	T	A	B	L	E	S	W

Unit 7

7a (page 40)

1 **a** autumn **b** spring **c** summer **d** winter

2 1 F 2 T 3 F

3 1 live 2 speak 3 speak 4 understand 5 have 6 teach

4 1 One million people live in Zanzibar.
 2 It is a group of islands in the Indian Ocean.
 3 We speak Swahili and English.
 4 They teach their sons how to make them.
 5 We don't have cold winters.

5 1 They don't speak Swahili in Zanzibar.
 2 We don't live on an island.
 3 The fishermen have boats.
 4 I don't understand Swahili.
 5 You don't teach English.

7b (page 41)

1 1 teacher 4 pencil
 2 board 5 book
 3 student 6 pen
 classroom

2 2 Do they live in the capital?
 3 Do they go to school every day?
 4 Do they like their school?
 5 Do they study English?

3 1 Do you understand Arabic?
 2 Do your friends speak German?
 3 Do we have an Internet connection?
 4 Do the students in your class study online?
 5 Do they live with their parents?

4 1/2 in a city, in Oman
 3/4 two children, the Internet
 5/6 English, at college

7c (page 42)

1 1 cloudy 2 rainy 3 snowy 4 sunny 5 windy

2 2 eat 3 watch 4 stay 5 read 6 cook 7 play 8 take

3 1 outside
 2 beach
 3/4 biking
 3/4 swimming
 5 college

7d (page 43)

1 5 Is it 6 It's 7 It's

2 1 c I don't feel well
 2 g Why don't you
 3 a Are you OK
 4 f I'm thirsty
 5 d I don't like tea
 6 e I don't understand
 7 b Here you are

3 2 have a sandwich 4 use a dictionary
 3 take a walk 5 go to bed

7e (page 44)

1 **a** biking **e** biking
 b Pacific Technical College **f** Saturdays
 c married **g** two children
 d teacher **h** two bikes

2 1 b, d 2 c, g 3 a, e, f, h

3 1 d I'm a teacher.
  b I work at Pacific Technical College.
 2 c I'm married.
  g I have two children, a boy and a girl.
 3 a I like biking.
  h I have two bikes.
  e We go biking in the mountains.
  f We meet on Saturdays.

4 Example answers:
 1 I speak Japanese.
 2 Today is Tuesday.
 3 This month is June.
 4 My favorite season is fall.
 5 I study at the Escola Oficial d'Idiomes.

Learning skills / Check! (page 45)

3 1 Pacific 3 how 5 reindeer 7 Canada
 2 winter 4 teacher 6 Holi 8 islands

P	R	E	T	N	I	W	R	P
A	N	S	R	L	I	E	K	B
C	J	B	D	L	I	R	D	Q
I	L	A	O	N	E	T	N	Q
F	J	H	D	H	A	X	K	D
I	N	E	C	A	D	L	N	W
C	E	A	M	T	N	H	S	L
R	E	R	X	T	Y	A	O	I
T	G	G	J	Z	M	D	C	W

Unit 8

8a (page 46)

1 1 breakfast 2 lunch 3 dinner 4 work 5 bed

2 Jeff; nine and a half hours

3 3 Jeff doesn't start work at seven thirty. He starts work at eight thirty.
4 Jeff doesn't have lunch at eleven o'clock. He has lunch at twelve thirty.

Example answers:

4 Jeff doesn't have breakfast.
Jeff goes to bed at ten o'clock.
Tommy starts work at six o'clock.
Tommy doesn't have lunch.

8b (page 47)

1 1 journalist   3 businesswoman 5 receptionist
2 waiter   4 nurse   6 salesperson

2 1 Waiters <u>usually</u> work late.
2 Journalists <u>sometimes</u> write books.
3 A businesswoman <u>often</u> travels to different cities.
4 A waiter <u>never</u> works at home.
5 A salesperson <u>always</u> talks to customers.
6 A nurse <u>often</u> works late.

3 1 What does he do?
   He's a doctor.
2 Where does he work?
   He works in a hospital.
3 Does she live in Miami?
   No, she doesn't.
4 Does she write for the *Miami Times*?
   Yes, she does.

4 1 do (you) do   6 do
2 works   7 finishes
3 Does (your husband) do 8 start
4 doesn't   9 don't work
5 Do (you) like

8c (page 48)

1 scientists at a "sleep laboratory"

2 1 a 2 c 3 e 4 b 5 d

3 1 How many days do you work?
2 How does he watch people?
3 How often do nurses change their routine?
4 How many hours do police officers work?
5 How does it work?

4 1 She goes to work <u>every</u> day.
2 Do you change your routine <u>every</u> week?
3 We meet <u>every</u> month.
4 I talk to my mother <u>every</u> evening.
5 Does he watch TV <u>every</u> night?
6 We go to the beach <u>every</u> Sunday.

8d (page 49)

1 1 e Can I help you
2 d Can I speak to
3 a one moment
4 e Can I help you
5 d can I speak to
6 c I'm sorry
7 b I'll call back later

2 1 yes
2 yes
3 yes
4 yes
5 yes

8e (page 50)

1a meet, noon, meeting, boss, see, will, will, dinner, I'll, call, tomorrow, usually, free, weekends, weekend, off, too, soon

1b The words *tourist*, *friends* and *job* don't have double letters.

2a 1 time   2 place

2b 3 night   4 the morning   5 work   6 Italy

3 1 a an Italian restaurant
2 d I'm a waiter
3 g the customers are usually tourists
4 c have pizza or pasta
5 e in the morning
6 b get up late
7 f on Mondays

4 boss, difficult, noon, usually, week

5 Example answer:
Hi Craig,
Yes, I'm in Italy. I have a new job too. I work in a call center.
It's boring, but it isn't difficult.
I finish work at eight o'clock. Let's talk at nine o'clock.
Oscar

Learning skills / Check! (page 51)

2 1 breakfast   4 lunch   7 movie
2 receptionist   5 exercise   8 bed
3 cats   6 dinner

Unit 9

9a (page 52)

1 1 a hat 2 a scarf 3 a jacket 4 a sweater 5 a pair of jeans

2 1 a T-shirt   3 a shirt   5 a pair of pants
   2 a pair of boots   4 a coat   6 a pair of shoes

3 1 there are   4 there are   7 there are
   2 There's   5 there is   8 there's
   3 There are   6 there are

9b (page 53)

1 1 table   4 chair   7 bath
   2 lamp   5 desk   8 closet
   3 bed   6 TV

2 Executive

3 2 Is there a sofa in the Club rooms?
   3 Is there an ocean view in the Executive rooms?
   4 Is there a bath in the Superior rooms?
   5 Is there a desk in the Executive rooms?
   6 Is there a fridge in the Superior rooms?

4 2 Yes, there is.   4 Yes, there is.   6 Yes, there is.
   3 No, there isn't. 5 Yes, there is.

5a A: Let's go <u>to</u> New York for New Year's Eve.
   A: Yes, there are. There are flights from Monday <u>to</u> Friday.
   A: And there's a bus from the airport <u>to</u> the hotel.

5b 1 T   2 T

9c (page 54)

1 1 b 2 a 3 d 4 c 5 f 6 e

2 1 Can I take two <u>suitcases</u> on the plane?
   2 Can I take photos in <u>the plane</u>?
   3 Can I take a <u>bus</u> to the airport?

3 1 Start 2 Don't drive 3 Stay 4 Visit 5 Go

9d (page 55)

1 1 wake-up call   3 laundry   5 business center
   2 room service   4 medical service

9e (page 56)

1a 2 You can swim every day <u>because</u> the beach is next to
   the hotel.
   3 Stay in bed and breakfasts <u>because</u> they're cheap and
   friendly.
   4 Don't go in winter <u>because</u> it's very cold.
   5 There are a lot of hotels <u>because</u> it's a popular place.
   6 Don't take a bus <u>because</u> they aren't comfortable.

1b 1 d 2 c 3 a 4 b 5 e

2 1 b   2 c   3 d   4 a

3 Example answer:
   Legoland is a great place for families. It's near London. There
   are a lot of attractions. Don't go in August because there are
   a lot of people at that time. There's a hotel in the park. Don't
   miss the children's train because it's great for young children.

Learning skills / check! (page 57)

1 take a photo, take a suitcase
   book a hotel, book online
   travel by bus, travel to Africa

2 Example answers:
   go: to school / work, home, to the beach, to bed, to a class, to
   Africa, into the forest, swimming, for walks, out, on vacation;
   temperatures go up
   have: classes, a meeting, teachers, children, a camera,
   a bottle of water, breakfast / lunch

3 1 Peru   5 Lisbon
   2 Russia   6 a pyramid
   3 ice   7 Wellington
   4 the Trans-Siberian railway   8 yes

4 1 table 2 beds 3 fridge 4 sofa 5 bath tub

5 wardrobe

Unit 10

10a (page 58)

1
b second	**e** fifth	**h** twelfth
c third	**f** tenth	**i** thirteenth
d fourth	**g** eleventh	**j** twenty-first

2
2 December sixteenth, nineteen sixty-four
3 August third, fifteen twenty-three
4 October seventeenth, sixteen seventy-six
5 February twenty-eighth, two thousand thirteen

3
1 October	3 Sweden	5 engineer	7 rich
2 scientist	4 parents	6 brothers	

4 1 was 2 were 3 was 4 were 5 was 6 was

Example answers:

5
2 He was an engineer and inventor.
3 He was the inventor of television.
4 His parents were from Scotland.
5 He was born in Scotland.
6 His children were born in England.

10b (page 59)

1 1 famous 2 interesting 3 good 4 great 5 friendly

2 1 boring 2 unfriendly 3 bad 4 unhappy

3 1 F 2 T 3 F 4 T 5 F 6 F

4
2 His parents weren't rich.
3 His first job wasn't in a movie.
4 His first movie roles weren't big.
5 He wasn't a happy child.

10c (page 60)

1
1 <u>Where</u> were your parents from?
2 <u>When</u> was your father born?
3 <u>What</u> was your grandmother's name?
4 <u>Who</u> was your best friend at school?
5 <u>When</u> is your birthday?

3 1 Who 2 Where 3 What 4 When 5 Why

4 1 ago 2 At that time 3 Today 4 ago 5 Today

5
1 The <u>first</u> Aztec ruler was Acamapichtli.
2 Modern Mexico's <u>first</u> president was Guadalupe Victoria.
3 Who was the <u>first</u> president of your country?
4 Which Russian president was born on February <u>first</u> 1931?
5 What was President Yeltsin's <u>first</u> name?

10d (page 61)

1
b vacuuming / cleaning
c in traffic
d on the phone / busy at work
e sick
f busy

2
1 b I was at home.
2 d I was sick.
3 a Don't worry.
4 e I'm sorry I'm late.
5 g That's OK.
6 f I was busy at work.
7 c I'm very sorry.

3 1 e 2 c 3 d

10e (page 62)

2
1 When I was five, my brother was born.
2 When I was in school, I was good at English.
3 When I was in high school, I was in the sports club.
4 When my parents were children, their families were poor.
5 When I was a child, my favorite food was pizza.

Learning skills / Check! (page 63)

1 1 d 2 a 3 b 4 g 5 e 6 f 7 i 8 j 9 h 10 c

4
1 Apache	3 Japanese	5 South	7 Maya
2 Russia	4 Portugal	6 Norway	

5 history

Unit 11

11a (page 64)

1 2 h 3 e 4 a 5 d 6 f 7 b 8 g

2 2 finished – R   4 found – I   6 took – I
   3 went – I   5 called – R

3 1 called   4 finished   7 started
   2 died   5 killed   8 studied
   3 discovered   6 lived   9 walked

4 1 lived   3 died   5 walked
   2 started   4 studied   6 finished

11b (page 65)

1 1 actor and writer
   2 because he loved travel and exploration
   3 2005
   4 an adventurous person
   5 met and filmed local people

2 2 discovered   6 wrote   9 met
   3 loved   7 traveled   10 filmed
   4 changed   8 walked
   5 went

3 2 He didn't write *Around the World in 80 Days*.
     Jules Verne wrote *Around the World in 80 Days*.
   3 He didn't travel to the South Pole in 2012.
     He traveled to the South Pole in 2010.
   4 He didn't go around the Pacific Ocean in two months.
     He went around the Pacific Ocean in ten months.

4 2 Did you read Jules Verne's story?
   3 Did you drive to the South Pole?
   4 Did you meet interesting people?
   5 Did you make a movie on every trip?
   6 Did you have an adventure last year?

5 2 I did   3 I didn't   4 I did   5 I did   6 I didn't

11c (page 66)

1 1 two men – Borge Ousland and Mike Horn
   2 the North Pole   3 sleds   4 a polar bear

2 1 Who did Borge Ousland travel with?
   2 When did they go to the North Pole?
   3 What did the polar bear eat?
   4 Where did Mike Horn fall?
   5 Why did Mike Horn fall?
   6 Why did Borge Ousland start a fire?

3 1 Mike Horn   4 into the sea
   2 in 2006   5 because the ice broke
   3 their boat   6 to dry Horn's clothes

4 1 Who did you go on vacation <u>with</u> last year?
   2 Did you reserve the tickets <u>with</u> a travel agent?
   3 Did you stay in a hotel <u>with</u> wi-fi?
   4 Who do you live <u>with</u>?
   5 Students' own answers

11d (page 67)

1 conversation 1: 2 c   3 e   4 b   5 d   6 f
   conversation 2: 1 b   2 e   3 d   4 c   5 a   6 f
   conversation 3: 1 b   2 f   3 c   4 e   5 d   6 a

2 2 h 3 f 4 g 5 d 6 c 7 a 8 e

11e (page 68)

1 1 Dear / Hi
   2 Regards, / Best wishes, / Love, / All the best,
   3 Dear / Hi
   4 Regards, / Best wishes, / Love, / All the best,
   5 Dear
   6 Regards, / Best wishes, / All the best,

2a a

2b 1 no: We visited the park. Then we went home.
   2 no: We had dinner. Then we went to bed.
   3 yes
   4 no: I fell on the ice. Then my friend helped me.
   5 no: I didn't have any money. Then my friend gave me ten
     dollars.

3 1 a, e   2 d, h   3 c, f   4 b, g

4 Example answer:
   Dear Eve,
   Thanks for the DVDs. They were really interesting. I watched
   the first one last night and the second one this morning!
   Thanks again. Talk to you soon.
   Love,
   Rachel

Learning skills / Check! (page 69)

1 do – did, drive – drove, fall – fell, find – found, go – went,
   have – had, leave – left, make – made, meet – met,
   say – said, see – saw, send – sent, take – took

3 1 Ötzi   5 Madagascar
   2 Italy   6 very sharp
   3 knife   7 animal
   4 Austria   8 skis

Unit 12

12a (page 70)

1 2 I eat lunch in the dining room / kitchen / living room.
3 I cook in the kitchen.
4 I sleep in my / the bedroom.
5 I take a bath in the bathroom.

2 1 Kolkata, India
2 in the living room of the grandfather's house
3 eight

3 1 The man is sitting on a chair.
2 The children are sitting on the floor.
3 The boy is looking at the camera.
4 The girl is standing near a small table.

4 2 Are the children watching TV?
No, they aren't.
3 Is the man reading a book?
No, he isn't.
4 Are the children sitting?
Yes, they are.
5 Is the girl making tea?
No, she isn't.
6 Are the boys wear shorts?
Yes, they are.

5 1 Are they making lunch?
2 He isn't reading the newspaper.
3 You're watching TV.
4 We're washing the car.
5 Are you eating?
6 She isn't sitting on the floor.

12b (page 71)

1 1 have   4 go out   7 get up   10 go
2 visit   5 go   8 go   11 go
3 play   6 meet   9 read   12 go

2 2 Adela and Naomi are meeting friends on Saturday evening.
3 Mike is visiting his family this weekend.
4 Gary is reading the newspaper.
5 Kayla is going out to eat with colleagues tomorrow.
6 Joe and Sue are going shopping with their children on Saturday morning.

3 2 on Saturday evening   5 tomorrow
3 this weekend   6 on Saturday morning
4 now

12c (page 72)

1 1 travel – PR
2 go – PR
3 took – P
4 'm taking – F
5 do – PR
6 went – P
7 'm going – F

2 1 works   5 're going   9 'm learning, 'm taking
2 's meeting   6 goes   10 came
3 went   7 made
4 read   8 visit

3 1 What do you do?
2 What are you doing?
3 What do you usually do on the weekend?
4 What did you do last weekend?
5 What are you doing this weekend?

12d (page 73)

1 a T b T c O d O e T f O g T/O h T

2 1 a A ticket to New York, please.
2 h Would you like a one-way or round-trip ticket?
3 b Are you coming back today?
4 e What time is the last bus?
5 c Four tickets for the history exhibition, please.
6 g Would you like a family ticket?
7 f Would you like to buy a brochure?
8 d What time does it close?

12e (page 74)

1 1 c to the marriage of their daughter
2 b at the Inn on the Lake
3 d We're having a garage sale
4 a 2 Fountain Street

2 1 b 2 c 3 d 4 a

3

	Present continuous	Present simple (he/she/it)	Past simple
arrive	arriving	arrives	arrived
come	coming	comes	came
do	doing	does	did
drive	driving	drives	drove
fly	flying	flies	flew
get	getting	gets	got
have	having	has	had
leave	leaving	leaves	left
lie	lying	lies	lay
make	making	makes	made
move	moving	moves	moved
phone	phoning	phones	phoned
run	running	runs	ran
see	seeing	sees	saw
sit	sitting	sits	sat
smile	smiling	smiles	smiled
study	studying	studies	studied
swim	swimming	swims	swam
travel	traveling	travels	traveled
work	working	works	worked

4 1 a, c   2 b, d

Learning skills / Check! (page 75)

3 1 newspaper   3 ironing   5 builder
2 castle   4 window   6 motorcycle

My top ten photos

Videoscript

Tom Brooks: Hi. My name's Tom Brooks. I'm a photographer. This is my top ten, my favorite National Geographic photos of people and places.

Number 1 is a photo by Alex Treadway. The woman is from Nepal in the Himalayas. She's Nepalese.

Photo number 2 is in Asia, too. The man is from Mongolia. He's a hunter. This photo is by Charles Meacham.

This is photo number 3. It's by James Stanfield. It's in Mongolia, too. It's evening. The woman is happy.

Number 4 is a photo by Michael Melford. This is Ina Bouker. Ina is American. She's from Alaska in the United States. She's a fisherwoman.

Now number 5. This photo is by Jim Blair. He's an American photographer. This photo is in Dhaka in Bangladesh. It's a photo of water buffalo in a river … and a man.

Photo number 6 is fantastic. It's by Brian Skerry. The photo is in the ocean of New Zealand. It's a photo of a man and a whale.

Photo 7 is by Jimmy Chin. This is Kate Rutherford. She's from the United States. She's a climber.

And now three photos from Africa.

Photo number 8 is by David Cartier. He's Australian. He's a student. This is a photo of a student, too. She's a student from South Africa.

This photo is of people from Namibia in Africa. It's by Chris Johns. He's a National Geographic photographer. This is photo number 9.

And this is photo number 10. It's my favorite. It's by Chris Johns, too. It's a lion. It's in South Africa. It's the evening. The lion is beautiful. This photo is fantastic.

Antarctica

Videoscript

Narrator: Antarctica is a continent. It isn't hot. It's cold.

The temperatures in Antarctica are below freezing. Temperatures of 30 degrees below zero are typical.

Antarctica is a good place for scientists and explorers, but the people on this boat are on vacation!

Boats to Antarctica come from South America, Australia, New Zealand, and South Africa.

Is it a good place for a vacation?

The beaches aren't beautiful yellow beaches.

And the sea is gray and cold.

But, the animals are amazing. These whales and penguins are from Antarctica.

In Antarctica, the mountains are white.

In the sea, the ice is white and blue.

The temperature of the sea is from four degrees below zero to ten degrees.

For the animals in Antarctica, cold temperatures are good.

Life is difficult for scientists and explorers.

But Antarctica is a beautiful continent.

A Mongolian family

Videoscript

Narrator: This is Ochkhuu's home. It's a ger in Ulaan Baatar.

Ochkhuu's daughter, Anuka, is six years old.

Ochkhuu's wife's name is Norvoo. Norvoo's family isn't from the city. These are her parents. Their ger is in the country. This is Jaya—Norvoo's father. He's a farmer.

Jaya and his wife, Chantsal, are sixty-five years old.

They are happy in the country. Jaya's life and Ochkhuu's life are very different.

Ochkhuu is a taxi driver now.

Where's that?

Videoscript

Narrator: Four cities around the world. What are their names?

City 1

F: OK, so this is in Asia.

M: Ah, it's at night. Look at the lights.

F: Yeah, they're shops. It's a shopping street.

M: And the cars and the people …

F: Yes, it's big. Well, it's the capital.

F: And this is in the day.

M: That's beautiful. Where's that?

F: It's in the city. It's a park with a lake.

M: Who's that? Is that you next to the lake?

F: No, it isn't.

City 2

M: And now this is in Europe.

F: Of course, this museum is really famous: the Prado.

M: Oh, yes! Is it an art museum?

F: Yeah, that's right. It's popular with tourists and local people, too.

M: Is that in the capital?

F: Yes, it is.

M: And where's that?

F: That's the train station.

M: Where are the trains?

F: Ah, this is the old station.

M: What's that? A park?

F: Well … a garden … and a nice café next to the garden.

M: Oh, yes. It's beautiful … for a train station!

City 3

F: Now we're in the United States.

M: That's a great photo.

F: I know. The bridge is famous.

M: It's the symbol of the city …

F: Yeah … this is about seven o'clock in the morning.

M: Look at the buildings in the city. And the mountains, too. Where's this? Is it in a parking lot?

F: No, it's a snack bar. It's near the beach. Look at the sign—eat, drink, surf.

M: Oh, yeah! Well, the surfing and the beaches are famous.

City 4

M: Ooh, that's cold!

F: Yes. Well, it's Europe!

M: What's this building? Is it a museum?

F: No, it isn't. It's old and famous but it isn't a museum.

M: Is that next to the river?

F: Yes, in the capital.

M: And look at the two people. Why are they there?

F: I don't know.

M: Aha! That's opposite the Houses of Parliament!

F: Yeah.

M: Look at the river and the bridges. Great! Who are the people?

F: Erm, they're tourists, I think.

Narrator: Four cities around the world. What are their names?

The Owl and the Pussycat

Videoscript

Narrator: In northern Spain, falconer Jordi Amenos regularly takes his young barn owl on training flights.

The owl, named Gebra, sharpens her flying skills, especially her takeoffs and landings.

Jordi's young cat begins to tag along on these walks. The cat watches the owl with interest.

And then, one day, Fum— meaning smoke in Catalan—goes airborne as well.

Most cats are agile, but Fum's moves belong in the Cirque du Soleil.

Fum leaps from his predatory instinct. But luckily, this is all in good fun.

Jordi Amenos Basora: In the beginning, I was not amused by the game because I saw that it could turn for the worst.

After a few days, I realized that the game was quite harmless and innocent.

And as it turns out, their games are really a sight to behold.

So, Jordi begins to capture the air show on tape for his own amusement.

When he edits the video and posts a link to his Facebook page the web traffic explodes.

His good friend, Ferran Marti, a web developer, remembers how surprised they both were.

Ferran Marti: On the seventh of May, Jordi put the video up on YouTube and I remember, one day, you put it on your Facebook profile and there were, like, a thousand visits, or something. I was surprised.

Jordi: Yes, I remember it that way, too. First it had one thousand visits, or something like that. And then, I went to sleep and the next day there were three hundred thousand visits. I thought, "What happened?"

After this, Ferran helps Jordi create a Fum and Gebra website where visitors post comments.

Ferran: They all love the story and want to find out more. That's why we had the idea of making the website to talk about Fum and Gebra's lives.

At the market

Videoscript

Interviewer: Is this your local market?

Jan Szafranski: Yes, this is my local market and it's really great. You can buy a lot of things: fish, meat, fruit, vegetables, bread.

Amy Mills: Yes, it is. My house is in this street, so this is my local market.

Richard Lewis: Well, yes and no. I'm a teacher and my school is near this market.

Interviewer: Which stalls do you like?

Richard Lewis: Ah, my favorite stall is this cheese stall. I love cheese. That's my favorite—Brie—but I like Camembert, too. English cheese is good, but French cheese is great. I love it.

Amy Mills: Well, probably this fruit and vegetable stall. These peaches are from Spain … hmm, that's fantastic.

Jan Szafranski: I like the cheese stall. It has cheese from all around the world.

Interviewer: Tell us what you don't like.

Jan Szafranski: Fish, actually! My wife likes it but I don't. It has bones. I don't like them. And I can't cook it. No, I don't like fish very much.

Richard Lewis: Erm, I can't think. Maybe tomatoes. I don't like them very much.

Amy Mills: Well, I'm a vegetarian. I don't like meat. I like vegetables, rice, pasta, bread … but meat? No, I don't like it.

The people of the reindeer

Videoscript

Narrator: The Sami people's reindeer move in spring. The Sami people go with them.

These are Nils Peder Gaup's reindeer. On the journey, the people live in tents. These Sami people have traditional lives. The children travel with the reindeer, too.

This snow is hard.

After snowy weather, it is soft.

Soft snow is good for the reindeer. Well, that's all. It's time to sleep.

The elephants of Samburu

Videoscript

Narrator: Nick Nichols takes photos of the elephants in their family groups, and of individual elephants, too.

Nick takes a lot of photos, about 10,000 in total.

Daniel Lentipo works for *Save the Elephants*.

He can identify individual elephants in Samburu Reserve.

Daniel teaches Nick how to identify individual elephants.

Nick and Daniel follow the elephants for ten hours every day.

The elephants drink.

They have a bath.

They eat.

Elephants are gentle and intelligent.

Nick explains that Daniel sometimes puts his hand up to the elephants.

The elephants put their trunks up.

It's a greeting—like "hello."

This ten-year-old elephant greets Nick.

The Samburu Reserve is a very good place for these elephants.

The elephants greet their family members with their trunks … and by calling.

At night, the elephants lie down to sleep.

In the morning, Nick and Daniel get up early and start work again.

Along the Inca Road

Videoscript

Narrator: Karin Muller is in South America. She's in a village in Ecuador and there's a market today.

Karin buys some food before she starts her trip.

It's day one on Karin's trip. They walk along the mountain track. There's something unusual. Two helicopters fly above them.

Then there's a very loud bang. One of the helicopters crashes.

The men are OK.

Karin helps them with their things.

There are many ways to travel through South America: by canoe, hitchhiking, by truck, on foot.

And there are many people to meet with their donkeys, horses, and of course, llamas.

The Inca Road takes Karin from Ecuador to Chile on one long adventure.

The space race

Videoscript

Narrator: <u>John F. Kennedy, the president of the United States,</u> in 1961.

In the 1950s and 1960s, there was a race between the United States and the Soviet Union—the space race.

Kennedy's famous speech about space was on May 25th, 1961. <u>Alan Shepard was the first American in space,</u> on May 5th, 1961.

But he wasn't the first person in space. That was the Russian, Yuri Gagarin.

<u>Sputnik was the first satellite.</u> It was part of the Soviet Union's space program in 1957.

On April 12th, 1961, the Soviet Union was the first country to send a person into space.

In the United States, Alan Shepard, John Glenn, Gus Grissom, and four more astronauts were part of the <u>Mercury program.</u>

<u>John Glenn was the first American to orbit the Earth,</u> on February 20th, 1962.

The next goal was <u>to put a man on the Moon. This was the Apollo program.</u>

There was a tragedy on January 27th, 1967, when there was a fire on Apollo 1. Three astronauts, including Gus Grissom, died.

On July 20th, 1969, there was success for Apollo 11.

For the first time in history, there were men on the Moon. The first man was Neil Armstrong and the second was Buzz Aldrin.

The next American space program was the Shuttle program.

There were also tragedies on this program, in 1986 with the <u>Challenger shuttle and in 2003 with the Columbia shuttle.</u> The shuttle was also part of the International Space Station program. <u>This is a program by the United States, Russia, Canada, Japan, and Europe.</u>

Perfumes from Madagascar

Videoscript

Narrator: Madagascar is a fantastic island. There are some very unusual plants in the forests.

It's a very interesting place for scientists.

These scientists are from Switzerland.

They went to Madagascar last year.

They wanted to find plants for perfumes. Some plants and flowers have fantastic scents.

The scientists traveled into the forest by boat.

Then they flew in a balloon. They looked for interesting flowers and fruit.

When they were back in Switzerland, they studied the new scents in the laboratory.

Roman Kaiser: I'm quite happy. It's already very close to this beautiful stephanotis scent as I experienced it on the Tampolo River.

Narrator: There are many natural and man-made scents in this laboratory.

Last year, this scientist found two new plants.

One plant had green fruit.

The second plant had red fruit.

They cut the fruits and they tasted them.

But they didn't like them.

There are many things to discover in Madagascar.

It's a natural paradise.

Saturday morning in São Tomé

Videoscript

Narrator: It's early on Saturday morning in São Tomé. Children are playing. Some people are resting.

The main beach near the city of São Tomé is very busy. Boats are arriving with fish. There are a lot of flying fish today.

In the mountains, people are taking vegetables to market.

Oswaldo Santos is from São Tomé. He's usually at home on Saturdays. Oswaldo is a musician. He's in a group called Grupo Tempo. He plays the guitar, he sings, and he writes music.

This Saturday morning, Oswaldo is visiting his friends, Guillerme and Nezo.

Oswaldo and Guillerme are driving to the south of the island.

Nezo lives in a small town here.

Oswaldo, Guillerme, and Nezo are playing a new song. They're giving a concert next week. Today they're preparing for the concert.

Guillerme and Nezo are painters, too. They paint things from local life: the people, the colors, and the animals.

Their music and art is about life in São Tomé.

Photocopiable tests

Unit 1 Test

Grammar

1 Choose *a* or *an* to complete the sentences about jobs.

1 It's *a / an* very good job.
2 I'm *a / an* explorer.
3 Sally is *a / an* writer.
4 He's *a / an* artist.
5 Tom is *a / an* engineer.

(5 points)

2 Complete the sentences with *'m* or *'re*.

1 Hi! I _____ Sally!
2 You _____ a student.
3 I _____ a teacher.
4 You _____ Robert Ballard!
5 I _____ a doctor.

(5 points)

3 Complete the sentences with *He's*, *She's*, or *It's*.

1 Barack Obama is from the US. _____ American.
2 Peru is a country. _____ in South America.
3 Mattias is a photographer. _____ from Sweden.
4 Silvia is Spanish. _____ from Madrid.
5 Curry is from India. _____ fantastic!

(5 points)

4 Complete the conversations with *my* and *your*.

Anna: What's ¹ _____ name?
Tom: ² _____ name's Tom.
Anna: Hi Tom. ³ _____ name's Anna.
Tom: Anna? Nice to meet you, Anna.

Joe: What's ⁴ _____ phone number, Sally?
Sally: It's 202-555-1292, and ⁵ _____ mobile number is 875-555-4415.
Joe: OK. Thanks.

(5 points)

5 Complete the description. Use one word in each space.

Hi! ¹ _____ name is Mike. I ² _____ a writer and ³ _____ explorer. It ⁴ _____ a fantastic job! I'm ⁵ _____ England.

(10 points)

Vocabulary

6 Match the letters that have the same sound.

B	Y	L	U	K

1 I, ___
2 M, S, N, ___
3 A, H, J, ___
4 D, P, C, ___
5 Q, W, ___

(5 points)

7 What are the jobs? Look at the pictures. Write the letters in order.

1 testcisni _____

2 rewirt

3 eroopptghrea _____

4 fmmrekail _____

5 perloxre _____

(5 points)

8 Write the nationalities.

1 Sally is from Australia. She's ___Australian___.
2 Stefan is from Germany. He's _____.
3 Yoko is from Japan. She's _____.
4 Pilar is from Mexico. She's _____.
5 Paul is from Great Britain. He's _____.
6 Simone is from France. She's _____.

(5 points)

9 What are the continents? Write the letters in the correct order.

1 Italy, Spain, and Poland are in _____ (porepu).
2 China, India, and Vietnam are in _____ (saai)
3 Brazil, Argentina, and Bolivia are in _____ (othus cramiea)
4 Nigeria, Kenya, and Somalia are in _____ (cafira)
5 The US and Canada are in _____. (ronth ramicae)

(10 points)

10 Write the numbers.

1 seven + one = _____   4 four + five = _____

2 six + four = _____   5 five + one = _____

3 two + three = _____

(5 points)

Functions

11 Complete the sentences. Put the sentences in order (1–5).

from	you	to	are	thanks

a Hi Joe. How _____ you?   ____

b Nice to meet _____ too.   ____

c Fine, _____. And you?   ____

d Nice _____ meet you Dan.   ____

e I'm OK. This is Dan. He's _____
Sydney in Australia.   ____

(10 points)

Writing

12a Write the sentences correctly. Use capital letters.

1 yourefiona   You're Fiona   .

2 imdavid   _____

3 mynamespaulmurray   _____

4 imfromscotland   _____

5 hesamerican   _____

6 imanengineer   _____

(5 points)

12b Write your personal profile. Answer the questions.

What's your name?

Where are you from?

What's your nationality?

What's your job?

Personal profile
_____
_____
_____
_____
_____
_____
_____
_____
_____
_____
_____
_____
_____
_____
_____
_____
_____
_____
_____
_____
_____
_____
_____
_____
_____
_____
_____
_____
_____

(15 points)

Speaking

13 Work in pairs. Ask and answer questions from 12b.

(10 points)

Unit 2 Test

Grammar

1 Choose the best option (a, b, or c) to complete the sentences.

1 I'm Jack and this is Tom, and _____ friends.
  a they're   **b** we're   **c** you're

2 Fiona and Kate are on vacation, and _____ happy.
  a they're   **b** we're   **c** you're

3 Your name is Ken and _____ Australian.
  a they're   **b** we're   **c** you're

4 In this photo, I'm with Sue, and _____ in a boat.
  a they're   **b** we're   **c** you're

5 Javier and Ana are from Chile, and _____ Chilean.
  a they're   **b** we're   **c** you're

(5 points)

2 Write the negative form of the verbs in parentheses.

1 We <u>aren't</u> (not be) French.
2 You _____ (not be) happy.
3 I _____ (not be) from the US.
4 Henry _____ (not be) on a beach.
5 Amy and Claire _____ (not be) Scottish.
6 It _____ (not be) Chinese.

(10 points)

3 Put the words in order to make questions. Then match the questions (1–6) with the answers (a–e).

1 hot / you / Are / ?   _____

_____

2 from / she / Russia / Is / ?   _____

_____

3 a / they / on / Are / boat / ?   _____

_____

4 Tom / Is / in / hotel / a / ?   _____

_____

5 London / in / we / Are / ?   _____

_____

  a No, he isn't.   **d** No, they aren't.
  b Yes, we are.   **e** Yes, she is.
  c No, I'm not.

(10 points)

4 Complete the sentences with the plural form of the noun in parentheses.

1 London and Cardiff are two British _____ (city).
2 The _____ (mountain) in Switzerland are beautiful.
3 Are they old _____ (bus)?
4 The _____ (beach) in Mexico are fantastic!
5 Argentina and Peru are South American _____ (country).

(5 points)

Vocabulary

5 Write the letters in the correct order.

1 untoanim   Everest is a _____.
2 ekal   Titicaca is a _____.
3 ase   The Mediterranean is a

_____.

4 yict   London is a _____.
5 andlis   Hawaii is an _____.

(5 points)

6 Write the missing numbers.

1 sixteen, seventeen, _____, nineteen, _____
2 twenty, _____, forty, fifty, _____
3 fourteen, thirteen, _____, _____, ten
4 ninety-one, ninety-two, ninety-three, _____,

_____

5 _____, seventy, eighty, ninety, _____

(10 points)

7 Write the colors of the flags.

1 The French flag is red, _____ (itweh), and _____ (ubel).
2 The German flag is _____ (ablck) and _____ (der) and gold.
3 The South African flag is red, blue, _____ (nerge), _____ (wollye), black, and _____ (hitwe).
4 Ireland's flag is green, white, and _____ (gorane).
5 The Newfoundland flag is white, _____ (gnree), and _____ (kinp)!

(10 points)

8 Match the questions (from 1 to 5) to the answers (a to e).

1 What's your zip code? ____
2 What's your license plate number? ____
3 What's your address? ____
4 What's your telephone number? ____
5 What's your email address? ____
  a It's 3 Lindall Street, Springfield
  b It's paul@mail.com
  c It's 04046
  d It's 1365 FRV
  e It's 977-555-0886

(5 points)

Functions

9 Put the words in order to make questions. Then write the questions in the correct place in the conversation.

a here / on / Are / vacation / you / ?

b your / email / Is / address / this / ?

c telephone / in the US / What's / number / your / ?

d you / from / are / Where / ?

e zip code / What's / the / ?

A: Good evening, Mr. Smith.

¹ _____ B: Yes, I am.

A: ² _____ B: I'm from Cleveland.

A: OK. This is your address.

³ _____ B: It's 25424.

A: ⁴ _____ B: Oh, it's 878-555-9789.

A: ⁵ _____ B: No, it isn't. My email address is smith@mail.com.

(10 points)

Writing

10 Complete the reservation form with this information. Add the correct capital letters.

cole@post.youmail.com	ms. sarah cole
14 buswell street. boston, massachusetts, usa	02215

Title: ¹ _____

First name: ² _____

Last name: ³ _____

Address: ⁴ _____

Zip code: ⁵ _____

Email address: ⁶ _____

(10 points)

11 Complete the reservation form with your own information.

Title: ¹ _____

First name: ² _____

Last name: ³ _____

Address: ⁴ _____

Zip code: ⁵ _____

Email address: ⁶ _____

(10 points)

Speaking

12 Work in pairs. You are on vacation. Take turns to ask and answer the questions.

Where are you?

How are you?

Is it hot or cold?

Are you happy?

(10 points)

Unit 3 Test

Grammar

1 <u>Underline</u> 's when it is the possessive, and circle 's when it means *is*.

1 (It's) John's book.

2 She's Paul's sister.

3 Oliver's boat's green.

4 What's your brother's name?

5 Where's Patrick's house?

6 Tim's son's eighteen today.

(10 points)

2 Choose the correct option to complete the sentences.

1 My brother is eighteen. *His / Her* name is Tom.

2 They're sisters, and *their / our* names are Emma and Amy.

3 We're married. *Our / Her* anniversary is in December.

4 Jo and Andy are from New Zealand. *Our / Their* house is on the beach.

5 Mr. Hayes is poor but *his / her* brother is rich.

(5 points)

3 Rewrite the sentences. Use *his, her, our,* or *their*.

1 My mother's family is big.
   Her family is big.

2 Mr. Hall's children are young.
   _____

3 The children's parents are here.
   _____

4 My daughter's name is Susie.
   _____

5 My and Fiona's house is small.
   _____

6 Anna's friends are at work.
   _____

(5 points)

4 Write the plural forms of the nouns in parentheses.

1 Carl's _____ (daughter) are thirteen-year-old _____ (girl).

2 Two _____ (man) and three _____ (woman) are in the boat.

3 Twelve _____ (person) are on two _____ (bus).

4 Forty _____ (child) are at the party. They're happy _____ (boy)!

5 My _____ (grandmother) are old _____ (woman).

(10 points)

Vocabulary

5 Write the missing months. Use these words.

July	October	March	January	April	August

1 January, February, _____

2 May, June, _____

3 November, December, _____

4 August, September, _____

5 February, March, _____

6 June, July, _____

(6 points)

6 Choose the best answer (a–c) for the questions.

1 Who is old?
   a my grandson   **c** my granddaughter
   b my grandmother

2 Who is a woman?
   a my sister   **b** my brother   **c** my father

3 Who is a man?
   a my daughter **b** my brother   **c** my mother

4 Who isn't my parent?
   a my brother   **b** my mother   **c** my father

5 Who isn't my grandchild?
   a my grandfather   **c** my granddaughter
   b my grandson

(5 points)

7 Look at Claire's birthday book. Complete the sentences.

1 John's birthday is in January.

2 Annie's birthday is _____.

3 Paul's birthday is _____.

4 Susan's birthday is _____.

5 Emily's birthday is _____.

6 Sophie's birthday is _____.

7 Patrick's birthday is _____.

1/3	John
3/12	Annie
4/22	Paul
7/19	Susan
10/7	Emily
11/3	Sophie
12/19	Patrick

(6 points)

8 Write the opposite adjectives.

1 big _____   2 old _____   3 rich _____

(3 points)

9 Complete the text with *in* or *at*.

I'm not [1] _____ work [2] _____ the office today. I'm [3] _____ a wedding [4] _____ a friend's house [5] _____ Chicago. And it's my birthday [6] _____ February! My birthday party isn't [7] _____ home. It's [8] _____ a hotel [9] _____ the Bahamas [10] _____ the Atlantic Ocean.

(10 points)

Functions

10 Choose the best option (a or b).

1 This is for the baby.
   a That's very kind.   **b** You're welcome.

2 Congratulations!
   a Oh, hello!   **b** Oh, thanks!

3 Happy Birthday!
   a Thanks for the present.   **b** I'm very happy for you.

4 Happy anniversary!
   a Thanks for coming to my birthday party!
   b Thanks. Wow! Married for twenty years!

5 Thanks for the lovely card.
   a You're welcome.   **b** It's very nice.

(10 points)

Writing

11 Rewrite the sentences with contractions.

1 It is Paul's birthday.
   It's Paul's birthday.
   _____

2 Amy is sixteen tomorrow. It is her birthday.
   _____
   _____

3 Jo and Dan are not married, but they are engaged.
   _____
   _____

4 Sally's wedding is in May. I am the bridesmaid.
   _____
   _____

5 Oh! You are eighteen. When is the party?
   _____
   _____

6 Fiona is not single. She is married.
   _____
   _____

7 It is not our birthday today. We are thirty on Friday.
   _____
   _____

8 I am not married. It is not my wedding!
   _____
   _____

(14 points)

12 Complete the greetings cards with words from the box.

your	to	happy	wishes	on	from

---

¹ _____ Amy,
Many ² _____
returns ³_____ your
birthday!
Love ⁴ _____
Aunt Claire

Hi Matto and Louise!
Congratulations on
⁵ _____
engagement!
Best ⁶ _____ ,
Gary

(6 points)

Speaking

13 Talk about your family. Answer the questions.

Who are the people in your family? What are their names? What do they do? How old are they? When are their birthdays?

(10 points)

Unit 4 Test

Grammar

1 Look at the street map. Choose the correct option to complete the sentences.

café | museum | movie theater | park

High Street

bus station | bank | information center | parking lot

1 The café is *on / at* High Street.

2 The bank is *opposite / next to* the information center.

3 The bus station is *near / next to* the museum.

4 The museum is *opposite / next to* the bank.

5 The park is *on / opposite* High Street.

(5 points)

2 Look at the street map in Exercise 1. Complete the sentences with *opposite, next to,* or *near*.

1 The movie theater is _____ the information center and _____ the museum.

2 The parking lot is _____ the movie theater and _____ the park.

3 The café is _____ the museum and _____ the bus station.

4 The information center is _____ the museum and _____ the parking lot.

5 The bank is _____ the movie theater and _____ the museum.

(10 points)

3 Tom is next to the bank and the bus station. Look at the map in 1 and choose *this* or *that* to complete the text.

¹*This / That* is the bank and ²*this / that* is the bus station here. ³*This / That* is the museum, and ⁴*this / that* is the movie theater, over there. Oh, and ⁵*this / that* is the parking lot, opposite the park.

(5 points)

4 Complete the questions with *Where, What, When,* and *Why*.

1 "_____ is Astana?" "It's in Kazakhstan."

2 "_____ is the bus to Cambridge?" "It's at 7:30."

3 "_____ is the parking lot?" "It's next to the park."

4 "_____ is this?" "It's a guidebook."

5 "_____ are you happy?" "It's my birthday!"

6 "_____ does the museum open?" "It opens at 9."

7 "_____ are you now?" "I'm in the park."

8 "_____ is the party?" "It's in June."

9 "_____ time is it?" "It's 9 o'clock."

10 "_____ is your brother?" "He's in Italy."

(10 points)

Vocabulary

5 Write the number of the picture next to the word.

a café _____	a parking lot _____	a movie theater _____
a market _____	a park _____	a train station _____

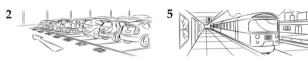

(10 points)

6 What are the days of the week? Write the letters in the correct order. Then number the days in order 1–6.

Sunday 1

a amnyod _____ **c** yadrif _____

b yutrshad _____ **d** wsdadeeny _____

e sedutya _____

(10 points)

7 Match the times (1–5) to the numbers (a–e).

1 It's eight thirty. a 7:00

2 It's seven o'clock. b 9:15

3 It's five forty-five. c 8:30

4 It's nine fifteen. d 1:00

5 It's one o'clock. e 5:45

(5 points)

8 Match the times (1–5) with these words.

midnight	in the morning	in the afternoon
in the evening	noon	

1 12:00 p.m. _____ **4** 3:00 p.m. _____

2 7:45 a.m. _____ **5** 9:00 p.m. _____

3 12:00 a.m. _____

(5 points)

Functions

9 Put the words in order to complete the dialogs.

1 help / Can / you / I / ?

_____

2 water / have / I / Can / , / please / a / ?

_____

3 are / Here / you / . / else / Anything / ?

_____

4 coffees / A / two / tea / two / and / , / please / .

_____

5 dollars / That's / twelve / .

_____

(10 points)

Writing

10 Join the sentences with *and*.

1 It's big. It's old. <u>It's big and old.</u>

2 The park is old. The park is famous.

_____

3 The city is new. The city is beautiful.

_____

4 My brother is young. My brother is rich.

_____

5 The market is open on Sundays. The market is open on Mondays.

_____

6 I'm happy at home. I'm happy at work.

_____

(5 points)

11 Write the postcard. Make sentences from the prompts. Use *and*.

1 The hotel / big / old
2 The people / nice / friendly
3 The beach / small / beautiful
4 The food / hot / great
5 I / fine / happy

See you soon

Mark x

Hi Jane,

We're in Portugal. _____

_____

_____

_____

_____

_____

_____

_____

_____

_____

_____

_____

_____

_____

_____

_____

_____

_____

_____

_____

_____

_____

_____

(10 points)

Speaking

12 Describe three places in your favorite city. For example, talk about a park, a movie theater, and a market.

(10 points)

Unit 5 Test

Grammar

1 Complete the sentences with *can* or *can't*.

	Speak French	Speak German	Play football	Play tennis
Paul	✓	✗	✓	✗
Annie	✗	✗	✓	✓

1 Paul _____ speak French.

2 Annie _____ speak French.

3 Paula and Annie _____ speak German.

4 Paula and Annie _____ play football.

5 Annie _____ play tennis.

6 Paul _____ play tennis.

(6 points)

2 Put the words in order to make questions.

1 you / Can / Chinese / speak / ?

_____

2 cook / food / Can / Chinese / you / ?

_____

3 your / Chinese / speak / brothers / Can / ?

_____

4 cook / Can / they / ?

_____

5 Can / write / you / in Chinese / ?

_____

(10 points)

3 Choose *have* or *has* to complete the sentences.

1 I *have / has* a computer.

2 Penny *have / has* two sisters.

3 We *have / has* a big house.

4 It *have / has* a camera.

(4 points)

4 Rewrite the sentences with the adjective in brackets.

1 This is my house. (new)

_____

2 I have a cell phone. (great)

_____

3 It's a café. (small)

_____

4 Jack has friends. (nice)

_____

5 You have a bag. (blue)

_____

(5 points)

5 Put the words in order to make sentences.

1 This / cheap / phone / very / is / .

2 Sally's / very / old / grandfather / is / .

3 boat / really / is / fantastic / Our / .

4 small / town / Their / is / very / .

5 really / My / is / computer / great / .

(5 points)

Vocabulary

6 Match the prices to the money and the countries.

1 $12   euros   the UK

2 €19   dollars   the EU (Germany, France, etc.)

3 £10   pounds   the US and Canada

(6 points)

7 Match the verbs (1–7) to the nouns (a–g).

1 cook	**a** a bike
2 speak	**b** table tennis
3 play	**c** a car
4 ride	**d** Chinese food
5 drive	**e** the piano
6 play	**f** English
7 swim	**g** in the lake

(7 points)

8 Complete the sentences with verbs from Exercise 7.

1 Jo can _____ French and Spanish!

2 Harry can't _____ the guitar.

3 Andy can _____ Indian food.

4 Jerry can _____ basketball and soccer.

5 Anne can _____ in lakes.

6 Tom can _____ a Ferrari.

7 Sally can't _____ her new bike.

(7 points)

9 Match the words to the pictures (a–j).

1 a camera _____   6 a laptop _____

2 headphones _____   7 a tablet _____

3 a camcorder _____   8 a battery _____

4 a webcam _____   9 a cell phone _____

5 an MP3 player _____   10 a robot _____

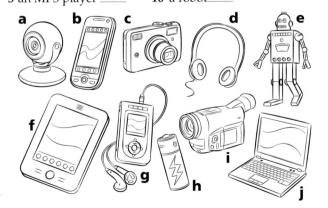

(10 points)

Functions

10 Put the words in order to make questions. Then match the questions (1–5) to the answers (a–e).

1 help / Can / you / I / ? _____

2 this / much / is / How / ? _____

3 card / pay / Can / I / a / with / ? _____

4 these / are / much / How / ? _____

5 Can / cash / with / I / pay / ? _____

_____**a** Yes. Is it a credit card?

_____**b** Yes. I'd like this camera, please.

_____**c** They're $200.

_____**d** Of course. That's $300.

_____**e** It's $60.

(10 points)

Writing

11 Rewrite the sentences with *but*.

1 This computer is old. It's very good.

_____

2 My laptop is big. It's easy to use.

_____

3 The cameras are light. They're good quality.

_____

4 I have a new cell phone. It isn't expensive.

_____

5 This tablet is old. It's fast.

_____

(10 points)

12 Read the email. Then write a reply. Use *but* and the information 1–5.

> Hi,
>
> I'd like a new cell phone. Can you help me?
>
> Best wishes,
> Dan

1 small / easy to use

2 new / not expensive

3 can take photos / can't make films

4 has a good memory / light

5 cheap / fantastic

> Hi Dan,
>
> Buy the Galaxy X 480! _____
> _____
> _____
> _____
> _____
> _____
> _____
> _____
> _____
> _____
> _____
> _____
> _____
> _____
> _____
> _____
> _____
> _____
> _____
>
> All the best

(10 points)

Speaking

13 Talk about what you can and can't do.

What sports can you play?

What types of food can you cook?

What other things can you do?

(10 points)

Unit 6 Test

Grammar

1 Put the words in order to write sentences.

1 weekend / the / They / like / .

_____

2 We / like / vegetables / don't / .

_____

3 like / I / soccer / .

_____

4 don't / their / They / house / like / .

_____

5 like / You / don't / food / Chinese / .

_____

(5 points)

2 Look at the example. Write questions.

1 "you / like / pizza / ?" <u>Do you like pizza?</u>   "Yes,
I do."

2 "you / like / pasta / ?" _____ "No,
I don't."

3 "your parents / like / pasta / ?"
_____ "Yes, they do."

4 "they / like / vegetables / ?" _____
"Yes, they do."

5 "you / like / salad / ?" _____ "No,
I don't."

6 "you / like / chocolate / ?" _____
"Of course! Yes, we do!"

(10 points)

3 Complete the text with the negative or question form of the verb in brackets.

Our favorite sports.

My brother Ben ¹ _____ (like) soccer and
rugby, but he ² _____ (not like) tennis or
golf. My favorite sports are basketball, handball, and volleyball.
³ _____ Ben _____
(like) basketball? Well, no, he doesn't. And he
⁴ _____ (not like) handball. But Ben
and I ⁵ _____ (like) volleyball. In fact,
we play volleyball every Wednesday!

(10 points)

4 Choose the correct word.

1 I have a new computer. I really like *it / them*.

2 I like golf, but I can't play *it / him*.

3 Tom has two cameras. He loves *it / them*.

4 Our friends are English. We like them, and they like
us / her.

5 My sister's name is Sally. I love *her / him*, of course!

(5 points)

Vocabulary

5 Write the numbers. Use these words.

twelve	hundred	million	one	thousand	twenty	and

1 112 _____

2 12,000 _____

3 1,000,000 _____

4 20,100 _____

5 120 _____

(10 points)

6 What are the foods? Write the letters in the correct order.

1 tufir _____

2 dalas _____

3 gegs _____

4 atem _____

5 ecir _____

6 heecse _____

7 sevegbalte _____

(7 points)

7 Write these words in the correct places.

pop	wildlife shows	comedies	scuba diving
novels	birds	jazz	swimming

1 animals: fish, _____

2 books: detective stories, _____

3 films: action, _____

4 music: rock, _____, _____

5 sports: football, _____, _____

6 TV: reality shows, _____

(8 points)

8 Choose the best option (a or b).

1 We don't like reality TV.
  a It's boring.   **b** It's fantastic!

2 I love football.
  a It's great!   **b** It's horrible!

3 I don't like cold eggs. Ugggh.
  a They're horrible!   **b** They're great!

4 I like comedies.
  a They're boring.   **b** They're fantastic!

5 I don't like cold coffee. Yuk!
  a It's boring.   **b** It's horrible!

(5 points)

Functions

9 Complete the sentences with these words. Then put the sentences in the correct order 1–5.

Let's	How	That's	What's	great

___ **a** Hum…two movies. _____ about *The Bourne Ultimatum*? It's a film with Matt Damon.

___ **b** _____ watch TV tonight.

___ **c** _____ on?

___ **d** Oh yes, that movie's _____!

___ **e** OK. _____ a good idea.

(10 points)

Writing

10 Complete the text with five of these words.

she	it	he	they	her	his	its	their	him	them

The Dark Knight Rises

This is a fantastic movie. I love [1] _____. The stars are Christian Bale and Anne Hathaway. [2] _____ are great in the movie. I love [3] _____! I think Christian Bale is a really good actor. [4] _____ is very intelligent, and I like all [5] _____ movies.

(5 points)

11 Look at the notes. Then write a review.

> *Film: The Amazing Spider-man (very good***)*
> *Stars:*
> *Andrew Garfield (great ****)*
> *Emma Stone (great*****)*
> *Opinion:*
> *Emma Stone (fantastic actor*****)*
> *beautiful*
> *all films good*

The Amazing Spider-man***

_____

_____

_____

_____

_____

_____

_____

_____

_____

_____

_____

_____

_____

_____

_____

_____

_____

_____

_____

_____

_____

_____

(15 points)

Speaking

12 Talk about your favorite things.

Your favorite sport

Your favorite food

Your favorite film or TV program

(10 points)

Unit 7 Test

Grammar

1 Look at the example. Write negative sentences.

1 I live in Norway. _I don't live in Norway._

2 We have the Internet. _____

_____

3 Oliver and Mary speak French. _____

_____

4 You work at home. _____

_____

5 They study mathematics. _____

_____

6 I understand you. _____

_____

7 David and I like our classes. _____

_____

(6 points)

2 Write Jo's questions. Then complete Mark's answers.

Jo: Hi Mark. ¹ you / have a job / ?

_____

Mark: Yes, I ² _____ .

Jo: OK. ³ you / work in an office / ?

_____

Mark: No, I ⁴ _____ .

Jo: What about your children? ⁵ they / go to school / ?

_____

Mark: Yes. Yes, they ⁶ _____ .

(9 points)

3 Complete the questions with these words.

What	Where	Who	When	Why

1 "_____ do you go in summer?" "To Miami Beach."

2 "_____ do you go with?" "My friends."

3 "_____ do you go?" "In July."

4 "_____ do you do?" "We go swimming."

5 "_____ do you go?" "It's fun!"

(5 points)

4 Complete the conversation with the correct form of the words in parentheses.

"Where ¹ _____ (Simon and Diane / live)?"

"Oh, I think they ² _____ (have) a house near Cambridge. They ³ _____ (not live) in Boston."

"What ⁴ _____ (they / do) on the weekend?
⁵ _____ (they / stay) at home and watch TV?"

"Oh, no, they don't. They ⁶ _____ (go) to the beach.
They ⁷ _____ (not like) TV!"

(10 points)

Vocabulary

5 What are the seasons? Write the letters in the correct order and complete the sentences.

1 mermus   In _____ , it's very hot.
2 terniw   In _____ , it's very cold.
3 allf   In _____ , it's brown and cold.
4 ginspr   In _____ , it's green.

(4 points)

6 Write these words in the correct category.

college	board	student	pencil
university	classmate	book	teacher

1 people: _____ , _____ , _____

2 places: _____ , _____

3 things: pen, _____ , _____ , _____

(8 points)

7 Match these words to the pictures.

1 cloudy	2 sunny	3 rainy	4 windy	5 snowy

a _____   b _____   c _____   d _____   e _____

(5 points)

8 Complete the sentences with these adjectives.

cold	thirsty	bored	wet	hot	tired	hungry

1 Drink! Where's the water? I'm _____ .
2 Brrr. It's 2 degrees here. I'm _____ .
3 I don't have things to do. I'm _____ .
4 It's late. I want to sleep. I'm _____ .
5 Food! I want to eat. I'm _____ .
6 It's rainy and I'm outside. I'm _____ .
7 It's 90 degrees! I'm _____ !

(7 points)

9 Complete the sentences with *to*, *for*, or – (no word).

1 I go _____ work every day.
2 We go _____ skiing in winter.
3 I go _____ walks with my family.
4 We go _____ the beach in summer.
5 I go _____ home at 6 o'clock.
6 They go _____ cycling every spring.

(6 points)

Functions

10 Put the words in order to complete the conversations.

A

1 matter / What's / the / ?

_____

2 feel / I / well / don't / .

_____

3 down / you / lie / Why / don't / ?

_____

B

4 very / I'm / bored / !

_____

5 don't / beach / Why / you / to / go / the / ?

_____

(10 points)

Writing

11 Match the sentences 1–6 to a–f in the personal profile.

Personal profile
Paragraph A: professional information
a _____
b _____
Paragraph B: family and lifestyle
c _____
d _____
Paragraph C: interests
e _____
f _____

1 I'm single and I don't have children.
2 I like cycling.
3 I go for walks.
4 I'm a teacher.
5 I live in a big city.
6 I work in a middle school.

(6 points)

12 Write your personal profile.

A: professional information

_____

B: family and lifestyle

_____

C: interests

_____

(14 points)

Speaking

13 Talk about what you do in spring, summer, fall, and winter.

(10 points)

Unit 8 Test

Grammar

1 Complete the sentences using the correct form of the verb in parentheses.

1 Andrea _____ up at 7 o'clock. (get)

2 Jill _____ breakfast with her family. (have)

3 Karen _____ on the weekends. (not work)

4 My brother _____ work in the evening. (finish)

5 Sally _____ to bed at midnight. (not go)

(10 points)

2 Choose the correct word to complete the sentences.

1 She works *in / at* Mexico.

2 My sister goes to work *at / on* eight-thirty.

3 The office is open *on / at* Wednesdays.

4 I have a cup of coffee *at / in* the morning

5 We don't watch TV *in / at* night.

(5 points)

3 Put the words in order to make sentences.

1 He / gets / late / always / up

_____

2 usually / my / have / with / I / colleagues / lunch

_____

3 She / writes / often / reports

_____

4 finish / We / sometimes / late / work

_____

5 breakfast / never / in / I / the / have / morning

_____

(5 points)

4 Write questions. Use the correct form of the verbs.

1 What / Sylvia / do / ?

_____

She's a geologist.

2 Where / she / work / ?

_____

She works at the university.

3 How often / she / give lectures / ?

_____

Every week.

4 When / she / go to work / ?

_____

She goes to work at 9.

5 What / she / have for lunch / ?

_____

She has a cup of tea and a sandwich.

(10 points)

Vocabulary

5 Complete the words to make jobs.

1 bu_____ld _____r

2 sal_____s_____er_____o_____

3 r_____c_____pt_____ _____n_____st

4 wa_____t_____r

5 n_____rs_____

6 wr_____t_____r

7 j_____ _____rn_____l_____st

(8 points)

6 Complete the sentences with a job from Exercise 5.

1 A _____ works in a café.

2 A _____ works in a shop.

3 A _____ writes books.

4 A _____ works in a hospital.

5 A _____ works outside and builds houses.

6 A _____ writes stories for newspapers.

7 A _____ works in an office and answers the telephone.

(7 points)

7 Complete the sentences about a typical day with these words.

have breakfast   get up   finish work   go to bed   start work

1 I _____ at 7 a.m.

2 I _____ at 8 a.m. I usually eat eggs.

3 I _____ in the office at 9 a.m.

4 I _____ at 5 p.m and go home on the bus.

5 I _____ at 11 p.m.

(5 points)

8 Complete the text using these words.

work	give	travel	write	have

My name's Angela and I'm a writer. I [1] _____ books and articles. I usually [2] _____ at home from 9 to 5. I often [3] _____ to different cities, and sometimes to other countries, too. I [4] _____ meetings and [5] _____ lectures about my job.

(10 points)

Functions

9 Complete the sentences with these words. Then put the sentences in the correct order 1–5.

| morning | to | moment | back | help |

___ **a** Goodbye.

___ **b** I'm sorry. He's out of the office at the _____.

___ **c** Good _____, Regent School. Can I _____ you?

___ **d** Yes, can I speak _____ Mr. Thompson, please?

___ **e** OK, thank you. I'll call _____ later. Goodbye.

(10 points)

Writing

10 Write the missing double consonants to complete the words.

1 busine _____ man

2 di _____ erent

3 co _____ ege

4 su _____ er

5 di _____ er

(5 points)

11 Write an email to a friend about your job. Answer these questions.

1 What do you do?

2 When do you start and finish work?

3 What do you do at work?

4 Is it easy or difficult?

5 Do you like it?

Hi Tony,

I'm _____

_____

_____

_____

_____

_____

_____

_____

_____

_____

_____

_____

_____

_____

_____

_____

_____

_____

_____

_____

Best wishes,

(Your name)

(15 points)

Speaking

12 Work in pairs. Talk about your day. Ask and answer the questions.

1 What time do you get up?

2 What do you have for breakfast?

3 What time do you go to work?

4 What do you have for lunch?

5 When do you finish work?

6 What do you do in the evening?

7 When you go to bed?

(10 points)

Unit 9 Test

Grammar

1 Choose the correct word to complete the sentences.

1 There *is / are* some T-shirts.

2 There *is / are* two scarves.

3 There *is / are* a skirt.

4 There *is / are* a pair of shoes.

5 There *is / are* a camera.

(10 points)

2 Choose the correct option (a–c) to complete the sentences.

1 There _____ a beach.
  a isn't   **b** are   **c** aren't

2 There aren't _____ youth hostels.
  a some   **b** a   **c** any

3 _____ there an airport?
  a Are   **b** Is   **c** Does

4 Are there _____ hotels in the city?
  a a   **b** some   **c** any

5 There are _____ restaurants.
  a some   **b** any   **c** an

(10 points)

3 Choose the correct option to complete the sentences.
Travel Tips

Always ¹*plan / don't plan* your trip before you go to a different country. ²*Book / Don't book* your tickets on the Internet, because it's cheap. If you travel a long distance, ³*sleep / don't sleep* on the plane for some time. If you don't have money, ⁴*don't stay / stay* in an expensive hotel. ⁵*Have / don't have* fun on your trip!

(10 points)

Vocabulary

4 Match these words to the pictures (a–j).

| a dress | a skirt | a coat | a sweater | a pair of jeans |
| a hat | a scarf | a shirt | a T-shirt | a pair of boots |

(10 points)

5 Choose the correct option (a–c).

1 You can watch programs on a…
  a TV   **b** desk   **c** fridge

2 You can't sit on a / an…
  a chair   **b** closet   **c** armchair

3 You can relax and read a book in a / an…
  a fridge   **b** armchair   **c** desk

4 You can wash in a…
  a bed   **b** bath tub   **c** TV

5 You can cook dinner in a / an…
  a fridge   **b** table   **c** oven

6 You can sleep in a…
  a bed   **b** shower   **c** desk

7 There's a dress and a pair of boots in the…
  a oven   **b** closet   **c** fridge

8 There are some cold bottles of water in the…
  a fridge   **b** bath   **c** shower

9 You can do your homework on a…
  a TV   **b** desk   **c** bath

10 In the afternoon, you can relax on a…
  a small table   **b** closet   **c** sofa

(10 points)

6 Check (✓) the words that go with the verb.

1 go
  a home [✓]   **b** shopping [✓]   **c** TV [ ]

2 take
  a a bus [ ]   **b** a photo [ ]   **c** a hotel [ ]

3 stay at
  a home [ ]   **b** a country [ ]   **c** a hotel [ ]

4 drive
  a a bike [ ]   **b** a bus [ ]   **c** a car [ ]

5 leave
  a home [ ]   **b** work [ ]   **c** from east to west [ ]

6 use
  a an email [ ]   **c** a travel agent [ ]
  b a computer [ ]

(10 points)

Functions

7 Put the words in order to complete the sentences in the hotel.

1 call / like / 7 a.m. / please / I'd / at / a / wake-up /.

_____

2 I'd / evening / to / have / dinner / in / like / this / my / room /.

_____

3 taxi / like / to / book / o'clock / I'd / for / eight / a /.

_____

4 a / Is / bank / the / near / there / hotel / ?

_____

5 night / like / extra / stay / an / to / I'd / please / .

_____

(10 points)

Writing

8 Rewrite the sentences with *because*.

1 Don't take a taxi. It's expensive.

_____

2 Tourists come here in the summer. It's a popular place.

_____

3 Don't take your sweater. It's hot.

_____

4 Take a picture of the river. It's very beautiful in the evening.

_____

5 There isn't an airport. It's a small city.

_____

(5 points)

9 Your friend wants to visit your city. Complete the email. Answer the questions.

1 What's the name of your city?
2 How can you travel there?
3 Where can you stay?
4 What can you eat?
5 What can you see?
6 What can you do?

Hi Anna,

_____

_____

_____

_____

_____

_____

_____

_____

_____

_____

_____

_____

_____

_____

_____

_____

_____

_____

_____

_____

_____

_____

_____

_____

Best wishes,
(Your name)

(15 points)

Speaking

10 Talk about your travel experiences.

How do you usually travel to work or school?

How often do you travel to different places? Where do you go and why?

(10 points)

Unit 10 Test

Grammar

1 Complete the sentences about famous British explorers of the sixteenth century. Use *was* or *were*.

1 Sir Francis Drake _____ a famous explorer.

2 He _____ born in 1540.

3 Sir Walter Raleigh _____ a writer and explorer.

4 Sir Francis Drake and Sir Walter Raleigh _____ born in Devon in southwest England.

5 Drake _____ the first Englishman to go around the world.

6 They _____ very important people in history.

(6 points)

2 Complete the text with the past form of *be*. Use affirmative and negative forms.

At home with a history book

Yesterday, I ¹ _____ (not be) at school. I ² _____ (be) at home with my friend Simon. We ³ _____ (be) in my bedroom with a fantastic book. It ⁴ _____ (be) about explorers. These explorers ⁵ _____ (not be) from Europe. They ⁶ _____ (be) Chinese. In the 15th century, Chinese explorers ⁷ _____ (be) in America. Their ships ⁸ _____ (be) amazing! We ⁹ _____ (not be) hungry or tired because the book ¹⁰ _____ (be) very interesting.

(10 points)

3 Write questions. Use *was* or *were*. Then match the questions (1–5) to the correct short answers (a–e).

1 he / an explorer / ?

_____

2 they / in the mountains / ?

_____

3 you / on an expedition / ?

_____

4 she / on a boat / ?

_____

5 it / an important expedition / ?

_____

a Yes, it was.   **d** Yes, they were.
b No, we weren't.   **e** Yes, she was.
c No, he wasn't.

(10 points)

4 Complete the sentences with these words.

past	ago	time	now

1 I'm in history class _____.

2 Two years _____, I was in Mexico.

3 In the _____, people were very poor.

4 At that _____, there weren't cars or good roads.

(4 points)

Vocabulary

5 Look at the example. Complete the dates.

1 7/6/67   *the sixth of July, 1967*

2 2/18/79   the _____ of _____, 1979

3 11/1/90   the _____ of _____, 1990

4 4/3/50   the _____ of _____, 1950

5 1/22/29   the _____ of _____, 1929

6 3/12/19   the _____ of _____, 1919

7 6/25/99   the _____ of _____, 1999

8 5/11/87   the _____ of _____, 1987

9 8/30/31   the _____ of _____, 1931

(16 points)

6 What are the adjectives? Write the letters in the correct order. Complete the sentences.

1 derfilyn   William is very _____. He always says hello. I like him.

2 saftacnti   Jo's work is _____. She's really, good —my favorite artist!

3 ecni   Rachel is _____. I really like her.

4 yhapp   Steve is always _____. He likes people and has a good time.

5 grentinise   Andrew is _____. He has good stories.

6 oafsmu   Peter is _____. He's a pop star on TV.

7 tager   Sir Roy was the first explorer on that mountain. He's a _____ explorer.

8 doog   Penny is _____. She always listens to her parents.

(8 points)

7 Match these words and expressions to the pictures.

asleep   at home   busy   in traffic   sick   on the phone

a _____

b _____

c _____

d _____

e _____

f _____

(6 points)

Functions

8 Complete the conversation with these words.

hello	busy	worry	were	late	OK
sorry	take	about	very		

Student: Hi.

Teacher: [1] _____.

Student: I'm [2] _____ I'm [3] _____.

Teacher: That's [4] _____. Don't [5] _____.

Student: The bus was [6] _____ late.

Teacher: What [7] _____ yesterday? Where [8] _____ you then?

Student: Humm… I was very [9] _____ then. Sorry!

Teacher: OK. Well, [10] _____ a seat.

(10 points)

Writing

9 Rewrite the sentences with *when*.

1 I was born. It was snowy outside.

_____

2 I was a child. I was very happy.

_____

3 My parents were young. They weren't rich.

_____

4 The bus was late. We were late for school.

_____

5 My sister was sixteen. She was on TV.

_____

(10 points)

10 Write a blog about your childhood memories. Answer the questions.

Where and when were you born?

What do you remember about your house, your family, and your friends?

Childhood memories

_____
_____
_____
_____
_____
_____
_____
_____
_____
_____
_____
_____
_____
_____
_____
_____
_____
_____
_____
_____
_____
_____
_____
_____
_____

(10 points)

Speaking

11 Talk about a friend, a hero, or a famous person.

Who was he or she?

Why was he or she famous or important?

(10 points)

Unit 11 Test

Grammar

1 Complete the sentences with the simple past form of the verb in parentheses.

1 Scientists _____ (find) a body in the ice.
2 Explorers _____ (go) to the Arctic.
3 Andy _____ (take) a photo.
4 We _____ (have) lunch in the city center.
5 They_____ (be) very old.

(5 points)

2 Complete the sentences with the simple past form of these verbs.

finish	study	live	walk	start

1 Tom _____ French at university when he was young.
2 Philippa _____ from Paris to Madrid in 2006 for charity.
3 Dave _____ work at 6 p.m. and went home.
4 We _____ in a small house in the country from 2000 to 2003.
5 Tony _____ work at 8 o'clock this morning. He's very busy.

(10 points)

3 Complete the sentences with the negative simple past form of the verb in bold.

1 Sally **left** the party at 10, but Tim _____ until midnight.
2 Gary **walked** home, but Jo _____. She took a taxi.
3 Emma **went** to Italy last year, but Ruth _____ on vacation.
4 Pete **ran** the marathon, but Paul _____ in the race.
5 Sue **studied** German, but Emily _____ languages in college.

(5 points)

4 Put the words in order to make questions.

1 Did / leave / at / she / nine / ?

_____

Yes, she did.

2 you / play / yesterday / Did / soccer / ?

_____

Yes, I did.

3 When / Carole / home / did / arrive / ?

_____

At 9.

4 night / you / What / last / do / did / ?

_____

I stayed at home.

5 they / Did / see / movie / the / ?

_____

No, they didn't.

(10 points)

Vocabulary

5 Match verbs 1–8 with similar meanings a–h.

1 find	**a** end
2 arrive	**b** go away
3 leave	**c** study
4 start	**d** discover
5 finish	**e** name
6 call	**f** get there
7 investigate	**g** visit
8 go to	**h** begin

(8 points)

6 Match 1–5 with a–e to make sentences. Write the sentence using *with*.

1 I saw a bird…	**a** my parents
2 I had dinner…	**b** a travel agent
3 I booked tickets…	**c** long legs
4 I bought a computer…	**d** friendly people
5 I work…	**e** a big memory

(10 points)

7 What are the adjectives? Write the letters in the correct order. Complete the sentences.

1 abuteiflu   This lake is blue and very _____.
2 sdraneguo   These mountains are _____. Be careful!
3 tantfacis   This food is _____. It's great!
4 ginretniset   This book is _____. There is a lot of information in it.
5 uualnus   His films are _____. They are different from other movies.
6 zacry   She's _____! She does amazing things!

(6 points)

8 Choose the correct option to complete the sentences.

1 We went out *in / on* Friday.
2 *Before / Last* night, we saw a movie on TV.
3 Where did you go on vacation *in / on* the summer.
4 I didn't talk to her *on / –* yesterday.
5 I worked there two years *last / ago*.
6 What did you do *last / on* weekend?

(6 points)

Functions

9 Write past simple questions. Then match them to the answers (a–e).

1 you / have / a good vacation / last month / ?

_____

2 they / go swimming / on Sunday / ?

_____

3 you / have a good time / last night / ?

_____

4 your parents / have a nice trip / last weekend/ ?

_____

5 you / have a nice meal / on Saturday / ?

_____

   a No, they didn't! There was a shark in the water!
   b Yes, they did. They visited an old castle.
   c Yes, we did. It was sunny and hot every day.
   d Yes, thanks. I did. It was delicious!
   e Yes, thanks. It was a fantastic evening.

(10 points)

Writing

10 Complete the email with these words.

Love	for	Hi	again	soon

> ¹ _____ Bob,
>
> Thanks ² _____ your help yesterday. I got home OK, but it was midnight!
>
> See you ³ _____,
>
> Thanks ⁴ _____.
>
> ⁵ _____,
>
> Mark

(5 points)

11 Read the situation then write a thank you email.

Your friend Susan helped you when you didn't have money for the bus. She loaned you ten dollars.

Thank you email

_____
_____
_____
_____
_____
_____
_____
_____
_____
_____
_____
_____
_____
_____
_____
_____
_____
_____
_____
_____
_____
_____
_____
_____
_____

(15 points)

Speaking

12 Talk about what you did last weekend.

Where did you go?

Who did you go with?

What did you see, play, or do?

(10 points)

Unit 12 Test

Grammar

1 Write the correct form of *be* to complete the present continuous sentences.

1 Penny _____ cooking in the kitchen.

2 We _____ playing tennis in the park.

3 They _____ talking to friends.

4 It _____ raining.

5 I _____ living in Spain at the moment.

(5 points)

2 Complete the sentences with the present continuous form of the verbs in parentheses.

1 I _____ (go) to Joe's party.

2 Jenny _____ (study) Spanish at college.

3 We _____ (not get) up.

4 Amy _____ (not feel) well.

5 Tim _____ (lie) on the sofa.

(10 points)

3 Write present continuous sentences.

1 What / you / do / on Saturday / ?

2 I / play / tennis with Mark / .

3 OK. What / Karen / do / on the weekend / ?

4 She / not stay / in Houston / .

5 OK. / she / come / to Los Angeles / ?

(10 points)

4 Complete the sentences with the correct form of the verbs in parentheses.

1 Last Tuesday, I _____ (go) to San Francisco.

2 Next Friday, we _____ (visit) Jerry in Hawaii.

3 Every day, Tom _____ (go) to work on the bus.

4 Susie _____ (sit) outside now.

5 Dan and Marie _____ (get) married four years ago.

(5 points)

Vocabulary

5 Which rooms are they? Answer the questions.

1 In which room do you find a bath tub, a shower, and a toilet? _____

2 In which room is there a TV, an armchair, and a sofa?

_____

3 In which room do you find a bed and a closet?

_____

4 In which room is there a refrigerator and an oven?

_____

5 In which room do you eat dinner? _____

(10 points)

6 Match 1–5 with a–e to make sentences.

1 She's cooking…	a coffee
2 He's ironing…	b his shirt
3 She's bathing…	c computer games
4 They're drinking…	d her children
5 He's playing…	e lunch

(5 points)

7 Write the letters for these words in the correct order. Complete the sentences with the words.

terccno	trapy	ninred	sohgnipp
usemmu	vieom rethate	preapsnwe	alet
klaw	ylfmai		

1 I often go _____ for clothes with my friends in the Roxy Center.

2 We love jazz and often go to a _____ at the Festival Hall.

3 It's my birthday on Saturday and I'm having a _____. All my friends are coming.

4 My dad reads the _____ every Sunday. He likes the news.

5 On Sundays, I get up _____. At 10 a.m. sometimes!

6 I went to the _____ yesterday, and saw a great movie!

7 Can we go for a _____ in the country? I want to be outside.

8 We went out for _____ in a beautiful restaurant.

9 We usually visit _____ on the weekend— grandparents and my aunt.

10 I went to a _____ and saw old, historical objects.

(10 points)

8 Complete the sentences with these words.

court	museum	brochure	exhibition	return ticket

1 There is an interesting _____ of Van Gogh's paintings at the National Gallery.

2 We have a new tennis _____ at the sports center.

3 Can I have a _____ to Montreal, please?

4 Did you read the _____? There is interesting information in it.

5 There are historical objects in our local _____.

(5 points)

Functions

9 Put the words in order to make sentences and complete the conversation.

1 exhibition / the / Two / for / tickets / please /

_____

2 twelve / That's / please / dollars /

_____

3 in / brochure / Would / like / a / English / you / ?

_____

4 thank / Yes / you /

_____

5 in / now / Would / go / like / to / you / ?

_____

(10 points)

Writing

10 Read the replies to Paul's party invitation. Complete the gaps with missing words.

> Hi Paul,
>
> We'd ^{1} _____ to come. Is it ^{2} _____ if we arrive late?
>
> Dan and Petra xo

> Dear Paul,
>
> Thanks ^{3} _____ the invitation. But I'm ^{4} _____ —I'm busy and I can't come.
>
> Doug

> Thank you very ^{5} _____ for the invitation to the party. Unfortunately, we can't come because we're on vacation.
>
> Dave and Meg

(5 points)

11 Read Annie's invitation. Write a reply. Say that you can't come and why.

> Hi!
>
> Please come to my party on 8 September at 9 p.m.
>
> It's my birthday!
>
> Annie!! xo

_____

_____

_____

_____

_____

_____

_____

_____

_____

_____

_____

_____

_____

_____

_____

_____

_____

_____

_____

_____

(15 points)

Speaking

12 Talk about your plans for next weekend.
Where are you going?
What are you doing?
Who are you doing things with?

(10 points)

Photocopiable tests: answer key

Unit 1 Test

1 1 a   2 an   3 a   4 an   5 an

2 1 'm   2 're   3 'm   4 're   5 'm

3 1 He's   2 It's   3 He's   4 She's   5 It's

4 1 your   2 My   3 My   4 your   5 my

5 1 My   2 'm   3 an   4 's   5 from

6 1 Y   2 L   3 K   4 B   5 U

7
1 scientist   2 writer   3 photographer
4 filmmaker   5 explorer

8
2 German   3 Japanese   4 Mexican
5 British   6 French

9
1 Europe   2 Asia   3 South America
4 Africa   5 North America

10 1 eight   2 ten   3 five   4 nine   5 six

11
a are 1   b you 5   c thanks 2   d to 4   e from 3

12a
2 I'm David.
3 My name's Paul Murray.
4 I'm from Scotland.
5 He's American.
6 I'm an engineer.

Unit 2 Test

1 1 b   2 a   3 c   4 b   5 a

2
2 aren't   3 'm not   4 isn't
5 aren't   6 isn't

3
1 Are you hot?   c   2 Is she from Russia?   e
3 Are they on a boat?   d   4 Is Tom in a hotel?   a
5 Are we in London?   b

4
1 cities   2 mountains   3 buses
4 beaches   5 countries

5
1 mountain   2 lake   3 sea
4 city   5 island

6
1 eighteen, twenty   2 thirty, sixty
3 twelve, eleven   4 ninety-four, ninety-five
5 sixty, one hundred

7
1 white, blue   2 black, red
3 green, yellow, white   4 orange
5 green, pink

8 1 c   2 d   3 a   4 e   5 b

9
1 a   Are you on vacation here?
2 d   Where are you from?
3 e   What's the zip code?
4 c   What's your telephone number in the US?
5 b   Is this your email address?

10
1 Ms.   2 Sarah
3 Cole   4 14 Buswell Street, Boston, Massachusetts, USA
5 02215   6 cole@post.youmail.com

Unit 3 Test

1
2 She's Paul's   5 Where's Patrick's
3 Oliver's boat's   6 Tim's son's
4 What's...brother's

2 1 His   2 their   3 Our   4 Their   5 his

3
2 His children are young.
3 Their parents are here.
4 Her name is Susie.
5 Our house is small.
6 Her friends are at work.

4
1 daughters, girls   2 men, women
3 people, buses   4 children, boys
5 grandmothers, women

5
1 March   2 July   3 January
4 October   5 April   6 August

6 1 b   2 a   3 b   4 a   5 a

7
2 in March.   3 in April.   4 in July.
5 in October.   6 in November.   7 in December.

8 1 small   2 young / new   3 poor

9
1 at   2 in   3 at   4 at
5 in   6 in   7 at
8 at   9 in   10 in

10 1 a   2 b   3 a   4 b   5 a

11
2 Amy's sixteen tomorrow. It's her birthday.
3 Jo and Dan aren't married, but they're engaged.
4 Sally's wedding's in May. I'm the bridesmaid.
5 Oh! You're eighteen. When's the party?
6 Fiona isn't single. She's married.
7 It isn't our birthday today. We're thirty on Friday.
8 I'm not married. It isn't my wedding!

12
1 To   2 happy   3 on
4 from   5 your   6 wishes

Unit 4 Test

1 1 on 2 next to 3 near 4 opposite 5 on

2
1 opposite, next to   2 near, opposite
3 next to, opposite   4 near, next to
5 near, opposite

3 1 This 2 this 3 That 4 that 5 that

4 1 Where 2 When 3 Where 4 What 5 Why
6 When 7 Where 8 When 9 What 10 Where

5
1 a park   2 a parking lot   3 a café
4 a market   5 a train station   6 a movie theater

6
a Monday 2   b Thursday 5   c Friday 6
d Wednesday 4   e Tuesday 3

7 1 c   2 a   3 e   4 b   5 d

8
1 noon   2 in the morning   3 midnight
4 in the afternoon 5 in the evening

9
1 Can I help you?
2 Can I have a water, please?
3 Here you are. Anything else?
4 A tea and two coffees, please.
5 That's twelve dollars.

10
2 The park is old and famous.
3 The city is new and beautiful.
4 My brother is young and rich.
5 The market is open on Sundays and Mondays.
6 I'm happy at home and (at) work.

11
1 The hotel is big and old.
2 The people are nice and friendly.
3 The beach is small and beautiful.
4 The food is hot and great.
5 I'm fine and happy.

Unit 5 Test

1 1 can 2 can't 3 can't 4 can 5 can 5 can't

2
1 Can you speak Chinese?
2 Can you cook Chinese food?
3 Can your brothers speak Chinese?
4 Can they cook?
5 Can you write in Chinese?

3 1 have 2 has 3 have 4 has

4
1 This is my new house.
2 I have a great cell phone.
3 It's a small café.
4 Jack has nice friends.
5 You have a blue bag.

5
1 This phone is very cheap.
2 Sally's grandfather is very old.
3 Our boat is really fantastic.

4 Their town is very small.
5 My computer is really great.

6 1 dollars, US / Canada 2 euros, the EU 3 pounds, the UK

7 1 d 2 f 3 b / e 4 a 5 c 6 b / e 7 g

8
1 speak   2 play   3 cook
4 play   5 swim   6 drive
7 ride

9
1 c   2 d   3 i   4 a   5 g
6 j   7 f   8 h   9 b   10 e

10
1 Can I help you? b
2 How much is this? e
3 Can I pay with a card? a
4 How much are these? c
5 Can I pay with cash? d

11
1 This computer is old, but it's very good.
2 My laptop is big, but it's easy to use.
3 The cameras are light, but they're good quality.
4 I have a new cell phone, but it isn't expensive.
5 This tablet is old, but it's fast.

Unit 6 Test

1
1 They like the weekend.
2 We don't like vegetables.
3 I like soccer.
4 They don't like their house.
5 You don't like Chinese food.

2
2 Do you like pasta?
3 Do your parents like pasta?
4 Do they like vegetables?
5 Do you like salad?
6 Do you like chocolate?

3 1 likes 2 doesn't like 3 Does…like 4 doesn't like 5 like

4 1 it 2 it 3 them 4 us 5 her

5
1 one hundred and twelve
2 twelve thousand
3 one million
4 twenty thousand one hundred
5 one hundred and twenty

6
1 fruit   2 salad   3 eggs
4 meat   5 rice   6 cheese
7 vegetables

7
1 birds   2 novels
3 comedies   4 pop, jazz
5 scuba diving, swimming   6 wildlife shows

8 1 a 2 a 3 a 4 b 5 b

9 a How 4 b Let's 1 c What's 3 d great 5 e That's 2

10 1 it 2 They 3 them 4 He 5 his

Unit 7 Test

1

2 We don't have the Internet.
3 Oliver and Mary don't speak French.
4 You don't work at home.
5 They don't study mathematics.
6 I don't understand you.
7 David and I don't like our classes.

2

1 Do you have a job?
2 do
3 Do you work in an office?
4 don't
5 Do they go to school?
6 do

3

1 Where	2 Who	3 When
4 What	5 Why	

4

1 do Simon and Diane live?	2 have
3 don't live	4 do they do
5 Do they stay	6 go
7 don't like	

5 1 summer   2 winter   3 fall   4 spring

6

1 student, classmate, teacher
2 college, university
3 board, pencil, book

7

a 2 sunny	c 1 cloudy	e 3 rainy
b 5 snowy	d 4 windy	

8

1 thirsty	2 cold	3 bored
4 tired	5 hungry	
6 wet	7 hot	

9 1 to   2 –   3 for   4 to   5 –   6 –

10

A
1 What's the matter?
2 I don't feel well.
3 Why don't you lie down?

B
4 I'm very bored!
5 Why don't you go to the beach?

11

a/b 4/6	c/d 1/5	e/f 2/3

Unit 8 Test

1

1 gets	2 has	3 doesn't work
4 finishes	5 doesn't go	

2 1 in   2 at   3 on   4 in   5 at

3

1 He always gets up late.
2 I usually have lunch with my colleagues.
3 She often writes reports.
4 We sometimes finish work late.
5 I never have breakfast in the morning.

4

1 What does Sylvia do?
2 Where does she work?
3 How often does she give lectures?
4 When does she go to work?
5 What does she have for lunch?

5

1 builder	2 salesperson	3 receptionist
4 waiter	5 nurse	
6 writer	7 journalist	

6

1 waiter	2 salesperson	3 writer
4 nurse	5 builder	
6 journalist	7 receptionist	

7

1 get up	2 have breakfast	3 start work
4 finish work	5 go to bed	

8

1 write	2 work	3 travel
4 have	5 give	

9

a 5	c morning, help 1	e back 4
b moment 3	d to 2	

10

1 businessman	2 different	3 college
4 summer	5 dinner	

Unit 9 Test

1

1 are	2 are	3 is	4 is	5 is

2

1 a	2 c	3 b	4 c	5 a

3

1 plan	2 Book	3 sleep
4 don't stay	5 Have	

4

a a coat	e a skirt	i a scarf
b a sweater	f a shirt	j a dress
c a hat	g a pair of boots	
d a T-shirt	h a pair of jeans	

5

1 a	2 b	3 b	4 b
5 c	6 a	7 b	
8 a	9 b	10 c	

6

2 a [✓] b [✓]	3 a [✓] c [✓]	4 b [✓] c [✓]
5 a [✓] b [✓]	6 b [✓] c [✓]	

7

1 I'd like a wake-up call at 7 a.m. please.
2 I'd like to have dinner in my room this evening.
3 I'd like to book a taxi for eight o'clock.
4 Is there a bank near the hotel?
5 I'd like to stay an extra night, please.

8

1 Don't take a taxi because it's expensive.
2 Tourists come here in the summer because it's a popular place.
3 Don't take your sweater because it's hot.
4 Take a picture of the river because it's very beautiful in the evening.
5 There isn't an airport because it's a small city.

Unit 10 Test

1

1 was	2 was	3 was
4 were	5 was	6 were

2

1 wasn't	2 was	3 were
4 was	5 weren't	6 were
7 were	8 were	
9 weren't	10 was	

3

1 Was he an explorer? c
2 Were they in the mountains? d
3 Were you on an expedition? b
4 Was she on a boat? e
5 Was it an important expedition? a

4 1 now 2 ago 3 past 4 time

5

2 the eighteenth of February, 1979
3 the first of November, 1990
4 the third of April, 1950
5 the twenty-second of January, 1929
6 the twelfth of March, 1919
7 the twenty-fifth of June, 1999
8 the eleventh of May, 1987
9 the thirtieth of August, 1931

6

1 friendly	2 fantastic	3 nice
4 happy	5 interesting	6 famous
7 great	8 good	

7

a on the phone	b asleep	c busy
d sick	e in traffic	f at home

8

1 Hello	2 sorry	3 late
4 OK	5 worry	6 very
7 about	8 were	
9 busy	10 take	

9

1 When I was born, it was snowy outside.
2 When I was a child, I was very happy.
3 When my parents were young, they weren't rich.
4 When the bus was late, we were late for school.
5 When my sister was sixteen, she was on TV.

Unit 11 Test

1

1 found	2 went	3 took
4 had	5 were	

2

1 studied	2 walked	3 finished
4 lived	5 started	

3

1 didn't leave	2 didn't walk	3 didn't go
4 didn't run	5 didn't study	

4

1 Did she leave at nine?
2 Did you play soccer yesterday?
3 When did Carole arrive home?
4 What did you do last night?
5 Did they see the movie?

5 1 d 2 f 3 b 4 h 5 a 6 e 7 c 8 g

6

1 c I saw a bird with long legs.
2 a I had dinner with my parents.
3 b I booked tickets with a travel agent.
4 e I bought a computer with a big memory.
5 d I work with friendly people.

7

1 beautiful	2 dangerous	3 fantastic
4 interesting	5 unusual	6 crazy

8

1 on	2 Last	3 in
4 –	5 ago	6 last

9

1 Did you have a good vacation last month? c
2 Did they go swimming on Sunday? a
3 Did you have a good time last night? e
4 Did your parents have a nice trip last weekend? b
5 Did you have a nice dinner on Saturday? d

10

1 Hi	2 for	3 soon
4 again	5 Love	

Unit 12 Test

1 1 is 2 are 3 are 4 is 5 am

2

1 am going	2 is studying	3 aren't getting
4 isn't feeling	5 is lying	

3

1 What are you doing on Saturday?
2 I am playing tennis with Mark.
3 OK. What is Karen doing on the weekend?
4 She isn't staying in Houston.
5 OK. Is she coming to Los Angeles?

4

1 went	2 are visiting	3 goes
4 is sitting	5 got	

5

1 bathroom	2 living room	3 bedroom
4 kitchen	5 dining room	

6 1 e 2 b 3 d 4 a 5 c

7

1 shopping	2 concert	3 party
4 newspaper	5 late	6 movie theater
7 walk	8 dinner	
9 family	10 museum	

8

1 exhibition	2 court	3 return ticket
4 brochure	5 museum	

9

1 Two tickets for the exhibition, please.
2 That's twelve dollars, please.
3 Would you like a brochure in English?
4 Yes, thank you.
5 Would you like to go in now?

10

1 love / like	2 OK	3 for
4 sorry	5 much	